Personality
Assessment

Personality Assessment

Second Edition

Richard I. Lanyon

Leonard D. Goodstein

1807 1982

A Wiley-Interscience Publication

JOHN WILEY & SONS

New York • Chichester • Brisbane • Toronto • Singapore

Library of Congress Cataloging in Publication Data:

Lanyon, Richard I., 1937-
  Personality assessment.

  "A Wiley-Interscience publication."
  Bibliography: p.
  Includes index.
  1. Personality assessment. I. Goodstein,
Leonard David. II. Title.

BF698.4.L34 1982	155.2'8	81-23081
ISBN 0-471-04087-8		AACR2

Printed in the United States of America

10 9 8 7 6 5 4 3 2 1

*To Barbara
and Jeanette*

PREFACE

The ten or so years that have elapsed since the publication of the first edition of this book have seen a number of changing emphases and new directions in psychology that have affected the field of personality assessment. Perhaps the most far-reaching is the rapid expansion of professional psychology as a career area together with other human services that are related to or based upon psychology as a science. Because of this proliferation, we have reached somewhat further afield in the second edition in order to cover the wider range of settings in which the formal assessment of personality and psychodiagnostic characteristics is useful. As with the first edition, however, we have been guided by the requirement for personality assessment to be anchored in work that meets accepted scientific standards, and we have attempted to portray clearly which assessment procedures do have a demonstrated empirical base and which do not.

The 1960s was a time in which many basic ideas were developed and much research was conducted that was relevant to the improvement of personality assessment procedures. A sampling of topics that were popular at that time might include social desirability, acquiescence, and other sources of potential response distortion, actuarial versus clinical description and prediction, the study of clinical judgment, and psychometric issues in test construction. Consistent with the expansion of professional psychology, the 1970s was a period in which *applications* of existing principles and technologies were a primary focus. These developments are reflected in the following major changes in this edition over the first. (a) The original chapter on behavioral assessment and biographical data has now been expanded into two separate chapters (5 and 6) to deal with each of these topics at greater length. In particular, Chapter 6 reviews some of the many structured instruments for collecting and recording interview and case history data that have appeared over the last ten years. (b) There is a new chapter (10) on automated personality assessment—the use of computers in the administration, scoring, and interpretation of personality and psychodiagnostic tests. (c) A new chapter (9) describes several special areas of personality assessment, including children, law-related settings, and clinical neuropsychology. (d) Other major changes include a wider view of the various historical influences that have shaped the field of personality assessment (Chapter 1), a more complete account of the research on the technology of assessment (Chapter 8), a greater emphasis on industrial and organizational applications as well as clinical applications, and a sensitivity to the increasingly legalistic atmosphere in which practitioners of personality assessment must now operate (Chapter 11).

We are thankful for the many comments and criticisms of the first edition that have been offered by our students and colleagues, and we hope that the second edition has benefited from this input in the way it was intended. Also acknowledged with gratitude is the assistance of the secretarial staff at Arizona State University, but especially Mrs. LaVaun Habegger and her unflagging efforts to make sense out of Lanyon's handwriting. Our wives, Barbara P. Lanyon and Jeanette Treat Goodstein, have continued to be uniquely helpful in this project and in all our professional work.

RICHARD I. LANYON
LEONARD D. GOODSTEIN

January 1982

CONTENTS

Personality
Assessment

1 HISTORY OF PERSONALITY ASSESSMENT

The way in which people behave has always been of interest to others. It is of immediate interest to their family, friends, and neighbors, since people's behavior is likely to have direct consequences for those who are close to them. Also, most of us like to feel that we have at least some understanding of human behavior in general. Thus, the development of a capacity to understand and predict individual human behavior is of both immediate interest and general social interest.

The field of personality assessment—our *systematic* efforts to understand and predict the behavior of individuals—has a long history. If a prehistoric man attempted to gauge the intentions of a stranger approaching his campsite by observing the stance of the visitor, or the cast of his eyes, this might be regarded as an early effort at personality assessment. The later use of soothsayers and oracles to determine the veracity of peace offers from the enemy could be similarly viewed. There are many such early, informal procedures that precede the development of modern scientific and professional psychology. Because of their historical value and because they illuminate some of the methodological issues involved in all personality assessment, we discuss several of them here, concentrating on those that are still practiced to some degree in our society, despite their ascientific develop- ment and rather dubious contemporary status. They are astrology, palmistry, and phrenology, methods that are considerably older than any current professional assessment technique.

Astrology, Palmistry, and Phrenology

Astrology, the attempt to forecast events on earth through observation of the fixed stars and other heavenly bodies, is thought to have originated about 25 centuries ago in Mesopotamia. The belief that the stars were powerful gods led the ancients to conclude that human affairs could be foretold by study of the heavens. The personality of each individual, and the cause of events in his/her life, was determined by his/her horoscope (the configuration of the stars at the time of birth). Personality assessment for an individual was accomplished by noting the moment of

1

birth and then getting the appropriate predictive information from one of a number of elaborate manuals or almanacs, not unlike the daily horoscopes that are still to be found in many newspapers. The extensive knowledge of the physical world developed during the scientific revolution has done much to reduce serious interest in astrology, but it still remains popular with many people.

What are the reasons for the continued popularity of astrology? The basic notion that our lives are predetermined by the configuration of the stars at the moment of our birth seems extremely naïve, and there is absolutely no serious evidence for the existence of a relationship between time of birth and personality. Nevertheless, the popularity of the notion persists, much to the discomfort of most professional psychologists. One reason for this persistence is the Barnum effect (described later). Another is the general fascination which cosmic or supernatural notions hold for the public. Books such as *Cosmic Influences on Human Behaviors* (Gauquelin, 1973) and *Supernature* (Watson, 1973) cater to this fascination by dressing up the pseudoscientific notions of astrology in the trappings of formal research and scholarship. It might perhaps be most appropriate to view astrology and similar areas of interest as a part of the entertainment industry, with its emphasis on packaging whatever will ''sell'' irrespective of most other considerations.

Analogous to astrology is the technique of *biorhythms,* a method for personal prediction developed initially by Sigmund Freud's colleague Wilhelm Fliess and more recently promoted by George Thommen (1973). According to the theory of biorhythms, our day-to-day effectiveness is governed by our position on three ''cycles''—physical, emotional, and mental—which are fixed according to the moment of our birth and are not otherwise modifiable. Since each of the cycles has a different period, they can periodically combine to produce ''triple-low'' days, on which things are likely to go badly, and ''triple-highs,'' when the opposite will be true. The more cycles stacked against us on any particular day, the more things are likely to go wrong, and vice versa. With the advent of the preprogrammed hand microcomputer, people can predict their potential effectiveness for any given day almost instantaneously.

There is no apparent reason why this scheme would give any useful information, and a number of empirical studies (e.g., Shaffer, Schmidt, Zlotowitz, and Fisher, 1978) have shown conclusively that it does not. Certainly there are changes in one's energy level and motivation over time. What is inconceivable is that the pattern of these changes should be fixed absolutely by the moment of one's birth. Nevertheless, the notion of biorhythms has attracted a growing cult of ''true believers'' and is being commercially promoted as a viable approach to the prediction of human behavior.

Palmistry refers to the determination of an individual's characteristics by interpreting the various irregularities and folds of the skin of the hand. Palmistry is known to have existed as a standardized system in China as early as 3000 B.C., although its early beginnings and theoretical roots are lost in antiquity. In palmistry, importance is given to the lines of the hand, as well as to the swellings, or monticuli, between these lines. Each of these ''signs'' is interpreted in a specific manner. Thus a large Mound of Saturn, that portion of the palm directly below the third joint of the middle finger, indicates wisdom, good fortune, and prudence. Palmistry provides for a complete personality assessment of individuals by the reading of these signs. The complete absence of any reasonable explanation for the interpretative inferences, coupled with the clear knowledge that the monticuli and other characteristics of the hand can be changed by physical exercise, leads to a dismissal of palmistry as superstition and quackery.

Nevertheless, people claiming to be practitioners of this ancient art can still be found with little difficulty today and they have their ardent adherents. Much of the claimed success of palmists would seem to depend upon their ability to respond to cues such as voice, general demeanor, and dress, which are more relevant for assessing personality than are the "signs" of palmistry. Still another possibility is that the palmist offers such generalized trivial statements (e.g., "Although you have considerable affection for your parents, there have been times of great discord") that they could apply to virtually anyone.

Meehl (1956) suggested the phrase *Barnum effect* to "stigmatize those pseudo-successful clinical procedures in which patient descriptions from tests are made to fit the patient largely or wholly by virtue of their triviality; and in which any nontrivial, but perhaps erroneous, inferences are hidden in a context of assertions or denials which carry high confidence simply because of the population base rates" (p. 266). Tallent (1958) labeled this kind of personality assessment as involving the *Aunt Fanny error* because it contains mostly information that would be true of anybody's "Aunt Fanny." The degree to which any personality assessment procedure involves the Barnum or Aunt Fanny effect because it produces trivial, highly generalized personality descriptions always needs to be carefully evaluated.

Phrenology, the art of personality assessment through the measurement of the external shape of the human skull, was given its major impetus by Franz Joseph Gall, a German physician and anatomist, late in the 18th century. This comparatively recent attempt to develop a complete system of personality measurement deserves a more careful scrutiny for several reasons: (1) there were reasonable theoretical assumptions underlying the system, (2) the system is completely empirical and thus open to scientific inquiry, and (3) the history of phrenology is recent enough to have provided fairly complete documentation.

Gall's basic assumption was that the human brain was the locus of control over human behavior, a view which is now uniformly accepted by psychologists. At the turn of the 19th century, however, the operation of the cerebral cortex was poorly understood, and the current scientific view favored a strict localization of cortical action, with each function or faculty centered in a definite and specific region of the brain surface. The sizes of these regions created corresponding and observable alterations in the shape of the skull, which could be used by the phrenologist to assess the many characteristics of the individual, including personality. For example, a protrusion of the skull in the area of "honesty" would indicate an honest individual. As was the case with astrology and palmistry, phrenology enabled its practitioners to give a complete personality assessment, based in this case upon the protrusions and contours of the skull. The basic assumptions concerning the specificity of cerebral functioning and the formation of the skull have now been clearly disproven, and thus the theory upon which phrenology rests is discredited.

It is worthwhile to note that Gall was essentially empirical in his approach to the development of phrenology, attempting to relate behavior to brain functioning and skull shape through personal observation. To gather information about the brain, he examined the skulls of living persons and then attempted to study their brains through autopsy after death. He also examined the skulls of persons in mental hospitals, prisons, colleges, and other places where individuals of exceptional deficiencies or endowments could be found, hoping to be able to relate skull shape with the characteristics which had brought these persons together. Although this early attempt at the development of an empirical science of personality assessment is both noteworthy and laudable, it also points up the danger of unverified personal observations as the sole source of data in a scientific endeavor. The need for cross-validation of personal observations—that is, the objective demonstration of the same relationships in an independent setting—is as critical today as it was in Gall's time.

Paradoxically, it was not the lack of scientific validity of Gall's position that drew the most serious objections. Rather, the most strenuous indictments were based upon philosophical grounds (Davies, 1955). The critics of phrenology insisted that Gall's position was not unproved but unprovable; and even if provable, it was immoral. The confirmation of phrenology, according to these critics, would involve an acceptance of atheism and fatalism, and a denial of moral responsibility, the same issues which are raised in objection to contemporary deterministic views of human behavior. In the face of this violent and emotional criticism, however, the phrenologists themselves became defensive and dogmatic. What had originally been regarded as tentative and experimental now became dogma and gospel. Phrenology thus deteriorated from an experimental science, albeit one based upon inadequate assumptions, into a religionlike cult which was closed to any self-examination or modification based upon new data. The change doubtlessly served to hasten its fall from the respectability it once enjoyed.

The use of stable physical signs to assess personality characteristics is common to both palmistry and phrenology. The search for clear-cut relationships between the physical attributes of an individual and his/her psychological characteristics has been a continual one, reminiscent of our unending concern about the relationship between mind and body. This concern had an early expression in the humoural theory, an ancient physiology which remained current through the Middle Ages. The theory proposed four "ingredients": blood, phlegm, yellow bile (choler), and black bile (melancholy). The particular proportion of these four ingredients in different people determined their "complexions" (or personality characteristics), their physical and mental qualities, and their unique dispositions. It was thus claimed possible, by reading the physical signs of the relative amounts of these humours in a given individual, to determine his/her distinctive personality.

Although our more complete understanding of the physiology of the human body has long put the humoural theory into disuse, the assumption that human personality is a reflection of the physical body is also to be found in the modern work of Sheldon and his colleagues (Sheldon, Stevens, and Tucker, 1940). Sheldon's theory of *somatotypes* divides people into three major types: the ectomorph, who is thin and fragile; the mesomorph, who is powerful and muscular; and the endomorph, who is round, soft, and fat. According to the theory, each of these ideal types has a specific personality that is an innate consequence of that particular body build. The personality characteristics of most individuals, who are combinations of these three body types, are determined by the relative proportions of these body-type factors in their individual somatotype. Sheldon's theory has been the subject of considerable controversy, and the evidence for its validity is at best equivocal. Nevertheless, it is consistent with the age-old concern for discovering a simple link between mind and body.

It is not to be denied that there *are* significant relationships between certain physical signs (e.g., trembling, sweating) and personality characteristics (e.g., anxiety), nor that these relationships, though far from perfect, can be utilized in assessment. The unsuccessful attempts throughout history to rely on physical signs appear to have at least one of the following two characteristics: first, reliance on a theory which postulated that personality characteristics were *caused* by particular physical attributes; and second, lack of any logical connection between the physical sign and the personality attribute.

Astrology, palmistry, and phrenology—together with such methods as crystal ball gazing, tea leaf reading, and physiognomy (personality assessment from facial features)—have not survived scientific investigations of their usefulness, and the practice of such dubious procedures is considered charlatanism today. Yet, as we have seen, certain aspects of these approaches continue to be identifiable in current psychological thinking, indicating that these notions do have some current influence. Also, it should not be assumed that their practitioners can never do better than chance in personality assessment. In many cases such persons are sensitive to the same subtle cues that trained clinical psychologists and psychiatrists use in their own intuitive personality assessments. The charge of charlatanism arises from the attempts of phrenologists and palmists to insist that their understanding of the person being studied results from the application of some technique or procedure that has now been demonstrated to be ineffective or useless for that purpose, rather than from their superior intuitive assessment skills.

Influence of Psychological Measurement

Scientific personality assessment has its roots in the study of individual differences through psychological measurement. Most students of individual differences identify the opening of this area of inquiry as 1796, when a Greenwich astronomer's assistant, Kinnebrook, was dismissed because he had constantly observed the times of stellar transits almost one second later than his superior. It was later realized that this difference in reaction time was a stable one, and that people differed from each other in this and other measurable characteristics in a similarly stable fashion.

The study of individual differences was given considerable impetus by Darwin's work on evolution. In order to study the effects of human genetics, it would be necessary to identify clearly individual differences in those behaviors that had adaptability and survival value for humanity. Sir Francis Galton, a famous British scholar of the 19th century, became interested in the inheritance of these differences and devoted the later portion of his life to their study. Although there had been previous attempts to categorize and measure what Galton called "intellectual faculties," Galton himself was the initiator of the measurement of the nonintellectual faculties, known more commonly at that time as "character and temperament."

Galton discussed the measurement of several such faculties in the *Fortnightly Review* of 1884. His statement "that the character which shapes our conduct is a definite and durable 'something,' and therefore . . . it is reasonable to attempt to measure it," bears a strong resemblance to most contemporary views of personality, a topic to be explored further in the next chapter. Further, Galton proposed that the measurement of character should involve the same approach as "that which lies at the root of examinations into the intellectual capacity," and he briefly discussed methods for the measurement of "emotion" and "temper," using what we might term the *behavior sample approach*. For example, he suggested measuring emotion by means of instruments to record physiological changes in the individual during real-life stress situations. To investigate the practicality of this procedure, Galton himself actually wore a pneumocardiograph over his heart while delivering an important public lecture. He also suggested measuring pulse rate and changes in limb volume with the withdrawal of blood, all measures which are still used in psychophysiological research laboratories for studying emotional reactions. With regard to temper, Galton pointed out that small boys were expert in measuring the temper of a dog (i.e., how much teasing a dog would tolerate before responding negatively), and he was convinced that similar techniques could be developed for the assessment of good and bad temper in humans.

The study of individual differences in the United States was pioneered by James McKeen Cattell, who took his doctorate in Leipzig with the pioneer of experimental psychology, Wilhelm Wundt. Cattell also worked briefly with Galton in England, then returned to the United States in 1888 and established the Psychological Laboratory at the University of Pennsylvania. Although his interests were mainly in the areas of psychophysics, perception, and reaction time, Cattell nevertheless had a strong influence upon the development of other psychological measurement devices, including personality tests, through his support for the practical utilization of psychological knowledge (Boring, 1929, pp. 532–540).

At about the same time in France, Alfred Binet, who had become enthusiastic about Galton's work on individual differences, began a series of studies of eminent persons in the arts and sciences. Binet used a standard series of experimental tasks, including observations on body types, head measurements, and handwriting. Some of these interests appeared to reflect the influence of phrenology (which was then current) and other prescientific notions, and Binet, who was a careful and objective investigator, later discarded them as not leading to useful understanding of the persons being studied. Binet also began a series of investigations into mental functioning, which included personality, using a wide variety of tasks such as word knowledge, reasoning, and numerical ability. These investigations led to the development of the now famous Binet tests of intelligence. Some of his tasks, which involved telling stories about pictures and identifying inkblots, were antecedents of what are now known as the "projective" tests of personality.

Thus, prior to 1915, research on the measurement of personality was preceded by work on the measurement of skills or abilities, and it grew out of the early academic interest in the measurement of human individual differences. The faculties of character or temperament were considered to be "real," along with reaction times and perceptual abilities, in much the same sense as physical characteristics such as height and weight. Galton had introduced the use of direct behavior samples in real-life situations, and his work had stimulated considerable interest in both the United States and France. Two of Galton's followers, Karl Pearson and Charles Spearman, were playing a major part in the development of statistical procedures that provided powerful tools for later work in assessment.

At about this time, an English scientist named Webb (1915) published what seems to have been the first major attempt to summarize the important aspects of character through the intensive study of a large number of subjects. He obtained ratings of a large group of school- and college-age males on 40 or more qualities which had "a general and fundamental bearing on the total personality." The ratings were obtained from persons who knew the subjects well, and the resulting data were treated by an early form of statistical procedures which are now known as *factor analysis*. They were interpreted to indicate that the most basic aspect of personality was the "consistency of action resulting from deliberate volition, or will." Webb's study is noteworthy both for its use of judges' ratings (i.e., estimates by experts) and for its sophisticated statistical techniques. Webb also summarized two previous studies which had approached the scientific study of personality in a different way—through the use of what he called the "biographic method," an analysis of written personal life histories. These can be regarded as forerunners of the present-day "biographical data blank" approach to personality assessment.

Influence of Abnormal Psychology

At about the same time that academic psychologists were developing their interest in the measurement of normal human capacities and individual differences, other investigators were becoming involved in the formal assessment of *abnormal* human behavior. This interest stemmed from the practical need to classify and categorize the various kinds of psychopathology as well as the more theoretical need to gain a better understanding of the phenomena under scrutiny. Closely related to these efforts were the parallel attempts of Binet to develop clinical tests that would identify children who lacked the mental capacity to benefit from schooling and provide theoretical information about their intellectual limitations.

It is generally considered that the earliest attempts at personality assessment with psychopathological cases involved word association procedures. Emil Kraepelin, the renowned German psychiatrist who was primarily responsible for our current psychiatric classification procedures, made some use of a "free association test" as early as 1892, and Sommer, one of his colleagues, suggested its use for differentiating various kinds of mental disorder in 1894 (Anastasi, 1967, p. 18). In the word association technique, the subject is presented with a stimulus word, frequently from a standardized list of such words, and is asked to respond as quickly as possible with the first word that comes to mind. The list is usually presented more than once, since the giving of different responses to the same word is believed to indicate a problem area. A record is made of the responses given and of the reaction time to each presentation. It is noteworthy that the technique had been also used by Galton and Cattell for assessing individual differences.

The use of word association as a method for the identification of unconscious personality conflicts was initially proposed by Carl Jung. Jung (1910) developed a standardized list of words that were regarded as especially useful in detecting areas of conflict or disturbance, indicated by excessively long reaction times, failures to respond, misunderstandings of the stimulus words, and other emotional reactions, such as stammering and blushing.

Another, more formal approach to the use of word association was developed by Kent and Rosanoff (1910). Their standardized list deliberately omitted words which were especially likely to call up personal experiences, and they developed norms of common responses by administering the list of 1,000 normal persons. By comparing the responses of normals with those of psychotics, they were able to demonstrate that the psychotics gave strikingly fewer common responses than normals and that these differences were large enough to be of diagnostic significance in individual cases. Thus, the word association test can be regarded as the first practical psychometric device for identifying emotionally disturbed persons, although it is little used for this purpose today.

A similar concern with problems of adjustment led Heymans and Wiersma (1906) to develop a list of symptoms indicative of psychopathology. This list, revised by Hoch and Amsden (1913) and later by Wells (1914), was influential in generating the self-report personality inventory. The first such inventory was Woodworth's (1919) Personal Data Sheet, which was developed during World War I to diagnose the ability of soldiers to adjust satisfactorily to the strains and stresses of military life. Since it was obvious that there were not enough psychologists or psychiatrists available to interview each draftee personally about his emotional status, some more economical method was sought. A Committee on Emotional Fitness was appointed by the National Research Council to work on this problem under the chairmanship of Robert S. Woodworth. Their solution was a paper-and-pencil inventory (entitled the Personal Data Sheet to allay suspicion about its real purpose), which was a standardized psychiatric interview in printed form (see Symonds, 1931). The questions were based upon common neurotic symptoms and upon the reports of symptoms which were actually observed in men who had not been able to adjust to war and its stresses. The questions dealt with physical symptoms ("Do you ever feel an awful pressure in or about your head?"); fears and worries ("Are you troubled with the idea that people are watching you on the street?"); adjustment to the environment ("Do you make friends easily?"); unhappiness and unsociability ("Are you troubled by shyness?"); dreams, fantasies, and sleep disturbance ("Are you frightened in the middle of the night?"); plus some miscellaneous items. The score on this questionnaire was the number of items answered in the direction considered to be typical of maladjustment or psychoneurosis. Over 200 different questions were initially assembled, all capable of being answered yes or no. On the basis of preliminary testing with both college men and draftees, the list was reduced to 116. However, the armistice came before the final form could actually be used in practice. Later called the Woodworth Psychoneurotic Inventory, this self-report inventory was the forerunner of the many paper-and-pencil personality tests in use today.

Following Woodworth's original work, there were several rather immediate attempts to adapt his questionnaire to other groups (such as schoolchildren, juvenile delinquents, and college students), essentially by modifying the wording of the questions. A variation of the questionnaire procedure was developed by Pressey and Pressey (1919), whose X-O Test presented the subject with lists of words rather than questions. Subjects were asked to read the list and to cross out (hence the title of the test) the words that they regarded as wrong (such as spitting, smoking, recklessness), that made them nervous or anxious (such as loneliness, sin, pain), or that involved their likes or interests (such as camping, reading, kissing).

Thus, by 1920 there was a firm beginning of a structured and empirically based approach to personality measurement—one based upon the academic study of individual differences and the clinical assessment of psychopathology. In the subsequent decades there has been an explosion of interest in personality assessment. The lines of development are much less clear, however, and there is much cross-fertilization of ideas and research. Let us try to untangle the basic threads of the later influences on this burgeoning field.

Influence of Psychoanalysis

As we noted, one strong influence in the development of personality assessment was an interest in the clinical assessment of single individuals suffering from some form of psychopathology. Within this context, an influence which became predominant was psychoanalytic theory, with its view that personality is best understood as a series of levels and that the causes of psychological disturbances are hidden deep below the level of conscious awareness. In the psychoanalytic view, the most important and useful means of understanding of an individual is an analysis of the hidden elements of a person's functioning, and not the overt behavior which is readily available for superficial scrutiny. To psychoanalysts, the data yielded by the self-report inventories previously discussed would be of limited utility. Of related importance was the rising influence of Gestalt psychology, with its implication that the personality of the whole individual was more than the simple sum of discrete behaviors or traits.

These trends came together in a well-known development in the history of personality assessment for clinical purposes. Hermann Rorschach, a Swiss psychiatrist, had been using the perception of inkblots as an approach to theoretical problems in psychology when he made the empirical discovery that the results could be used for making differential psychiatric diagnoses. His major work was published in German in 1921 but did not appear officially in English until 1942 (Rorschach, 1942). Although earlier investigators had used inkblots as free association material, they had limited themselves to an analysis of the thematic content. Rorschach's contribution was to attempt a systematic analysis of the subject's concern with the *formal* aspects of the blots (such as color, shading, apparent movement) and whether the subject preferred to consider the blot as a whole or in parts. He believed that these different perceptual approaches were related to different psychological processes, or "structures," of the personality, and he advocated further research into this perceptual task, using an empirical, statistical orientation. Rorschach's work was seminal both in stimulating research with his inkblots and in the development of other minimally structured stimulus situations, to which responses can be elicited and analyzed for the purpose of personality assessment. Rorschach's plans for greater validational research on his technique were interrupted by his untimely death at the age of 37.

Rorschach's inkblot technique soon found favor among clinicians, especially those of a psychoanalytic orientation, as a means for assessing the state of the unconscious mind. Its use in this manner is somewhat ironic, since Rorschach's interests were primarily in using his inkblots as a means of addressing theoretical problems in experimental psychology, and secondarily as an empirical means of assigning patients to psychodiagnostic categories (Rorschach, 1942). In fact, he specifically stated that "the test cannot be considered as a means for delving into the unconscious" (p. 123). Nevertheless, the technique eventually became the most widely used procedure for exploring both the content and structure of the deeper aspects of personality within psychoanalytic theory.

The popularity of the Rorschach technique and the development of other, similar procedures for examining the hidden or covert aspects of personality led Frank (1939) to term these approaches to personality assessment *projective* techniques. Projective methods were conceptualized as those which present the subject with a situation for which there are few clearly defined cultural patterns of response, so that he/she must "project" upon that ambiguous field "his way of seeing life, his meanings, significances, patterns, and especially his feelings" (Frank, 1939, p. 403). According to Frank, a projective test involves the presentation of a stimulus situation that elicits the private idiosyncratic meaning and organization of the individual's private world that is brought to the testing situation and which is called into play in responding to the test demands. Frank regarded these methods as indirect ones which tap the pattern of internal organization and structure of personality without disintegrating or modifying the pattern as it exists, much in the manner of an X ray of the body.

What are the other projective methods? We have already discussed the word association method, which is seldom used nowadays in clinical practice. A group of procedures which Lindzey (1961) has called *constructive techniques* was developed by Henry A. Murray and his colleagues at Harvard University in the 1930s (Morgan and Murray, 1935; Murray, 1938, 1943). Murray, with a strong interest in literary creation, developed the Thematic Apperception Test (TAT), in which subjects create stories about ambiguous pictures. According to Murray, the content of the stories reflects the subjects' past experiences and present needs. A similar constructive approach is to be found in Van Lennep's (1951) Four Picture Test, developed initially in the 1930s, and in such later instruments as the Blacky Pictures (Blum, 1950) and the Children's Apperception Test (Bellak, 1954). Another widely used group of projective procedures involves an analysis of the subject's own creative drawings and paintings. Although figure drawings of a man had been used for some time as a convenient method of estimating intelligence (Goodenough, 1926), it remained for Buck (1948a, 1948b) and Machover (1949) to popularize them as a projective method for personality assessment.

Influence of Psychometrics

At the same time that some psychologists were busy developing and using projective approaches to the assessment of personality, others were busy with the further development and refinement of personality inventories. This work, although directly related to Woodworth's original Personal Data Sheet (Symonds, 1931), was conducted by psychologists who in many cases possessed sophisticated skills in test construction and statistics, together with a clear understanding of the complex problems of test reliability and validity. It emphasized the measurement of a person's discrete traits or aspects rather than a global assessment of the whole personality.

The advantages of inventories were that they could be readily administered to many individuals in a group, scoring was rapid and objective, and statistical procedures could be used in establishing norms, internal consistency, the relationship between test scores and other behavioral measures, and other characteristics of the instruments. There were difficulties also. The test items involved in these instruments often reflected the more superficial and obvious aspects of overt behavior, and their susceptibility to deliberate faking posed many problems in interpreting the scores obtained. Goldberg (1971a) has published an exhaustive historical survey of personality scales and inventories, and the interested reader is referred to his work for more extensive information in this area.

The item content of most early inventories was chosen for its *face validity;* that is, items were included if the test developer thought that they would elicit different responses from well-adjusted and poorly adjusted subjects. The Bell Adjustment Inventory (Bell, 1939) is an example of this approach to item selection and test construction.

A different and more sophisticated technique for item selection is the empirical approach, where the actual responses of different subject groups are examined in order to determine which responses are characteristic of each group. Only those items that can be actually shown to differentiate the groups are included in the final form of the test. The empirical approach, used by Rorschach in the original development of his psychodiagnostic procedure, was employed by Edward K. Strong (1927) in the development of the Strong Vocational Interest Blank. Although a full discussion of interest measurement is beyond our scope here, Strong's work is noteworthy because it presents an important early model of the empirical approach to test construction. The empirical technique was also involved to some extent in the construction of the Bernreuter Personality Inventory (Bernreuter, 1939) and in the Humm-Wadsworth Temperament Scale (Humm and Wadsworth, 1935). The latter was a direct predecessor of the more carefully developed Minnesota Multiphasic Personality Inventory (Hathaway and McKinley, 1940, 1951).

We have already alluded to the troublesome problem caused by the tendency of some subjects to avoid giving socially undesirable answers to inventory items, such as failing to admit to being nervous, rather than making the more personally appropriate responses. The Minnesota Multiphasic Personality Inventory (MMPI) attempted to deal with this problem by including several *validity scales,* such as the lie scale, which give some measure of the tendency to respond in the socially acceptable manner. Concern with this problem also led to the development, in the 1940s, of the forced-choice technique, which was subsequently used by Edwards (1953) in his Personal Preference Schedule. Since the forced-choice procedure requires subjects to endorse one of two items matched for social desirability (or undesirability), it was presumed that responses would have to reflect something more than the social desirability of the items.

Goldberg (1971b), commenting upon the current proliferation of personality inventories, made a distinction between two kinds of inventories, based on the reasons for their development. The first group of inventories was developed in response to pressures from society to deal with specific applied problems. This category included the inventories dealing with the problem of personal adjustment as previously discussed, those measuring satisfaction and success in vocational choice, and those tapping aspects of academic achievement beyond that is predictable from measures of scholastic aptitude or intelligence. The second group of inventories was based more upon conceptions of the structure of individual differences than upon any societal or real-life considerations, and was viewed as stemming from theoretical concepts about the nature of personality. This group included the inventory measures of introversion-extroversion and masculinity-femininity, and also the inventory measures based upon two influential theories of individual differences, Spranger's (1928) classification of "personal values" and Murray's (1938) scheme for ordering manifest needs. Although Goldberg's classification scheme was developed only for inventory measures of personality, it has clear relevance for other personality assessment methods.

Psychoanalysis versus Psychometrics

Most of the specific instruments and the methodological issues introduced in the preceding sections will be discussed in greater detail later. What, however, can be said about the present relationship between these two major historical influences—psychoanalysis and psychometrics—and the two major approaches to assessment they spawned—the projective technique and the self-report inventory? Over the years there has been a persistent tendency on the part of most followers of these two traditions to have a strong negative emotional bias toward work in the other tradition. This tendency was undoubtedly heightened in 1939 by Frank's use of the label "projective techniques" with the explicit statement that these instruments provided indirect measures of personality structure, and by the implication that the era's more traditional inventories were not coming to grips with the real stuff of personality. The most important consequence of this development of two antagonistic points of view has been the loss of much clinical and scientific interchange between the two opposing camps—and the loss of cross-fertilization that might have advanced the entire process of personality assessment. With the possible exception of the Holtzman Inkblot Technique (Holtzman, Thorpe, Swartz, and Herron, 1961) and a few other developments (e.g., Gleser and Ihilovich, 1969; Lanyon, 1972), there have been negligible developments that would represent any synthesis of the two traditions.

Some psychologists (e.g., Levy, 1963) have argued that the distinction between projective and inventory devices is a spurious one. It is pointed out that self-report inventories can be, and most often are, responded to "projectively," and that the resultant personality "profiles" are used by skilled clinicians as the basis for a global interpretation of personality, in terms that involve far more than a simple description of overt behavior. On the other hand, the traditional projective techniques can be, and often are, objectively scored and then interpreted according to normative data and empirical evidence about the meaning of certain discrete response categories.

In a recent review of projective techniques, Klopfer and Taulbee (1976) concluded that these methods "often reveal much more about a person's conscious preoccupations and goals than they do about the unconscious" (p. 562). While their final conclusion was that the primary contribution of projective techniques is in "revealing aspects of motivation and personality that do not fit neatly into either the self-concept or behavioral category" (p. 563), these characteristics are by no means unique to projectives and do not seem to justify the distinctive category typically provided for them. Granted that the independence of the histories of projectives and inventories has been real enough to demand formal recognition, we see no reason to perpetuate a distinction which serves no useful purpose, and we shall attempt in the remaining chapters to transcend many of the usual differences between the two.

Influence of Vocational and Industrial Psychology

While clinical psychologists were directing their efforts toward the detection and evaluation of maladjustment through either inventories or projective techniques, interest was also developing in the assessment of other aspects of human personality, especially non-skill characteristics that might contribute to vocational success. Although maladjustment per se was seen as often an important factor in determining vocational failure, interest was focused more specifically on factors within the range of normal functioning that determined people's choices of vocation and their long-range vocational satisfaction.

The Strong Vocational Interest Blank (now the Strong-Campbell Interest Inventory), noted earlier, was originally developed in 1927 by empirically comparing the expressed interests of successful persons in a variety of occupations. By asking persons who were established in different occupations to express their preferences among activities such as "visit an art gallery" and "collect coins," Strong was able to identify a number of interests that were differentially correlated with success in specific occupations. He reasoned that, if successful persons in a vocation could be differentiated on the basis of their expressed interests, then new persons with similar interests would more likely be successful in that vocation than those with dissimilar interests. More than 50 years of research with Strong's instrument and its successor has shown substantial support for this basic hypothesis. The Strong Vocational Interest Blank and a number of similar interest inventories began to be routinely used by vocational counselors for career guidance and by industrial psychologists for selection purposes.

Vocational and industrial psychologists began to assess still other variables. For example, it became apparent that large differences existed in effective job performance among persons of approximately equal ability level. Those who did well seemed to have more drive or a stronger motive to achieve than those who did poorly. It was hoped that the assessment of this characteristic would result in improved counseling and selection procedures. McClelland, Atkinson, Clark, and Lowell (1953) responded to this particular challenge by developing a highly reliable scoring scheme for achievement motivation, based on the Thematic Apperception Test. The development of the Edwards Personal Preference Schedule (Edwards, 1953, 1959), using a modified self-report inventory approach, was also a response to the need for instruments to assess motivational aspects among normal persons.

These psychologists also started to realize that as people progressed up the vocational ladder from assembly line worker through supervisory roles and into management, interpersonal relationships became more and more important as a determinant of success. Consequently, it began to become necessary for psychologists to evaluate interpersonal factors as part of their routine work of management selection and management development. The earlier paper-and-pencil inventories, with their focus on psychopathology, were clearly unsuited for such purposes, and a new generation of inventories was developed, tapping aspects of everyday psychological functioning such as sociability, dominance, flexibility, and various dimensions of interpersonal style. Instruments whose origins were motivated in part by the needs of vocational and industrial psychology include the California Psychological Inventory (Gough, 1967/1975), the Fundamental Interpersonal Relations Orientation (FIRO) Scales developed by Schutz (1967), Jackson's (1967/1974) Personality Research Form, and the Jackson Personality Inventory (Jackson, 1976).

Another product of the real world of work was the observation that items of personal history, as recorded on a written application blank, appeared to have value in predicting success in specific work settings. This observation resulted in the development of the weighted biographical data sheet (England, 1961), which provides an alternative to the established psychological "testing" approach to assessment.

To digress for a moment, the use of biographical data for clinical purposes has been well established. For example, the Phillips (1953) scale for predicting outcome in schizophrenia is a method of estimating the premorbid adjustment of psychiatric patients by assigning differential weighting to various items in the patient's case history, mainly those behaviors involving heterosexual interests and relationships. Biographical data have also been used for many years in the development of "base expectancy tables" to predict whether or not a prisoner is likely to violate parole if it is granted. Such tables were discussed in detail in the July 1962 issue of the *Journal of Crime and Delinquency*. In view of the central role accorded case history information in professional mental health work, it is somewhat surprising that no widely used clinical instrument of this type exists. The promising start made by Briggs (1959) indicates that such instruments can be developed and shows their potential for clinical use.

Another approach to personality assessment is the behavior sample technique, pioneered by Galton (1884), as we have previously described. Here, the behaviors of interest are evoked in the laboratory or in a controlled field setting. The primary assumption underlying this approach is direct and simple—that the frequency, or ease with which the behaviors are aroused in the test situations, is related to the frequency with which they occur in ordinary, real-life settings.

Perhaps the best known of the early attempts to use this approach is that of Hartshorne and May (1928) in their studies of honesty and deceit. A more complex use is found in the *assessment center* procedure, which is designed to gain a better understanding of particular groups of individuals or to select candidates for difficult or high-level positions. The use of this procedure for assessing a particular group of individuals, such as architects or mathematicians, was pioneered by psychologists at the University of California's Institute of Personality Assessment and Research (IPAR). Their research reports (e.g., MacKinnon, 1975) tend to offer strong support for this type of complex, behavior sample approach.

One of the first uses of the assessment center method for personnel selection was the U.S. Office of Strategic Services' clinical assessment project during the Second World War (OSS Assessment Staff, 1948), involving the selection of persons for intelligence and spying operations. The individuals to be evaluated were brought together in small groups for several days of evaluation by a group of assessors at a remote residential site or assessment center. Many different kinds of data were made available to the panel of assessors, including psychological test and interview data. What was unique, however, was observation of the participants in a variety of situational tests which were developed as representative behavior samples of the work to be done. For instance, one of the situational tests developed for the OSS assessment program was a stress interview in which interrogators attempted to break down the "cover story" which the candidate developed. Despite considerable difficulty, data were obtained to indicate the positive contribution of the assessment center concept for selecting spies. Among the several problems inherent in this approach are how the many behavioral indices (such as test scores and ratings) should be weighted, how to combine them into a single predictor, and how to develop criterion measures. Taft (1959) has provided an interesting and illuminating summary of many of the issues involved in the multiple-method approach to assessment and selection.

Motivated in part by the OSS experience, a multiple-method assessment program was conducted to study the selection process for the profession of clinical psychology (Kelly and Fiske, 1951; Kelly and Goldberg, 1959). However, results were disappointing. Using ratings of later professional success as the criteria, neither the individual measures nor the combined ratings yielded useful predictions. In trying to explain the relative failure, the authors noted that the subjects involved were already highly selected and rather homogeneous in a number of important respects, all of which would attentuate the obtained correlations. A similar study with more promising results was reported by Holt and Luborsky (1958), using psychiatric residents as the subjects.

The assessment center methodology has been widely adopted as the procedure of choice in the selection and development of middle-level managers. Based upon the early work of the American Telephone and Telegraph Company (Bray and Grant, 1966), these centers have been shown to provide reliable and valid predictions against ratings of job success. Predictions have been based upon situations with a high degree of real-life behavioral relevance. One advantage of the behavior sample approach in this situation is its relatively high degree of acceptance by participants; another is that its predictive validity and its obvious face validity make it less susceptible to legal objections based upon equal employment opportunity legislation. Research indicating the superiority of multimethod assessment, of which assessment center technology is an example, is discussed in Chapter 8.

Influence of Modern Behaviorism

The mainstream of American academic psychology has always been rather behavioral in orientation, and the 1960s and 1970s saw a strong movement to extend this orientation into clinical psychology. This movement, largely associated with the rise of behavior modification and behavior therapy, also has its implications for personality assessment. It should be recognized that traditional personality assessment, based either on self-report inventories or projective techniques, has its antecedents in a kind of trait or factor psychology. Assessments prepared by persons working from the traditional position have typically emphasized the underlying personality structure or the inner predispositions of the person, and there has been little interest in considering the contextual or situational determinants of the person's behavior. Rather, the assumption in traditional assessment has been that an understanding of personality, referring to inner dispositions, is all that is necessary for making predictions about future behaviors. Within this orientation, little or no concern has been shown with the relatively limited predictive value of most traditional personality measures.

Behaviorally oriented psychologists have called for greater specificity of predictions, and most particularly, for a thorough study of the environmental circumstances that are necessary for a particular behavior to be evoked (Mischel,

1968, 1977). Many behavioral psychologists, including Mischel (1972) himself, believe that an individual's self-statements and self-predictions are often as accurate in predicting the person's behavior as the more indirect and expensive evaluations by trained personality assessors. The underlying rationale is phenomenological: the crucial determinant of the person's behavior in a situation is believed to be the person's awareness of the behavioral contingencies in the situation, and only the person has access to that awareness.

Another important characteristic of the behavioral approach is its emphasis on the person's overt behavior, or what a person *does* in various situations, rather than on inner dispositions, or what a person *is*. Thus, instead of relying upon generally available and commercially published personality tests, behavioral psychologists prefer to develop "tailor-made" assessment devices in which the particular stimulus situation of interest to the psychologist is represented in as accurate and detailed a manner as possible. As an early example, in measuring fear, a population of potentially fear-arousing stimuli is identified and a representative sample of items is drawn from it and presented to the person in a variety of ways (Geer, 1965; Lang and Lazovik, 1963; Wolpe and Lang, 1964). In assessing fear of snakes, for example, the items could include written descriptions; slides, pictures, or movies; vivid fantasies of snakes; and actual snakes. The similarity of this approach to the behavioral sample approach of the assessment center should be readily apparent. The growing field of behavioral assessment is considered in detail in Chapter 5.

Influence of Social Psychology

We began the chapter with a discussion of our abiding interest in understanding the behavior of others and the manner in which "naïve" persons have gone about achieving this understanding. We conclude with the same topic but from a different perspective. Social psychologists have long been interested in understanding how nonpsychologists go about understanding others, assessing other people's intentions, motives, interpersonal likes and dislikes, and other important characteristics. Social psychologists term this area *person perception,* and we can assume that at least some of the operations engaged in by clinical psychologists during interviewing and therapy also fall within this topic. Clinicians were naïve perceivers of others long before they became psychologists, and these early patterns of perception probably continue to function largely unchanged.

Not unexpectedly, it has been shown that a primary determinant of how we are perceived by others is our physical appearance. A large number of research studies support the conclusion that the impression we make is influenced by physical attractiveness and neatness of dress and grooming, plus a number of other immediately obvious characteristics such as the wearing of glasses. To cite a specific example, Dion, Berscheid, and Walster (1972) found that physically attractive people are seen by others as more sensitive, more interesting, more sociable, more exciting, and kinder than less attractive people.

The impressions which we form of others come not only from various static or structural elements of appearance but also from a variety of kinetic or fluid elements such as gestures and body movements. Among the various elements which have been studied are body contact, proximity, orientation of body, posture, looking or gazing, and the nonverbal elements of speech (Argyle, 1972). In general, these cues are utilized to make judgments about such characteristics as attractiveness or likability, about emotional states such as depression or anxiety, and about status and role. It appears that judgments rely heavily upon "display rules," or conventions which have established the appropriate behaviors for a variety of situations (Goffman, 1959).

One important finding from the research on person perception is that, as we collect data about other people, we tend to rely upon *central traits* in forming our impressions. That is, certain bits of data about a person are given greater weight than other bits, and we ordinarily use these more central bits to organize our impressions. The seminal experiments of Asch (1946) demonstrated that one such central trait was represented by the *warm-cold dimension.* For instance, when the adjective *warm* was used to describe another person who was to be judged, over 90 percent of the experimental subjects described the target person as *generous,* and more than 75 percent used *humorous* as a descriptor. Other constructs, such as *polite* or *blunt,* when supplied to the subjects did not generate such a strong halo effect about the target person, leading Asch to conclude that only certain descriptors or traits were central ones. Asch's work, supported and elaborated by a number of subsequent investigations, is useful in helping us understand how we often form a rather clear impression of another person, even with a minimum of information.

A basic question is, of course, the accuracy of such impressions. There is no clear answer to this question. However, there is evidence (Norman and Goldberg, 1966; Passini and Norman, 1966) that central traits or dimensions of personality are at least in part a function of the way in which observers tend to use the trait names rather than of the observed person's actual characteristics. In other words, our judgments about others can be in part a function of the way we structure our interpersonal world and might not be primarily a function of the way others behave.

There appear to be three kinds of central traits around which observers organize their judgments of others: *evaluation,* where we organize our judgments around a good-bad dimension; *potency,* where we use strong-weak or hard-soft as the dimension; and *activity,* where the dimension is active-passive or energetic-lazy (Rosenberg and Sedlak, 1972). These dimensions are particularly apparent in direct ratings of traits and in trait-sorting tasks, where judges are asked to describe a target person by selecting from a list of traits those that best describe themselves. There is obvious congruence between these three dimensions and those previously identified by Osgood in his work with the Semantic Differential (Osgood, Suci, and Tannenbaum, 1957).

One important reason why people observe another person is to know the person's intentions or motives (Heider, 1958). Such knowledge makes that other person's behavior understandable and predictable. Two basic models of this process have been proposed—the intuitive and the inferential. The phenomenological and Gestalt psychologists have argued that the person-perception process is intuitive, immediate, organized, and direct; and based more upon some innate, human mechanism than upon learning (e.g., Allport, 1937, 1961). The inferential view, on the other hand (e.g., Sarbin, Taft, and Bailey, 1960), suggests that judgments about others are built up from cues provided by the person and are based upon learned, general principles of human behavior. The inferences operate much like syllogisms in which the underlying characteristics of the person are judged in terms of *general constructs* or postulates.

Consider the syllogism:

People who wear glasses are intelligent; this person wears glasses; therefore this person is intelligent.

The major premise (''People who wear glasses are intelligent''), the one upon which the entire inferential process depends, is a general construct which developed either from (1) past experience, (2) an organized set of beliefs that constitutes in effect a personality theory, (3) analogy, or (4) the uncritical acceptance of a proposed construct from others. It is these constructs, part of what the observer brings to the person perception, that produce the beauty in the beholder's eye. Obviously, the usefulness of such constructs depends upon their ''truthfulness,'' or predictive validity.

One general set of constructs is called *stereotypes* (Lippmann, 1922), widespread beliefs about the characteristics of persons who belong to certain definable groups—racial, ethnic, national, social, sex, or age; or who possess certain salient physical qualities—height, weight, hair coloring, facial characteristics, handicaps, or deformities. While many stereotypes do contain a germ of truth, these truths are typically distorted and exaggerated by the language which is used to express them. More important, there is considerable danger that people tend to use them in an overspecific manner and that every member of a certain group is assumed to have exactly the same characteristic. Nevertheless, stereotypes do constitute one important source of our initial constructs about other people.

The minor premise (''This person wears glasses'') involves classification of the person as a member of the class defined in the major premise. This process involves an examination of the many cues provided by the person. When the cues clearly establish class membership, we draw a conclusion based upon that membership. Hathaway (1956a) has demonstrated that there is only a handful of cues (which include gender, age, and intelligence) that provide an adequate basis for assignment to group membership, and that much of our inaccuracy in making predictions about others stems from using cues that are insufficiently valid. To summarize, whether or not the inferential model of Sarbin et al. (1960) accurately reflects all instances of person perception, it would seem to be useful in understanding a great many of them.

Social psychologists recently have centered much of their research attention on the process of *attribution;* namely, how people go about assessing and evaluating the intentions and motives of others. When we observe a behavior of others, we usually explain what we observe in one of two ways. Either we believe that the person did it by *volition* or else because of situational *circumstances*. For example, a person who is successful is seen to have succeeded either by trying hard or because the task was easy. Analogously, failure is explained either by insufficient effort or because the task was too difficult.

It is important to recognize that people tend to be held responsible for their behavior when they are free to choose but are not seen as responsible for responding to external compulsion. Many of our judgments about the moral quality of others depend upon how we attribute motivation or responsibility. Did some POWs become traitors voluntarily, or did they simply yield to the inevitable and overwhelming pressure of their captors? Was Patty Hearst a voluntary colleague of her bank-robbing captors or did she simply break down under extreme duress?

The body of research now available suggests that the answer to such questions is different for actor and observer. As summarized by Jones and Nisbett (1971), there is a "persistent tendency for actors to attribute their actions to situational requirements, whereas observers tend to attribute the same actions to stable personal dispositions" (p. 2). In other words, we tend to perceive that our own actions are controlled by the environment and not by some internal need or predisposition, while we believe that others act in the same way because of their personal dispositions and not due to the influence of their environment. Thus, we may regard our affectional overtures to another person as due to a covert invitation (or possibly inebriation), but we are much more likely to regard such behavior in others as evidence of their licentiousness. "I am just a victim of circumstances, but he's a dirty old man."

Perhaps the simplest way of explaining this pervasive finding is that we have a great deal more information available about our own inner needs, our own past history, and about how we experience our own environment than we do about other people. Also, we have a large library of data about our own past reactions in similar and dissimilar situations, whereas we must interpret the behavior of others from a normative or modal frame of reference. These tendencies tend to combine to produce a view of other people as a package of personality traits, while we see ourselves as a package of underlying values and strategies that are brought into behavior by particular circumstances. Some psychologists, like Mischel (1968), believe that this approach to ourselves is also a potentially more accurate way of perceiving other persons than our typical way of seeing them as driven by underlying traits. In any event, the data seem rather clear. We tend to attribute our own behavior to external causes, but the behavior of others to internal causes.

Attribution theory has considerable relevance to the practical problems of personality assessment (Brehm, 1976). Psychologists make many attributions concerning their clients; indeed, much of our clinical work is motivated by the need to reach some conclusion about the underlying intentions or motives of those with whom we are working. As Shaver (1975) has noted, "insight" by a client in therapy can be seen as basically a correct attribution of causation (or at least, one that matches that of the psychologist), and much of our therapeutic work with clients has the goal of changing their attributional systems. Valins and Nisbett (1971) have expanded upon this idea. In their analysis, clients frequently make attributions of abnormality or inadequacy about themselves which have very negative consequences. These attributions are developed without any checking with peers because the behavior for which causation is sought is bad or shameful, or because it is assumed that others would not have had similar experiences. The erroneous causal attribution ("I am emotionally disturbed" or "I am sick") exacerbates the problem by creating even further distance between the person and his/her peers.

In summary, it is clear that attribution theory, which began as a theory of "naïve psychology," has important implications for the process of personality assessment in a broad sense. In particular, we need to beware of the general tendency to attribute the behavior of others to underlying, internal traits without considering how such attributions may be a function of a pervasive tendency to externalize causation that has little to do with the target person.

Summary

A number of assessment methods such as phrenology, astrology, and palmistry are fascinating to many laymen but are not regarded as having the documented utility required for their serious consideration by trained professional workers in personality assessment. Turning to the professionally recognized assessment instruments, two historical trends can be seen in their development. The first is traceable to the original academic interest in measuring individual differences, and it has its most important consequences in contemporary paper-and-pencil inventories, the self-report personality tests. The second originated in the need for understanding clinically abnormal behavior, and it is seen as leading to the interest in and development of projective techniques.

There has been long-standing conflict between the proponents of projective techniques and psychologists interested in psychometrically oriented assessment procedures. While some differences may exist between the two approaches, especially in their historical development, the overemphasis placed upon the differences has probably been detrimental to the development of the science of personality assessment.

Several other areas have had a significant impact on personality assessment. Within the fields of vocational and industrial psychology, procedures such as the Strong Vocational Interest Blank (now the Strong-Campbell Interest Inventory) were developed for career guidance and vocational selection. Also, a variety of inventories have been developed for assessing motivation and personality variables within the normal range, and biographical data and behavior samples have been used for assessment purposes. Such procedures came together in the assessment center technique, which was used for the selection of intelligence agents during World War II and has been widely adopted as the procedure of choice in selecting middle-level management personnel in business and industry.

Modern behaviorism has been another influence in the development of personality assessment, with its emphasis on a thorough study of the environmental circumstances that are necessary for a particular behavior to be evoked, as opposed to the more traditional approach of viewing the causes of behavior as residing within the person. A further influence has been the field of social psychology, and particularly the area of person perception, referring to the study of the manner in which lay persons go about achieving an understanding of others. One manner of organizing judgments about others involves three dimensions: evaluation, potency, and activity. A recent framework for studying how people assess others (the intentions and motives of others) is attribution theory. Research findings in this area show that the perceived reasons for a person's behavior differ for the actor and the observer; namely, we tend to view our own behavior as controlled by the environment but that of others as due to personal dispositions.

2 CONCEPTS AND DEFINITIONS

In understanding any human enterprise, it is important not only to understand *what* is being undertaken, but also to understand *why* a particular course of action is being pursued. Why do psychologists undertake the task of personality assessment? What are the benefits that this enterprise can offer? In general, psychologists assess personality for two reasons: first and primary, to assist our understanding of the behavior of a particular person, that is, the *clinical assessment* of a single individual; and second, in the context of psychological research and theory building, to advance our *general knowledge* of human behavior.

The major use of personality assessment instruments in professional psychology has been in the first context, the assessment of the single person. Here, the aim is to come to some decision about the future course of action of a specified individual or to make a prediction about his/her unique future behavior. It is this professional use which has been the main reason for the development and continued existence of most of the better known assessment devices.

With regard to the second use of assessment, researchers in psychology employ personality assessment techniques for a number of reasons. Some wish to study a particular personality concept—such as authoritarianism, ego strength, or loss of control—either for its own sake or within the framework of some theoretical approach to personality. Another research reason for utilizing assessment techniques could be in the context of achieving a better understanding of a certain pattern of behavior, such as managerial behavior or a particular clinical syndrome. A third reason might be to reduce the range of individual differences within subject groups on a research task by sorting the subjects according to a distinctive personality characteristic. For example, a researcher evaluating the effects of a psychotherapy procedure such as relaxation training might decide to examine high-anxiety and low-anxiety subjects separately because it is suspected that these subjects will differ in their ability to relax. Or, it might be decided to separate field-dependent and field-independent persons in an investigation of ability to solve a managerial In-Box problem. In research uses of assessment, the interest is typically in group differences rather than in a particular individual or in understanding the implications of the findings for the single person. Researchers are primarily interested in how the overall results shed light on some general fact or behavioral law which is reflected in the behavior of people in their experiments.

It would thus appear that the two major themes or influences which have defined and shaped our current knowledge in personality assessment are our involvement in solving applied, practical problems and our interest in a better theoretical understanding of human functioning. We have previously noted that Goldberg (1971a) drew a similar conclusion after discussing the rise of interest in personality inventories. His conclusion might well be extended to include the entire field of personality assessment, as it seems clear that the interplay between these two themes—the applied or individual, and the general or theoretical—has strongly influenced our present stage of development in personality assessment. Let us further examine these themes in order to enhance our understanding of basic concepts and issues. We focus our discussion on the clinical or practical role of assessment and introduce theoretical aspects as appropriate.

Personality Assessment: The Empirical Approach

We begin with an analysis of personality assessment procedures that utilize empirical knowledge. Taking a simple example, assume we have evidence that a particular response or set of responses (for instance, a score on a self-report personality inventory or a set of responses to the ambiguous stimuli of a projective test) is highly correlated with some nontest behavior (the criterion). It might be that high scores on the ABC Test are known to be highly correlated with success in door-to-door selling, or that a large number of animal responses on the XYZ Test are highly correlated with unsuccessful rehabilitation following release from a mental hospital.

In the *empirical approach* to personality assessment, the psychologist would need only to administer either of these tests, compare the obtained results with the empirical research findings, and make a prediction as to the probability of success or failure of the individual in either door-to-door selling or posthospital rehabilitation. The psychologist usually neither knows, nor is concerned about, the psychological or theoretical connection between the individual's test responses and the behavior to be predicted. In the empirical approach it is not necessary to understand *why* there is a connection between high scores on the ABC Test and selling behavior; it is sufficient to know that such a relationship reliably exists. Naturally, it is important to know the limiting conditions of this empirically derived relationship; that is, to know the particular groups of individuals and kinds of selling for which this relationship holds, and the circumstances under which it might break down. If we presume, however, that such information is available and that the individual is drawn from the segment of the population covered by a known empirical relationship, we can use this knowledge for prediction or decision making about that individual. The empirical approach might be schematically represented as follows:

Information from assessment procedures	→	Previous empirical findings	→	Decision about the individual

Depending upon such factors as the size of the relationship between the predictor and the criterion, the representativeness of the original empirical data, and the similarity of the current criterion to the original one, the professional psychologist will be more or less correct in the prediction or decision. Since there are a relatively small number of steps and inferences between the data and the decision, and it is not difficult to make periodic checks on the accuracy of the previously reported relationship, the probability of serious error is not great. However, it has been argued by Peak (1953), Loevinger (1957), and others that a purely empirical approach, with a total reliance upon observed relationships, is limited and superficial because the psychologist will not be able to develop any understanding, except on a primitive correlational level, of *why* the decision was a useful one.

The empirical approach to assessment involves a basic assumption. This is the assumption of interpersonal behavior consistency; that is, that there are enduring patterns of behavioral responses which transcend situations and which can be tapped and used for understanding particular individuals and people in general. The search for an understanding of these enduring characteristics of persons serves to identify the entire field of personality as an area of inquiry. Although a concern with the *nature* of these enduring characteristics is clearly the province of the more theoretically based approaches to personality assessment, the empirical approach must also assume their existence. It is particularly important to understand this assumption, because some psychologists who are identified with the behavioral approach to assessment have questioned the existence of significant enduring characteristics. This theoretical trend, which minimizes the importance of general and enduring characteristics as determinants of behavior, was seen in its most radical form in the 1960s (e.g., Kanfer and Saslow, 1965; Mischel, 1968; Peterson, 1968). The major question asked today is not so much whether enduring interpersonal characteristics can be identified, as whether they have importance for the field of personality theory, and in particular for assessment. In the *behavioral assessment* movement, primary emphasis is placed on the current situational determinants of behavior and on the relevant rewards and punishments which are contingent on these behaviors. Thus, the understanding and prediction of individual behavior is based not so much on an assessment of "underlying personality" as on an analysis of the actual behavior and the context in which the behavior occurs. We return to these issues later in the chapter.

Personality Description and Personality Assessment

In the empirical approach to personality assessment, the professional psychologist moves directly from the obtained data to the prediction or decision without considering any intervening processes. The empirical approach is data based, and its use is limited to those situations in which the test data, usually psychometric in nature, have been shown to be of predictive value. In actual practice, this limitation turns out to be a serious one. While the data which we have may predict door-to-door salesmanship, we are also interested in sales potential in a whole variety of situations. Similarly, while our empirical data may refer to success in posthospital rehabilitation, we are also interested in postprison rehabilitation and other related situations.

We could argue that all that is required under these circumstances is to extend the empirical approach to these new situations; that is, to collect additional new empirical data in each specific situation of interest. Unfortunately, because of the high cost of collecting and processing data—in terms of time, money, and other resources—this is usually not what happens in practice. Rather, the existing data are interpreted in more general terms, using the nonspecific language of personality description, and then they are used for prediction or decision making. Thus, persons scoring high on the ABC Test become characterized in general terms such as high in "salesmanship"; and persons giving many animal responses to the XYZ Test, as low in "rehabilitation potential." The personality description approach to assessment might be schematically represented as follows:

Information from   Personality   Decision
assessment   →   description   →   about the
procedures   individual

It is possible to regard this approach to clinical or individual assessment as a theoretical one, but we prefer not to do so. Our reasons are that there is very little "theory" involved other than common sense, and the choice of the concepts involved in this kind of procedure is primarily determined by pragmatic rather than theoretical considerations. Thus, our decision to use the ABC Test of "salesmanship" or the XYZ Test of "rehabilitation potential" would be made because we are interested in the behaviors that presumably can be predicted by these instruments, and there is minimal "theory" involved either in developing the tests for this use or in employing them in this practical manner.

It seems advisable at this time to state more precisely what we mean by a *theory*. Marx and Hillix (1973) have identified three general meanings of "theory" in contemporary psychological writings. The most general use is in reference to any conceptual process in science in contrast with the empirical, or observational, aspects. A second use is in reference to any generalized explanatory principle, one which ordinarily involves a statement of functional relationships among variables. The third usage, which both Marx and Hillix and the present writers endorse as the preferred one, refers to a group of logically organized or deductively related laws, usually based upon empirical observations. This usage is more closely aligned with those of the more developed sciences, and it also has a closer relationship to the concept of a *system,* in that this latter term broadly refers within psychology to a cluster of theoretical propositions and methodological biases. Taking the third usage as the criterion, it is readily apparent that there are few viable personality theories. In the remainder of our text, the term *theory* is restricted to this third usage, and much of what is often termed "theory" is regarded by us as rational, a priori, or commonsensical.

The reader should note that there is nothing intrinsically incorrect, either theoretically or methodologically, with the procedure of assessment through description. Indeed, if there were data available to suggest that the ABC Test did identify those who would become successful salesmen in a variety of settings or that the XYZ Test could predict who would respond unfavorably to rehabilitation efforts under a number of different circumstances, no serious objections to this kind of procedure would be raised. Unfortunately, the literature in personality assessment is replete with examples demonstrating that this is not the case. Rather, it would appear that indices developed for predicting a characteristic such as salesmanship in a particular setting are often relatively specific to that particular setting, and that they become much less effective when the situation to be predicted differs in any substantial way. Therefore, it is always necessary to make an empirical check on the generality of the prediction. The ABC Test must be checked to see whether it works with new samples of men, who may be older or younger or better educated than the original sample, or to see whether it will predict life insurance sales as well as door-to-door sales of encyclopedias. If we do not empirically verify the generality of our conclusions, we run the risk of making incorrect predictions and bad decisions, and sometimes we will perform worse than if we had used pure chance to make our choices. In summary, the major problem involved in using such descriptive constructs as "salesmanship" or "rehabilitation potential" is that their looseness represents a clear invitation to many potential users for abuse.

Because nontest criteria for generalized tendencies such as salesmanship or rehabilitation potential are often extremely difficult to obtain, it is sometimes argued that psychologists should use peer ratings or expert ratings of these tendencies as the criteria against which to compare the test responses. The major problem with this approach is the unknown validity of the ratings. On what basis can we assume that peer or "expert" ratings of some generalized behavioral tendency are themselves correlated with the behaviors in question? The question is an empirical one, and without evidence it cannot be assumed that ratings can be substituted for more empirically based criterion data.

The procedure of using the empirical relationships between test scores and nontest behaviors to support the utility of an abstract, generalized construct introduces the important concept of *construct validity* (Cronbach and Meehl, 1955), which is further discussed in Chapter 6. What should be understood at this point is the existence of a frequent problem in the applied use of personality assessment procedures—the assumption that a test score or index is indicative of some generalized internal characteristic of the respondent in cases where there are precious few data available to support such as assumption.

The Language of Personality Description

Before becoming involved with matters of theory in personality assessment, let us discuss the language that we tend to use to describe personality characteristics. Phrases like "sleeps more than usual," "works energetically on a problem," and "has never been observed to cry" represent rather clear and specific descriptions of directly observable behavior. In describing personality, however, either in our ordinary conversation or as professional psychologists, we usually wish to go further than this. We are usually interested in descriptive concepts that tap the more basic characteristics of the individual. Thus we tend to use general descriptive concepts such as "lethargic," "energetic," and "stoic" rather than the more behaviorally specific phrases given above. Our language usage involves many of these general descriptive words that are employed in both lay and professional conversations to describe ourselves and others.

Cultural anthropologists have suggested that a study of the words used in ordinary conversation by a culture will provide clues as to what the culture regards as basic and important. The observation that the Eskimo language has many single words denoting different kinds of snow (variations that could only be described in English using multiword phrases) and that the Polynesian dialects contain single words indicative of complex kinship relations (e.g., my father's brother's wife) is seen as evidence that snow and kinship are important concepts in these cultures. It is usually the case that those personality characteristics which are regarded as the more basic ones in our culture tend to be denoted by single words.

This view—that those individual differences which are of most importance to us in our daily human transactions have been encoded into our natural, everyday language as single-word descriptors—was initially proposed by Allport (1937) and has been strongly supported by Norman (1963c) and Goldberg (1972a, 1978a). A related assumption is that our language contains many synonyms to provide the culture with nuances of meaning for these important human characteristics. To illustrate, there are a large number of single words which describe a person with high energy level; for example, vigorous, energetic, active, lively, spry, brisk, pushy, and busy. However, there is no single-word descriptor of persons with skill in wiggling their ears.

We have just seen that one way of looking at the importance of an individual difference is its representation in natural language. Both Gough (1965) and Cattell (1950, 1957), in their development of personality measures, have deliberately used the occurrence of single-word descriptors in natural language to identify characteristics that are worth measuring. Thus, Gough selected "variables used for the description and analysis of personality in everyday life and in social interaction. It is theorized that such folk concepts, viewed as emergents from interpersonal behavior, have a kind of immediate meaningfulness and *universal relevance*" (1965, p. 295).

While Gough relied upon informal procedures for developing his list of important characteristics, Cattell used the 17,954 trait names which Allport and Odbert (1936) had developed from *Webster's Second Unabridged Dictionary*. Allport and Odbert had synthesized this list into a briefer list of 4,504 which they regarded as "real traits." Cattell further reduced the list to 171 items by eliminating synonyms. A cluster analysis of peer ratings using the 171 descriptors yielded 36 clusters which Cattell regarded as "surface traits." Several different factor analytic studies based upon peer ratings of these surface traits led Cattell to conclude that there were 15 to 20 distinct factors, or "source traits," underlying the surface traits, the so-called primary personality factors, which are now measured by his Sixteen Personality Factors Test (Cattell, Eber, and Tatsuoka, 1970). Thus, by a distillation process involving a combination of common sense and statistics, Cattell was able to reduce almost 18,000 characteristics to a list of 16.

More recently, Norman (1967) used the 17,954 characteristics of Allport and Odbert plus an additional 170 terms selected from *Webster's* third edition to develop a list of 7,300 descriptors by eliminating those terms which were obscure, ambiguous, purely physically descriptive, or purely evaluative (such as awful, bad, or fine). The 7,300 trait words were then sorted into three categories by Norman and his colleagues using the criterion of consensus. The three categories were: (1) stable traits (e.g., daring, imaginative, lazy, persistent), which accounted for approximately 40 percent of the total list; (2) temporary states (e.g., hesitant, sad, peeved, ranting), which also accounted for about 40 percent; and (3) social roles, relationships, and effects (e.g., employed, manageable, noted, respected), which accounted for the remaining 20 percent. In this manner the list was differentiated into *traits,* or enduring response predispositions which have implications for intrapersonal and interpersonal adjustment, and *states,* which are more transitory and ephemeral. For example, anxiety as a trait would suggest a continuing, generalized condition of the individual, while anxiety as a state would suggest a more transitory or temporary condition. One of the common confusions in personality description is that traits are often assumed from behaviors which are only indicative of states. When we are developing a personality description, as opposed to predicting a specific behavior in a specific situation, we are presumably trying to identify the individual's underlying, enduring response predispositions.

Dispositional versus Situational Determinants of Behavior

Earlier in this chapter we indicated that there are a number of psychologists who have minimized the significance of underlying, enduring response predispositions, in particular Mischel (1968, 1973, 1977). Let us now examine in greater detail the objections to the significance of dispositional determinants. For convenience, we use the term *traits* for these underlying dispositional determinants, a usage typical of the field. (As we shall see, this term is problematic and somewhat difficult to define.) Hogan, DeSoto, and Solano (1977), in summarizing the objections that have been raised to both the theoretical and practical utility of traits, have discerned six major criticisms. First, "critics seem to assume that personality researchers define traits as enduring psychic or neurological structures located somewhere in the mind or nervous system" (p. 256). Or as Mischel (1976) has suggested, "traits are likely to have both a genetic and a biochemical source" (p. 166). Such a position, of course, tends to reify traits as much more than convenient abstractions or intervening variables, perhaps even suggesting that the neural or biochemical substrata can be specifically identified.

A second criticism involves the assumption that the bulk of personality assessment procedures measure traits, and it charges that validation of these procedures is impossible because there are no independent measures of traits. The third criticism involves the assumption that psychologists who use personality tests are necessarily wedded to trait theory. Since tests measure traits, psychologists who use tests must believe that "traits form the molecular structure of personality" (Hogan et al., 1977, p. 257).

A fourth criticism is that traits lack explanatory power. To explain an individual's hostility by recourse to an underlying trait of aggression is seen as essentially circular. The fifth objection is that there is little evidence for the consistency of traits within individuals across situations. Within subjects, it is argued, trans-situational differences in behavior are larger than any trait theory suggests they should be. The early Hartshorne and May (1928) studies on deceit are often cited as typical evidence for the lack of intraindividual consistency. Hartshorne and May concluded from their data that children's behavior was less a function of any internalized predisposition to be honest and more a function of the particular temptation, and proponents of the situational view of behavior (e.g., Mischel, 1968, 1973, 1977; Peterson, 1968) believe that the succeeding 50 years of research have done nothing to change this conclusion. As Peterson has stated: ''This research suggested very strongly that traditional conceptions of personality as internal behavior dispositions were inadequate and insufficient'' (p. 23). It should be understood that this is not an argument against the feasibility of understanding and predicting behavior, but against the view that prediction is best approached from internal rather than external determinants.

The sixth and last objection is that traits are concepts constructed by the external perceiver rather than some inner state of the actor. Here the argument is that personality traits are best viewed not as properties of the individual but as value judgments placed upon the behaving individual by observers. We encountered this position in Chapter 1 in our discussion of attribution theory (Jones and Nisbett, 1971). It assumes that people's generalized tendencies to attribute the behavior of others to internal dispositions and their own behavior to external factors have produced a universally consistent way of understanding behavior, but one that distorts the true nature of human personality.

In the last few years these objections have been increasingly held to signal the demise, or at least the decline, of personality assessment as a useful enterprise (Bersoff, 1973; Cleveland, 1976; Mischel, 1977). However, each of the objections can be countered on both theoretical and empirical grounds. First, are traits really seen as biophysical systems? While Allport (1937), Cattell (1950, 1957), and a few other writers seem to have favored that position, the bulk of trait-oriented psychologists are nonspecific about the underlying nature of traits. Most psychologists who favor a trait do appear to agree that trait terms refer to stylistic consistencies in interpersonal behavior, but there is no agreement about the origins of the consistencies. Hogan et al. (1977) have pointed out that it is reasonable to criticize these psychologists for not attempting to define traits, but it is not proper to assume that they necessarily adopt Allport's definition.

Second, are most personality tests really assumed to measure traits? As we noted earlier, most test authors tend to be negligent in providing an explicit rationale for selecting their scales, or information as to how one should regard the behaviors that are presumably tapped. Some authors, such as Gough (1957/1975), have explicitly specified that traits are *not* being measured. Rather, Gough intended that the scales of the CPI be used ''to predict what an individual will do in a specified context, and/or to identify individuals who will be described in a certain way'' (p. 56). Most test authors, however, are much less clear than Gough in regard to their intentions.

This argument applies also to the third criticism, that persons who use tests are necessarily committed to some kind of trait theory. As pointed out by Hogan,

DeSoto, and Solano (1977), "one can use personality tests and adopt any of a number of views on the structure of personality, just as one can use a particle accelerator and adopt any of a number of views on the structure of matter" (p. 257). All that is necessary is clear evidence of the reliability and validity of the particular instrument for the intended purpose. Underlying this usage, of course, is also the assumption that individuals' behavior is significantly consistent from situation to situation.

The fourth criticism involves the explanatory power of traits. To some extent, taking a position on this issue depends upon the *level* of explanation that is desired. One can "explain" the illumination of the room either in terms of flicking the light switch, or by a more thorough examination of the electrical generating system which provided the current that illuminates the light bulb, or by raising questions about the nature of light. Each of these levels of explanation is useful at certain times and inadequate at other times. In the same way, traits as explanations can be seen both as adequate and as inadequate. The fact that there are certain regularities in human behavior and that one can use these regularities for purposes of individual prediction can be seen as an example of a low-level general law and thus as a valid explanation on that level. Obviously, such explanations give rise to further questions, and it is up to the individual scientist or practitioner to decide what particular level of explanation will be adequate for his/her particular purpose.

The fifth and most critical objection to trait theory is that there really is no evidence to support it. Citing as their primary evidence the generally low correlations of behavioral ratings across situations (typically no higher than .30, accounting for less than 10 percent of the total variance), the critics of trait theory have argued that there is no trans-situational consistency in human behavior except for that which occurs as a function of the similarity of environmental cues.

This situational argument, however, is open to rebuttal. First, trait theorists have never denied the importance of situational determinants of behavior. It is clear that situations differ widely in the constraints which they place upon human behavior. Some situations, such as participating in a church service or attending a lecture, provide substantial constraints. The expected behaviors are well known, and only grossly deviant persons significantly violate the behavioral norms involved. Other situations provide considerably more behavioral options, such as attending a large party or going to a public beach. Trans-situational consistency can only be expected to occur in situations where the relevant behaviors can be freely demonstrated.

A second point in rebuttal is that individual differences occur even in the face of strong situational cues. For example, some church goers carefully follow the church service, some are obviously asleep, and some daydream. Hogan et al. (1977) have reminded us that in the now notorious Milgram (1974) obedience studies, in which the situational variables were extremely powerful, over 30 percent of the subjects were nevertheless disobedient, refusing to administer the electric shocks. Such individual differences between people are clearly contrary to the situational position, just as findings of low trans-situational consistency are contrary to the position of trait theory proponents.

Traits differ in importance—importance to the culture, importance to the behaving individual, and importance to observing others. For instance, the stealing of pennies in the early work of Hartshorne and May (1928) involved a rather trivial behavior from most points of view, and thus is perhaps not a very compelling base from which to make generalizations. On the other hand, the McClelland et al. "Need for achievement" (1953) is a much more central and important characteristic for which some consistency is necessary in order to regard it as a viable concept. Thus, a reasonable position would seem to be that only certain personal characteristics should be expected to have a high degree of generality across situations, and that conclusions regarding trans-situational consistency in general should be based on findings in regard to important traits rather than trivial ones.

More recent investigators have concluded that there is greater consistency of individual behavior across situations than believed by Mischel and other trait critics (e.g., Oskamp, Mindick, Berger, and Motta, 1978; Sechrest, 1976). As examples, Hogan, DeSoto, and Solano (1977) have drawn attention to Block's (1971) work using Q-sort methodology to demonstrate the high stability of a number of personality characteristics over long periods of time, and to Strong's (1955) report of exceptionally high stability in vocational interests as measured by his Vocational Interest Blank over a 22-year-old period. Thus, a careful consideration of the relevant literature would appear to merit the conclusion that the state of affairs regarding trans-situational consistency and stability of traits is not as dismal as has been suggested. A careful reading of Mischel's latest writings (1973, 1977, 1979) shows some changes away from the extreme view and toward an emphasis on the importance of person-environment interactions, to be discussed below.

An interesting and potentially important insight into the trans-situational consistency of behavior is found in the work of Bem and Allen (1974). These investigators obtained self-ratings on a number of traits such as friendliness and conscientiousness, plus ratings by parents and peers on the same traits. Subjects were also asked to rate their perceived *consistency* (vs. variability) on each characteristic. Bem and Allen hypothesized that trans-situational consistency would only be found in behaviors where the individuals perceived themselves as consistent. The results strongly supported their hypothesis: correlations between self-ratings and others' ratings were much stronger for the low-variability subjects than for the high-variability subjects. For instance, the mean correlation on "friendliness" was + .57 for the low-variability subjects but only + .27 for the high-variability group. Bem and Allen concluded that it is possible to "predict some of the people some of the time" (p. 517), and that people are able to identify their own consistencies in a fairly direct fashion. One could further ask whether consistency itself might be a source trait worthy of further investigative efforts.

The sixth and final criticism is that people tend to overestimate the degree to which behavior of others is caused by underlying traits and underestimate the degree to which it is caused by external factors. While the research findings (e.g., Goldberg, 1978a; Nisbett, Caputo, Legant, and Marecek, 1973) apparently tend to support the actor-observer differences as postulated by attribution theory (Jones and Nisbett, 1971), a more careful analysis of the data raises serious questions about the strength and generality of these conclusions. As Goldberg (1978a) has clearly pointed out, despite the strong tendency for subjects to use the situational response in describing themselves and the trait response for describing others, the fact that the situational response is also the "middle, neutral, average, uncertain, and ambiguous response" (p. 1028) makes these findings more difficult to interpret than it would initially seem, since the situational response can be viewed as "an amalgam of inconsistency, neutrality, and uncertainty" (p. 1027). The last word on this topic has by no means been written, but it would appear that there may not be as much support for the attribution theory interpretation of trait concepts as the trait critics had once believed to be the case.

In sum, a careful review of the theoretical and empirical underpinnings of the six major criticisms which have been raised against the dispositional view of human behavior indicates that these arguments are themselves flawed and are less conclusive than their proponents have suggested. Personality assessment is still a healthy and thriving enterprise, and there is a steadily growing data base to support the empirical utility of many of the standard assessment instruments, a data base which is described and analyzed in the remainder of this volume. There are, of course, many existing personality assessment instruments which lack the psychometric properties required for legitimate use, and there are a number of important but unresolved theoretical and methodological questions in this field. These problems and issues are also covered, hopefully in balanced fashion.

Situational and Dispositional Determinants of Behavior

While there is little question that the situational critics of internal dispositions have overstated their position, it is equally true that psychologists, especially those interested in personality assessment, have paid too little attention to the situational determinants of behavior. As Bowers (1973) has concluded: "Although it is undoubtedly true that behavior is more situation specific than trait theory acknowledged . . . situations are more person specific than is commonly recognized" (p. 307). Bowers, among others, believes that an interactionist view of human behavior, one in which neither the main effects of traits nor of situations are seen as adequate to account for behavior, is the only viable approach.

Bowers (1973) reviewed 11 published investigations in which it was possible to evaluate the relative magnitudes of the person and situation variables involved in the dependent behavior that was studied. Using analysis of variance techniques, he was able to partition the variance attributable to situations, to persons, and to the person-by-situation interaction. His conclusion was that, while the percentage of variance due to situations was less than the variance attributable to persons, the interaction of persons and settings accounted for a higher percentage of the total experimental variance than the effect of either person or situation alone. Similarly, an independent review of the research literature by Endler and Magnusson (1976) supports a view of behavior as a function of a continuous interaction process between the individual and the situations that he/she encounters.

In summary, with the current waning of enthusiasm for the situational view of human behavior, we see a rise in an *interactional view,* in which it is argued that the causes of behavior lie in the interaction between person and environment. Endler and Magnusson (1976) have gone even further in postulating a *reciprocal causation* position. In their view, not only do events affect the behavior of people, but the person is also an active agent in influencing environmental events.

The interactional view of human behavior is not a new one in psychology. The early works of Woodworth (1920) and Murray (1938) are clearly in this tradition, as noted by Ekehammer (1974) and others. However, there is a clear lack of methodology and tools for assessing and classifying situations and environments. It is not enough to argue for an interactional point of view; a methodology for implementing this point of view is also needed, as well as theory to guide the efforts. Without theory and methodology, research into the prediction of human behavior will continue to focus heavily on traits or dispositions, because it is here that there is a plentiful supply of both theory and methodology.

Structure of Personality

As we have just indicated, the development of a viable interactional approach to the study of personality requires the existence of an adequate taxonomy of environments and situations, hopefully with an appropriate theoretical basis. Obviously, the same is true for the area of personality characteristics. The challenge is how to arrange the many traits and characteristics in some systematic, understandable, and logical fashion, such as the chemists have done for the elements in the periodic table. We have already noted that some work along these lines has been accomplished (Cattell, 1950, 1957; Norman, 1967), but there is little or no agreement about the structure of personality nor even about the importance of work in this area. The situation has changed little since Carlson (1975), in reviewing the recent personality literature, bemoaned the fact that "not a single published study attempted even minimal inquiry into the organization of personality variables within the organism" (p. 209).

If one considers science to be essentially a matter of the discovery of truth, then the problem is to determine how these personality characteristics are arranged in nature—that is, to discover nature's "building blocks." If, on the other hand, one's view of science is that scientists impose explanatory constructs upon their observations of the natural world in order to assist them in understanding certain phenomena and that there is no "real order" to the universe, then the task is to develop useful explanatory constructs. In this latter view, the primary problem in the study of personality is to develop useful ways of organizing or conceptualizing personality structure and functioning. Cattell's work (1957, 1965) is a carefully reasoned presentation of the former, or "discovery of the truth," viewpoint as applied to the organization of personality traits, while George Kelly (1955) has been a vigorous proponent of the latter, or "creative," point of view. It should be emphasized that in the discovery point of view it is presumed that there is only a single correct view of personality structure, while the creative view accepts the proposition that there may be several different, and even equally useful, ways of viewing the structure of personality. Since most psychologists would appear to be implicitly, if not explicitly, committed to the creative view, the reader may begin to understand why there are so many different concepts and ideas about personality, personality structure, and personality assessment.

Definitions of Personality

The problem of defining personality is a difficult one, and a very wide variety of definitions have been suggested over the years. Thus, Allport (1937) was able to delineate no fewer than 50 meanings for this term. Allport's analysis exhaustively traces the history of the concept of personality, beginning with the early antecedent *persona,* which referred to the theatrical mask first used in Greek drama, and documents its diverse meanings in such fields as theology, philosophy, sociology, linguistics, and psychology.

Even when the matter of defining personality is approached from a purely psychological viewpoint, the diversity is great. In their text on personality theory, Hall and Lindzey (1978) stated that "no substantive definition of personality can be applied with any generality" (p. 9). The historical and theoretical reasons for this diversity of thought and lack of agreement among psychologists are complex and lengthy, and the reader is referred to the chapter by Sanford (1963) entitled "Personality: I's Place in Psychology" for a careful discussion of the issues.

Hall and Lindzey (1978) have argued that personality is best defined by "the particular empirical concepts which are part of the theory of personality employed by the observer" (p. 9). The typical *measures* of personality in use today, however, tend to be atheoretical. As early as 1941 Angyal was concerned that most personality tests involved the measurement of elements of personality that are random or arbitrary, such as leadership, dominance, or anxiety. Although these kinds of measures may be of practical utility, they do little to advance either the science of personality study in general or the technology of personality assessment in particular. More than 30 years later, Goldberg (1972a) noted similarly that there existed only a handful of personality questionnaires for which there is a discussion of the rationale underlying the selection of their scales and that the most potent factor in scale development would seem to be simple historical precedent. The few exceptions include the previously mentioned scales developed by Gough (1957/ 1975) and by Cattell (1950, 1957), in which attempts were made to use the natural language of personality description as a base, and the Myers-Briggs Type Indicator (Briggs, 1959), which is based upon the typology of Carl G. Jung.

In light of the lack of unification in both personality theory and personality measurement, it is difficult to develop a definition of personality that adequately comprehends all the diverse and contradictory elements involved in this complex and difficult field of endeavor. The best approximation that we can offer, one that reflects the concern of most psychologists for utility ahead of theory, is that personality is an abstraction for those *enduring characteristics of the person which are significant for his/her interpersonal behavior.* In using this definition we are also mindful of Allport's (1937) insistence that personality is what the person *really is;* that is, it involves what is most typical and deeply characteristic of the individual. In using the concept of personality we need to concentrate upon those individual differences which are of greatest significance in the daily transactions of human beings with each other. Only by identifying and focusing our attention on such factors will we be able to discover those trait-by-situation interactions that can enable us to make more valid differential predictions than those obtainable from the individual effects of traits or situations.

All definitions of personality suggest many questions, and ours is no exception. What are the antecedents of these "enduring characteristics?" To what extent are they inherited, learned in early childhood, or developed in later life? Under what conditions and to what degree can they be expected to change? These and related questions bring us deeper into the subject of personality theory; indeed, it is around such questions that the major differences in personality theory are found. These problems are actively dealt with by most of the major contemporary personality theorists (see Hall and Lindzey, 1978, for lucid and readable accounts), each of whom takes a somewhat different stand. From the viewpoint of personality assessment, however, they need not directly concern us, since we can pursue our subject with only minimal involvement in personality theory per se.

Personality Theory and Personality Assessment

Although it would be useful to have a universal, internally consistent conceptual language for personality description, none exists. As indicated in our brief discussion of the structure of personality, there is much disagreement about how best to even approach this task. Instead, each of the major personality theorists has attempted to develop his/her own conceptual system, which has little or no integration with any other system. Most approaches to assessing personality have been theoretically neutral, but the personality descriptions produced by each have tended to involve the language of one or another personality theory. For example, in psychoanalytic, or Freudian, theory, it is considered that differences in personality stem from individual differences in the amount of available psychic energy (libido) or in the methods of handling this energy. Concepts such as ego, superego, and Oedipal conflict refer to mechanisms and processes in the flow of energy. Thus, if we were to explain an individual's behavior as due to a strong ego, or to unresolved Oedipal striving, we would be using the language of Freudian personality theory. In another language system, that of "trait and type" personality theory, personality is described as a simple additive combination of many separate characteristics. Using this language, we might say that the individual was very hostile, or had strong dominance characteristics, or was extroverted. As yet another alternative, if we were to employ the language system of stimulus-response learning theory as applied to personality, we might describe the individual as having failed to learn an appropriate discrimination or as behaving according to a certain reinforcement schedule.

To repeat, personality descriptions resulting from assessment procedures are often couched in the language of a particular personality theory. We must not be misled, however, into believing that the assessment procedures are therefore based on careful theoretical considerations. A few of the major methods of personality assessment do have some theoretical identification, but most are theoretically neutral, and the language of the assessment procedure is chosen according to the theoretical sympathies of the test constructor rather than because the assessment procedure is derived directly from the theory or satisfies its assumptions. It is too often a simple matter to rename the concepts used in a procedure with those of another theoretical language system, without any significant difference either in the procedures involved or in the level of understanding achieved.

Which theory offers the best language to use in the description of personality? There are no simple rules for assessing the relative merits of the existing sets of personality concepts, and certainly none upon which the major theorists would agree. Hall and Lindzey (1978, Chapter 1) have suggested that the critical test of the utility of a theory is the amount of significant research it generates. Using this criterion of utility, the generally atheroretical nature of personality assessment procedures is perhaps an indictment of the current state of personality theory.

Theoretical Approaches to Personality Assessment

Let us try to see what is involved in the theoretical approach to clinical assessment. For the purposes of this discussion we shall ignore the issue of which assessment procedures the psychologist chooses and how the information produced by these procedures is collected, analyzed, and integrated. We shall simply note that the information is processed and a description of the individual's personality is offered by the psychologist, phrased in the language of a particular theory of personality. For example, let us suppose that an individual being considered for psychotherapy is referred to a psychologist of Freudian persuasion for a personality evaluation. After completing the steps involved in a clinical personality assessment, the psychologist forwards a report, which includes the finding that the patient has an unresolved Oedipal conflict. The psychologist further recommends that the patient be seen in therapy by a dominant male therapist as the optimal arrangement for the resolution of the conflict. It should be clearly apparent that the conclusion that the patient requires a male therapist does *not* stem directly from the assessment data but rather from some theoretical considerations on the part of the psychologist. This process might be schematically expressed as follows:

Information from assessment procedures		Personality description		Personality theory		Decision about the patient
	→		→		→	

In order for this decision to be a useful one for the patient, three conditions must hold true: (1) the psychologist's interpretation of the assessment data must be correct within the framework of the particular personality theory that is being used; (2) the psychologist's understanding of the theory must be adequate enough to enable a decision to be made which is consistent with the demands of the theory; and (3) the theory itself must be a useful one. If the patient subsequently *deteriorates* in therapy with a dominant male therapist, the psychologist will be somewhat at a loss to know why, because of the lengthy chain of inferences leading to the original decision. Any one or any combination of the three conditions might not have held true. Or the failure may have been a function of therapist incompetence, unfavorable changes in the real-life circumstances of the patient, or a multitude of other considerations.

On the other hand, suppose the patient did improve in therapy. What could be concluded from this event? Success with the one single individual does not validate this rather long chain of inference; for one thing, the same extraneous factors just listed (favorable real-life circumstances of the patient or extreme competence of the therapist) may have been operating. Success by several dominant male therapists with several similar patients takes us further toward the desired validation but not the whole distance, since the chain of inferences might well contain redundancies or compensating errors. The validity of this approach to individual assessment cannot be adequately determined by observing the outcomes of decisions based upon it, but must be investigated through careful step-by-step study of the inferential chain. In other words, validating the assessment technique is closely tied to validating the personality theory utilized in the chain.

Comparison of Theoretical and Empirical Approaches

Let us contrast the steps involved in this theoretical or inferential approach with those which would be involved in the empirical approach to the same problem. We would assume that the psychologist knows, from previously reported empirical research, that patients with certain kinds of responses on a particular assessment instrument improve more quickly with male than with female therapists. When faced with the decision of recommending the sex of a therapist for a prospective patient, the psychologist would administer this assessment instrument, compare the patient's responses with the empirical research findings, and make a decision as to a male or female therapist solely upon that basis. Given the current state of personality theory, the clinician has a greater probability of correctness in decision making if the empirical rather than the theoretical approach is used. There are fewer steps and inferences between the data and the decision, which reduces the probability of error, and it is comparatively easy to recheck the correctness of the previously reported relationships.

It is possible to argue that the empirical approach is not personality assessment at all, at least not in any strict sense. The inferential step of attributing some underlying enduring characteristic to the respondent—that is, of making inferences about his/her personality—has in a sense been bypassed. However, empirical processes have traditionally been so closely tied with personality assessment, particularly in the context of establishing the "validity" of personality tests (see Chapter 6), that they must be regarded an integral part of the field.

One might reasonably ask which of the two approaches—theoretical or empirical—generally should be the better one to use. There is no simple answer to this question. On one hand, the existing theories of personality are not sufficiently explicit to offer any superiority to prediction through the theoretical approach. On the other hand, this approach offers more for the ultimate advancement of the field, so that its development will be slowed if empirical procedures are always favored for applied work.

It is possible, in principle, to develop an assessment instrument directly from a theory of personality. In such a case, the individual's responses would be immediately meaningful within the context of the theory, and no additional inferential activity by the clinician would be necessary. Thus, the step labeled "personality description" in the last diagram would be eliminated. One of the few instruments which are clearly and explicitly based upon theory is the Blacky Pictures Test (Blum, 1949), which is discussed in Chapter 3. Although such approaches are scientifically rather sophisticated and offer much hope for the development of basic knowledge about personality, once again it must be stated that personality theorizing is not sufficiently advanced for them to be generally useful at the present time.

Methods of Personality Assessment

The term *personality assessment* refers to the process of gathering and organizing information about another person in the expectation that this information will lead to a better understanding of the person. Understanding the personality of another individual typically involves making some prediction about the future behavior of that person in rather specific terms. Among the kinds of predictions to be made could be probability of vocational success in a variety of areas, response to different kinds of psychological treatments, or probability of demonstrating certain socially undesirable behaviors. The task of the professional psychologist often involves participating in a variety of decisions concerning other people, based upon the assessment of their personality.

All of us, however, are continually involved in gathering a variety of unsystematic information about the behavior of people around us, and we are continually, if not with complete awareness, making inferences about their personality characteristics from our observations. Statements such as "I know her pretty well" or "I've known him for a long time but I don't understand him at all" reflect our everyday ways of talking about our knowledge of another's personality. The study of these informal processes of data collection and of the ways we organize and analyze the information is a fascinating one. How well can one get to know another's personality in this manner? Are some people more effective in this respect than others? On what basis? What psychological processes are involved? It is nowadays common to address these questions within the framework of attribution theory, as discussed in Chapter 1. Other analyses can be found in the writings of Korchin (1976) and Sarbin, Taft, and Bailey (1966).

The informal, or intuitive, processes by which we get to know and understand people with whom we are closely involved are similar to those employed by the psychotherapist in understanding a patient. The informal approach is characterized by the large amount of time which it requires, and also by the lack of specificity about the manner of both data collection and data analysis. Observers are expected to proceed with the task of understanding the other person at their own pace and in their own, nonspecified fashion.

Although the informal, intuitive approach is fascinating, it is not considered beyond this chapter. We are primarily concerned with the formal, systematic ways of going about the assessment task—the methods used by the professional psychologist in the formal role of expert assessor of personality. We shall emphasize the situations in which the psychologist or other professional person uses standardized assessment instruments in a systematic manner in the assessment situation. The interview, an unstandardized personality assessment technique but a major assessment method in use today, is also considered briefly.

How might standardized assessment tools be classified? Here we can identify three groups of instruments, the first consisting of those generally regarded as *personality tests*. The discussion of personality tests, both inventories and projective techniques, and of the many problems surrounding their use and interpretation, fills the major portion of this book. A second group of procedures uses either models of real-life situations or real life itself, in which the behavior of interest can be observed directly. For example, an instrument for assessing the subject's stress tolerance would consist of a structured and standardized situation in which the individual would be required to perform under some artificially produced stress. The situation normally would be arranged so that the behavior could be directly observed without the person being aware of what was happening. This method of assessment, through the use of *behavioral observation,* is discussed in Chapter 5. A third group of instruments makes use of specific factual information about the individual's present status and past history, the kind of information which might be obtained from a biographical data blank or a carefully structured interview. This method, the *biographical data method,* is widely used in personnel selection in industry, and it is discussed in Chapter 6.

Some psychologists have felt that certain personality tests, notably the projective techniques, are more appropriately regarded as standardized situations for eliciting a behavior sample. They consider that the projective testing situation represents a standardized model of an interpersonal interaction with ambiguous demands and that the entire situation—the projective test materials (such as inkblots or pictures), plus the examiner, plus the instructions, plus the immediate environment— constitutes the assessment "instrument." This is a fruitful approach to the analysis and understanding of projective tests and their contribution to personality assessment; we, however, have taken the more straightforward and traditional direction of grouping projective techniques together with the other personality tests.

Choice of Assessment Procedures

How does the psychologist decide upon which instruments to use in a particular assessment situation? The psychologist traditionally uses an interview, tests, biographical and other case data such as supervisory ratings or school records, and additional assessment tools, in order to provide information about the individual under study. Although the steps involved in normal clinical assessment may be more organized than those in the informal intuitive method of assessment, there is still much variability among psychologists in their manner both of data collection and of data analysis. There are no standard procedures for gathering data that are followed universally by psychologists, and the assessment instruments chosen by a particular psychologist will be a function of training and experience, idiosyncratic preferences, and familiarity with the current literature.

One recurring problem in choosing assessment methods involves deciding between formal personality tests and the informal intuitive methods. Although it is usually not the case, let us assume for the purposes of this discussion that the end results of the two methods would be comparably useful; that is, both methods would yield equally correct predictions.

In choosing between the methods, the *time factor* is one important consideration. It may well be that a decision must be reached about a patient by noon tomorrow because he/she is going on court trial or is being considered for discharge. To initiate a lengthy informal intuitive procedure at this stage would not be expedient. However, if the patient had previously been seen in psychotherapy for several months, the therapist could give an intuitive assessment very quickly.

Economic factors must also be considered in making a decision about which method to use. To assign an individual to an informal assessor for an extended period of time is obviously an expensive business and would rarely be done for the sake of assessment alone. However, if the person were a hospital patient in a well-staffed ward, a routine duty of the ward staff might well be to gather the informal data needed for such an assessment. Another situation where intuitive assessment would be prohibitively expensive is in the routine screening of large numbers of persons, such as for draft into the armed forces. Standardized assessment techniques, which can be administered to large numbers of persons simultaneously in a short time, have an obvious economic advantage.

Thus, the choice between these or any other assessment procedures will be influenced by considerations of practical efficiency. In this regard, a crucial factor will often be the availability of a person or persons who have been able to make the kind of observations necessary for an informal intuitive assessment over an extended period of time. If competent assessors of this type are available, they should generally be utilized. To state the conclusion another way, the decision as to which assessment method to use should ultimately be determined by the *relative gain* or payoff of the alternative courses of action.

There may be occasions when it is not justifiable to apply any assessment procedure at all. Taking all factors into consideration, if the losses (in time, expense, increased hostility of the patient, loss of staff morale) more than offset the gains (additional pertinent information about the individual, increased probability of making the optimal prediction or decision), then it would be better not to use any assessment procedure. Unfortunately, there has been little systematic research on the relative payoffs of assessment techniques. Further, many hospitals, clinics, industries, and schools have been using the same assessment procedures routinely over many years with little information about, or even interest in, the efficiency of these procedures. More than 20 years ago Hathaway (1959) considered the time actually spent by clinical psychologists in routine clinical assessment and estimated that if an empirical evaluation of their efficiency were made, much of this activity would be abandoned.

Personality Tests and Ability Tests

We have previously indicated that the major focus of this book is upon personality assessment through the medium of standardized assessment instruments, typically referred to as *personality tests*. The more general term *psychological tests* includes, in addition to personality assessment instruments, an extensive array of devices for measuring *abilities*.

How might we differentiate between ability tests and personality tests? Some of the attributes of an individual which are typically regarded as personality traits could also at times be considered as abilities, especially for tasks involving interpersonal interactions. For example, are leadership and persuasiveness more appropriately considered as personality or ability factors? Any distinction between these two kinds of domains is to some degree arbitrary. Traditionally, the term *ability tests* has been used to identify instruments which assess skills or achievement in cognitive, intellectual, and motor areas. As an alternative to the term *ability tests,* Cronbach (1970) has suggested *"maximum performance test,"* a term which conveys the following concepts: (1) individuals are expected to perform as skillfully as they can; and (2) there are specific right and wrong answers to the test items. Cronbach further suggested that personality tests might be better regarded as tests of *typical performance,* or instruments which are expected to identify the individual's typical modes of responding, where no particular response can be singled out as "right." While the arbitrariness of the distinction is not eliminated by Cronbach's suggestions, the types of individual differences involved in these two categories are made more specific.

One reason for discussing ability tests in the present context is that the methods and techniques employed in ability testing have provided important models for the development of personality tests. However, the degree of success enjoyed by ability tests has not yet been realized in the field of personality assessment. Although the predictions about real-life situations made from carefully constructed ability tests can be considered fairly satisfactory, the same cannot be said for personality tests. Some of the reasons for this difference lie in the lack of widely accepted personality concepts; others involve fundamental questions as to what is meant by "measurement." Nevertheless, personality tests modeled on the traditional ability-testing procedures have probably now reached their maximum degree of refinement. Thus, further improvements in personality assessment will probably have to come from new approaches to the problem rather than from further refinements of the traditional methods.

Summary

Psychologists undertake personality assessment for two reasons, corresponding to two general themes underlying the development of the field: for the clinical assessment of single individuals and to advance knowledge of human behavior through research and theory. In clinical assessment, the simplest approach is prediction based on known empirical relationships between the assessment results and the behavior to be predicted. A disadvantage of this procedure is that it adds little to a broader understanding of the processes involved. One assumption basic to all traditional personality assessment procedures is that one's interpersonal behavior has some consistency over time and across different situations. This assumption is questioned in recent theoretical approaches to personality through behavioral learning theory, in which much greater emphasis is placed on environmental conditions in determining behavior at any time.

A common approach to personality prediction is first to construct a personality description by generalizing from known empirical relationships, and then to make predictions on the basis of the description. This approach is sometimes regarded as "theoretical," but the term *theory* in this text is reserved for more rigorous procedures involving sets of related laws. A serious problem with prediction from a general personality description is that the known empirical relationships are frequently generalized beyond their applicability.

There has been considerable debate as to whether personality is determined by traits or dispositions, as opposed to situational factors. Critics of the trait position point to the difficulty of obtaining independent evidence of their existence, their limited utility for predictive purposes, their limited explanatory power, and other problems. A reasoned position would seem to suggest that behavior is determined in part by both situations and dispositions, and that the causes of behavior probably lie in the interaction between person and environment. Further, it is suggested that each actively influences the other in a reciprocal manner.

Researchers have attempted to ascertain the structure of personality in our culture by identifying and analyzing the many thousands of trait words in the English language. There are two points of view about personality structure: (1) that a "true" structure exists and will be eventually discovered, and (2) that any number of structures may be imposed upon natural human behavior in an attempt to understand it better. There is no agreed-upon definition for the term *personality,* and in this text we adopt an atheoretical, practical definition, which regards personality as *those enduring characteristics of the person which are significant for his/her interpersonal behavior.* Personality descriptions resulting from assessment procedures are usually couched in the specific language of one or another theory of personality, but this does not mean that the assessment is based on the theory. In fact, the science of personality is not yet sufficiently developed to permit a truly theoretical approach to personality assessment.

There are a variety of methods of personality assessment: informal and intuitive methods, interviewing, formal standardized procedures, biographical data, and behavior samples. Most of this book is devoted to a consideration of standardized assessment procedures. The choice of which assessment procedure to employ in any given situation depends on economic factors, the available time, and other aspects of practical efficiency.

In the development of personality assessment procedures, the well-established methods for assessing skills and abilities have generally been used as models. However, it appears that personality assessment procedures based on these models have now reached their maximum degree of refinement, and further developments will have to come from new approaches.

3   RATIONAL-THEORETICAL APPROACHES TO ASSESSMENT

We have touched upon a number of basic issues involved in developing and using personality assessment instruments. They include the problems of how the test situation can be standardized, what stimuli can be used to evoke meaningful and useful responses from test takers, and what type of responses should be observed in order to understand and predict those human behavior usually subsumed under the rubric *personality*. Chapters 3 and 4 are specifically concerned with these issues. Following a discussion of the characteristics of assessment techniques, we examine the most widely used assessment devices. This procedure serves to present and illustrate the problems mentioned above and to give the reader some familiarity with current assessment devices and practices.

CHARACTERISTICS OF STANDARDIZED ASSESSMENT PROCEDURES

An examination of the standardized assessment procedures in common use shows that they tend to meet the following conditions: (1) the stimuli to be used in the assessment process are identical for all respondents and are always presented in the same fashion; (2) there are available *norms,* or frequency distributions of responses, either formal or informal (intuitive), so that responses can be assigned to a specific place within an anticipated range; and (3) there are useful personality and behavioral correlates of the to-be-observed responses. We say that assessment procedures *tend* to meet these criteria because the strictness with which the criteria are employed, particularly the latter two, varies. Nevertheless, each of these elements is present to some extent in all techniques which are considered formal assessment procedures.

The previously mentioned conditions suggest three dimensions that could be useful in characterizing personality assessment procedures. The first dimension concerns the variety of relevant responses made by the test taker and observed by the examiner, and might be turned the *degree of response structure*. It should be clearly noted that here we are *not* referring to differences in the degree of structure which is imposed upon the testing situation by the examiner. A high degree of structure or standardization of procedure is an important condition for any formal assessment device. Thus, the procedures for administering the Rorschach are, or should be, just as inflexible as those for giving the Minnesota Multiphasic Personality Inventory (MMPI). Most paper-and-pencil personality inventories, such as the MMPI, also can be regarded as rather highly structured with respect to respondent behaviors, since the only responses to be made and observed are indications of "true" or "false" to a series of personal statements. Whatever other responses the test taker might otherwise make are discouraged by the preliminary instructions and tend to be ignored if they are made despite the instructions. Since the MMPI is taken either by sorting cards into "true" and "false" piles or by marking an IBM answer sheet, variations in such behaviors as vigor or response time are not recorded, and neither the MMPI scoring procedure nor its interpretive system permit the use of such data. Rorschach's inkblot test, on the other hand, would be regarded as relatively unstructured in the present sense because the examiner generally observes and records a wide range of respondent behaviors, and considers all of them to be relevant response material. Included are the portion of the blot to which the person has responded; the stimulus characteristics of that portion of the blot—for example, the form, color, or shading—that determined each given response; the actual content of each response; the respondent's body position and movement; changes in pitch, volume, loudness, and rate of speech; any spontaneous comments about the situation; and other features of the respondent's style of expression.

A second dimension on which assessment procedures differ is the degree to which published formal norms are available. Structured inventories, such as the MMPI, with a smaller range of relevant responses, more readily lend themselves to the development of formal norms. These norms are usually developed by the test authors and are presented in tabular form, frequently with conversion tables for easy translation into some standard score form. For example, the MMPI scales employ "T-scores," with a mean of 50 and a standard deviation of 10. Later research often provides specific norms for working with homogeneous groups of various sorts (e.g., Lanyon, 1968). Projective techniques, on the other hand, with a larger range of responses to be considered, generally do not have formal norms available. Instead, the clinician who uses these procedures must build informal norms based upon personal experience, so that the development of skills in the use of projective techniques becomes complex and time consuming. While there have been some attempts to develop formal norms for these assessment procedures, especially for the Rorschach (e.g., Beck, Beck, Levitt, and Molish, 1961; Hertz, 1951), the results have by no means been generally accepted or integrated into clinical practice.

A third dimension which might be useful for characterizing personality assessment devices is the usefulness of the instrument. By usefulness, we mean the extent to which the test taker's responses will permit understanding and prediction of some of his/her nontest behaviors. A very useful instrument would enable relatively precise predictions to be made about socially important behaviors, such as success in a particular occupation or prognosis in psychotherapy. Less useful instruments are either less precise in their predictions or deal with socially less significant behavior, such as performance on an experimental laboratory task. The term *validity* is similar to usefulness, but it is more precise and refers to the existence of a demonstrated relationship between certain test responses and a particular nontest characteristic of the person. Thus the number of validities, or valid relationships, that a test possesses, and the importance or significance of these relationships, determine the test's usefulness. This topic is discussed more fully in Chapter 6.

The position of an assessment instrument on each of these three dimensions— degree of response structure, availability of norms, and usefulness—to some degree is established by a more basic aspect of the instrument. We are referring to the method of construction of the instrument, and more particularly, to the method employed in selecting the stimuli. In general, there are three major approaches to or strategies in the construction of formal assessment devices: (1) rational-theoretical, (2) empirical, and (3) internal consistency.

1.   A test may be based upon purely rational, face-value, or commonsense considerations. For example, we might include the item "I frequently find myself worrying about something" in a test of manifest anxiety, since it would be reasonable to assume that on an a priori basis, manifestly anxious subjects would be more likely to respond affirmatively than nonanxious subjects. Rationally derived tests are developed by selecting or constructing stimulus materials that *seem* to tap the behavior in which the test author is interested. A test might conceivably also be devised to be congruent with a particular theoretical view of personality, and it would assess concepts within that theory. The Blacky Pictures Test (Blum, 1950), which involves drawings portraying the adventures of the pup Blacky and its family, best approximates a theoretically derived personality test, in this case based on traditional psychoanalytic theory. The test taker's responses to the drawings are scored and interpreted as indices of the amount of conflict in the various psychoanalytic stages of psychosexual development. Since there are no theories of personality which, strictly speaking, meet our preferred definition of a theory (see Chapter 2), and since most rationally based tests do involve some theoretical considerations, the discussion to follow considers rational and theoretically based tests together. Thus, a continuum of *rational-theoretical* derivation is concep- tualized, with a priori inventories nearer to the rational end and tests such as the Blacky Pictures nearer to the theoretical end.

2.   The basis for a test can be *empirical;* that is, there is an empirical basis for believing that the test should work in the manner described by the test author. Each test item might be selected according to its power to discriminate between two groups of interest, such as people with sales potential from people in general, or it might be that a global score of some kind is shown to discriminate between two groups.

3.   A test might be developed on the basis of the *internal consistency* of the items. For example, a fairly large number of test stimuli might be administered to a group of respondents, and those items whose responses are closely related or intercorrelated are assumed to tap the same psychological variable. Such statistically defined variables are then used as indices of aspects of personality functioning.

It should be emphasized that these three approaches to test development are not mutually exclusive. For example, the development of the so-called empirically derived instruments has almost always involved an initial rational or theoretical selection of items to be put to an empirical test. Similarly, the internal consistency approach typically follows some rational or theoretical assembling of the items. In fact, it is nowadays most common for serious test developers to employ all three procedures in the course of developing an instrument. What we have done, however, is to classify instruments as predominantly based upon one approach or another. As stated previously, psychologists interested in personality and assessment have often tended to employ the word *theory* in a loose or colloquial sense. Thus they might consider certain tests to have a stronger theoretical base than we give them credit for here.

RATIONAL-THEORETICAL APPROACHES

Perhaps the most obvious approach to test development is the strictly rational one, where we expect the test items to act as stimuli for directly eliciting the information in which we are interested. Woodworth's Personal Data Sheet, described in some detail in Chapter 1, is an early example of purely rational derivation. It asks the same questions that a psychiatrist or a clinical psychologist would ask when directly examining a patient to determine level of adjustment. As already noted, the assumption is made that the responses to such test items as "Do you sleep well?" or "Do you get rattled easily?" are valid indices of the level of adjustment of the respondent, in the same way as the responses to an oral examination are assumed to be. We shall have more to say about these assumptions later in the chapter; first we describe some of the more widely used instruments in the rational-theoretical category. Tests which fall toward the rational end of the continuum are considered first.

Sentence Completion

Sentence completion is a technique or a method rather than a single specific instrument, although commercially marketed instruments representative of the method are readily available (Forer, 1950; Rohde, 1957; Rotter and Rafferty, 1950). The respondent is presented with a series of items consisting of the first few words of a sentence, and the task is to provide an ending for each of these beginnings or stems. The stems are developed to elicit responses that illuminate various aspects of the individual's feelings and behaviors. Thus, the person's attitudes and feelings toward his/her mother are assumed to be tapped by the stem "My mother and I . . .," and techniques for handling strong emotions are presumably seen in responses to the item "When I am angry or upset, I. . . ." Sentence stems in the third person are also employed, such as "His greatest wish was . . .," and the projective hypothesis is used as a basis for reasoning that the responses to these third person stems are informative about the subject's own desires.

Of the several commercially available instruments, the Rotter Incomplete Sentences Blank (Rotter and Rafferty, 1950) has perhaps enjoyed the widest use. In addition to qualitative, clinical inferences that might be drawn from the content of the individual's responses, the Rotter Incomplete Sentences Blank (ISB) also contains a rationally derived quantitative scoring scheme that yields a single index of adjustment-maladjustment. There are 40 sentence stems, all of which are rather brief and nonspecific, such as "I feel . . .," and "Marriage. . . ." Each response is scored, with the aid of the examples provided in the manual, on a seven-point rating scale for degree of maladjustment. The reasonably high levels of reliability and validity reported in the manual for this maladjustment index have tended to be substantiated in latter studies (Goldberg, 1965).

In general, the available evidence about the usefulness of the sentence completion method can be summarized as follows (Goldberg, 1965):

1.   There is little research evidence to indicate that any of the formal aspects of responses to sentence completion items—such as reaction time, response length, or grammatical or spelling errors—are systematically related to any personality-relevant behaviors. There is also little evidence to support the use of impressionistic or clinical analyses of the content of the responses, although adequate studies of such an approach are difficult to conduct.

2.   The more structured approaches to content analysis, such as Rotter's scoring procedure, have been demonstrated to be useful. This finding is intuitively reasonable, since an instrument developed to assess a single, clearly defined variable or dimension like adjustment-maladjustment can be expected to be valid or useful for that particular purpose. Further, the focus upon a single dimension tends to result in relative homogeneity of items, enhancing the consistency or reliability of the instrument, which in turn enhances usefulness. However, it should be pointed out that the clinician interested in describing and understanding a broad range of personality and behavior will probably be dissatisfied with an instrument yielding only a single score.

3.   Employing first person stems seems to provide somewhat more useful responses than third person stems, although the evidence is not unequivocal.

4.   The specificity of the content of a response can be controlled by the specificity of the sentence stem. That is, the stems can be worded so that the responses are more or less delimited. For example, the stem "Marriage . . ." elicits a wider range of responses than the stem "My marriage has been. . . ." It is yet unclear which of these two types of stems elicits the more significant responses.

In order to illustrate the use of the sentence completion method, the first five sentence stems of the Rotter Incomplete Sentences Blank are given here, together with the completions which were provided by an 18-year-old college male freshman seeking help for personal problems.

1. I like . . . music, leisure time, and sports.

2. The happiest time . . . is when I'm performing.

3. I want to know . . . what I don't know.

4. Back home . . . it's very nice.

5. I regret . . . many things, but only slightly.

The nature of the objective scoring system for degree of maladjustment is as follows. The scoring manual (Rotter and Rafferty, 1950, p. 55) would give a score of *6*, representing the extreme of maladjustment, to a response such as ". . . to know if I am going crazy," given to the first stem, "I like. . . ." The response ". . . most everything" to this stem would receive a score of *0*, representing the extreme of adjustment. The response ". . . to observe people" would receive a score of *3*, the neutral category with respect to adjustment-maladjustment. The particular response which was given by this client would be scored *2*, or slightly on the "adjusted" side of the neutral point. With the aid of similar scoring examples, the response given by the client to the second sentence stem would be scored *3*. The complete set of 40 responses given by this client yielded a total score of 134, placing him at about the 70th percentile with respect to maladjustment according to the norms provided in the ISB manual.

Qualitative or subjective inferences typically also are drawn from sentence completion responses. For example, the client's response to the second stem might be taken to suggest exhibitionistic needs, and further evidence to support or contradict this tentative hypothesis would be sought from the remainder of the test. Likewise, strong dependency needs might be inferred from the fourth response. The fifth response, which contains a mild contradiction, might be interpreted as reflecting a personality conflict, perhaps involving guilt.

Lanyon (Lanyon, 1972; Lanyon and Lanyon, 1980) developed a sentence completion test designed to yield scores on three variables: hostility, anxiety, and dependency. What is noteworthy about this test, the Incomplete Sentences Task, is that it represents the application of all three test construction procedures to the development of what has traditionally been regarded as a projective test. Thus, preliminary sentence stems were written on the basis of a rationally developed universe of content for each characteristic, refined through factor analytic procedures. Final selection of the stems was made empirically, by contrasting the responses of junior high school students rated high and low on the criterion measures by their teacher. Empirical cross-validation data continued to support the validity of each scale.

Edwards Personal Preference Schedule

A commonly used paper-and-pencil inventory is the Edwards Personal Preference Schedule (EPPS), which is also one of the more psychometrically sophisticated of the rational-theoretical instruments. Edwards' (1959) avowed purpose in developing the test was "to provide quick and convenient measures of a number of relatively independent normal personality variables" (p. 5). The 15 variables were selected from the list of "manifest needs" listed in the theoretical writings of Murray (1938) and include such needs as achievement, affiliation, deference, nurturance, and order. To assess each need, the EPPS uses nine brief statements that bear a rational, commonsense relationship to that need. Thus, the need for achievement is tapped by such statements as "I like to do my very best in whatever I undertake" and "I would like to accomplish something of great significance." Although the EPPS has sometimes been considered to be derived directly from Murray's theoretical writings on personality, its basic reliance upon commonsense considerations, particularly in item development, should be emphasized.

The sophistication of the EPPS is found in its *forced-choice* format. Pairs of self-reference statements are presented simultaneously to the respondent, who in each case is to choose the statement which is the more self-descriptive. There are 210 such choices for the respondent to make, and he/she can endorse the set of statements related to each need from zero to 28 times. Every need is paired three or four times. The strength of a particular need is determined by the number of times, out of the 28 options, that the respondent chooses or endorses the statements representing that need. Fifteen additional pairs are included in order to evaluate the consistency or reliability of an individual's responses.

Why was the forced-choice technique employed? Edwards (1953, 1957) was concerned by his finding that the frequency of endorsement of any self-descriptive statement was highly related to the judged *social desirability* of that statement. The general issue of the complex effects of social desirability upon personality test responses is dealt with in some detail in Chapter 7; we shall simply indicate here its role in the construction of the EPPS. Edwards decided, upon the basis of his findings, that people ordinarily respond to a test item according to the social desirability of that item rather than according to its specific personality content. Thus, the failure to control for social desirability led to a failure to fairly evaluate the respondents' personality characteristics. Edwards attempted to circumvent this difficulty in his construction of the EPPS by arranging the statements in pairs within which the alternatives were approximately matched on social desirability, and by requiring respondents to endorse one statement from each pair. He reasoned that the choice could not now be made on the basis of social desirability, so that persons must choose according to their own personality characteristics.

The development of the EPPS represents an innovative attempt to deal with the problem of social desirability, although later research (e.g., Heilbrun and Goodstein, 1961a, 1961b, Rorer, 1965) has shown that the problem is far from resolved. Briefly, the research tends to suggest that the forced-choice format reduced but failed to remove the influence of social desirability; more important, however, is the finding that the predictive usefulness or validity of such questionnaires appears to be determined in part by the extent to which the factor of social desirability is still present. As already mentioned, this problem is explored in detail in Chapter 7 under the heading "Response Sets."

The use of a forced-choice format also raises other problems. In the case of the EPPS, the respondent is in effect asked to distribute 210 endorsements over 420 items. Put another way, the respondent must indicate 210 points' worth of personality needs, regardless of whether or not this degree of "need" exists. The result is an EPPS profile which reflects a rank order of needs as they apply to the respondent. Such procedures, which allow comparisons of an individual's intraindividual characteristics but are limited in the degree to which they permit interindividual comparisons, are termed *ipsative,* and they raise special problems in the interpretation of test scores. Still another problem posed by the forced-choice format is that the scale scores thus obtained are not statistically independent of each other since, by the nature of the forced choice, an elevated score on one dimension will force a lower score on another dimension. Since most statistical operations assume the independence of scores, many studies involving the interrelationship of EPPS scores are difficult to interpret. Thus, it can be concluded that Edwards's attempts to deal with the problem of social desirability have not been completely successful and have created, in turn, several new and difficult problems.

Despite these problems, the rational derivation of the EPPS might lead us to expect it to be a reasonably useful or valid instrument. Edwards (1959, p. 19) has shown that the scores are reasonably stable or reliable. Yet the most recent reviews of the EPPS (Heilbrun, 1972; McKee, 1972) are consistent with previous reviews in concluding that the evidence for its utility is in general poor, despite the more than 1,000 reported studies which had examined it to that time (Buros, 1972, p. 148). More recent evidence has not served to alter this conclusion.

Study of Values

Another personality assessment instrument that utilizes a paper-and-pencil questionnaire format and which takes some account of a theoretical viewpoint is the Study of Values (Allport, Vernon, and Lindzey, 1960; Vernon and Allport, 1931). Utilizing the theoretical views of personality advanced by Eduard Spranger (1928), the Study of Values aims to measure the relative prominence of six basic interests or motives in personality: theoretical, economic, aesthetic, social, political, and religious. The theoretical person is dominated by the discovery of truth and his/her chief purpose in life is to bring order and systematization to his/her understanding of the world. The economic person is concerned with that which is useful and is very much in keeping with the typical stereotype of the successful American businessman. The aesthetic person is interested in form and harmony, and his/her primary concern is with beauty rather than truth or utility. The social person is concerned with love for other people in an altruistic or philanthropic sense, a selfless love for humankind. The political person is primarily dominated by power, by control over people and events, and by needs for personal influence and renown. The religious person is concerned with a sense of unity, a need for establishing a kind of transcendental understanding of the universe in some personal way.

The format of the test, like the EPPS, is ipsative. Part I consists of 30 forced-choice item pairs in which each value is paired twice with every other value, and Part II consists of 15 forced-choice item tetrads in which each value is compared with all other combinations of three other values. The test is self-administering and self-scorable.

The Study of Values was originally published in 1931 (Vernon and Allport, 1931) and was revised in its present form in 1951. Although there is good evidence for the stability, or reliability, of the separate scores, there is a serious question about their unidimensionality and degree of independence. Hundleby (1965) felt that even factor analytic studies were not conclusive about the nature of the interrelationships among the scores, a problem complicated by the ipsative format of the test. It should be noted that the fairly wide use of the Study of Values for demonstration and research purposes has been connected only minimally with Spranger's theoretical views, which have had little impact upon contemporary personality theory.

Much of the research into the usefulness of the Study of Values has involved comparisons among scores of different occupational groups and students in different colleges and different curricula, demonstrating the different values of such groups. These differences are interesting and lend some support to the use of the instrument for research purposes, but they are not sufficiently large to justify its clinical use for individual assessment. However, Hogan's (1972) review concluded that the test, when used with cooperative subjects, "provides dependable and pertinent information concerning individual cases" (p. 356).

Personality Research Form

During the decade of the 1960s a considerable amount of research was conducted on the methodology of constructing inventories. Jackson's (1967/1974) Personality Research Form (PRF) was one of the first to capitalize on this increased sophistication, making it, in a sense, one of a new generation of personality assessment devices. The PRF was designed to assess 20 traits adapted, as with the EPPS, from the theoretical writings of Murray (1938). When first published, the PRF was offered in two parallel 440-item forms (AA and BB) and two parallel 300-item forms (A and B). In 1974 an improved and simplified 352-item version (Form E) was published. Based on his belief (Jackson, 1971) that the most satisfactory approach to the development of personality test items is a rational one, Jackson initially developed more than 100 items for each trait and refined the pool using a variety of careful psychometric procedures. The resulting scales have high content validity and item homogeneity, relatively low correlations with social desirability, and relatively low correlations with each other. According to Hogan (1978), "it has been developed with extraordinary attention to psychometric detail and is in some ways a paragon of technical sophistication" (p. 1007). On the debit side, the normative samples involve mainly adolescents and college student samples, and relatively few validation data involving behavioral criteria are yet available. Overall, however, the PRF is considered one of the more promising instruments in personality assessment.

Jackson (1976) has more recently published another test, the Jackson Personality Inventory (JPI). Constructed (once again, using a rational approach) to assess traits that are somewhat more social or interpersonal in nature than those assessed by the PRF, the JPI was developed using essentially the same methods but with an even higher degree of psychometric sophistication. Details of construction are difficult to follow from the *Manual* but are summarized clearly by Goldberg (1978b). Correlations of the JPI scales with ratings of the traits by the respondents' peers show a high degree of empirical validity for some of the scales, and it would appear that the JPI has the potential for becoming a very useful test. Adequate data for its applied use have not yet been developed, however.

Rorschach Psychodiagnostic Technique

The Rorschach Psychodiagnostic Technique, or Rorschach, is usually classified simply as a projective technique. However, if we classify it according to the strategy employed in its development as a clinical instrument, the Rorschach is best regarded as rational-theoretical. The presumed relationships between Rorschach responses and the personality characteristics of respondents are based largely upon assumptions and hypotheses developed by Hermann Rorschach, the Swiss psychiatrist who invented the test, and several generations of his followers; and also upon commonsense considerations. In addition, there is a strong theoretical aspect to its development, since many of the interpretative dimensions stem from Jungian personality theory. There have also been a variety of attempts to conceptualize the Rorschach within other theoretical frameworks, and these efforts have been evaluated by Zubin, Eron, and Schumer (1965). As a further point of interest, the original derivation of the Rorschach was to some extent empirical, since Rorschach himself compared the responses of certain patient groups in developing his concepts about the instrument. However, the contemporary clinical use of the instrument— based upon the writings of Beck et al. (1961); Klopfer, Ainsworth, Klopfer, and Holt (1954); Rorschach (1942/1951); and many, many others—is based primarily upon rational considerations. Even here there is a wide variety of approaches. Exner (1974) has identified "at least five reasonably distinct Rorschachs. But when the potential combinations of these systems are considered, the possibilities become astronomical" (p. 14). Thus, the use of the Rorschach is essentially a subjective, individual enterprise.

In administering the Rorschach, the examiner shows the respondent a series of 10 symmetrical inkblots, five achromatic and five chromatic, and asks for a description of what he/she can see in these blots, or "what they remind you of." The order of presentation is invariant and the examiner records the individual's responses verbatim, including any spontaneous comments as well as nonverbal behavior such as card turning. The respondent is permitted to give as many or as few responses as he/she wishes. Following this initial free association period, there is an inquiry or posttest interview in which the examiner, bearing in mind an interest in the specific formal Rorschach scoring categories, repeats the individual's responses back and asks the respondent to specify the particular characteristics of the blot that determined each response. The introductory text by Klopfer and Davidson (1962) provides the basic information needed to administer and score the test.

Perhaps one way of understanding the development of the Rorschach is to examine Rorschach's initial work and how it has led to contemporary Rorschach interpretation with its emphasis on the formal characteristics of the responses. Hermann Rorschach's original interest was in fantasy (Zubin et al., 1965, p. 172), which he studied through perception of small, colored geometric forms. Finding that these geometric forms were too limited as stimulus material, he started to experiment with inkblots. When he began to use his patients as subjects for these perceptual experiments, he was surprised to note that there were stable relationships between certain inkblot perceptions and psychiatric symptoms. Encouraged by these findings, he began a more systematic investigation of the responses of a number of diverse patients groups and started to speculate about the reasons for these relationships.

Since Rorschach was primarily interested in perception, he paid particular attention to the formal aspects of the individual's responses rather than to the content. He noted the number of responses, the reaction time, whether the response was determined solely by the form of the response or whether color or perceived movement were also involved, and so forth (Rorschach, 1942/1951, p. 19). As part of his speculation, he developed fairly complex hypotheses about the relation of color and movement responses to the dimension of extroversion-introversion, based in part upon Jung's theoretical interest in this dimension.

The current clinical use of the Rorschach has varied little since the test's inception. As Zubin et al. have noted (1965, p. 178), most of the current rationale, procedures, and even interpretative phrases ascribed to various test response characteristics can be found in Rorschach's original monograph, which was initially published in German in 1921. Since Rorschach himself considered many of these relationships as highly tentative and requiring additional research, this is indeed a surprising state of affairs, the more so since the subsequent half century has seen the publication of several thousand articles and books dealing with this instrument. Rorschach's own empirical commitment and his feelings of tentativeness about his findings appear not to have strongly influenced the subsequent course of events.

The validity of the Rorschach is the subject of continuing controversy. Despite a total literature of nearly 5,000 references (Buros, 1978), the empirical basis for interpreting this test remains thin. Thus, psychometrically oriented reviewers (e.g., Knutson, 1972; Peterson, 1978b) are consistently negative about the appropriateness of continuing to use the Rorschach as an instrument for diagnosis and prediction. Reviewers who are more closely identified with the field of projective techniques and with psychoanalytic theory tend to acknowledge the lack of evidence for predictive validity, but they believe that the strength of the test lies in its ability to assess personality processes (Weiner, 1977), to serve as a general source of information about a patient (Dana, 1978), to reveal aspects of motivation and personality not assessed by other instruments (Klopfer and Taulbee, 1976), or as a standardized interview. Evidence for the utility of these applications, however, is mostly subjective in nature.

Despite the general agreement that the empirical basis for Rorschach interpretations is inadequate, a number of books have recently appeared which list different aspects of Rorschach responses together with proposed interpretations of these aspects (e.g., Gilbert, 1978; Ogdon, 1975). Since most of what is listed has no demonstrated validity, but is essentially a collection of clinical folklore, these interpretive guides should be used with great caution, if at all. A recent attempt to put the Rorschach on a sounder footing has been made by Exner (1974, 1978), who has developed an integrated approach to scoring and interpretation which attempts to draw the best work from each of the existing approaches to the test. Time will tell whether Exner's work is successful in its intended goal.

Careful analyses of different procedures for establishing the validity of the Rorschach have been made by Weiner (1977) and by Zubin, Eron, and Schumer (1965). The most frequently used approach has involved attempts to show the empirical validity of various signs, scores, indices, or clusters of scores in predicting behavior or discriminating different groups. Either formal scores (see following discussion) or aspects of response content can be involved. This approach clearly highlights the low reliabilities of most of the signs or scores, a difficulty which greatly restricts the validities that can be achieved. Traditional Rorschach enthusiasts criticize this approach because it does not accurately reflect the manner in which experienced clinicians are thought to interpret the test—by relying on patterns or configurations of scores rather than on simple signs or scores.

A second approach to validity involves the matching of a series of Rorschach protocols with the case history belonging to each respondent. Success in matching is said to demonstrate validity in a holistic sense for the test. However, a major criticism, sufficient to preclude further use of matching as a validation strategy, is that many protocols and case histories can easily be matched on the basis of trivial or irrelevant variables, such as references to a particular geographic location or to a specific occupation, or other personal data. A third approach, preferred by Weiner (1977) and termed the *conceptual approach,* is to assess construct validity (see Chapter 7). Here, the challenge is to "formulate theoretical relationships that adequately link the personality characteristics being assessed with the condition being assessed or the behavior being predicted" (Weiner, 1977, p. 597). This is a "theoretical" approach, as described in Chapter 2, in which it is assumed that personality characteristics serve as bridges between the test response and the behavior or prediction of interest.

A fourth approach, which the present authors regard as the simplest and most direct, is the global strategy, in which the clinician makes predictions and interpretations about each patient from the Rorschach results as a whole, according to some structured format such as a Q-sort, checklist, or questionnaire. The same structured format is used by an independent criterion judge to describe each patient from nontest sources of information such as therapy notes, and the two sets of derived information are compared for accuracy. Further details on the use of this approach are given in Chapter 7 in an extended discussion of the reliability of projective techniques. As indicated earlier, none of these approaches have been very successful in demonstrating validity for the Rorschach.

The manner in which the Rorschach is traditionally used clinically can best be illustrated by discussing responses that were actually given to one of the stimulus cards. Figure 3-1 shows a reproduction of Card IV from the 10 Rorschach inkblots. Klopfer and Davidson (1962, p. 10) have described the stimulus characteristics of this card as follows:

> The blot material of Card IV appears massive, compact, yet indistinct in shape. This card is black-gray all over and highly shaded. Because of its massive structure and dense shading, it appears ominous to some people. Thus monsters, giants, gorillas, or peculiar-looking people are seen sitting or approaching, or the blot looks like a dense forest with mountains and lakes. The frequency of the giant, ape, or monster type of response has prompted some clinicians to refer to this card as the "father card." They believe that attitudes toward paternal authority are revealed because of the combination of masculine aggression and dependent needs related to shading.
>
> Subjects who are prone to select details for their responses may perceive the large side areas as "boots," or the top side areas as "snakes" or a "female figure diving." Two other areas that are easily delineated are the lower center portion and the small top center area, frequently associated with sexual responses.
>
> The shading of the card, if not disturbing to a subject, may suggest furriness; in that case the blot is frequently seen as a fur rug.

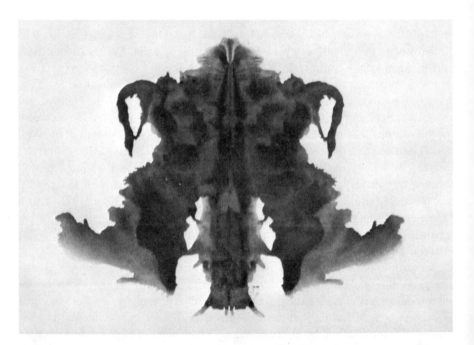

FIGURE 3-1. A reproduction of Card IV from the 10 Rorschach inkblots. From Rorschach (1942). Reproduced by permission.

A 23-year-old female psychotherapy outpatient gave the following responses to this card. The question marks in the inquiry phase indicate places where the examiner asked clarifying questions about the *location* of the percept (What parts of the blot are you referring to?) and its *determinants* (for example, What about the blot suggested a monster?).

Free Association Phase	Inquiry Phase
IV 1. Sort of looks like a monster with big feet.	A cute little thing. Really a dashing little monster. Such a friendly little guy. Got a big tail, though. (?) The whole blot. (?) Really looks like a monster, but a friendly one.
2. When I turn it round, it just looks like—when you mount an insect it has wings and legs—looks like a mounted insect. Sort of cute insect. Maybe a little moth.	You lay him out flat. Only partially mounted. Person hasn't finished yet. You can tell by the lighter color that its wings are turned over. (?) The lighter gray. (?) Again, the whole blot.

The first response would be scored W F+ (H), indicating that the location of the percept was the whole blot (W), that the determinant was form, or shape (F), that the form perceived was appropriate or realistic (indicated by the + sign), and that the content of the percept was humanlike, but not distinctly human [H]. The second response would be scored W FC′+ A, indicating a whole response (W), a realistic form integrated with the perception of achromatic color (FC′+), and animal content (A).

In traditional Rorschach interpretation, at least three kinds of material are considered to be significant: the formal scoring categories (namely, the distribution of percepts over the various location and determinant categories), the nature of the perceived content, and the general language with which percepts are described. Only the most tentative hypotheses would be made from each individual percept, and heavy reliance is placed upon the response pattern as a whole.

Predominance of W, or "whole," locations, when combined with a high level of form appropriateness, is traditionally interpreted as reflecting "the ability to organize material, to relate details, to be concerned with the abstract and the theoretical" (Klopfer and Davidson, 1962, p. 131). A high degree of form appropriateness is also considered to indicate a concern with the reality situation. The presence of achromatic color responses in any quantity is interpreted as indicating either hesitation in responsiveness to external stimuli or an unhappy mood. With regard to content and language, the client's recognition of a "monster" and the manner in which she divests it of its threatening nature ("cute," "little," "friendly") might be seen as illustrating one method of adjustment to perceived threat, by denying and even "reversing" the threatening elements. The fact that a satisfactory compromise is reached at the end of the inquiry ("a monster, but a friendly one") might be taken as a tentative indication that this particular defense mechanism operates satisfactorily for the client. This hypothesis might be tempered slightly after examining the next response, in which the percept has been reduced not only to an insect but a dead one, and the client again calls it "cute," perhaps suggesting that she is still finding it necessary to reassure herself that no threat exists. Pinning it out on a board might be seen as yet a further attempt to remove the threat. The use of "him" rather than "it" in the inquiry might be taken as a tentative cue that the threat has its basis in human interactions, particularly involving males. Obviously, such statements as these would only be regarded as tentative hypotheses, to be confirmed or negated by the client's responses to the other nine cards.

Holtzman Inkblot Technique (HIT)

Generally speaking, workers interested in unstructured or "projective" personality tests have tended to ignore problems of formal measurement, such as norms and unreliability. In 1954, however, a project was begun to develop "a completely new approach to inkblot testing, one which is designed from its inception to meet adequate standards of measurement while preserving the uniquely valuable projective quality of the Rorschach" (Holtzman et al., 1961, p. 10). The materials were specifically designed to tap the same variables as the Rorschach, yet the method was designed to obviate a number of serious psychometric problems inherent in any quantitative use of the Rorschach, problems which center about unreliability due to the great variation in responses from subject to subject. Out of a very large number of inkblots produced by a variety of methods, Holtzman and his coworkers developed two parallel forms of 45 cards each. In these preliminary investigations the stimulus cards were administered to samples of normal persons (college students) and mental hospital patients. The two major criteria for selecting the final stimulus blots were that they should provide maximum discriminatory power between the two groups, and that the blots should enable maximum reliability of the scoring categories being studied. These categories included many traditional Rorschach variables such as location, form appropriateness, color, shading, and movement, categories whose personality interpretation is based on rational grounds. Thus, we consider the HIT as a rationally derived instrument despite the empirical basis of the selection of the actual HIT stimuli.

The HIT cards are shown one at a time to the individual, who is to give a single response to each card. The responses are then scored for 22 different variables, selected for their relative independence, reliability of scoring, and judged relevance for understanding personality. In addition to the five scoring variables already listed, they include form definiteness, space, anxiety, pathognomic verbalization, and five different content categories. The advantages claimed for the HIT include: (1) simplified psychometric treatment, since all subjects would give the same number of responses; (2) independence of responses, since each would be given to a different stimulus; (3) utilization of recent Rorschach research to improve upon the response elicitation properties of the cards; and (4) the establishment of reliabilities through the correlation between parallel forms.

A great deal of reliability information has been developed by Holtzman et al.

(1961), all of which indicates that the stability or reliability of most scores is quite satisfactory, a considerable improvement over the Rorschach. An exception is found in the relatively low test-retest reliabilities, some of which are lower than .5, even with intervals of as little as one week between test and retest. Extensive normative data are presented on both normal persons and psychiatric patients. The manual reports substantial correlations of HIT scores with those obtained from the Rorschach, suggesting that the same variables are indeed being tapped by these two instruments. On the other hand, there are very few significant relationships reported between HIT scores and either scores from paper-and-pencil inventories or ratings of overt behavior. These findings are explained by Holtzman et al. as a consequence of the fact that the significant variables in personality and psychopathology are neither directly observable nor measurable by inventories.

More recent reviews of the utility of the HIT are mixed. In a handbook on the test, Hill (1972) took the view that interpretation is best regarded as a creative process, relying heavily on traditional beliefs regarding the meaning of projective responses. Reviews of the validity literature by Gamble (1972), Klopfer and Taulbee (1976), and Peterson (1978a) have adopted more scientific standards, and have concluded that the instrument has some degree of potential for personality assessment. While some reviewers have approached their evaluation of the HIT mainly in the context of comparing it with the Rorschach, it would seem more logical to regard it as a completely different test, to be evaluated on its own merits.

Thematic Apperception Test

The Thematic Apperception Test, more commonly known as the TAT (Murray, 1943), is another traditional projective device which is here classified as rational-theoretical. The stimulus materials consist of 31 cards, 30 depicting various scenes and people, and one blank card. In the standard presentation, the respondent is shown 20 cards chosen according to sex and age, although in the typical clinical presentation fewer than 20 cards are generally used. The TAT is introduced as a "test of imagination," and the respondent is asked to tell as dramatic a story as possible to each card. He/she is instructed that each story should include what has led up to the event depicted in the card, what is happening at that moment, what the people in the story are feeling and thinking, and finally the outcome of the story. The examiner records the stories verbatim as they are given. Murray (1943) also recommended that the examiner attempt, in a posttest interview, to determine the source of the story—whether personal experience, from friends, or from books or movies.

Although Murray was not the first person to use the picture-story method, he did the most to popularize it as both a clinical and research tool. Apart from one or two isolated studies in the early 1900s, the earliest clinical application of the procedure was that of Schwartz (1932), who used his Social Situation Picture Test as a diagnostic aid to psychiatric interviews with juvenile delinquents. The TAT was developed as a method for eliciting unconscious fantasy material from patients in psychoanalysis (Morgan and Murray, 1935). Indeed, the final selection of the TAT cards was based upon how much relevant information the TAT responses contributed to understanding the personality characteristics of individuals who had already been studied in detail by other methods.

The popularity of the TAT has given rise to a number of other story construction tests. The Children's Apperception Test (Bellak, 1954) and the Michigan Pictures Test (Hartwell, Hutt, Andrew, and Walton, 1951) are rather similar in procedure to the TAT. In the Four Picture Test (Van Lennep, 1951), the subject is presented simultaneously with four colored pictures and is instructed to incorporate them in a story. In Shneidman's (1951) Make-a-Picture-Story Test, respondents are given various background scenes and cardboard cutouts of a large variety of people from which to construct their own pictures, to be used as a basis for stories. In general, these techniques are based upon the same assumptions and utilize the same interpretative framework as the TAT, although there is much less evaluative research available on them.

Two rational assumptions that guided Murray's initial work with the TAT were: (1) that the attributes of the hero, or main character, in the story represent tendencies in the respondent's own personality; and (2) that characteristics of the hero's environment represent significant aspects of the respondent's own environment. Thus, the traditional use of the picture-story technique involves an interpretative analysis by the examiner, first, of the intrapsychic state of the individual, as reflected in descriptions of the story heroes; and second, of the environmental pressures experienced, as reflected in descriptions of the heroes' environments. For example, in the first TAT card, which shows a boy peering at a violin, the story might reflect the boy's resentment (an inner state) at his parents, who insist upon his practicing (an environmental pressure) when he wishes to do something else. Murray's (1938) own theoretical system would discuss these inner states as *needs* and the environmental or external pressures as *press*. However, the use of the TAT does not require the adoption of Murray's system, so that this instrument cannot be regarded as having a strong theoretical base.

As with the Rorschach, there have been a number of attempts both to develop quantitative scoring schemes and to construct formal norms for the data derived from an analysis of TAT responses. Perhaps the most widely used scoring system is that of McClelland (McClelland et al., 1953). McClelland was concerned primarily with the *need achievement* dimension, and with assessing motivation in various research endeavors rather than clinical diagnosis. Another system is Eron's (Zubin, Eron, and Schumer, 1965), which has been shown to be useful in research but appears to have found little clinical application. Murstein (1963) has provided an excellent summary of a variety of scoring and interpretative schemes for picture stories. However, the typical clinical use of the TAT and the other picture-story methods remains rather informal and idiosyncratic.

How useful or valid is the TAT as a personality assessment procedure? Although the volume of literature on the TAT is large (it is third in this respect, preceded only by the MMPI and the Rorschach), its status as a proven, clinically useful instrument is still in doubt. Many of the problems associated with the clinical use of the TAT—lack of standardized procedures and formal normative data, low reliabilities, overenthusiastic and undercritical acceptance of intuitive hunches about the supposed meaning of certain responses—are also present in the Rorschach and other unstructured techniques.

One particularly troublesome problem with the TAT is the difficulty of determining whether an indicated need or personality characteristic will be present in the subject's overt behavior in real-life situations as opposed to existing only on the fantasy or unconscious level. This is especially important since the TAT is commonly regarded as helpful in understanding the content, or "dynamics" of behavior; yet, for example, the person with strong needs for attention and recognition that are expressed overtly is very different behaviorally from the "Walter Mitty" character with equally strong needs that do not find behavioral expression because of some suppressive or inhibitory mechanism. Murstein (1963) has summarized the research pertaining to one specific aspect of this problem: the relationship between the judged aggressiveness of the heroes in TAT stories and the overt aggressive behavior of the subject. He concluded that the relationship was generally positive but was complicated by the operation of a number of other variables, such as guilt over aggression, the objective amount of hostility depicted in the TAT pictures, and the specificity of the aggressive acts. According to Swartz (1978), the research on the relationships of TAT stories to real-life behavior continues to be equivocal.

An additional consideration worth noting concerns the "hero assumption" described earlier. Lindzey and Kalnins (1958) were able to demonstrate the validity of this assumption in two rather important ways. First they were able to show that the figures identified by respondents in a clinical interview as most like themselves were, indeed, the same as those judged to be the heroes in the TAT protocol. Second, the aggression ascribed by the respondents to the TAT heroes increased following experimentally induced frustration, while the aggression ascribed to other figures did not. These findings tend to support the assumption that the picture-story hero often does possess characteristics of the story teller.

Figure 3-2 shows one of the stimulus cards of the Thematic Apperception Test. According to Henry (1956), the stimulus properties of this TAT card are as follows:

Murray's description. The portrait of a young woman. A weird old woman with a shawl over her head is grimacing in the background.

Manifest stimulus demand. An adequate accounting will include only the two figures plus some explanation of their being together in this position. Generally, the interpretation of subjects is about as Murray gives it. However, recently we have seen in female subjects over seventy interpretations in which the "weird old woman" becomes a gently smiling and helpful person. Close examination of the face of the older figure suggests that "weird" and "grimacing" are not necessary connotations.

Form demand. The two figures are the only major details, though the facial features of the older woman can be differentially perceived.

Latent stimulus demand. In subjects in the middle-age range, this appears to be a stimulus relating older to younger. Thus, for the mature woman, threats of old age appear prominent. In the younger adult, apprehension over control by an older woman appears more prominent. A basic stimulus selected by many subjects, especially women, is one

FIGURE 3-2. A reproduction of one of the TAT stimulus cards. From Murray (1943). Reprinted by permission. Copyright 1943 by the President and Fellows of Harvard College; © 1971 by Henry A. Murray.

which portrays the old woman as some symbolic representation of a part of the younger; her evil self, her self when aged, etc.

Frequent plots. Most generally, the younger woman bears a family relationship to the older woman who is influencing or advising in some way. In about one-third of the stories, the older woman is seen as adversely influencing. In about one-third of the stories, a second plot will appear in which the older woman is a symbolic representation of the younger woman.

Significant variations. Of importance here is the issue of whether the subject sees the two figures in the same reality plane (mother-daughter) or whether one is a symbolic representation (my bad self, me when old, etc.). In addition, if treated in this fashion, the particular ideas toward the good and evil or other parts of the self should be specially viewed. In the light of the possibility of some, especially older, subjects seeing the background woman as kindly, responses to her should probably be watched more carefully and attention paid to the extent to which projection rather than reality observation is involved in attributing adverse influences (pp. 254–256).

The following story was given by the same 23-year-old female who contributed the Rorschach material discussed earlier in this chapter.

Well, there's a young woman in the foreground and an older woman in the background, and the older woman looks as though she has planned something that will be harmful to the younger woman, who looks very naïve. And in fact the older woman has planned to keep the younger woman captive, and to make her serve her, for the rest of the older woman's life. But although the girl is naïve, she's also rebellious; and by asserting herself with other people and getting a group of friends she's able to move out of the—not exactly spell, but she's able to break the bond that the older woman has around her. Right now she's just beginning to realize that she is being put in a position like this, but she's still very much under the control of the older woman, because these two have lived together for a long time. In fact, the younger woman was raised by the older woman. She's still very much under her control as I said, and she has strong feelings of guilt and fear of facing the world on her own. But fortunately she is able to make friends. At this point, though, she hasn't broken the bonds and she feels very confused, like she's being drawn between two poles. Ultimately, she's able to go out and make friends, and getting to know people and the different ways they have from the ways the old woman had taught her, she's able successfully to face the older woman, and defy her control, and go out and live a life of her own.

This story follows the stimulus demands of the card to a considerable extent; that is, the client reacted to the card much like most people her age. Thus, we would not be justified in coming to an immediate conclusion that she has any special problem in her relationships with older women. Also, a typical TAT interpretation would draw material from 10 or more cards and would regard whatever hypotheses are gleaned from an individual story as quite tentative, to be strengthened or disconfirmed by the remainder of the stories. From the present story, the following details might be considered of interest.

The older woman's control over the younger is perceived as long-standing and as having caused some rather central personality problems. However, the younger woman is seen as taking the initiative in developing other friendships in order to provide emotional support for the break which she plans with the older woman. Her ambivalence over these plans is seen in the use of the words "rebellious," "guilt," and "confused." The younger woman is perceived as displaying perhaps a somewhat lesser degree of anger and resentment toward the older than one would expect after having been trained as a lifelong captive and servant; and the severity of the confinement, together with the younger woman's expression of guilt rather than anger, suggests a situation where anger is perhaps repressed. There is also the younger woman's determination and ultimate success, though this comes about through defiance of the older woman rather than a resolution of conflict, again suggesting more anger than is overtly acknowledged.

Although themes of apprehension over control by an older woman are relatively common in stories given by younger persons to this picture, the strength of the conflict as represented by the guilt, the severity of the control exercised, and the absence of appropriate expressions of anger by the younger woman suggest the tentative hypothesis that such a conflict does exist for this client. The client's inability to resolve the fantasy conflict successfully lends further support to this hypothesis. A TAT analyst might also suggest that the client's ability to put forward a rational plan for the younger woman while still acknowledging her confusion and naïvete suggests good potential for improvement in psychotherapy. Naturally the experienced clinician would search for additional support for these tentative hypotheses elsewhere in the client's TAT responses.

Picture-Drawing Techniques

It is widely believed that creative works (especially in the fine arts, and drawing and painting in particular) reflect the personality of the artist. It should be noted that a demonstration of the validity of this assumption for trained artists would not necessarily establish its validity for people with little or no formal artist training. It is, however, this latter assumption that underlies the use of picture-drawing techniques in the assessment of personality characteristics.

The use of drawings in psychological evaluation was first popularized by Goodenough (1926), who developed a standardized procedure for evaluating the intelligence of children from their drawings of a man. As a result of a growing interest in interpreting the qualitative asyects of such drawings, two techniques have become widely used. One of these is Buck's (1948a, 1948b, 1949) House-Tree-Person, or H-T-P, technique, in which the respondent is required to draw first a house, then a tree, and finally a person, each on a separate sheet of paper. In the second, Machover's (1949) Draw-a-Person (DAP) test, the respondent first draws a person of either sex and then is asked to draw a person of the opposite sex. In the interests of brevity, we shall confine our discussion to the Machover DAP, recognizing that most of our evaluative remarks are equally cogent for the H-T-P and other drawing procedures.

In administering the DAP, the respondent is given a pencil and an 8½ by 11 inch sheet of blank paper, on which he/she is instructed to "draw a person." The examiner inconspicuously observes the individual, noting such behavior as the total time involved, the sequence in which the drawing is completed, any spontaneous comments, and so on. When this drawing is completed the individual is given a fresh sheet of paper and told "Now draw a man (woman)." Machover recommends reassuring the respondent, if necessary, that the test has nothing to do with drawing skills, and also persuading him/her to draw any parts that appear to have been omitted. It is also recommended that the individual be asked a series of questions to encourage free associations to the drawings, such as "How old is the person drawn?" and "Is he (she) married?"

The major portion of Machover's (1949) book is devoted to rules of interpretation involving the qualitative aspects of the drawings. These rules were apparently derived from the author's clinical experience as well as a variety of rational considerations, most of which reflect a psychoanalytic orientation. The rules provide for a description of the personality characteristics of the respondent with a strong emphasis on psychopathology. They include the following sets of categories: head, parts of the face, facial expression, neck, contact features (arms and hands, legs and feet, fingers, toes), other body features, clothing, structural and formal aspects, conflict indicators (erasures and shading), and differential treatment of the male and female figures. One of the rules that can be regarded as representative of rational considerations involves the interpretation of the manner in which the shoulders are drawn: "The width and massiveness of the shoulders are considered the most common graphic expression of physical power and perfection of physique" (p. 71). The rationale underlying some interpretations is more difficult to comprehend; for example, "The Adam's apple . . . has been seen mostly in the drawing of young males an an expression of strong virility or masculine drive. Special interest in the Adam's apple has been restricted to the sexually weak individual who shows little differentiation between male and female characteristics and is uncertain about his own role" (p. 58).

Swensen (1957, 1968) and Roback (1968), in their reviews of the research literature on the DAP, concluded that there was little support for Machover's interpretations or hypotheses, and indeed that more of the data directly contradicted her contentions rather than supported them. Swensen further noted that the available evidence indicated the test-retest reliabilities of the various content and structural aspects of the drawings to be quite low, although the overall quality of the drawings (rated according to their realism or correspondence to life) was fairly constant. The research also suggested that the judged overall quality of the drawing is related to the gross level of adjustment of the subject. Swensen (1968) suggested the possibility that future research that controlled for overall quality of the drawings might lead to more satisfactory findings with respect to specific personality variables. A later review by Klopfer and Taulbee (1976), however, showed that these suggestions had not been taken up. Johnson and Greenberg (1978) did control for quality of drawings and found essentially no significant personality correlates of the drawings.

Despite these generally negative findings, the clinical use of picture-drawing techniques continues to be very high (Brown and McGuire, 1976; Piotrowski and Keller, 1978). The work of Chapman and Chapman (1967) on the phenomenon of illusory correlation, discussed in Chapter 9, offers some possible explanations for their unabated popularity despite minimal validity evidence.

Figure 3-3 shows two drawings which were reported and interpreted by Hammer (1968), another leading authority in this area. Hammer's interpretation is given here.

The nuanced language of drawing projection is particularly suited for stating the complexities and human contradictions as they balance and interrelate within a single personality. At such times, the apparent contradictions can be seen to possess an inner harmony, as in the musical statement and counterstatement of a fugue. Figure 3-3, drawn by an eighteen-year-old male caught stealing a TV set, constitutes such a pictorial statement. Beneath the obvious attempts at an impressive figure of masculine prowess, there are more subtle trends of the opposite: of inadequacy and inconsequentiality. The muscles of the drawn figure have been inflated beyond the hard and sinewy, into a puffy softness as if it is a figure made of balloons; the legs taper down to insubstantiality and,

FIGURE 3-3. Drawings by an 18-year-old male showing surface and subsurface personality levels. From E.F. Hammer, "Projective Drawings." In A.I. Rabin, ed., *Assessment with Projective Techniques: A Concise Introduction*, pp. 162–163. Copyright © 1981 by Springer Publishing Company, Inc., New York. Used by permission.

finally, absent feet, and an incongruous hat is placed on the boxer making comical his lifting of one gloved hand in victory. . . . On the one hand, emblematic of his defenses, his drawn achromatic person is the "twenty-year-old" boxer with muscles flexed and a weight-lifter's build. Beneath this inflated image, however, on the crayon drawing of a person—which, due to the impact of color, tends to tap the relatively deeper levels of personality (Hammer, 1958)—he offers now only a "six-year-old boy" who then looks even more like an infant than a child: with one curlicue hair sticking up and the suggestion of diapers on (. . . shown here in black and white). The ears are rather ludicrous in their standing away from the head and, all in all, the total projection in this drawing is that of an infantile, laughable entity, rather than the impressive he-man he overstated on the achromatic version of a person. Beneath his attempts to demonstrate rugged masculinity (which may have culminated into the offense with which he is charged), the patient experiences himself as actually a little child, dependent and needing care, protection, and affection (p. 163).

Blacky Pictures Test

In Chapter 2 we suggested that most attempts to develop personality assessment procedures have been theoretically neutral, although the personality descriptions which stem from them are often couched in the language of some particular personality theory. For an assessment procedure to be regarded as theoretically derived, the actual stimuli employed to elicit the relevant responses would have to be selected on the basis of a viable personality theory, and the entire assessment procedure would be closely interwoven with that theory. As stated previously, since there are no rigorous theories of personality, we have utilized a general classification of *rational-theoretical* tests; and within this framework, the best-established test toward the theoretical end of the continuum is the Blacky Pictures Test developed by Blum (1949, 1950). This test is based upon the traditional psychoanalytic theory of psychosexual development, which holds that children typically pass through three distinct and critically important stages in their personality development. In the first, or oral stage, the child's primary preoccupation is with oral satisfactions—eating, sucking, chewing, and other stimulation involving the mouth. The anal stage is the period in which the child is made aware of the need for controlling eliminative functions and learns to achieve the required control. In the phallic stage, there is an awareness of the sexual organs as a source of satisfaction and a preoccupation with this satisfaction. Psychoanalytic theory involves a vast number of additional complexities, but what is important for us is the notion that excessive deprivation, or excessive gratification, at any one of these stages may lead to the child becoming "fixated" at that stage. That is to say, later personality characteristics, especially ways of handling conflict, may reflect the child's experiences at the fixated stage of development. Thus, a child who received excessive gratification at the oral stage might develop an "oral dependent" personality, where he/she would handle psychological conflicts by expecting to have needs met by others with little effort on his/her part, in an adult restructuring of the helpless role of the suckling infant. A child who was deprived of gratification at the anal stage may develop "anal retentive" personality characteristics, such as strong feelings of possessiveness about material things, stubbornness, and hoarding behavior. These examples suggest how psychoanalytic theory regards the roots for adult behavior to be established in the early psychosexual development of the child.

It follows from the Freudian theory of psychosexual development that if we can discover an individual's reactions and attitudes connected with the oral, anal, and phallic aspects of psychosexual development, we will have obtained significant information about the person's personality and about the sources of any overt or latent personality conflicts which he/she may have. The Blacky pictures are specifically designed to yield such information. The test materials consist of 12 cartoons portraying the life of Blacky, a puppy of indeterminate sex, and its family, consisting of Papa, Mama, and another sibling. Each scene was developed in order to tap what should be a potential conflict area for Blacky according to the psychoanalytic theory of psychosexual development. For example, the second picture, designed to assess "oral sadism," shows the puppy snarling while vigorously shaking Mama's collar in its teeth. The other pictures are similarly designed to measure such psychosexual concepts as anal sadism, penis envy, sibling rivalry, and guilt feelings. The respondent is presented with each picture, asked to make up a story telling what is happening and why, and is then asked a series of multiple-choice questions about the pictures. The subject is also asked which cards he/she likes and dislikes. It is assumed that these evaluations, together with the respondent's report of Blacky's mood as unhappy, angry, frightened, and so forth, are indicative of the subject's own response to these potential conflict areas. Since the connections between the stimulus materials and the inferences to be drawn from responses to them are quite subtle, and since there is little general understanding of psychoanalytic concepts, the Blacky Test does not require self-awareness on the part of the respondent and is typically regarded as a projective technique.

The scoring and interpretation of responses to the Blacky pictures are relatively complex procedures. Blum (1950, 1951) initially provided scoring directions for assessing the strength of 13 different psychosexual areas, and more recently (Blum, 1962) he proposed a 30-variable scoring system, based upon factor analytic research on the previous scoring schemata. According to Sappenfield's (1965) review, the scoring of the Blacky test is sufficiently reliable for research purposes but is not adequate for individual clinical assessment.

How useful or valid is the Blacky Test? There is little published evidence concerning the utility of impressionistic clinical analyses of Blacky Test responses, although it is likely that the instrument is often used in this fashion (Sappenfield, 1965). On the other hand, there are positive research findings in which the Blacky Test has been successfully used to demonstrate the validity of certain aspects of psychoanalytic theory, one of the primary uses for which it was developed. Sappenfield, in reviewing some of these studies, considered that their success was facilitated by the availability of the careful and explicit scoring instructions contained in the manual. Thus, one study showed a connection between the development of peptic ulcers and oral erotic conflicts (Blum and Kaufman, 1952), while another confirmed the predictions made from psychoanalytic theory about paranoia, using the Blacky Test responses of paranoids and other psychotic patients (Aronson, 1953).

To summarize, the Blacky Pictures Test shows some evidence of being a useful instrument for testing certain aspects of psychoanalytic theory in a research setting, though there is little published evidence to support its use as a clinical assessment device. Despite its theoretical orientation, overall interest in the test seems to be on the decline at the present time (Klopfer and Taulbee, 1976).

Bender Visual Motor Gestalt Test

The Bender Visual Motor Gestalt Test (Bender, 1938, 1946), which was initially developed within the Gestalt school of psychology, also has an easily identified theoretical base. Originally an orientation for the study of perceptual phenomena, the Gestalt approach soon spread into virtually all aspects of psychological theorizing. Briefly, it was based in the notion that events could only be understood by studying them in their entirety, as opposed to studying their individual elements, because the *configuration* of the elements, a critical component of the "whole," would otherwise be lost.

Bender (1938) studied the visual-motor perceptual skill of young children from a Gestalt point of view, noting the gradual development of their ability to perceive "wholes" and relationships when shown drawings of incomplete figures and other simple patterns. Reasoning that the individual's entire psychological development was reflected in this particular aspect of his functioning, Bender proposed that overall level of mental skill could be assessed from visual-motor perceptual performance, and she based her development of test materials on that assumption.

The test stimuli for the Bender-Gestalt consist of nine 4 by 6 inch cards, each of which contains one of the original patterns used in early Gestalt perceptual research studies. The respondent is shown the cards one by one and is asked to copy the patterns on a single sheet of blank 8½ by 11 inch white paper. Bender (1946) originally interpreted the drawings according to the principle that "any deviation in the total organism will be reflected in the final sensory motor patterns in response to the given stimulus pattern" (p. 4). For guidance in interpretation, Bender presented illustrations of the responses of normal children at various age levels. She also presented illustrations of the response patterns of various psychologically disturbed groups which she considered to be identifiable with the instrument, based on the assumption that psychopathology is caused by early childhood trauma, which subsequently interferes with the maturation of the ability to perceive Gestalts, or "wholes."

Although it can be argued that any *quantitative* scoring of Bender-Gestalt responses would be inconsistent with the theoretical insistence of the Gestalt viewpoint that the "whole" is more than the sum of its parts, Bender (1938) did offer a tentative scoring scheme for measuring the maturational level of children using their responses to the test stimuli. A number of other scoring systems have been developed, probably the best known being that of Pascal and Suttell (1951). In this system the individual's drawings are assessed for their deviation from the standard on 105 different details. Numerical values are given and totaled to give a single score. The reliability of such scoring schemes is generally rather satisfactory, and they have served to point up the test's correlation with factors like intelligence and education.

The theoretical basis of the test indicates that its validity should be assessed, at least initially, from its degree of success in discriminating among subjects who differ in their development of the visual-motor Gestalt function, or the capacity to organize perceptual "wholes." A number of studies have shown that a fairly adequate mental age score can be derived from the test responses of children between the ages of 4 and 12 (Billingslea, 1963), a conclusion not inconsistent with Bender's initial assumption. It is also possible to make a gross differentiation of normal persons from various groups, especially those with cerebral brain damage, although these findings are somewhat less clear-cut (Billingslea, 1963; Golden, 1979). Specifically, the more severe the brain damage, the more readily it is reflected on the test. Use of Canter's (1970) Background Interference Procedure, in which designs copied on blank paper are compared with those copied on wavy-lined paper, showed some initial promise as a more accurate gross screening procedure for brain damage, but it has received little attention recently.

Many clinicians argue that a variety of qualitative aspects of a subject's Bender-Gestalt responses—such as the relative size of the drawing, the strength of the impression, and the relative placement of the figures on the page—are useful indices to the personality of the individual. Although much use is made of the responses in this manner, empirical efforts to demonstrate relationships with molar personality characteristics have been rather unsuccessful (Billingslea, 1963; Kitay, 1972). These negative findings should not be surprising in view of the fact that Bender's original theory and her selection of the test stimuli have only the most tenuous connection with personality functioning, at least on the level of the assessment of observable behavioral characteristics. Hutt (1977) reported significant differences between normals and a number of groups with various kinds of psychopathology. However, factors such as intelligence were not controlled and could well have been responsible for these differences.

In summary, the theoretical basis of the Bender Visual Motor Gestalt Test as a measure of personality functioning is not a sound one; neither the theory nor the test stimuli seem to be firmly grounded in personality functioning. It is thus not surprising to find that the test lacks validity for personality assessment.

RATIONAL-THEORETICAL ASSESSMENT DEVICES: SOME COMMENTS

In Chapter 2 we indicated that clinical assessment of personality initially involved collecting data about the individual, data that hopefully enable us to understand and predict other aspects of his/her behavior. The critical issue is how the psychologist decides which data are worth collecting—that is, which data will have predictive or informative value. It is clear that there are many different kinds of data that *may* be useful, and often it is difficult, if not impossible, to decide in advance which of them will yield worthwhile clues about an individual's personality characteristics. Indeed, the history of personality assessment is replete with techniques, such as phrenology and astrology, which have proven to be "blind alleys" because the data involved were not related to personality attributes.

Since the range of information that could have usefulness in personality assessment must be regarded as practically infinite, the selection of the data to be considered must involve some choice on the part of the assessor, unless it is to be completely random. In personality tests based on purely rational considerations, the initial selection of the test stimuli is based upon the assumption that there will be meaning or significance in the test responses because of the very nature of these stimuli. The more importance that is given to considerations of a particular theory of personality, the closer the test would be classified to the theoretical end of the rational-theoretical continuum. Let us first consider problems which arise from the purely rational aspects of this strategy.

In the case of the rationally derived *questionnaire,* the basis for item selection is obvious in the content of the items. Thus, the assumption is that anxious persons will admit their anxiety when directly questioned about how they feel. The rationale for the so-called projective techniques is not quite so obvious, especially to the nonprofessional. The assumption, for example, that emotional persons will respond more to the colored portions of a series of inkblots than nonemotional persons stems from several sources: from some crude theoretical notions about responsivitity to color in general, from a logical analysis of the nature of humans and how they behave, and from informal empirical observations of human behavior. For simplicity, we have lumped this all together and called it a *rational basis.* Some more strictly theoretical and empirical elements are perhaps also involved, but these elements tend to be of limited significance in the current literature and folklore surrounding projective techniques.

Rationally derived questionnaires seem to depend for their usefulness upon at least three specific assumptions. (1) It must be assumed that respondents are competent to judge themselves with regard to the questions asked. (2) We must rely upon them to share the truth about which they are assumed to be aware. (3) The test stimuli must be assumed to be clear and unambiguous in their meaning.

Most psychodynamic views of personality would tend to deny the validity of the first two assumptions. Such views hold that most people tend to hide unpleasant truths from self-awareness, as a way of avoiding the anxiety that the admission of these truths would arouse. Thus, individuals would be least likely to provide useful responses in the very aspects of personality where assessment is most important. In addition, most persons are well aware of the possibility of dissimulation, of deliberately not revealing unpleasant truths about themselves because of the social consequences of admitting them. Both of these considerations are among the most frequently mentioned objections to rationally derived instruments.

Concerning the third assumption, the psychological meaning of the stimulus can be thought of as varying among persons in two ways: (1) as a consequence of the defensiveness just discussed, and (2) because of individual differences in meaning stemming from differences in individual experience or personal learning history. Thus, the questionnaire stimulus "I often have headaches" may elicit an affirmative response from one subject for whom "often" is once a month, and a negative response from another subject for whom "often" is once a week. In other words, selecting unambiguous stimuli is by no means a simple task.

It is just these idiosyncratic differences in the psychological meaning of the stimulus materials that originally gave rise to the concept of using test stimuli "projectively." The major assumption underlying projection in this sense is that individual differences in responses to ambiguous stimuli are functionally related to some underlying, habitual characteristics of individuals, their personality. An allied assumption is that the relationships between the stimuli and responses are known or knowable to the test developer on some rational basis. However, because of the subtle nature of these relationships, they are not readily known to the subject, thus reducing the effects of defensiveness or deliberate simulation upon responses. As it turns out, it is this very subtle or tenuous nature of the relationship between test response and assumed personality characteristic that provides the most serious objection to the traditional projective instruments.

Although the rational selection of the content of test stimuli often may not be a *sufficient* basis for usefulness or validity, it seems to be a *necessary* basis. That is to say, without some rational connection between the test response and the characteristic to be assessed or criterion to be predicted, the likelihood of establishing a satisfactory level of validity is much reduced. Thus, an important consideration in selecting test stimuli would appear to be that the meaning of responses to the test stimuli should be inherent in the stimuli themselves or in the fashion they were selected.

A clear illustration of this point is found in the research reported by Norman

(1963a, 1963b) using questionnaire items. Faced with the problem of assessing the personality suitability of candidates for desirable jobs (where the defensiveness of the respondents could be assumed to be high), Norman attempted to develop "subtle" items whose meaning would not be clear to the respondents. For several groups of college students, friends' ratings were obtained on five personality dimensions. These ratings were then used as personality criteria to be predicted from the students' responses to three sets of test stimuli. The first test employed personality-descriptive adjectives (obviously related to the criterion), the second required preference ratings for various occupational titles (intermediate in their relationship to the criterion), and the third required preference ratings for geometrical designs (very subtle in their relationship to the criterion). Using the criterion group approach, described in Chapter 4, Norman constructed a series of personality scales from the results of each test. His results clearly indicated that only the scales based upon the first test (the self-descriptive adjectives), which were the most obvious in their meaning, were at all consistently related to the criterion.

The importance of rationality in test stimuli was also illustrated by Duff (1965) using the MMPI. Following the lead of Seeman (1952, 1953)—who had demonstrated that the MMPI contained both obvious and subtle items, and that subtle items were difficult for the test taker to simulate or "fake"—Duff listed the MMPI items which originally had discriminated normal persons from three particular psychiatric groups: conversion hysteria, psychopathic personality, and schizophrenia. Expert judges were then asked to indicate which items, on the basis of their content, appeared to be appropriate for one of these discriminations or another. That is, the judges were asked to pick out the items which one would rationally expect to be relevant for these discriminations. After identifying the rational or obvious (content-relevant) and the nonobvious or subtle (content-irrelevant) items in this manner, Duff compared the validity of the two kinds of items by examining the responses of patients in the appropriate diagnostic groups. His findings clearly indicated that the content-relevant items, that is, those with rational or face meaning, discriminated to a greater degree than did the so-called subtle items. Substantially the same point was made by Goldberg and Slovic (1967), whose findings are examined more carefully in Chapter 4. A more recent study by Gynther, Burkhart, and Hovanitz (1979) involving the MMPI *Pd* scale showed that while obvious items were the most powerful predictors of the criterion, subtle items made a smaller but unique contribution.

In a major theoretical paper, Jackson (1971) mustered many arguments to support his contention that rational derivation was an absolute necessity. He regarded the most useful personality assessment measures as those that are constructed rationally and "derived from an explicitly formulated, theoretically based definition of a trait" (p. 232). Jackson also emphasized the necessity of developing an item pool whose content adequately and representatively reflects the universe of content implied by the definition. He also advocated the use of items which could be regarded as both subtle *and* content relevant. For example, the item "I think newborn babies look very much like little monkeys" initially appears to have no particular content relevance, but a moment's thought indicates that it could well represent the negative pole of the nurturance dimension. The value of Jackson's paper is in providing a sophisticated rationale and model for the rational-theoretical development of personality test items in a way which maximizes their potential validity.

It should be noted that much of the evidence regarding the primacy of the rational approach has involved measures of normal personality functioning. It is possible that persons with psychological problems are less able to describe themselves accurately, and that the utility of rational procedures in assessing psychopathology is therefore much more limited. Research evidence is needed on this question.

Despite Jackson's exhortation, the present status of personality assessment instruments with a substantial theoretical base is equivocal. There are relatively few such instruments available, their contribution to our knowledge of personality function in either an applied or a theoretical sense has been minimal, and they tend to offer little to the practicing clinician who is concerned with describing and understanding an individual patient. Thus, their promise as the most sophisticated approach to the problem of understanding personality has not as yet been realized.

There are at least two reasons for this state of affairs. First, there are few approaches to personality which fully qualify to be called theories, as has already been noted. Further, contemporary psychological theorists have shown relatively little interest in developing new molar personality theories. Instead, far more attention is being given to constructing microtheories thas attempt to deal with more limited behavior sequences than those typically subsumed under the rubric of *personality*. The personality theory which has been most viable in instigating the development of personality tests has been Freudian psychoanalytic theory, which can claim the Blacky Pictures Test, the IES (Id-Ego-Superego) Test (Dombrose and Slobin, 1958), and others.

The second reason for the atheoretical basis of current assessment devices is the preoccupation of psychologists who are interested in test development with psychometric technical refinements rather than with clinical usefulness. The increasing demand for a high level of technical specialization amng psychometricians may have tended to isolate them from both the theorizing and research in other areas, work which may have important implications for test development (Anastasi, 1967). There is clearly a need for both technical sophistication and theoretical understanding in the area of personality test development.

Summary

This and the following chapter introduce basic issues in the development of standardized personality assessment procedures. Such procedures tend to meet several conditions: (1) The stimuli and their manner of presentation are invariant, (2) norms exist for the responses of interest, and (3) the personality or behavior correlates of these responses are known. These conditions suggest several criteria for the classification of assessment devices: degree of response structure, completeness of norms, and degree of usefulness or validity. We have chosen a more basic classification—the manner in which the assessment stimuli were originally selected.

Three categories are employed: (1) *rational-theoretical,* where the stimuli have commonsense appeal and are based to a lesser or greater extent in a particular theory of personality; (2) *empirical,* where the stimuli are chosen solely on the basis of their demonstrated utility; and (3) *internal consistency,* where the dimensions to be assessed are defined statistically. It is nowadays usual for all three procedures to be used in the course of developing a particular test. Described next are some common instruments whose development is predominantly rational-theoretical.

In the sentence completion method, subjects write endings to a variety of sentence beginnings designed to elicit personality-relevant material. This method has been most widely used in a "clinical" or impressionistic manner, though several scorable forms are available, and research findings suggest that standardized content scales have the best validity.

The Edwards Personal Preference Schedule (EPPS) is a paper-and-pencil inventory yielding scores on 15 "need" scales. In order to counter the tendency to answer all questionnaire items in a socially desirable direction, Edwards employed the forced-choice technique of presenting the statements in pairs matched for social desirability. However, later research has indicated that the validity of the test was not enhanced by this procedure. The Study of Values is another forced-choice paper-and-pencil inventory, developed to assess Spranger's six basic interests or motives in personality. There is some evidence for its utility in research applications and as an individual assessment device. Two more recent tests, both developed with considerable care and sophistication, are the Personality Research Form and the Jackson Personality Inventory.

In the Rorschach test, the subject is shown a series of 10 inkblots, and responses are categorized according to a number of formal characteristics. The original discovery of stable differences in response among groups of psychiatric patients was made accidentally, and Rorschach's tentative speculations about the reasons for these differences are still regarded by many clinicians as authoritative, despite much research evidence to the contrary. A global approach, in which the test is regarded as a standardized stimulus within the total context of a clinical interaction, might prove to be fruitful. The Holtzman Inkblot Technique (HIT) was designed to measure the basic variables assessed by the Rorschach, while avoiding a number of serious psychometric problems inherent in the Rorschach. Although the HIT does measure these variables satisfactorily, there is little evidence that it is useful in personality assessment.

Picture-story techniques, of which the Thematic Apperception Test (TAT) is the most popular, require the subject to make up stories about pictures depicting personality-relevant scenes. It is generally assumed that the behaviors and feelings of the main characters (heroes) of the stories reflect those of the subject. A number of standardized schemes exist for scoring the content and other aspects of the stories, but the clinical use of picture-story techniques is generally impressionistic. In picture-drawing methods, the subject is given blank paper on which to draw something, often a human figure. Apart from a gross relationship between the degree of realism of the drawing (if a human figure) and the subject's general level of adjustment, such drawings have as yet been demonstrated to have little value.

Perhaps the most theoretically oriented of the established assessment devices is the Blacky Pictures Test, based in the traditional psychoanalytic theory of psychosexual development. A standardized scoring system is available, and there is evidence to indicate that the system provides valid information for research purposes. The Bender Visual Motor Gestalt Test, designed within the theoretical framework of Gestalt psychology, assumes that all phases of human development, including personality, are reflected in perceptual functioning. It appears to yield a fairly satisfactory ''mental age'' score for children, but seems to have no demonstrated validity for assessing personality.

In general, how valid are assessment procedures which are based entirely on rational considerations? The assumptions which would need to be met in order for a rational basis to be *sufficient* for validity appear to have little support. However, there is evidence that a rational basis for stimulus materials is *necessary* if an assessment procedure is to have potential validity. There seem to be two main reasons for the lack of assessment instruments with a good theoretical base. (1) There is more interest in building ''microtheories'' to explain elemental aspects of personality than in developing the broader theoretical structures that would be needed as a basis for a general assessment device. (2) Test constructors have often tended to become absorbed in the technical refinements of their procedures at the expense of practical utility.

4 EMPIRICAL AND INTERNAL CONSISTENCY APPROACHES

In Chapter 3 we introduced three different strategies or approaches to the construction of formal assessment devices: (1) rational-theoretical, (2) empirical, and (3) internal consistency. We discussed in some detail the first of these approaches and the problems involved with it. We continue with a description of the remaining two strategies, together with some general comments about the issues involved in their use.

EMPIRICALLY BASED APPROACHES

In Chapter 2 we introduced the use of test responses for the *prediction* of behavior in real-life situations without the intervening step of involving any personality characteristics. In order to review this approach and to indicate that such a strategy is applicable to any kind of stimulus material, we draw some hypothetical examples involving the Rorschach inkblots. If, for example, every patient who gave responses of "decaying flesh" or "rotting flesh" on two or more cards of the Rorschach was later confirmed to be schizophrenic, the diagnosis of schizophrenia could be made directly from this sign without any intervening assessment of assumed personality characteristics.

Essentially the same approach can be used for the assessment of the underlying personality characteristics themselves. To illustrate again from the Rorschach, if all subjects who gave a response of "several people asleep" were later found to be unusually passive in their dealings with the environment, then we would have an *empirical predictor* for the personality characteristic of passivity.

In these examples from the Rorschach, it might be possible to infer a rational or even a theoretical connection between the individual's test response and the personality characteristic which was predicted. The recognition of such connections is irrelevant to empirical prediction. Although there will often be recognizable connections in addition to the empirical one, their nature is simply not of concern in purely empirical prediction. In a strictly empirical approach, the responses having predictive value would be determined by trial and error, and not by utilizing rational or theoretical hunches about possible relationships. However, such an approach is rarely followed, and most of the instruments discussed here include rational or theoretical considerations in their derivation, especially the former. For convenience, however, we refer to them as empirically based.

We now illustrate how the empirical approach can be used with paper-and-pencil questionnaires, using *dominance* as the personality characteristic to be predicted. The initial step is to identify a clear-cut and readily obtainable behavioral index of the attribute; that is, to formulate an *operational definition* of dominance. For our present purpose, we define dominance as "the characteristic involved in seeking elective public office." We then obtain a group of dominant persons (that is, people who sought or are seeking elective office) and a group of nondominant persons (those who have not sought office). It is assumed that both groups are equally willing to cooperate in our undertaking and that they are matched on relevant characteristics such as age, education, and socioeconomic status.

Both groups are asked to respond to a large number of questionnaire items, let us say 200. We could use items inquiring about subjects' likes and dislikes, their interpersonal relationships, their political orientation, or anything at all. In truly empirically based instruments, the items would be randomly selected from a universe of all such questionnaire items, if such a pool were available. In our hypothetical example, let us suppose that one of the items is "I like people with blue eyes," to be answered "true" or "false" insofar as the respondent is concerned.

Let us further suppose that we learn, by comparing the responses of our office-seeking, or dominant, or criterion group with those of the non-office-seeking, or nondominant, or control group, that 90 percent of the criterion group have responded "true" to this item, while only 15 percent of the control subjects have answered "true." We have discovered a diagnostic "sign" for identifying dominant people; and each of our 200 statements would be similarly examined, typically using rigorous statistical criteria, in order to determine whether or not it too is a sign of dominance. By identifying all the items that reliably differentiate our criterion and control groups, we would have constructed an empirical dominance scale, and a dominance score would be generated for each person by totaling the number of discriminating items which were answered in the criterion direction.

It should be obvious that, depending on the level of significance established for the selection of items, at least some proportion of the items would have been identified as valid on the basis of chance alone. For example, if a 5 percent probability level is used to identify discriminating items, then 5 percent of the items in the total item pool will be "selected" by chance alone. Inclusion of such chance items is what is typically referred to by statisticians as committing a Type One Error. In order to guard against errors of this nature, it is imperative that the items selected be *cross-validated*. That is to say, the item pool should be administered to further criterion groups which are demographically and otherwise rather similar to, but independent of, the original groups. In terms of this example, either the complete item pool, or a portion of it, should be administered to another group of persons identified as dominant and to another control group. Those items selected by chance alone would not be the same in both administrations (except for a negligibly small percentage), and therefore those which are selected in both procedures can be assumed to be "true" discriminating items. A less elegant, but more typical, procedure for cross-validation is simply to test on a new group the discriminating power of a scale which is composed of those items selected from the initial administration.

The method of empirical derivation, illustrated here with questionnaire items, can in principle be applied to any set of test responses, such as preference for geometric designs, responses to inkblots, or endorsement of self-descriptive adjectives. It is only necessary to establish that a reliable difference exists between the criterion and control groups in the proportions of responses to the stimuli.

There are certain disadvantages to assessment devices that are empirically derived. Although these instruments may be useful practically, they provide us with little basic or theoretical information about operation of personality variables in behavior. Further, there is no assurance that the procedure will yield *any* discriminating items, since the items in the initial pool may not be sensitive to whatever differences exist between the two groups. Last, it should be pointed out that extreme care is necessary in interpreting the personality attribute that an empirical scale is presumed to be measuring, since there may be other differences between the criterion and control groups which will distort the meaning of the scale. Thus, later research might demonstrate that our hypothetical dominance scale measures strength of political feelings rather than what is generally agreed to be meant by *dominance,* and it would therefore have little utility in identifying persons who are interpersonally dominant.

Duff (1965), Jackson (1971), and Norman (1963b), whose work was discussed in Chapter 3, took the position that it is most useful to have the content of the test stimuli related in some rational manner to the particular aspect of personality in which one is interested. However, Berg (1959) argued strongly that the rational content of the test stimuli is unimportant. He advocated the use of a greater variety of test stimuli, such as abstract geometric designs, requiring only that they should elicit enough variability of response to permit the discovery of empirical relationships. Berg's "Deviation Hypothesis" was tested by Goldberg and Slovic (1967), who investigated the relationship between content validity and empirical validity for a variety of kinds of possible personality inventory items, including nonverbal items. They found that "items of low face validity generally had low validity coefficients, while items of high face validity had validities that were distributed over the entire range of the distribution (e.g., some presumably relevant items actually were valid discriminators, while others were not)" (p. 467). These findings directly contradict Berg's point of view and give experimental support to the notion that content validity is a necessary but not sufficient basis for empirical validity. As indicated previously, most test constructors using empirical derivation techniques have tended to follow the method endorsed by Goldberg and Slovic—they employ rational considerations in selecting the original item pool and then focus on empirical comparisons of the responses of the criterion and control groups.

The general issue raised by Goldberg and Slovic seems to be a clear one. Their results raise a serious question about the usefulness of the Deviation Hypothesis as an explanatory concept in personality assessment. Although this hypothesis may be of limited use in explaining responses in procedures where the stimuli are highly ambiguous, it does not seem to apply in situations of low stimulus ambiguity; that is, it does not apply to most self-report questionnaires. The implications of this argument for the empirical approach to personality assessment also seem to be clear, and they are consistent with the conclusions reached in Chapter 3 that (1) the content of the items to be empirically evaluated is critical, and (2) test constructors need to spend considerable time and effort in selecting the items to be used. The Deviation Hypothesis is further analyzed in Chapter 7.

Minnesota Multiphasic Personality Inventory (MMPI)

The MMPI can be described as the most widely used personality or psychodiagnostic questionnaire and the most widely researched of all psychological tests. The *Eighth Mental Measurements Yearbook* (Buros, 1978) shows that the number of published references exceeds 5,000; of these references, 1,188 appeared in the approximate period 1972–1977, almost twice as many as for the next highest test, the 16 PF. Thus, it would seem that literature on the MMPI is continuing to appear at an accelerated rate.

Construction of the MMPI was begun in the late 1930s by Hathaway and McKinley (1940, 1951), who were motivated by their recognition of a need in both clinical psychiatric research and practice for an objective multidimensional instrument to assist in the identification of psychopathology. They were interested in developing an instrument that would provide for a comprehensive sampling of behavior of significance to psychiatrists, yet would involve a simple presentation so that it could be used with individuals of limited intelligence and education.

They compiled more than 1,000 items from psychiatric examination forms, psychiatry textbooks, previously published attitude and personality scales, and from the authors' own clinical experience, and prepared them in a self-report (true or false) format. The number of items was reduced to 550 through the course of revisions. The items are presented to the respondent either in a printed booklet or singly in a deck of small item cards. The test is scored for 10 or more basic psychiatric and personality scales, as well as three "validity" scales.

Generally speaking, each scale was empirically developed by contrasting the responses of nonpsychiatric control subjects with those of patients in a particular psychiatric diagnostic category, using the traditional system of diagnosis which stemmed from the work of Kraepelin in the late 19th century. More than 800 carefully studied psychiatric patients constituted the pool of clinical subjects, while approximately 1,500 control subjects were drawn from hospital visitors, normal clients at the University of Minnesota Tresting Bureau, local WPA workers, and general medical patients. The individual diagnostic criterion groups generally numbered 50 or fewer, although in some cases additional groups were utilized in efforts to improve the discriminating power of the scale. For example, more than a dozen scales were developed in an unsuccessful effort to obtain satisfactory discrimination among the subcategories of schizophrenia (Hathaway, 1956b, p. 108). The schizophrenia scale finally chosen for inclusion in the inventory was the fourth such scale attempted and proved to be the most satisfactory of previous and subsequent efforts.

The usual method of item selection was to consider a basic pool of those items which showed a statistically significant percentage frequency difference between the responses of the criterion group and the control subjects. Items were excluded if the frequency of response for both groups was very high or very low, if they failed to differentiate among additional relevant groups, or if the group difference appeared to have an irrelevant basis, such as marital status. Further items were often eliminated from a scale if they showed an overlap in validity with some other diagnostic category. No item, however, was ever eliminated from a scale because its manifest content appeared unrelated to the category in question. The articles documenting the original construction and validation of the MMPI have been reprinted by Welsh and Dahlstrom (1956).

In the construction of the basic MMPI scales, every effort was made to utilize responses only of psychiatric patients whose symptoms were clear-cut and who were relatively free from psychiatric signs other than those qualifying them for their particular diagnostic category. The categories and the resultant scales are as follows:

Scale 1. Hypochondriasis *(Hs)*.   These patients showed an exaggerated concern about their physical health, often with complaints about physical problems which in fact had a psychological basis.

Scale 2. Depression *(D)*.   Characterized by intense unhappiness, poor morale, and lack of hope about the future, these patients were relatively pure cases of depression.

Scale 3. Hysteria *(Hy)*.   These patients, who had been diagnosed "psychoneurosis-hysteria," had psychologically based physical symptoms coupled with *la belle indifference* or bland unconcern about their condition.

Scale 4. Psychopathic Deviate *(Pd)*.   All the criterion subjects used in developing this scale had shown notable difficulties in social adjustment, with histories of delinquency and other antisocial behavior.

Scale 5. Masculinity-Femininity *(Mf)*.   This scale was derived from the responses of a rather small group of homosexual males, all of whom were relatively free of other psychopathology.

Scale 6. Paranoia *(Pa)*.   Although rarely diagnosed as paranoia, these patients showed paranoid symptoms such as ideas of reference, suspiciousness, interpersonal sensitivity, feelings of persecution, and delusions of grandeur.

Scale 7. Psychasthenia *(Pt)*.   The subjects in this criterion group, mainly patients, showed unreasonable fears, high general anxiety, feelings of guilt, and excessive doubts.

Scale 8. Schizophrenia *(Sc)*.   These patients were all diagnosed as schizophrenic without regard to the various subtypes of the disorder.

Scale 9. Hypomania *(Ma)*.   These patients showed the milder degrees of manic excitement typically occurring in manic-depressive psychosis, characterized by excessive activity, easy distractibility, elevated mood, and a rapid but disjointed flow of speech.

One additional scale, social introversion-extroversion *(Si)*, was later added to the nine basic clinical scales.

The three validity scales developed in order to enhance the clinical usefulness of the MMPI were constructed as follows. (1) The *L*, or lie scale, designed to provide a basis for evaluating the subject's general frankness, contains 15 rationally selected items reflecting socially desirable but rather improbable behaviors. (2) The *F*, or infrequency scale, intended as an aid to recognizing random or other invalid respondents, contains items that are answered in the same direction by at least 90 percent of the normal subjects, and is thus a measure of how similar the subject's responses are to those of people in general. (3) The *K* or defensiveness scale was developed as a correction or "suppressor" scale to improve the discriminating power of several of the clinical scales by correcting for varying degrees of subtle test-taking defensiveness. It was constructed by comparing the responses of normals with those of patients whose clinical scale scores were in the normal range and who could thus be assumed to have responded to the items defensively.

It soon became apparent that the MMPI could not be used successfully in the manner originally intended, since high scorers on a scale often did not fit into that particular diagnostic category. Further, it was recognized that large numbers of apparently normal people achieved high scores on the clinical scales. However, it was found that useful clinical and personality discriminations could be made by examining combinations or *patterns* of scores, and it is in this manner that the MMPI is currently used. The large volume of research literature involving the MMPI has been summarized through 1975 by Dahlstrom, Welsh, and Dahlstrom (1972, 1975). A number of empirically based interpretation manuals are also available for adults (Drake and Oetting, 1959; Gilberstadt and Duker, 1965; Lanyon, 1968; Marks and Seeman, 1963) and adolescents (Marks, Seeman, and Haller, 1974). Other significant books on the MMPI have been published by Butcher (1969), Graham (1977), Lachar (1974), and Swenson, Pearson, and Osborne (1973). Lachar's book summarizes previous empirical and clinical literature on the MMPI and is set out in convenient form as an interpretive guide. The reader is reminded that a considerable amount of formal training and supervision with the test is needed in order to use these materials properly.

Although the MMPI has not been completely successful in its original purpose, the classification of psychiatric patients, there is much empirical support for its usefulness in identifying other aspects of personality functioning in the psychopathological domain. Empirical data bases, or "cookbooks," for interpreting the MMPI, as previously listed, became increasingly widely used in the 1970s, and these have substantially increased the validity of the MMPI's use. This topic is discussed in detail in Chapter 8. The development of computer interpretation services has had a further major impact on the use of this test. Automated interpretation is also discussed later in this text; for now, the reader should be aware that there are serious ethical and validity problems with most automated interpretation systems (Adair, 1978c; Butcher, 1978c).

The MMPI is open to a number of criticisms. Perhaps the most frequently voiced concern is that some of the scales are highly correlated, indicating a considerable degree of redundancy. Similarly, Block (1965) has shown that many of the "pathological" items are highly similar in nature, creating a redundancy in items as well as scales. Other common criticisms are that the test is too long, that it contains items about sex and religion which are offensive to many people, and, as previously noted, that many normal persons achieve high scores on the clinical scales. Finally, it should be clearly noted that the MMPI was not designed for the assessment of normal personality, so that neither the items nor the scales are optimal for this purpose.

Mindful of the fact that the MMPI is now about 40 years old, several experienced psychometricians have offered suggestions for improving or revising it. Meehl (1979) believes that the basic item pool, although redundant in many ways, has not been fully "milked," and that it should therefore be retained in new developments. He has suggested that attention be given specifically to developing improved criterion groups and to the use of technical improvements in item selection, somewhat like those employed by Jackson (1976). Norman (1972) has argued that in the redevelopment of basic scales, the criterion reference group should be a diverse pool of psychiatric patients rather than normals. He has also argued that predictions from profile configurations would be improved if each of the scales was homogeneous rather than heterogeneous in item content. Other points to be debated include the relative merits of different scale construction procedures, the proper use of factor analytic procedures, and a clearer understanding of whether the scales should be built to predict membership in a particular class of persons or one's place on a psychological dimension.

Ever since the publication of the MMPI, interested psychologists have heeded the suggestion of Hathaway and McKinley to develop further scales from the item pool, for particular purposes. Dahlstrom, Welsh, and Dahlstrom (1975) list a total of 455 scales, subscales, and indices which had been proposed up to that time. Unfortunately, most of this work beyond the original scales lacked the care that was put into the initial developments, so that the utility of much of the additional work is quite questionable. One project, however, merits special mention and can be seen as an attempt to improve upon the original scales by utilizing some of the suggestions already listed. We are referring to the development of the Wiggins Content Scales (Wiggins, 1966), a set of 13 scales which were developed to represent the "content" clusters in the MMPI item pool. These scales have high internal consistency, are moderately independent, and have some demonstrated validity for college undergraduates (Wiggins, Goldberg, and Appelbaum, 1971), for psychiatric inpatients (Jarnecke and Chambers, 1977), and for male clients at a military medical facility (Lachar and Alexander, 1978). Names of the scales are Social

Maladjustment, Depression, Feminine Interests, Poor Morale, Religious Fundamentalism, Authority Conflict, Psychoticism, Organic Symptoms, Family Problems, Manifest Hostility, Phobias, Hypomania, and Poor Health.

One of the major practical problems in using the MMPI has been the length of time required to complete it. Because there is considerable redundancy in the item pool, there have been a number of efforts to develop shorter forms of the instrument which would nevertheless retain the original meaning of the scales. In the first of these attempts, Kincannon (1968) selected a representative sample of 71 items, most of which appeared on more than one scale, and from these items he projected the full scores on each of the scales. Items on Kincannon's Mini-Mult were reworded for use in an interview situation. Other short forms include Dean's (1972) 86-item Midi-Mult, the MMPI-168 of Overall and Gomez-Mont (1974), Faschingbauer's (1974) abbreviated MMPI (the FAM), and others. Faschingbauer and Newmark (1978) have reviewed the development and validity evidence for the various short forms and have concluded that some of them, at least, are potentially useful. However, other authors have pointed to the relatively limited practical correspondence between the profiles based on the full MMPI and those derived from short forms (Hoffman and Butcher, 1975; Rand, 1979), and to weaknesses in the validity evidence (Butcher, Kendall, and Hoffman, 1980). The present authors believe that the short forms are best regarded as separate tests from the MMPI, and that their correlates need to be determined independently of the parent test (Lewis and Lanyon, 1979).

The contemporary clinical use of the MMPI is illustrated as follows. Figure 4-1 shows the MMPI profile of an adult male client seeking help in a community mental health center. The numbers on the sides of the chart represent a standard score system with a mean of 50 and standard deviation of 10. The *K*-correction (see text) has been added to the raw scores on the *Hs, Pd, Pt, Sc,* and *Ma* scales.

In order to give a satisfactory interpretation of these responses, we should have some idea of the *base rates,* or relative frequencies in the population of interest, of the various personal characteristics which are suggested by the test responses. This concept is discussed in detail in Chapters 6 and 8. The most noteworthy psychological features of persons giving MMPI profiles of the general pattern shown in Figure 4-1 are anxiety and depression; thus, in a community mental health center where the base rate of these characteristics is fairly high, we could suggest with considerable confidence that anxiety and depression are psychological problems of major concern to this client. If a psychiatric label is given, it would almost certainly involve some category of neurosis. Detailed information about such profiles, based upon both empirical and clinical findings, has been reported by Marks and Seeman (1963) and by Gilberstadt and Duker (1965). For example, according to the latter source, which is based upon the characteristics of male patients seen in the psychiatry service of a VA hospital, the most common (and discriminating) complaints of such clients include insomnia, obsessions, anxiety, depression, nervousness, tension, worry, tiredness, and gastrointestinal problems. Typically they have high standards of performance, are capable of developing good emotional ties, and tend to become overwhelmed and dependent under accumulated

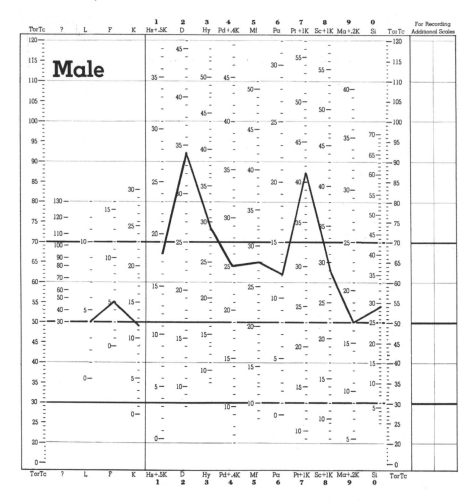

FIGURE 4-1. MMPI profile suggesting anxiety and depression. Reproduced by permission from the Minnesota Multiphasic Personality Inventory, Profile and Case Summary. Copyright 1948, renewed by The Psychological Corp., New York. All rights reserved.

stress. However, reality orientation remains good, and in a hospital setting, improvement is usually fairly rapid.

California Psychological Inventory (CPI)

The California Psychological Inventory, or CPI (Gough, 1957/1975), was specifically designed for the multidimensional or multiphasic description of normal personality—the task to which the MMPI had, less appropriately, been put. Gough, who had a strong interest in devising measures with broad psychological and sociological relevance, used the empirical approach with a variety of criterion groups. The CPI consists of 468 self-reference items, of which 200 appear in the MMPI, to be answered "true" or "false" in the same manner as the MMPI.

The CPI yields scores on 15 personality and three validity or response bias scales, most of which were constructed empirically. The empirical personality scales are: dominance, capacity for status, sociability, responsibility, socialization, tolerance, achievement via conformity, achievement via independence, intellectual efficiency, psychological mindedness, and femininity. For some of these scales, the criterion groups were identified by a directly obtainable behavioral index. Thus, the socialization scale was derived by comparing the responses of juvenile offenders and high school disciplinary cases with those of normal high school students (Gough and Peterson, 1952); and similarly, the achievement via independence scale employed criterion groups defined according to course grades (Gough, 1953). For other scales, where behaviorally based groups were more difficult to obtain, criterion groups were defined by judges' ratings. For example, the dominance scale was developed by asking fraternity and sorority members to nominate the five most dominant and five least dominant members of their group (Gough, McClosky, and Meehl, 1951).

Four additional scales were constructed through internal consistency analyses, utilizing a combination of the rational selection of items and statistical refinement of the initial item pool. These four scales are social presence, self-acceptence, self-control, and flexibility. The usefulness of all 15 scales was further demonstrated by comparing the scores of a number of additional behavioral and personality groups.

The three validity scales are similar in nature to the validity scales of the MMPI. The well-being scale, designed to identify persons who exaggerate their misfortunes, was empirically constructed by comparing the responses of normal subjects who simulated severe conflict with those of actual psychiatric patients. The good impression scale, also empirically developed, was designed to identify exaggeration of one's personality characteristics in the positive direction. The communality scale, similar to the MMPI F scale, indicates the degree to which one's responses are like those of most normal subjects.

To facilitate the clinical interpretation of individual CPI profiles, the 18 scales are organized into four groups or clusters: (1) measures of poise, ascendency, and self-assurance; (2) measures of socialization, maturity, and responsibility; (3) measures of achievement potential and intellectual efficiency; and (4) measures of intellectual and interest modes. This grouping of scales generally has been supported by independent factor analytic studies of the CPI (Crites, Bechtoldt, Goodstein, and Heilbrun, 1961; Mitchell and Pierce-Jones, 1960). In interpreting a test profile, the test manual suggests initially observing the overall elevation of the profile as an index of the respondent's social and intellectual functioning, and then comparing the relative levels of the four scale clusters. Further information is gained by observing the highest and lowest scale scores, and by studying combinations of scales. The manual also provides lists of adjectives that were chosen by judges in an assessment program as descriptive of high and low scorers on each scale. This list contains some awkward contradictions, which might be a function of the scales, the rating procedure, or some other inconsistency. The manual gives a considerable amount of normative and correlational information about the scales, as a basis for further interpretative hypotheses and research.

Although the redundancy of the scales makes for some problems in interpretation, the evidence presented in the manual demonstrates some validity for each of the scales when judged against behavioral criteria. An example of this type of validity evidence is seen in a study by Goodstein, Crites, Heilbrun, and Rempel (1961), who compared the mean CPI profiles of college undergraduates seeking counseling for personal adjustment problems with a comparable group reporting vocational-educational problems and a control group who had not sought counseling. The three groups differed in the anticipated manner on overall elevation of their CPI profiles and also showed psychologically meaningful differences in profile patterns.

Reviews of the CPI have in general been positive. A wealth of information about the development and validity of the CPI is provided in Megargee's (1972) handbook on the test. In a more recent and critical review, Gynther (1978) has indicated that the major research effort with the CPI has been in forecasting performance criteria, such as success in dentistry, computer programming, and nursing. Other research reported the mean personality profiles of a variety of groups, such as young adolescents and alcoholics. What is needed, both for the CPI and comparable tests, is research to identify useful correlates of different profile types, and also studies comparing the predictive validities of the various tests in the normal personality range, for different types of predictions.

The contemporary clinical use of the CPI is illustrated by Figure 4-2, which presents the CPI profile of a 41-year-old male research scientist who was tested as part of an industrial management development program. As was the case with the MMPI, the numbers on the sides of the chart represent a standard score system with a mean of 50 and a standard deviation of 10. The 18 CPI scales are presented along the horizontal axis in the same order in which they were described in the text.

Applying the interpretative rules suggested earlier would lead us to view this man as a self-assured, poised, rather forceful person with little self-doubt or uncertainty about himself. At the same time his sense of responsibility, his willingness to accept rules and proper authority, and his self-control seem less well developed; and his achievements, both those gained through conformance and those gained through independence, are probably modest. Quite aware of and sensitive to others, he is quite open to change and may even be impulsive at times. However, he appears rather satisfied with himself and can be rather closed-minded and intolerant of of others, especially when he feels that his principles are being violated. One might conclude that this man is an ambitious and socially skillful individual who lacks the impulse control and conscientiousness necessary to realize his ambition. His sensitivity to others coupled with his unwillingness or inability to respond completely to this awareness might lead others to view him as manipulative and controlling.

This characterization was very much in keeping with the man's supervisory evaluations, which noted that he "has never realized his potential as a scientist." These evaluations further noted his very high needs for autonomy, making it very difficult for him to hear or accept supervisory feedback. His impulsiveness and his impaired interpersonal relationships led to a variety of morale problems in his

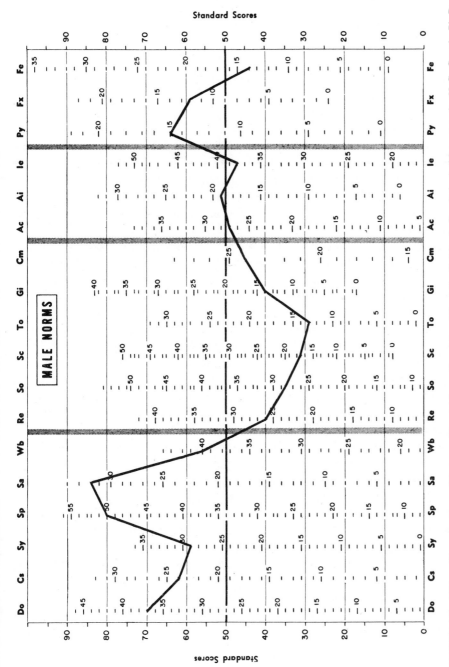

FIGURE 4-2. CPI profile suggesting mild personality problems. Reproduced from the California Psychological Inventory by H.G. Gough, Ph.D. Copyright 1957. Published by Consulting Psychologists Press, Inc.

87

laboratory, and he was generally regarded as having limited potential for higher managerial positions or promotions.

Empirical Personality Assessment Devices: Some Comments

Although the empirical development of the tests discussed in the preceding sections and others of this type offer built-in evidence of their ability to discriminate between groups, they can often be criticized on the grounds that the test authors have failed to cross-validate the scales on independent samples of the criterion and normal groups. The absolute necessity for cross-validation has already been strongly emphasized; as a concrete example, let us imagine a pool of 1,000 self-reference questionnaire items which can be answered positively or negatively. If we take two arbitrary groups—for example, people with blue eyes and people with brown eyes—the two groups will differ in their responses to some of the items by sheer chance. Specifically, if we noted the differences that would be expected to occur by chance less often than 5 percent of the time, we would identify about 5 percent, or 50 or the 1,000 items, that could be advanced as an empirically derived test for eye color differentiation. Yet these items would have been selected on the basis of a statistical artifact and would probably have no stable relationship to eye color. Thus, if we repeated the item analysis on two different groups of blue- and brown-eyed subjects, the second resultant scale would contain 50 *different* items— another chance selection from the 1,000 items. Needless to say, these two scales would be of no value in discriminating between further criterion groups. Since the extent to which empirically derived scales capitalize on chance variability is not always clear, independent demonstration of their discriminative ability is essential.

Other problems are raised by the use of the empirical method. The criterion groups are ordinarily selected to be pure and often extreme instances of the behavior domain to be tapped. Thus we would use rather "obvious" schizophrenics in developing a schizophrenia scale, and highly dominant versus perhaps passive individuals in developing a dominance scale, although we are typically interested in employing the scales to identify, not extreme individuals, but persons more in the middle of the continuum. It is frequently a moot point as to whether the items are either logically or empirically relevant for identifying less extreme instances of the phenomena.

We have already noted that empirically derived tests add little to our theoretical understanding of the characteristic under study, and that in practice it would seem best to combine the empirical approach to test construction with rational consid- erations, especially in the initial choice of the item pool. It is believed by many (particularly among psychometricians) that empirically based personality tests, because of their built-in evidence of practical usefulness, are the most promising instruments available at the present time.

INTERNAL CONSISTENCY APPROACH

The third approach to the construction of personality tests is the one based upon the internal consistency of clusters of test items. It can perhaps best be described by way of example. Suppose we have collected the responses of a large number of subjects to a number of test stimuli. The nature of the test stimuli is not important for the moment, except that they are usually selected to provide a balanced coverage of the particular behavior domain in which the test constructor is interested. Thus, most of the tests which have been developed on the basis of this strategy involve self-reference questionnaire items, though in principle they could equally well involve inkblots or geometrical forms. Let us further suppose that we have as stimuli 50 self-reference questionnaire items, all of which can be answered "true" or "false."

Since we are unsure, at this stage of our test development, about what characteristics our items are tapping, we might be seen as having responses to 50 different "scales," each of which had a possible "score" of 0 or 1. It would obviously be desirable to have a method for examining such a large mass of responses on other than an individual basis. We note that the responses to some items tend to be correlated, so that persons who answer "true" to item 13 may also be very likely to answer "true" to items 15, 25, and 36, and "false" to items 8 and 39. We would also expect other item clusters to exist. In other words, a subject's "score" on any item can to some extent be predicted by the "score" on other items; the items in each cluster are intercorrelated because they have a common basis for variability. The statistical procedure for identifying such clusters of items, or *factors,* is known as factor analysis. As might be expected, the first step in a factor analysis is to correlate every item with every other item. The resulting matrix of intercorrelations is then treated by a series of complex statistical procedures in order to identify the factors, or grouping of items. Incidentally, the same steps could be followed using scales rather than items in order to determine the factorial structure of a multiphasic instrument such as the MMPI or CPI.

When a factor, or cluster of items, is identified in this manner, it is assumed generally that these items are tapping the same psychological variable, because they tend to elicit consistent responses. In our example involving 50 items, let us suppose that we have been able to identify four clusters each involving 10 items, and that the remaining 10 items did not correlate significantly with each other nor with any of the four identifiable clusters. Factor analysis has reduced our original 50 variables to four, and we can describe individuals as they represent themselves by scores on four scales derived to represent these factorial variables. If these four factors are reproducible by the same steps in other, similar groups of normal persons, then we might assume that we have isolated four central traits of normal personality structure.

What do factor analytically derived scales really measure, and how do we know what these factors mean? Certainly they have a specific statistical meaning, since they are defined in part by statistical procedures. We can also look for rational meaning, both in the original selection of the items and in what items contribute to the particular factor. For example, the composition of Welsh's MMPI factor *A* (Welsh and Dahlstrom, 1956) was such that he described it as a measure of anxiety or emotional upset. The procedure for naming factors is always rational or clinical, and empirical validity evidence must be accumulated before it can be concluded that the behavior domain involved in the factor is the same as that typically described by that name. Thus, the decision about the usefulness of terming Welsh's MMPI factor

A an "anxiety factor" must depend partly upon whether persons with high scores on that scale are judged to be clinically anxious. Although the meaning of a factor is built into it in a statistical sense, the full nature of its meaning is not made clear by the statistical procedures.

An additional question is whether or not factors are *real* traits, the psychological essence of personality. This question is a highly complex one and has given rise to a variety of views among researchers in this area. On the one hand, Cattell (1965) views the particular factors that he has proposed as natural unitary structures in the domain of normal personality, natural elements that are logically equivalent to the atomic elements in the physical world. Eysenck (1953) has taken a similar, although less extreme view. On the other hand, Jackson and Messick (1958) have suggested that the major factors that are identified through the factor analysis of self-report inventories are mainly "response distortions" which should be regarded as distinct from the content of the scales. At the very least, however, it can be said that factor analysis is a useful technique for studying the internal composition both of individual scales and of the several scales in a battery or in a multiphasic instrument.

Guilford Tests

Guilford (1959), who favors a trait approach to personality description, has employed factor analysis to arrive at the most parsimonious set of traits for describing normal personality functioning. After several factor analyses of many sets of self-report questionnaire items, he developed three separate inventories: Inventory of Factors STDGR (Guilford, 1940), Inventory of Factors GAMIN (Guilford and Martin, 1943b), and the Personnel Inventory (Guilford and Martin, 1943a). The Guilford-Zimmerman Temperament Survey (Guilford and Zimmerman, 1949) was developed later to cover, in a single inventory, 10 of the 13 traits of the original three inventories. These were: general activity, restraint versus rhathmia, ascendance, sociability, emotional stability, objectivity, friendliness, thoughtfulness, personal relations, and masculinity. Two empirically derived falsification scales, similar to the validity scales of the MMPI and CPI, were added later, together with a "carelessness-deviancy" scale, similar to the MMPI *F* scale (Jacobs and Schlaff, 1955). Although there is some evidence that some of these factorially derived scales do measure the traits for which they were named (Guilford, 1959, pp. 185–187), their relationships to other indices of the same traits have generally been shown to be fairly minimal.

Thurstone Temperament Schedule

Thurstone (1949, 1951) performed his own factor analysis on Guilford's original data and concluded that seven rather than 13 factors were sufficient to describe the main dimensions of personality. He developed the Thurstone Temperament Schedule to measure these factors, which he named active, vigorous, impulsive, dominant, stable, sociable, and reflective. As might be assumed, the same evaluative comments directed toward the Guilford instruments can be applied to Thurstone's test.

Sixteen Personality Factor Questionnaire (16 PF)

Based upon extensive factor analyses of self-report inventories, biographical data, and behavior observation, Cattell (1965) has defined 16 factors which he regards as the "source traits" of normal personality structure, suitable for measurement on an inventory. Since some of Cattell's factors do not readily correspond to any readily named personality trait, he has developed his own nomenclature, such as *parmia* (implying parasympathetic nervous system domination) versus *threctia* (implying susceptibility to threat) (Cattell, 1965, p. 95).

The 16 PF questionnaire was developed to assess these factors. There are two sets of parallel forms (A and B, with 187 items each; and shorter forms, C and D), plus Form E for persons with low reading skills. To ensure adequate reliability, it is recommended that more than one form be used. Cattell, Eber, and Tatsuoka (1970) and Karson and O'Dell (1976) have published major reference works on the 16 PF, and the popularity of the instrument is shown by the fact that the volume of literature published in the period 1972–1978 was second only to the MMPI (Buros, 1978).

Despite the massive amount of psychometric effort that was devoted to the development of the 16 PF, the test has a number of serious deficiencies (Bloxom, 1978; Walsh, 1978). The writings on the construction of the test tend to be confusing and sometimes contradictory. While the handbook (Cattell, Eber, and Tatsuoka, 1970) contains an enormous amount of validity data, much of it is presented in a form that is very difficult to evaluate. Further, some of the claims about the uses of the test are simply not supported by the validity data (J.A. Walsh, 1978). Thus, the 16 PF should be used at the present time only with considerable caution or not at all.

Factor Analytic Personality Assessment Devices: Some Comments

The more one studies the literature on factor analytic approaches to personality measurement, the more bewildering becomes the array of factors that must be comprehended. The sheer number of different factors, coupled with the inability of factor analysts to agree about the factorial composition of the same set of data, would seem to render untenable Cattell's belief that there is anything "real" about factors. Fortunately, however, such a belief is not a necessary prerequisite for the use of the factor analytic approach.

The typical factor analysis does not involve a completely predetermined procedure; rather, certain decisions are based upon the "clinical" judgment of the factor analyst, which in turn partly determines the resultant factorial structure. This reliance upon judgment may help clarify why the factorial structure of a set of data suggested by one analyst does not resemble that proposed by another. Further, the degree of similarity between two different factor analyses is difficult to determine without a careful study of the statistical aspects of the data. For example, without such a careful study it would be impossible to determine that Norman's (1963c) emotional stability factor is not the same as the emotional stability factor described by Gordon (1963), but seems to be a combination of this and the ascendancy factor.

In recent years, one important area of agreement has emerged among factor analyses, at least the ones involving self-report inventories. There has been a fair degree of consistency in reporting the existence of two major independent or orthogonal factors (e.g., Block, 1965; Jackson and Messick, 1958; Welsh and Dahlstrom, 1956; Wiggins, 1968), and there has also been broad agreement on how these two factors should be named. They are appropriately described by the labels *extroversion* and *neuroticism,* which are the names chosen by Eysenck (1960) for the two factors which he articulated and described as centrally important to the theoretical understanding of personality.

An alternative to a two-factor theory of personality was demonstrated by Tupes and Christal (1961) and by Norman (1963c), who proposed a system of five relatively orthogonal (independent) and easily interpreted personality factors. The factor names and the polar anchoring adjectives for each of these scales are presented in Figure 4-3. The work leading to the delineation of these particular factors began with the identification by Allport and Odbert (1936) of 18,000 trait names. This list was reduced by Allport (1937), using personal judgment, to the 4,504 clearest and most stable traits, then to 171 by Cattell (1957), using empirical judgments of semantic meaning. Rating scales developed from further refinements of the list formed the basis for comparing a number of diverse subject groups by means of peer rating procedures (see Chapter 5), and the resulting personality factor

		Abbreviated Scale Labels	
Factor Name	Num-ber	Pole A	Pole B
I. Extroversion or Surgency	1	Talkative-Silent	
	2	Frank, Open-Secretive	
	3	Adventurous-Cautious	
	4	Sociable-Reclusive	
II. Agreeableness	5	Goodnatured-Irritable	
	6	Not Jealous-Jealous	
	7	Mild, Gentle-Headstrong	
	8	Cooperative-Negativistic	
III. Conscientiousness	9	Fussy, Tidy-Careless	
	10	Responsible-Undependable	
	11	Scrupulous-Unscrupulous	
	12	Persevering-Quitting, Fickle	
IV. Emotional Stability	13	Poised-Nervous, Tense	
	14	Calm-Anxious	
	15	Composed-Excitable	
	16	Not Hypochondriacal-Hypochondriacal	
V. Culture	17	Artistically Sensitive-Artistically Insensitive	
	18	Intellectual-Unreflective, Narrow	
	19	Polished, Refined-Crude, Boorish	
	20	Imaginative-Simple, Direct	

FIGURE 4-3. Personality factor structure suggested by Norman (1963c). Copyright 1963 by the American Psychological Association. Reprinted by permission of the publisher and author.

structure appeared to be highly consistent across the different groups. The data were collected by having each person in a rating group nominate one-third of the other members in the group for Pole A of each rating scale, and one-third for Pole B. Each member's score on a scale was then determined by averaging the ratings received.

Whether these five factors "truly" represent personality structure must be considered in light of the two positions on the structure of personality which were discussed in Chapter 2; namely, the viewpoint that there is a single "real" structure versus the view that any structure is necessarily man-made. Mischel (1968), arguing for a variant of the second position, had held that Norman's five factors reflect in part "behavioral consistencies that are *constructed* by observers rather than actual consistency in the subject's behavior" (p. 43). However, Norman and Goldberg (1966) were able to demonstrate that the factors are based on more than just semantic consistency, and at least in part reflect the nature of personality structure among the subjects. In a recent review of literature on the structure of major characteristics of personality, Goldberg (1980) reaffirmed that the five-factor structure is the most compelling one to date, and that it can be shown to subsume both the two-factor structure previously described and Cattell's 16-factor structure. Goldberg has also pointed out that descriptive adjectives differ in degree of abstractness versus specificity and has suggested that this dimension should also be represented in any comprehensive attempt to map the structure of personality.

To summarize, the major contribution of factor analysis is in understanding the relationships among items and scales of personality tests. Usefulness, in any predictive sense, is not an intrinsic property of factorially derived scales (unless, like Cattell, we consider them to be assessing some "real" properties of the organism), but must be demonstrated empirically. The reported empirical validities of factor scales have in general tended to be rather low, the major exceptions being the two-factor structure, which has been consistently replicated, and the five-factor structure, for which there is now increasing evidence.

OVERVIEW OF THE THREE STRATEGIES IN PERSONALITY TEST DEVELOPMENT

We have discussed three ways in which assessment procedures can be developed in order to obtain responses from an individual that will be meaningful in understanding behavior in the personality domain. The three procedures were carefully delineated and were presented separately for reasons of clarity, although this is not meant to suggest that combinations of methods cannot and have not been employed. Thus, a balanced and sophisticated method might involve the initial selection of test stimuli based upon theoretical or rational considerations, with factor analysis for the attainment of internal consistency and final refinement based upon clear-cut empirical findings. Although this type of test derivation is both time consuming and costly, it is generally becoming more widely used and should be regarded as a model for future efforts in test construction.

One question that can be raised is whether or not there is any clear superiority of one of these three strategies over the others. An empirical answer to this question is provided by the recent study of Hase and Goldberg (1967). These authors took the CPI items and constructed four sets of 11 scales each, developing each set by one of the major strategies of test construction, regarding the rational and theoretical methods as separate approaches. The 11 rational scales were the four rationally derived CPI scales plus seven other developed in the same fashion. The 11 theoretical scales were specifically developed for the purposes of this study using the Murray (1938) need system. The empirically derived scales were the 11 original CPI scales which had been developed empirically. The 11 factor scales were developed on the basis of a special factor analysis of the items done by the authors for this purpose. The predictive validities of these four sets of scales were then compared against 13 criterion measures obtained from 200 college women, such as college achievement relative to ability, an experimental test of conformity, sorority membership, dating behavior, and peer ratings on a variety of personality traits, such as dominance, sociability, and responsibility.

The main finding of this study was that the four sets of scales were equivalent in validity when measured against the 13 diverse criteria. Obtained validity correlations averaged over the criteria were: rational = .27; theoretical = .26; empirical = .26; and factor analysis = .26. These four mean correlations were all significantly higher than those obtained from two additional sets of scales which had been devised for control purposes. In a more detailed analysis of these data, Goldberg (1972b) was able to demonstrate some differential results. For example, the empirically derived scales predicted more of the criteria than the other two sets of scales, but their highest validity correlations were lower than those for the other two sets of scales. Stated another way, the empirical inventory had broader bandwidth but lower fidelity than the rational or theoretical inventories. The data also suggested a slight overall superiority for the "best" of the rational scales.

Ashton and Goldberg (1973) pursued this question further by testing Jackson's (1971) assertion that the validity of the typical empirically developed scales could be surpassed by rational scales composed of items developed intuitively by trained item writers, and even by inexperienced item writers. In a complex and extensive study, existing CPI and PRF scales were compared with scales intuitively developed by graduate students in psychology and by individuals with no formal psychology training. All scales were administered to 169 college females, and validity criteria consisted of the average rankings on the different dimensions by groups of peers. The most reliable of the intuitive scales constructed by untrained persons were essentially as valid as the empirical scales on the CPI, while "the most reliable scales constructed by psychology students and the PRF scales were of approximately equal validity, considerably higher than that of any of the CPI scales" (Ashton and Goldberg, 1973, p. 1).

While the highest average validity correlations in the Ashton and Goldberg study were only around .35, the study clearly demonstrated the advantages of the rational or intuitive approach to item development. The reader is again reminded that the most appropriate procedure for scale construction involves a combination of all three strategies—rational-theoretical, empirical, and internal consistency. Future research should now begin to address the question of how to best integrate the three approaches, bearing in mind that optimal strategies will presumably differ according to the characteristics to be assessed and, possibly, the different types of subjects involved.

Summary

In a purely *empirical* approach to test development, the recognition of rational or theoretical connections would be irrelevant, since the stimuli would be selected solely on the basis of their ability to lead to the desired description or prediction. The empirical approach is not often used alone but usually in combination with other methods. The Minnesota Multiphasic Personality Inventory (MMPI), perhaps the best known of all personality inventories, was originally developed as an aid in classifying psychiatric patients into diagnostic groups. The MMPI is currently scored on 13 scales, most of which represent psychiatric categories. It was derived from an original item pool of more than 1,000 rationally selected statements by contrasting the responses of patients in each category with those of normal subjects. Although the MMPI has a number of disadvantages, including item redundancy and the fact that many normals get high scores on the psychiatric scales, there is a large amount of evidence for its research and clinical usefulness. Since clinical interpretation involves *patterns* of scores rather than individual scales, a degree of skill is necessary in its use. The availability of empirical data bases, or "cookbooks," has substantially increased the validity of MMPI interpretation.

The California Psychological Inventory (CPI) is somewhat similar to the MMPI but was designed to assess significant aspects of normal personality functioning. Its 18 scales, most of which were derived empirically, are grouped into four clusters: poise, ascendancy, and self-assurance; socialization, maturity, and responsibility; achievement potential and intellectual efficiency; and intellectual and interest modes. A considerable amount of normative information is available for the CPI, and in spite of some redundancy among the scales, it appears to be a fairly useful device.

General problems with the empirical approach include its lack of contribution to theoretical understanding and a frequent lack of cross-validation information. Nevertheless, the empirical approach in combination with rational or theoretical considerations for the initial selection of the item pool is usually considered to be the most promising today.

In the *internal consistency* approach, complex statistical procedures are used to group items whose responses tend to be related to each other. The personality meaning of these item clusters, or factors, must be determined by other means. Guilford's several factor-analytically derived inventories, of which the *Guilford-Zimmerman Tempermanent Survey* is most representative, assesses 10 such variables. In the *Thurstone Temperament Schedule,* developed from similar data, seven factors are thought sufficient to cover the range of normal personality functioning. Cattell's *Sixteen Personality Factor Questionnaire* assesses 16 such factors, or "source traits," which Cattell considered to be natural unitary structures, logically equivalent to atomic elements in the physical world. In general, there has been considerable lack of agreement over the number and names of the necessary and sufficient factor traits for describing personality, which is not surprising since the definition of factors is partly arbitrary. However, there does seem to be good agreement that two factors, which Eysenck has named "extroversion" and "neuroticism," are clearly represented in self-report inventories. Recent work suggests that a five-factor structure may also be promising.

Our division of assessment development procedures into three categories has been for convenience of presentation, and any sophisticated device would certainly involve more than one of them in its development. Research has suggested that when considered alone, each approach is about as valid as the next, although different approaches show advantages for particular uses.

5   BEHAVIORAL ASSESSMENT

In Chapter 1 we discussed the influence of modern behaviorism on personality assessment. We saw that this influence has given rise to the development of an approach to assessment which differs considerably from the more traditional approaches which we have thus far considered. This behavioral approach to assessment is the subject matter of the present chapter.

Let us restate and clarify a possible source of confusion which we have touched on several times previously. If the topic of this book is *personality* assessment, what is the relevance of the direct assessment of *behavior?* The answer is that, as stated in Chapter 1, the purpose of the book is broadly conceived as the understanding and prediction of the behavior of individuals. It was once believed that such understanding could only come from the thorough study of "inner predispositions," or what people *are,* or what they *have;* in other words, their dynamics, needs, expectations, and underlying motivational forces. This view has been termed the "centralist" orientation to the study of humans (Murray, 1938), and we have also referred to it in Chapter 2 as the *dispositional* view of the determinants of behavior. In the more recent, behavioral view, however, it is believed that the best understanding comes from a greater emphasis on studying the behavior itself and the context in which it occurs. In particular, the behavioral assessor tries to identify the *controlling variables* for the specified behavior. Some of these variables may be external to the person and some internal. It is assessment of the external factors that has been the major contribution of the behavioral assessment movement; however, new and different ways of assessing the relevant internal variables are also now included in this framework. Some of the early and more radical behavioral psychologists believed that the assessment process could do without information about internal, or organismic, variables altogether. As we have previously discussed in Chapter 2, this situational view of the determinants of behavior has now given way to the interactionist view, which takes the position that the causes of behavior lie in the interaction between person and environment.

Development of Behavioral Assessment

Behavioral assessment procedures have been widely used for many years in industrial and organizational psychology, and in a variety of research applications (e.g., Hartshorne and May, 1928; OSS Assessment Staff, 1948). However, they did not become popular in clinically oriented applications until the late 1960s and early 1970s. There are a number of possible reasons for this lag, but the most obvious is that the overwhelming influence of the psychodynamic orientation, with its centralist philosophy, was not diminished until the rise of behavior therapy in the decade of the 1960s. Thus, many of the issues involved in the systematic observation of behavior were understood and documented well before the clinical use of behavioral assessment. What was introduced in the clinical context was the addition of behavioral learning theory with its premise that behavior is *controlled,* and that these controlling variables—antecedents (cues or stimuli) and consequences (reinforcers and punishers)—can be identified through systematic observation and then altered to result in more adaptive behaviors. Thus, the scope of behavioral assessment was significantly broadened by its acceptance into the realm of human adjustment problems.

There were other reasons why behavioral assessment procedures were slow to become a part of the clinical enterprise. For one thing, several generations of clinical psychologists had been taught to believe that the information that was critical to an in-depth understanding was "beneath the surface"; that is, neither accessible to consciousness nor displayed directly in overt behavior. A simple description of overt behavior might, in this view, be quite misleading in any attempt to understand what the individual was really like. Another reason was that direct observation is much more difficult to carry out successfully than is initially apparent. Much of the present chapter is devoted to an analysis of these problems.

Clinical Behavioral Assessment.   The clinical use of behavioral assessment made its formal appearance in the late 1960s, and a number of definitions and descriptions were offered (Kanfer and Phillips, 1970; Kanfer and Saslow, 1965; Mischel, 1968; Peterson, 1968). Peterson's description is worth repeating.

> What, in specific detail, is the nature of the problem behavior? What is the person doing, overtly or covertly, which he or someone else defined as problematic and hence changeworthy behavior? What are the antecedents, both internal and external, of the problem behavior and what conditions are in effect at the time the behavior occurs? What are the consequences of the problem behavior? In particular, what reinforcing events, immediate as well as distant, appear to perpetuate the behavior under study? What changes might be made in the antecedents, concomitants, or consequences of behavior to effect behavior change? (Donald R. Peterson, *The Clinical Study of Social Behavior,* © 1968. Reprinted by permission of Prentice-Hall, Inc., Englewood Cliffs, N.J.).

There are several further issues that relate specifically to the clinical use of behavioral assessment. The first and perhaps most important is one which we have already identified: Clinical behavioral assessment implies an interactionist view of the causes of behavior—a product of both organismic variables (such as current physiological state and past learning history) and current environmental variables (Nelson and Hayes, 1979). Thus, both kinds of variables need to be assessed, and their relationship to the problem behavior of interest must then be determined.

A second point involves the broadened definition of "behavior" which has accompanied the development of behavior therapy as a practical enterprise. Whereas mainstream behavioral psychologists once confined the term to *overt motor* events which can be publicly perceived and recorded, it is nowadays common for any type of activity to be called "behavior." Specifically, two other classes involving *covert* behavior: *thoughts,* or cognitive behavior, and *feelings,* related to emotional-psychological behavior, are now included within the realm of behavior that is amenable to assessment and scientific study. Some human problems involve more than one of these response systems. For example, anxiety involves all three, in varying degrees for various people, and there tends to be only a low or moderate degree of relationship among the three response systems (Lang, 1968). Thus, to talk about the behavioral assessment of anxiety is ambiguous; rather, one must talk about the assessment of a particular response system, or better, all three response systems. As we will see in Chapter 8, the use of multimethod assessment procedures, or multiple data sources in the assessment of a particular construct, results in a higher degree of overall validity.

A third topic of note in the clinical use of behavioral assessment is an extension of the expanded definition of behavior given previously. In clinical applications, not only is the behavior of interest observed but so are antecedents and consequences— the variables thought to be controlling the behavior of interest. These controlling variables can also be covert; that is to say, thoughts or feelings. For example, a feeling (such as anger) can trigger an overt motor behavior (such as a physical assault), which can be followed by a punishing thought ("That was bad; I shouldn't have done it"). It is tempting to take the simple view that exactly the same principles of learning theory that apply to overt behaviors also apply to covert behaviors, a hypothesis termed the "continuity assumption" (Thoreson and Mahoney, 1974). Bandura (1969) has extensively documented ways in which covert events, particularly thoughts, can function to control overt behavior. Whether this will prove to be a useful assumption for purposes of behavioral assessment is a question for the future.

A fourth topic has to do with the scope of the practical observations that are needed in a behavioral assessment for clinical purposes. The patient usually does not know what environmental events are controlling (triggering and/or reinforcing) the problem behavior. What, then, should be observed beside the problem behavior itself? It is here that a considerable amount of trial and error is usually involved. One common procedure is to have the client keep structured notes as to *when* each instance of the problem behavior occurs, *where* it occurs, and *what else* is happening at the time. Several sets of observations are usually needed, with feedback, in order for the client to become proficient at the kind of behavioral detective work that needs to be done. Because of the complexity of most clinical problems, we present here a somewhat oversimplified version of behavioral assessment as it applies to clinical practice, and we note that the development of practical skills in this area requires a considerable amount of experience and supervision.

Framework for Behavioral Assessment. The various definitions of behavioral assessment, both clinical and nonclinical, are in agreement on the two basic steps of the process: (1) selecting and defining the behavior of interest in concrete, observable terms; and (2) the use of standardized or systematic procedures for observing the behaviors and recording the observations in an appropriate manner. These two basic steps are reviewed here. In the case of assessment for planning clinical behavior change, three further steps are involved: (3) observation of the events that are controlling the behavior of interest, as already described; (4) behavioral formulation, in which an attempt is made to formulate in social learning theory terms exactly how this control is being maintained; and (5) survey of the available resources for behavior change and the selection or design of an optimal treatment strategy. The reader is referred to the work of Lanyon and Lanyon (1976, 1978) for a discussion of these three further steps.

SELECTING AND DEFINING THE BEHAVIOR

Behavioral Assessment

Definition is closely associated with observation. In the modified logical positivist philosophy that underlies modern behavioral psychology, *definition* is itself operationally defined as public and reliable observation. Even though the definition of a behavior of interest would seem to be obvious, numerous writers have stressed the need for care and precision in this regard. For example, consider a behavior as simple as fingernail biting. A young adult female client requesting treatment for this problem was given a simple event counter and asked to record every instance of fingernail biting each day for one week. On the next visit she reported that she had had difficulty in deciding exactly what should qualify as biting. Sometimes she would inspect a finger, wondering whether or not to bite. Sometimes she would put a finger to her mouth but not to her teeth. Sometimes she would close her teeth over a nail but not bite off any nail. After discussion, it was decided that fingernail biting should be defined to include all times when a finger touched the mouth, for any reason whatever except while eating or washing.

In addition to its use with concrete or easily observable events such as fingernail biting, behavioral assessment can also be employed with behaviors that are abstract or vague. For example, as part of a project to improve the quality of care in a hospital emergency room, Komaki, Collins, and Thoene (1980) reported the use of an instrument designed to define and measure "tender loving care." This instrument, shown in Figure 5-1, was utilized by personnel who were not directly involved in the provision of service, to record a sample of patient-staff interactions. It should be clear from this example how the *definition* of the variable of interest is essentially the same as the procedure for its *observation*.

In contrast to nailbiting, which was defined by specifying a simple physical position; and tender loving care, defined as the sum of a number of elements, some complex situations require a more complex approach. In their work with aggressive

Check the appropriate boxes for each patient-staff interaction:	Yes	No	N/A or N/O
1. Within 15-seconds	☐	☐	☐
2. Greeting	☐	☐	☐
3. Eye contact during greeting	☐	☐	☐
4. Introduction of ER Record	☐	☐	☐
5. Eye contact during introduction	☐	☐	☐
6. Individualized comment	☐	☐	☐
7. Eye contact during comment	☐	☐	☐
8. Within arm's reach	☐	☐	☐
9. Time→Dr.	☐	☐	☐
10. Next step	☐	☐	☐

FIGURE 5-1. Data sheet used to record care in a hospital emergency room. From Komaki, Collins, and Thoene (1980). Reproduced by permission.

children and their families, Patterson, Reid, Jones, and Conger (1975) developed definitions of 14 basic "noxious behaviors" and also reported norms for (or base rates of the occurrence of) these behaviors. Included were behaviors such as "yell," "whine," "tease," and "destructiveness." Also developed for the same project were definitions of 19 different behaviors that occurred in the classroom setting; some appropriate, such as "complies," "appropriate interaction with peer," and "attending"; and some inappropriate, such as "destructiveness," "noisy," and "inappropriate locale." Definitions of several of these behaviors are shown in Figure 5-2, and an illustrative segment of the recording sheet is shown in Figure 5-3. Obviously, a considerable amount of training is required in order for the observers to use such a scheme successfully. One recent extension of this multiple recording procedure is the use of a specially designed portable computer keyboard by which the trained observer can record observations directly onto a computer tape (e.g., Sanson-Fisher, Poole, Small, and Fleming, 1979).

Sampling and Recording Procedures

Regardless of the particular method of observation that is employed, it is necessary to specify in advance the exact procedures that will be used to sample the behavior and to record it. Careful sampling is necessary in order to assure that the measurements will be representative of the behavior as a whole, and this is particularly important in naturalistic observation because the behavior of interest may vary widely under different conditions. One technique that has been developed to heighten representativeness is *time sampling,* which involves the systematic observation of subjects' behavior according to a prearranged schedule of observations. The interval between observations is established to maximize the representativeness of the ongoing behavior that can be observed and recorded. The observations in a time sample are usually frequent and brief. For example, Barker, Kounin, and Wright (1943), in studying preschool children at play, observed and recorded the behavior of each child for one minute during each five minutes of a one-hour session. Barker and Wright (1955) suggested ways of collecting time

Appropriate Behaviors

CO—Complies. This category can be checked each time the person does what another person has requested. For example, the teacher asks class to take out notebooks and pupil does; she asks for paper to be turned in and pupil obeys; pupil asks for pencil and teacher or peer supplies one; teacher tells class to be quiet and pupil is quiet.

IP+ —Appropriate interaction with peer. Coded when the pupil is interacting with peer and is not violating classroom rules. Interaction includes verbal and nonverbal communication; for example, talking, handing materials, working on project with peer. The response for the peer is IP+ if the peer is *interacting* with the subject. The main element to remember in applying this code is that *an interaction is occurring* or one of the persons is attempting to interact. If two students are working on a social studies project, the code is IP+; if they are talking to each other or organizing a notebook *together,* the code is IP+; but if the subject is simply writing a report and the peer is writing, then the appropriate code is AT.

AT—Attending. This category is used whenever a person indicates by behavior that he/she is doing what is appropriate in a school situation: for example, looking at the teacher when he/she is presenting material to the class; looking at visual aids as the teacher tells about them; has eyes focused on his/her book while doing the reading assignment; writes answers to arithmetic problems; the teacher or peer looks at the child reciting. "Attending" is to be coded as a *response* when there is an indication that the subject is aware that a teacher or peer is attending to his/her actions.

Inappropriate Behaviors

DS—Destructiveness. Use of this category is applicable when a person destroys or attempts to destroy some object; for example, breaking a pencil in half, tearing a page from a book, carving name on desk, etc. This category is not to be used when the person is writing an answer or working out a problem on a desk with a pen or pencil.

NY—Noisy. This cateogry is to be used when the person talks loudly, yells, bangs books, scrapes chairs, or makes any sounds that are likely to be actually or potentially disruptive to others.

IL—Inappropriate locale. This category is not to be used if rules allow for pupils to leave seats without permission and what the pupil is doing is not an infraction of other rules; for example, a pupil going to sharpen pencil would not be classified IL, unless he/she stopped and looked at neighbors on the way or unless this activity takes permission from teacher, etc.

FIGURE 5-2. Examples of definitions of appropriate and inappropriate classroom behavior as coded by Patterson, Reid, Jones, and Conger (1975).

samples in order to maximize the usefulness of the obtained data. They also developed a "day record," or complete behavioral log, of an individual child by having trained observers accompany the child throughout the entire day (Barker and Wright, 1951). While such a log would be of considerable interest for some purposes, the question of the representatives of the particular day under study would limit its overall utility in many ways.

Obviously, the observer needs to strike a balance between completeness of observation, on the one hand, and efficiency, on the other. What is needed is to

Coding Sheet

Observer _____ Sheet No. _____1_____ Subject *Jimmy*

Date ____2-26-76_____ Academic Activity *arithmetic*

Structured ✓____ Unstructured _____ Group ✓___Individual__Transitional _____

```
_S_  AP CO TT+ IP+ VO AT  PN DS DI  _1_ NY NC PL TT- IP- IL SS (LO) NA IT _S_
_P_  AP CO TT+ IP+ VO (AT) PN DS DI  _2_ NY NC PL TT- IP- IL SS LO  NA IT _P_
_S_  AP CO TT+ IP+ VO (AT) PN DS DI  _3_ NY NC PL TT- IP- IL SS LO  NA IT _S_
_P_  AP CO TT+ IP+ VO AT  PN DS DI  _4_ NY NC PL TT- IP- IL (SS) LO NA IT _P_
_S_  AP CO TT+ IP+ VO AT  PN DS DI  _5_ NY NC PL TT- (IP) IL SS LO  NA IT  ·
_P_  AP CO (TT+) IP+ AT   PN DS DI  _6_ NY NC PL TT- IP- IL SS LO N
_S_  AP CO TT+ IP+ VO AT  PN (DS) DI _7_ NY NC PL TT- IP- IL SS
_P_  AP CO TT+ IP+ VO AT  PN DS DI  _8_ NY NC (PL) TT- IP
_S_  AP CO TT+ IP+ (VO) AT PN DS DI  _9_ NY NC P
_P_  AP (CO) TT+ IP+ VO AT PN DS DI  10  NV
_S_  AP CO TT+ IP+ VO AT  PN DS DI
_P_  AP CO TT+ IP+ VO AT  PN
_S_  AP CO TT+ IP+ VO
_P_  AP CO TT+                        _29_ (NY) NC PL TT- IP- IL SS LO NA IT _S_
_S_  A                         PN DS DI 30 NY NC PL TT- IP- IL (SS) LO NA IT _P_
              VO AT PN DS DI  31  NY NC PL TT- IP- IL SS (LO) NA IT _S_
           IP+ VO (AT) PN DS DI 32  NY NC PL TT- IP- IL SS LO  NA IT _P_
     CO TT+ IP+ VO AT  PN DS DI  33  NY NC PL TT- (IP) IL SS LO  NA IT _S_
_P_  AP CO TT+ IP+ VO AT  PN DS (DS) DI 34 NY NC PL TT- IP- IL SS LO NA IT _P_
_S_  AP CO TT+ IP+ VO (AT) PN DS DI  35  NY NC PL TT- IP- IL SS LO NA IT _S_
```

FIGURE 5-3. Illustrative segment of recording sheet used to code the observations of appropriate and inappropriate classroom behaviors. From Patterson, Reid, Jones, and Conger (1975). Reproduced by permission.

denote sufficient time to pilot observations to become fully aware of the range of variability of the behavior under different conditions, and then to design a time-sampling procedure that adequately incorporates this variability. In the observation system of Patterson and his colleagues for classroom behaviors, illustrated in Figure 5-2, "the target subject is observed at 15-second intervals for 12 minutes, and then randomly selected peers are observed in the same manner for six minutes" (Patterson, Reid, Jones, and Conger, 1975, p. 74). These authors also recommended that classroom behavior should be sampled in both group and individual academic work. Haynes (1978, p. 78) has listed five characteristics to be considered in deciding how to sample: (1) the rate of the behavior, (2) its variability, (3) its situational specificity, (4) possible changes over time, and (5) complexity of the recording system. The question of low-rate behaviors poses a special problem in time sampling. Here, it might be necessary to use continuous observation methods, perhaps through a participant observer rather than an outside observer.

Several other sampling questions must also be considered beside time sampling. For problems in which there is a wide variety of potentially relevant behaviors, such as in Patterson's work with families of aggressive children, a choice must be made as to which events to sample. The question of *subject sampling* also arises when it is not realistic to observe all available persons; for example, in setting out to assess the overall level of discipline that is maintained in a city school system. Representative sampling of situations must also be achieved, since the frequency of the target behavior will vary according to the many different stimulus components of the context in which it occurs. Haynes (1978) has provided a more complete discussion of each of these topics.

Methods of recording observational data have been briefly mentioned previously, and Figure 5-3 illustrates a complex recording system for parent-child interactions. With both simple and complex behaviors, there is usually a choice to be made between recording *frequency* and recording *duration*. The nailbiting client described earlier was asked to record frequency by activating the event counter for every instance of the behavior. At regular intervals, perhaps immediately before each meal (which serve as a reminding cue), the tally would be transferred to a data sheet. For behaviors such as asthma attacks, studying, or insomnia, the duration of the behavior might be more important than the frequency, and a recording procedure such as a log sheet is often appropriate. Figure 5-4 shows an abbreviated portion of such a sheet for a patient suffering from depression.

METHODS OF OBSERVATION

Procedures for behavioral observation can be grouped into four categories: uncontrolled, or naturalistic observation; controlled, or structured observation; self-observation; and written self-reports. These procedures focus mainly on the target behaviors themselves, and there is relatively little literature on the assessment of controlling variables as required in clinical applications, except on an informal basis, as exemplified in Figure 5-4.

Time	Circumstances	Additional information elicited by therapist
8 A.M.	Woke up feeling depressed; sat on side of bed	
10:15 A.M.	Felt less depressed; got dressed and made coffee	Telephone rang; patient hates its sound and answered it to stop the ringing
10:30 A.M.	Depressed again; sat in kitchen	
11:45 A.M.	Less depressed; got ready for work and left apartment	Patient became anxious about being late, which would result in a reprimand and possibly being fired
5:30	Became depressed when arrived home; depressed all evening; watched TV	

FIGURE 5-4. One day's self-observation sheet for a depressed patient, recording all changes in depressive feelings, together with time and place. On the right are the therapist's notes after questioning the patient concerning correlated events. [From R.I. Lanyon and B.P. Lanyon, (1976). Reprinted by permission of John Wiley & Sons.].

Naturalistic Observation

Naturalistic observation refers to the observing and recording of the behavior of interest by an independent observer exactly as it occurs in real life. For clinical applications, this approach has a substantial advantage over laboratory observation, since the real-life antecedent stimuli and the consequences of the behavior can also be observed directly.

A major disadvantage of naturalistic observation is its cost. However, it is often argued that, particularly in a clinical situation, anything other than naturalistic observation is of limited value, since it is only there that the relevant controlling variables can be detected. Unfortunately, scientific methodologists in psychology have traditionally regarded data gathered by naturalistic observation as an unsatisfactory basis for the development of knowledge (e.g., Underwood, 1966), even though it has been frequently pointed out (e.g., Sarason, 1974, p. 56) that the controlling variables for behaviors in the laboratory are usually different from those in the natural environment. This is particularly important in the assessment of real-life problem behaviors for which the controlling variables are obscure. In such situations, which are frequently encountered by psychologists interested in real-life problems, naturalistic rather than laboratory observation is essential, at least until sufficient knowledge is gained so that an appropriate situation for controlled observation can be be designed.

A second difficulty in naturalistic observation involves possible changes in the behavior under observation due to the observational process itself. In other words, the knowledge that one is being observed or judged often has direct consequences on the behavior under scrutiny. The result could be increased motivation and higher performance, or anxiety and lowered performance, or studied indifference with no apparent performance change. Consider, for example, a student teacher being evaluated by a supervisor sitting in the room, or an assembly line worker who knows that there is a time-study engineer on the line. It can readily be appreciated that the subject's awareness of being observed might produce nontypical behavior at a time when the occurrence of typical behavior is an absolute necessity. Campbell (1957) called these influences "reactive effects of measurement," and Selltiz, Jahoda, Deutsch, and Cook (1959) used the term "guinea pig effects." An illustration of guinea pig effects was reported by Moos (1968), who studied the behavioral effects of having psychiatric inpatients wear wireless transmitter microphones. In general, the effects were very small, but there was a tendency for some of the more disturbed individuals to show substantial reactions to being observed.

A third difficulty of direct observation involves invasion of privacy of the subject by the observer. This problem is especially important in personality assessment, since many of the behaviors which should be observed, such as affection, aggression, and sexual identification, are typically regarded as personal and private. Problems of invasion of privacy are considered in more detail in Chapter 11.

One technique for reducing guinea pig effects involves *participant observation,* in which the observers are themselves actively engaged in a spontaneous fashion with the individual or group under study. Participant observation has been widely used by anthropologists studying other cultures (see Williams, 1967, for a representative overview) and also by psychologists for a variety of purposes. In one interesting example, psychologists joined a "Doomsday" sect that met together to await the end of the world (Festinger, Riecken, and Schachter, 1956). The psychologists, whose professional role was not revealed to the sect, observed and recorded the group behavior before and during the time it became clear that the prophecy would not be fulfilled. Two of the difficulties mentioned earlier are raised by this example: the question of the observer's objectivity in observing and recording data under such circumstances, and the ethical question of invasion of privacy.

Another strategy to reduce guinea pig effects has been to provide for invisible or hidden observation, so that the subject is not aware of the observer's presence. Hidden microphones, "candid cameras," one-way vision mirrors, and elec-tromechanical devices to record subjects' movements in a chair or other piece of furniture represent some of the currently available devices for unobtrusive observa-tion (Webb, Campbell, Schwartz, and Sechrest, 1966, p. 142−170).

Other sources of natural behavior samples may be found in historical records available on individuals; for example, official school records, high school and college yearbooks, medical and dental records, and records of military service. Thus, Barthell and Holmes (1968) were able to demonstrate that the high school yearbook entries of persons who were later diagnosed as either schizophrenic or neurotic differed in expected ways from a control group. Although Schwarz (1970) has raised questions about the adequacy of controls used in this particular study, the utility of the method appears promising.

Although the continual development of sophisticated instruments for obtaining behavioral samples is making this approach more and more useful, the invasion of privacy problem is once again clearly apparent. It is obviously possible to secure prior permission of subjects to obtain the observations; but in such a case, the guinea pig effects might not be greatly reduced. Soskin and John (1963) reported an interesting example in which married couples, in exchange for an expense-paid vacation at a summer resort, permitted the recording of all of their verbal behavior during that time by means of miniaturized radio transmitters.

Despite the various problems inherent in naturalistic observation, it represents an important aspect of behavioral assessment, and there is currently a considerable amount of interest among psychologists in finding ways to deal with the various difficulties that accompany this approach. Two further methodological difficulties, bias due to the observer's own expectancies and problems of reliability, apply equally to controlled observations and are discussed under that heading. One additional limitation that will not be solved by better methods is that it tends primarily to permit the recording of public and frequent behavior, whereas many of the behaviors required for personality evaluation tend to be private and relatively infrequent. Responsiveness to stress, the handling of anger or sexuality, and reactions to tragedy fit this description and may not be observable naturalistically, even with improved methodologies.

Controlled Observation

The difficulties involved in data collection in naturalistic settings have led to the development of procedures for sampling behavior under more closely controlled conditions. Here there is the opportunity for more careful and thorough observation, as well as the potential for sufficient environmental control to elicit behaviors of special interest. Of considerable importance are laboratory situations in which subjects are presented with a number of tasks or experiences under conditions more or less similar to real life, and are expected to function with the same degree of effectiveness as they would in real life. These laboratory or controlled naturalistic observations have been used for many years in the context of personnel selection, industrial psychology, and personality research, where they have been referred to as *situational tests* or *work samples.*

Among the earliest situational tests were those employed by Hartshorne and May (1928, 1929) and Hartshorne, May, and Shuttleworth (1930) in their investigation of character, incorporating such traits as honesty, truthfulness, self-control, and persistence. Hartshorne and May assumed that character consisted of a series of responses or habits, and they attempted to measure these responses by sampling them directly. For example, in assessing honesty with money, children were given boxes of coins which had been secretly identified so that the experimenters could later determine which child had a particular box. Since the children were unaware of this arrangement, their honesty in handling money could be determined without their knowledge under relatively naturalistic but controlled conditions. Recognizing that honesty with money might be unrelated to other kinds of honesty, Hartshorne and May also collected behavior samples involving the possibility of other types of dishonesty. Thus, children were given an impossible task to perform and were then asked to report their own scores. The extended work of these authors involved a wide repertoire of tasks, concerned with the generality of behaviors such as honesty and persistence. Although these and similar tasks have been used in a variety of research studies (e.g., Brock and Guidice, 1963), the procedures have neither been standardized nor widely used as routine assessment devices for practical purposes.

Situational tests have also been utilized to assess suitability for military and intelligence operations, with a special emphasis upon determining characteristic modes of responding to stress. The principal feature of this type of assessment has been the intensive study by a highly trained staff of observers of a small group of candidates in a live-in program lasting several days and typically held at a remote and secluded site. These programs have made use of the traditional testing devices discussed in Chapters 3 and 4, but particular emphasis has been placed upon observing the candidates' reactions to the novel situation, to the continued pressure of scrutiny and evaluation, and to a series of specially designed stress situations.

In one such situation, designed to assist in the selection of military personnel for the Office of Strategic Services, candidates were required to construct a five-foot "Tinker Toy" cube with the aid of two supposed helpers, who were really members of the evaluation team who had been instructed to criticize, ridicule, and otherwise impede the candidate in completing the task (OSS Assessment Staff; 1948). The helpers carefully observed the candidate's reaction to this continual stress and frustration. In another instance, a group of candidates were given the task of crossing a stream and were provided with some materials to build a primitive bridge. They were then observed in their efforts to organize themselves into an effective work group to solve the task. Since the successful candidates operated throughout the world and performed a great variety of tasks, criterion measures were hard to obtain, making it difficult to assess the effectiveness of these particular selection procedures. Nevertheless, the correlations between overall suitability ratings and success in the field, as evaluated by such criteria as judgments by field commanders, ranged from .08 to .53, varying with the particular group studied and the criteria used (OSS Assessment Staff, 1948, p. 428). Further, it should be noted that the assessment program had a fairly rigorous set of selection standards, which served to decrease any correlation between the observers' predictions and judged criterion performance.

The live-in assessment procedure was also used for selecting members of the British Civil Service (Vernon, 1950). The situational tasks employed here were based upon a thorough job analysis of the work for which the candidates were applying, and included committee tasks and the handling of routine paper work. There was much opportunity for informal observations of the candidates throughout a three-day period, but there were no deliberately stressful situations built into the assessment procedure. With a rather homogeneous group of university graduates, the median correlation between ratings of trained observers and independent on-the-job evaluations collected two years later was .41. The median correlation between the more traditional written ability tests and the evaluations was only .12, indicating that the trained observers were able to identify significant elements of potential success that were not otherwise detected.

It is important to reemphasize that, in this example, the assessors had a clear understanding of the psychological requirements of the criterion task and were able to arrange for assessment situations to elicit relevant behaviors. Similar positive results have been reported with candidates for United States Army Officer Candidate Schools using leadership performance exercises as the situational task (Holmen, Katter, Jones, and Richardson, 1956) and by Mills, McDevitt, and Tonkin (1966) for selecting police cadets using a "clues" test, a situational exercise in police detection. On the other hand, assessment procedures based upon more traditional psychological tests, including a wide variety of personality tests, have not been so successful in predicting success in psychiatry (Holt and Lubor-sky, 1958) or in clinical psychology (Kelly and Fiske, 1951; Kelly and Goldberg, 1959).

One technique which is often used in live-in, or "house party," assessments is the *leaderless group discussion* (LGD). In this procedure, which originated in the German and British military assessment programs (Ansbacher, 1951), a small group of candidates, typically fewer than 12, are asked either to "discuss something" or to discuss a specific problem, perhaps a topic of current political or social interest. For a management group, the topic might be a management problem such as how to deal with an unsatisfactory employee. Since the procedure is otherwise unstructured and the group members are usually strangers to each other, the situation is rather ambiguous. There is opportunity to observe and rate behaviors like leading and following, social poise and self-presence, and "goal facilitation," which refers to the degree the individual helped the group accomplish its goal through making suggestions or by enabling others to contribute.

Initial participation in an LGD is usually equated with attempted leadership (Bass, 1960, p. 115), since most of the talk is directed at influencing other members either with procedural suggestions or with opinions on the topic under discussion. Attempted leadership, as defined in this manner, could be measured by determining the amount of time spent talking, in terms of total number of responses, rated participation, or total time talked. Other ways of assessing the members of an LGD have included ratings of behaviors such as "motivating others to participate" and checklists of behaviors such as "led the discussion," to be completed by either the participants themselves or external, nonparticipating observers.

Perhaps the most extensive and formal way of categorizing the various kinds of behavior observable in this and other social interactions is by means of the Bales Interaction Check List (Bales, 1950). In this technique, observers categorize every response made in the group into one of 12 predetermined categories, such as *shows solidarity* (gives help or reward), *shows tension release* (jokes, laughs), and *asks for orientation* (asks for information, confirmation). At the present time, however, the Bales Interaction Check List is more of a research instrument than a functional assessment device.

In general, there is excellent evidence for the reliability of observing LGD behavior. For most of the available methods of quantifying the behavior, the average correlation between any two observers is typically between .8 and .9 (Bass, 1954, p. 472). There is also sound evidence for the predictive value of LGD behavioral indices. For example, Bass and Coates (1952) reported correlations of .40 to .45 between LGD scores and ratings of military officers by their superiors. Similar findings have been reported for British foreign service officers (Vernon, 1950), British Civil Service employees (Vernon, 1950), and fraternity and sorority leaders and sales trainees (Bass, 1954).

The LGD procedure is a very good example of the utility of the situational test or work sample approach to personality assessment, particularly in the evaluation of characteristics such as leadership. Leadership involves the behavior of individuals in group settings, particularly their ability to structure, organize, and generally influence the group; and clearly such behavior is elicited and observable in the LGD. It should not be surprising, therefore, that the behavior displayed in the sample does provide information about the individual's behavior in other situations that require similar responses for effective performance.

One portion of a study by Gordon (1967) examined the relative utility of several assessment procedures, including individual situational work samples, in predicting failure of Peace Corps trainees to be selected for an overseas assignment. The subjects were 178 trainees in three different training programs, all of whom were subjected to an intensive one-week live-in assessment program. The program included a variety of paper-and-pencil personality inventories of the type discussed in Chapter 4, a foreign-language learning task, and four specially devised situational work samples, in which the subject was required to develop a plan to build an infirmary on a South Seas island, describe to a foreign national the American governmental system of checks and balances, discuss American culture with an anti-American, and enlist the aid of an Indian government official in a project to raise poultry. Prior to overseas departure, 74 trainees were rejected as unsuitable, although the personnel making this decision did not have access to the earlier assessment data. In general, each of the various assessment approaches enabled predictions of failure to be made that exceeded chance expectation, but there were no worthwhile differences in efficiency of prediction among the various approaches. Gordon argued that the simplest and most economical method of predicting success in the overseas assignments should be used operationally for screening—in this case, the paper-and-pencil inventories. These issues of cost and efficiency need further careful research involving a variety of criterion situations. The additional question of the relative utility of these procedures for predicting success in overseas assignments is as yet unanswered.

Clinical Use of Controlled Observation

The use of controlled observation procedures for the assessment of clinically related problems in a relatively recent development. Such procedures can be discussed under four headings: structured interactions, role-playing tests, experimental analogs, and physiological measures. Except for physiological measures, these procedures are analogous to the situational tests and work sample methods discussed earlier in the context of personnel selection.

Structured Interactions.   The assessment of interpersonal interactions through structured tasks employs the same definition and recording procedures as already described for naturalistic observation. Thus, Patterson, Hops, and Weiss (1975) extended the earlier work with families of deviant children (Patterson, Reid, Jones, and Conger, 1975) to develop a system for the assessment of husband-wife interaction. The laboratory situation consisted of 10-minute sessions in which the couples attempted to resolve several areas of conflict. Similar structured observational assessment procedures have also been developed for assessing components of mother-child interaction (e.g., Forehand and Scarboro, 1975), the social behavior of psychiatric patients (e.g., Wallace and Davis, 1974), and general social skills with anxious or unassertive college males. A somewhat different kind of example is found in the work of Bernal, Duryee, Pruett, and Burns (1968) with uncontrollable children and their mothers. Bernal made videotapes of the mothers interacting with their children in the clinic situation, and then used the tapes as teaching materials to help the mothers learn more appropriate behaviors.

Role-playing Tests.   In this procedure, the subject knows that the situation is simulated but is asked to react as though in real life. McFall and Marston (1970) and McFall and Lillesand (1971), for example, developed a tape-recorded behavioral role-playing test to assess assertive behavior. Subjects were required to respond to 16 hypothetical situations requiring assertiveness, and the degree of assertiveness that they displayed was determined by independent judges. A sample item from the test is shown in Figure 5-5. It should be pointed out that these items were developed by an extensive test construction process; they began with a list of over 2,000 situations calling for assertive behavior and reduced these through screening, factor analysis, and additional procedures. Other situations in which behavioral role-playing tests have been employed include social skills in delinquent boys (e.g., Freedman, Rosenthal, Donahoe, Schlundt, and McFall, 1978) and other populations, adaptive skills in alcoholics, and heterosexual skills. Goldfried and D'Zurilla (1969) took particular care in their development of procedures for assessing social competence among college students, and their work can be regarded as a model for future endeavors.

Role-playing tests have been subjected to a number of criticisms, and much research remains to be done to put this technique on a sound footing. For example, Bellack (1979) reported that the use of audiotaped or videotaped situations resulted in data of low validity as compared to the use of real-life models for the role playing. Based on a series of studies investigating the validity of role-playing tests for social skills with psychiatric patients, he offered the following recommendations for the future development of this procedure. (1) Because short or single responses might not permit an adequate sample of behavior in a particular situation, each item should allow for multiple responses by both the subject and the model. (2) Since the entire procedure appears to be highly stressful and may thus result in a distorted view of the subject's response skills, ways of making it less stressful should be

---

The format for the presentation of each stimulus situation is illustrated by the following excerpt from the script:

NARRATOR: In this scene, picture yourself standing in a ticket line outside of a theatre. You've been in line now for at least ten minutes, and its getting pretty close to show time. You're still pretty far from the beginning of the line, and you're starting to wonder if there will be enough tickets left. There you are, waiting patiently, when two people walk up to the person in front of you and they begin talking. They're obviously all friends, and they're going to the same movie. You look quickly at your watch and notice that the show starts in just two minutes. Just then, one of the newcomers says to his friend in line:

NEWCOMER: "Hey, the line's a mile long. How 'bout if we cut in here with you?"

PERSON IN
LINE: "Sure, come on. A couple more won't make any difference."

NARRATOR: And as the two people squeeze in line between you and their friend, one of them looks at you and says:

NEWCOMER: "Excuse me. You don't mind if we cut in, do you?"

            (Bell sounds as cue for S to respond.)

FIGURE 5-5. Sample item from the Behavioral Role-playing Test for Assertiveness. From McFall and Marston (1970). Copyright 1970 by the American Psychological Association. Reprinted by permission of the publisher and author.

explored. (3) In order for the subject to have an adequate understanding of what is required in each role-playing situation, it is suggested that more detailed descriptions be provided and that subjects preview them before responding. (4) Because some situations elicit highly specific or idiosyncratic responses, careful attention should be paid to the degree to which certain situations have specific demand characteristics which might lead to the same response for all subjects.

Experimental Analogs.   This term refers to laboratory situations that are arranged to be as parallel as possible to real-life problem situations, and these tests usually involve the assessment of specific instances of *nonverbal* behavior. One example can be seen in the *behavioral avoidance test* for assessing specific fears such as phobias of snakes or spiders. To make a quantitative assessment of snake phobics, Lang and Lazovik (1963) asked their subjects to move systematically closer and closer to a harmless snake, under structured laboratory conditions. Each successive step earned them a lower behavioral avoidance score. Thus, subjects who refused to go into the room at all earned a score of 19, those who were willing to get within two feet of the snake received a 4, and those who picked it up earned a 1. In addition to the behavioral avoidance score, Lang and Lazovik had subjects rate their subjectively experienced anxiety on a 10-point scale. In a similar assessment procedure involving fear of spiders, Lanyon and Manosevitz (1966) in addition had unobtrusive observers rate each subject on a checklist of observable signs of fear, such as trembling, hesitating, and sweating. In an experimental analog situation to assess fear of public speaking, Paul (1966) recorded all of these measures plus measures of pulse rate and palmar sweat. Thus, the behavioral avoidance test is suitable for gathering data in several different response modalities.

Another kind of experimental analog situation has involved a laboratory model not of the behavior itself but of the *process* thought to be involved. This method was pioneered in 1953 by Lindsley (1960), who arranged a simple operant reinforcement task for psychiatric inpatients, in which reinforcers such as candy or cigarettes could be earned by systematically pulling a plunger. This situation was seen as a "model" for assessing the nature of the factors that influenced the patients' behavior, and it revealed certain response characteristics that had direct clinical relevance (Kazdin, 1979). In a more recent application of this procedure, Marlatt (1978) has summarized the use of operant methods to assess the intensity of alcoholics' need to drink and factors which can cause the intensity of the need to vary.

Physiological Assessment Procedures.   The fourth laboratory assessment procedure to be considered is the assessment of physiological states. It would indeed be convenient if psychologists were able to assess personality characteristics by measuring bodily responses, and in science fiction they often can do so. In reality, however, there are only a few systems that can be assessed and which may be relevant to personality and interpersonal behavior. Psychophysiological (or electrophysiological) assessment, as it is called, has made definite advances as a field since the mid-1960s, due to the development of sensitive and sophisticated electronic equipment to monitor bodily responses.

The most commonly assessed psychophysiological response is overall level of bodily arousal. Because of recent research and theory suggesting that the common element in such pleasant states as deep relaxation and meditation is a bodily state of low psychophysiological arousal (Blanchard and Epstein, 1978), there is increasing interest in measuring this state. The elusive notion of increasing one's level of mental health by reducing one's overall level of "stress and tension," which are themselves ambiguous and poorly defined terms, is probably related to the interest in learning to reach a state of physiological hypoarousal. Bodily measures which appear to be relevant here include degree of electrical activity in the muscles (electromyographic, or EMG levels), heart rate, blood pressure, electrodermal activity (correlated with sweat gland activity), and certain EEG (brain wave) patterns. Because each individual's patterns of these responses in relation to stressful stimuli is unique, research progress on using them in structured assessment procedures is slow. However, there does appear to be some overall relationship between reduced psychophysiological activity and reduced physical and mental "tension." In addition, some more specific positive research findings are available, such as relationships between the occurrence of headaches in certain sufferers and EMG levels about the head and neck. The topic of psychophysiology is a highly complex one, and psychologists interested in psychophysiological assessment procedures require a comprehensive training in the basic knowledge of this area.

Two other uses of psychophysiological processes in assessment deserve specific mention. The first involves the assessment of sexual functioning, either in a research context or for planning treatment strategies for sexual dysfunction problems. Reviews of this area have been provided by Barlow (1977) and by Zuckerman (1971). For males, the usual measurement procedures involve the degree of increase in the size of the penis while viewing pictures or other stimuli causing varying degrees of sexual arousal. This is done either with a strain gauge, registering changes in electrical resistance as the circumference of the penis changes, or with a pneumatic plethysmograph, consisting of an airtight hollow cylinder by which changes in penis size are reflected in changes in air pressure. The laboratory assessment of sexual arousal in women is a more recent development. Geer (1977) has described preliminary work involving the assessment of vaginal changes by means of photoplethysmography, in which a small instrument containing a photoelectric cell and a light source inserted into the vagina registers changes in vaginal blood volume.

The second additional use of physiological assessment procedures is in the lie detection industry. Lie detection test procedures record multiple measures of overall physiological arousal (such as heart rate, blood pressure, skin resistance, and EMG levels) while the individual is answering questions related to the topic of interest, and the procedures are based on the premise that the pattern of such responses while lying will be different from the pattern while telling the truth. Despite the rapidly growing popularity of lie detection procedures, research reviews on this topic tend to conclude that most of the claims for accuracy made by the lie detection industry are exaggerated. Thus, Lykken (1980) has maintained that the most prevalent test is correct only two-thirds of the time, and that it is more likely to err in the direction of erroneously classifying innocent subjects as having lied. However, out of the many complex procedures employed in lie detection work, one in particular, the guilty-knowledge technique, does appear to have the potential for much higher accuracy in those cases to which it is applicable (Yarmey, 1979). Unfortunately, many professional polygraphers are ignorant of these matters, and the field continues to flourish on the basis of its popular appeal and its economic success.

Self-Observation

The view that self-reports can contain useful information about actual behavior has had a stormy history in psychology. Individuals' reports about their own behavior have usually been regarded with considerable suspicion, both by psychodynamically oriented psychologists and by classical behaviorists. It has been fashionable to believe that self-observation does not usually correlate adequately with observation made by independent observers, and that it is therefore not a valid assessment procedure. Such a view is expressed, for example, in the review by Wolff and Merrens (1974). Recently, however, there has been increasing support for the view that accurate and reliable self-observation is a learnable skill that can be efficiently taught by behavioral methods such as modeling and shaping. One very important factor gives overriding support to the practical use of self-observation: its *economy*. The self-observer is always ready and available, and is free of charge. Self-observation is particularly important in making an assessment of *covert* events, because it provides the only means of identifying and quantifying these events.

Methods of Self-Observation.   The importance of self-observation as an integral part of behavioral evaluation and change is only now beginning to be appreciated, and its technology is still in the early stages of development (Haynes, 1978). Most methods of self-observation involve systematic written note taking, such as on index cards or in a notebook. Special tally sheets have also been prepared for specific behaviors, such as eating (Stuart and Davis, 1972) and particular thoughts (Thoreson and Mahoney, 1974). Wrist counters (Lindsley, 1968) and other similar devices such as golf or supermarket counters can also be used, although they only enable the recording of frequencies and not the antecedent stimulus conditions (e.g., time and place) under which the behavior occurs, nor its consequences.

Obviously, a person who is recording instances of nailbiting, which may occur many times each day, would approach self-observation differently from a person recording instances of anxious feelings, which may occur only once or twice per day but last several hours. Watson and Tharp (1977) have presented an excellent discussion of a wide variety of practical self-observation techniques, and Mahoney (1977) has also given sound practical advice on how to self-monitor. One common procedure is for the behavior therapist to have patients construct their own recording sheets, as illustrated in Figure 5-3 for a depressed patient. Taken over a one-week or two-week time interval and expanded through inquiry by the therapist, such observations provide an overall frequency count of depressive episodes and their length, plus a listing of the stimuli associated with their onset and termination.

Teaching Self-Observation.   Procedures for the teaching of self-observation skills are not systematized at the present time. As pointed out by Thoreson and Mahoney (1974), individuals are not "naturally" accurate self-observers, so that specific training is in most instances essential. These authors have listed a number of factors that have been shown to enhance the learning of self-observation: modeling, immediate accuracy feedback, systematic reinforcement, and the gradual transfer of the responsibility for recording from an external source to oneself.

Problems in Self-Observation.   Many of the methodological difficulties encoun- tered in self-observation are similar to those encountered when naturalistic observa- tions are made by an independent observer. However, one specific type of problem, the reactive effects of measurement, takes on additional complexities. The reactive effect of self-observation has itself been successfully used as a behavior change procedure, although unsuccessful outcomes have also been reported (Nelson, 1977). A simple operant explanation of this effect might be given in terms of either self-punishment or self-reward. Thus, recording one's problem behaviors might call forth a self-statement such as "This is bad; I should do it less often" or "I'm doing a good job of cutting back." Kazdin (1974) has analyzed in detail the behavior change properties of self-observation and has shown that its behavior change effects are highly varied and usually temporary, and that a variety of theoretical explana- tions are possible in addition to a simple operant view.

Problems and Challenges in Behavioral Observation

The area of the systematic observation of direct behavior has developed very rapidly in the recent past, and these developments are generally regarded as positive. However, critics consistently point to one serious area of difficulty, which encompasses several different facets. They refer to the fact that behavioral assessment procedures have in general failed to incorporate the usual psychometric standards of validity and reliability that are expected of any structured psychological assessment method (e.g., Curran, 1979; Goldfried, 1979). Ironically, Rabin (1968) once offered exactly the same warning in regard to the proliferation of projective techniques (Hartmann, Roper, and Bradford, 1979).

Reliability.   A major area of concern is reliability of observation. The topic of reliability (defined as the *repeatability* of measurement) is discussed in detail in Chapter 7; we examine here specific questions as they apply to behavioral assessment. We have already discussed the need to gather adequate samples (over time, situations, and subjects) of the behaviors to be assessed, and we have discussed the reactive effects of the observation process on the behavior itself. Another problem related to reliability involves the observational skill of the observers. A significant problem here is bias due to the observer's own expectancies. This effect is closely related to the better-known effect of expectancies on the outcome of psychological research (e.g., Orne, 1962; Rosenthal, 1966). Lipinski and Nelson (1974) have listed three factors that appear to improve the accuracy of observers' reports: knowledge of expected results, evaluative feedback from another person, and knowledge that reliability measurements are being made. In an interesting study that experimentally manipulated observers' expectancies of therapeutic change, Kent, O'Leary, Diament, and Dietz (1974) demonstrated that expectancies were not a significant factor when a highly structured observational procedure was employed, but that the observers' subjective impressions about the behavior being observed nevertheless did show significant bias.

Observer reliability may be developed through specific training. Of considerable interest is the fact that the process of measuring reliability is itself reactive, so that different results may be obtained depending on the contingencies available to the observer. Romanczyk, Kent, Diament, and O'Leary (1973) showed that not only was reliability higher when the observers knew that they were to be monitored, but it increased even more when they knew against whose work it would be checked.

Validity.   As discussed in more detail in Chapter 7, an assessment procedure is valid to the extent that it indeed measures what it is supposed to measure. Because behavioral assessment involves the *direct sampling* of the behaviors of interest, the most important aspect of validity is content validity—namely, the degree to which the assessment procedure does indeed take a representative sample of the "universe of content" of the behavior to be assessed. A more detailed discussion of this topic has been given by Linehan (1980).

The use of contrived or laboratory assessment situations poses special threats to content validity. In the case of clinical assessment, in which the variables controlling the behavior (antecedents and consequences) must also be assessed, the use of contrived situations is even riskier. Thus, it is legitimate to ask whether such an approach can be valid at all. An appropriate response is that the potential for validity exists to the extent that the controlling variables that maintain the problem behavior in real life are also present in the laboratory situation. In other words, a basic condition must be that the laboratory situation resembles the real-life situation in all essential ways.

Two other psychometric concerns should be noted. First, there have been relatively few attempts to standardize behavioral observation procedures, and even fewer efforts to develop norms for the various procedures. Second, and of importance ranging beyond behavioral approaches to assessment, there is a strong need for multiple sources of assessment information regarding a particular behavior or concept. This principle is related to the recognition that many human events involve three simultaneous response systems: overt motor activity; thoughts or cognitive behaviors; and feelings, related to emotional-physiological behavior (see p. 99); and that a satisfactory assessment procedure should sample all three. It should also be understood that each particular method or mode of assessment suffers from biases or limitations inherent in that mode, so that "multimethod" or "multimodal" procedures are needed to provide unbiased assessment. We discuss this topic further in Chapter 8 in regard to personality assessment on a broader scale.

Unsystematic Observations

To this stage we have concentrated upon situations where a trained observer studies a subject in some specific type of behavioral situation. Obviously the subject has also been "behaving" in a wide variety of real-life situations where untrained observers have been present. The child's behavior in the classroom, the employee's on-the-job performance, and the patient's behavior on the ward are all observed and should provide useful data for the purposes of personality assessment. The major problem in making use of informal and unsystematic observations is the manner in which these observations are to be collected from the observers and, particularly, the form in which the observations are to be reported.

One approach is to ask the observer of an individual or group to keep an *anecdotal record*. Observers, who will often be teachers or supervisors, are asked to make notes of whatever behavior in their daily routine contact they regard as "significant." They are encouraged to record exactly what they observe as soon as possible after the observation, and to be as objective and descriptive in their reports as possible. Whatever inferences observers make should be clearly identified as such. An anecdotal record developed over a period of time provides a rich though nonquantified account of behavior that is unrivaled for developing an individualized behavioral description. It is the consistency and individuality of certain behavioral observations—for example, seeking affection, refusing help, working diligently at a task, or volunteering for responsibilities—that permit the reader of the anecdotal record to construct a personality "picture." The artistic, clinical nature of this process is clearly apparent.

In order to develop greater focus in anecdotal records upon behaviors of particular interest to the investigator, it is possible to utilize the *critical incident technique* developed by Flanagan (1954). This technique asks the observer to consider instances of behavior that are illustrative of a particular personality characteristic. Thus, a supervisor might be asked to observe and record examples of good or poor work performance, or a psychiatric ward nurse might be asked to record all instances of aggression. The observer is again required to record objectively the actual behavioral incidents, and it is the difficult task of the reader to draw inferences from this record. It can be appreciated that the values and attitudes of the observer are clearly a factor in making the observations. For example, a supervisor who regards quantity of output as the most important indicator of good work performance will probably record different critical incidents than would a supervisor who is primarily concerned about quality of product.

Anecdotal data are perhaps more widely used in another context. Potential employers often attempt to ascertain the suitability of a job candidate through *references*—that is, by requesting letters of recommendation or by a telephone inquiry about the applicant. Reference checks are usually of limited use, since they typically consist of positive but vague generalities. One comprehensive study of reference checks made by the United States Civil Service Commission (Goheen and Mosel, 1959) indicated that such inquiries did not even identify disqualifying factors, such as alcoholism, which were readily uncovered by field investigations. Letters which are negative take on particular weight because of their rarity in actual practice. An exception to these findings has been the experience of the Peace Corps where, in our personal experience, reference checks have produced considerable frankness on the part of respondents, yielding useful comparative information about applicants. In this area, a significant relationship has been demonstrated between quantified ratings of reference checks and overseas success (Stein, 1966).

Summary

Behavioral approaches to assessment are consistent with the view that important determinants of human behavior are to be found in environmental variables as well as personal variables, and more specifically, in the interaction between person and environment. Behavioral assessment procedures have been widely used for many years in industrial and organizational psychology, but their widespread use in clinical contexts is relatively new. In clinical assessment, covert behaviors (thoughts and feelings) tend to be included within the general definition of behavior, and attention is also given to gathering information about the variables (antecedents and consequences) thought to be controlling the behavior. Two basic steps in all behavioral assessment are (1) selecting and defining the behavior of interest and (2) systematic observation and recording. For clinical uses, further steps include observation of controlling variables, behavioral formulation, and design of an appropriate treatment strategy.

Observation can involve complex behaviors as long as they are defined in operational terms. Sampling and recording procedures must be specified in advance; a common procedure is time sampling, using a predetermined schedule. Behaviors may be observed according to either frequency or duration. Naturalistic observation refers to the observing and recording of the behavior of interest exactly as it occurs in real life. Difficulties include its cost, the reactive effects of measurement, and possible invasion of privacy. Reactive effects can be reduced through participant observation.

Controlled observations, also referred to as situational tests, involve structured or laboratory settings and have been employed for assessment purposes in personnel work for many years. One technique of note involving structured interaction is the leaderless group discussion, in which a small group of people are called upon to discuss a specific topic. An opportunity is thus provided for the observation of interpersonal characteristics such as leadership and social poise. Clinical uses of structured interaction have included the assessment of couples, families, and parent-child interactions. In role-playing tests, the situation is more obviously simulated, but the subject is asked to respond as though in real life. Uses of role-playing tests have included the assessment of social skills, assertiveness, and job-related behaviors. Experimental analogs involve laboratory situations that are arranged to duplicate the salient components of the real-life problem situations, under highly structured conditions. Specific fears such as phobias of snakes, spiders, and public speaking have been assessed in this manner. Physiological assessment has also been employed for clinical purposes in the measurement of sexual responses and for blood pressure, heart rate, and other responses correlated with psychophysiological arousal. The lie detection industry also involves psychophysiological assessment.

Self-observation, despite traditional criticisms of this procedure, is becoming more widely used and can be viewed as a learnable skill. Structured procedures include the use of notebooks and tally cards. Many methodological difficulties remain to be solved, particularly the reactive effects of measurement. General criticisms of all behavioral observation procedures include the inadequate attention that has been paid to basic psychometric considerations such as reliability and validity.

Unsystematic observations are also employed in assessment. An observer might keep an anecdotal record, in which everything is noted that appears significant in daily contact with the individual. In the critical-incident technique, note is made of instances of behavior which the observer considers particularly illustrative of the individual's behavior. Letters of reference also constitute unsystematic observations about interpersonal behavior. Problems of the representativeness of the behavior reported are an obvious drawback in this approach.

6 BIOGRAPHICAL DATA AND INTERVIEWS

The use of biographical information and data regarding recent and current events forms the very core of the traditional assessment process in a wide variety of uses. In selecting from among job applicants, for example, the selection officer typically gathers background information and then interviews to get a "feel" for the person. The traditional procedure for diagnosing medical diseases has been to ask questions about previous health status and then to assess current complaints. In the mental health area, diagnosis has traditionally been based on a current status interview by a psychiatrist and an extended case history taken by a social worker.

Research findings in the technology of assessment over the past three decades, discussed in Chapter 8, have conclusively demonstrated the great importance of *structure* and *objectivity* in gathering personal data. The use of structured instruments for gathering biographical data and for coding interviews has been an integral part of assessment in personnel selection for many years; however, their introduction into the mental health assessment field is relatively recent. Another relatively recent development is the blurring of a conceptual distinction between biographical or historical data, on the one hand, and current status or recent data, on the other. The traditional distinction between written self-report methods versus interview methods of data collection is also being eroded to some extent. For convenience in our own presentation, however, we first review the use of biographical information (which usually involves written self-report methods) and then discuss interview procedures. Since these categories are obviously not mutually exclusive, there is some degree of overlap in the two sections.

BIOGRAPHICAL INFORMATION

The predictive power of biographical data has been well established, with studies in both personnel and clinical fields showing that it is comparable or even superior to the use of formal tests (e.g., Alker and Owen, 1977; Sines, 1959). A common approach in personnel selection is the weighted biographical data sheet (England, 1961). In this method it is assumed that personal history items, obtainable from a formal written application blank, have predictive value for success or failure in a particular occupational setting. The items can be *demographic* (such as age, sex, marital status, and number of dependents), *experiential* (such as number of schools attended, age when first married, number of jobs held, and arrest record), or *behavioral* (such as recreational pursuits, hobbies, current reading matter, and consumption of alcohol). Items that correlate with some criterion of success or failure are identified statistically and are given differential numerical weights according to how predictive they are. In operational use, applications are "scored" according to these weights, and applicants are accepted or rejected depending upon whether or not their totals surpass some "cutting score" which has been previously established by empirical means. This procedure closely resembles the development of empirically derived personality inventories like the MMPI.

The weighted biographical data technique was successfully applied to the selection of life insurance salesmen as early as 1919. Using nine personal history items with weights ranging from -2 to $+3$ and a cutting score of $+4$ on the complete blank, Goldsmith (1922) reported that 84 percent of the successful salesmen would have been selected and 54 percent of the unsuccessful ones would have been rejected. During World War II, scores on the Air Force Biographical Data Blank were found to correlate .30 with pilot success (Guilford, 1947). More recently, this technique has been successfully used to select unskilled factory workers (Scott and Johnson, 1967), management personnel (Scollay, 1957), and clerical employees (Lee and Booth, 1974). The criteria used have included job tenure or longevity, productivity, amount of absenteeism, and size of salary. Since these criteria are not always highly correlated, it is important for investigators to decide which criterion is of primary importance in a particular setting.

There is controversy about the need for continual cross-validation or rechecking of the weighted application blank. One study (Hughes, Dunn, and Baxter, 1956) reported that the usefulness of the application blank "disappeared" within two years after it was put into operational use. It was surmised that the field management staff, who knew the item weights, were leading or guiding the applicants so that their blank would "pass" the cutting score. On the other hand, Brown (1978) demonstrated that a scoring key developed in 1933 was still as valid 45 years later. Further research is needed to determine the conditions under which such scoring procedures retain their validity.

This approach has also been used for other kinds of vocational and achievement predictions. James, Ellison, Fox, and Taylor (1974) demonstrated the use of biographical data to predict artistic performance, while Helmreich, Bakeman, and Radloff (1973) used life history data to predict performance in Navy distress training. Freeburg (1967) wrote a positive review of the literature on biographical material as a predictor of scholastic achievement, using grades, nonclassroom achievements, persistence, and curriculum choice as the criteria, while Owens and Henry (1966) surveyed the literature on the successful use of biographical data to predict creativity in a variety of work settings.

Another major application of the biographical or personal history data method is in psychopathology. Such information has traditionally formed an important basis for predictions and decisions about clients in mental health settings. Let us review some of these applications, both early and recent.

It has long been noted that patients in mental hospitals, especially those diagnosed as schizophrenic, differ in prognosis, with some showing rather prompt and good recovery while others make little or no change. Beginning with the work of Wittman (1941) at Elgin State Hospital, a number of investigators have attempted to identify particular aspects of case history or biographical data that are associated with good and poor prognosis in schizophrenia. Kantor, Wallner, and Winder (1953) and Phillips (1953) have provided prominent examples of this approach, although Kantor et al. included information about current symptoms in addition to case history data. In general, those schizophrenics with good prognosis (who subsequently recover) are found to have been better adjusted prior to the onset of the illness, with less family psychopathology, more satisfactory heterosexual experiences, better vocational adjustment, and more general stability than the group with poor prognosis (who recover very slowly or not at all). The terms *reactive* and *process schizophrenia* have traditionally been used as more or less synonymous with good and poor prognosis, respectively. In general, studies relating scores on life history prognostic scales to actual outcome have yielded moderately positive results (Buss, 1966; Garfield and Sundland, 1966), and these findings have led several investigators (e.g., Rodnick and Garmezy, 1957) to regard as essential the inclusion of a life history measure of prognosis in research with schizophrenic patient populations.

Zigler and Phillips (1960) extended this work with biographical data beyond schizophrenia by developing a technique to evaluate the relative premorbid adjustment level of psychiatric patients in general. Their procedure was based upon six personal history variables: age, measured intelligence, education, occupational level (unskilled or semiskilled), employment history (usually unemployed, seasonally employed, part-time employed, and regularly employed), and marital status. These variables were used to produce a composite measure of social competence that was significantly related to the type of symptoms shown by the patients. Those with higher social competence scores tended to show symptoms which can be regarded as "turning against the self," and those with lower scores tended to show symptoms indicative of "avoidance of others" or "self-indulgence and turning against others." Since these latter symptoms are typical of schizophrenia, it was concluded that patients diagnosed as schizophrenic tend generally to have relatively poor premorbid social competence. Zigler and Phillips (1962) were further able to show that within schizophrenics, those who exhibited a relatively good level of premorbid social competence were more likely than the poor premorbid patient to show symptoms characterized by "turning against the self." From these findings, they concluded that the reactive-process distinction in schizophrenia might be better regarded as a social competence or social maturity dimension which can be assessed through personal history data, and that this dimension was potentially applicable to all of psychopathology rather than to schizophrenia alone.

Instruments based on biographical data have been developed for the assessment of a variety of other specific characteristics. For example, Lanyon (1967a) developed a brief self-report questionnaire of 20 items to measure social competence in male college students. Sample items from this questionnaire are shown in Figure 6-1. Validity was established by showing the relationship of scores to other measures of social effectiveness, including ratings by peers. Another specific instrument is the Survey of Heterosexual Interactions (SHI), reported by Twentyman and McFall (1975). The SHI, a written self-report measure of heterosexual avoidance in shy males, was derived after pilot study interviews with college females. It includes a biographical section, containing questions about subjects' past dating behavior, and a section with questions assessing their ability to initiate and carry out interactions with women in specific social situations. A list of other questionnaires for specific functions has been developed by Haynes and Wilson

---

2. How many *different* girls did you date *up to the end* of your senior year in high school? <u>2 and more</u>

4. How frequently do you date at present? <u>more often than once a month</u>

5. How old were you when you began to date regularly? <u>up to and including 17</u>

6. How many serious physical illnesses have you had during your lifetime (those that have incapacitated you for 2 weeks or more)? <u>0 or 1</u>

8. Have you ever made a trip as much as 200 miles away from home (without your parents or other guardian) where you stayed overnight, *other than* visiting relatives? <u>yes</u> (yes or no)

9. Have you ever made such a trip as much as 1,000 miles away from home without a parent or other guardian? <u>yes</u> (yes or no)

10. How do you approach your school assignments?
    - __x__ Get them done ahead of schedule
    - __x__ Do them in the last few days, but always get them in on time
    - _____ Rush them at the last minute, and sometimes get them in late
    - _____ Have habitual problems with getting them done on time, in spite of adequate ability

11. How many times, in your lifetime, have you been spoken to by a policeman for any possible *traffic* offense, except parking? <u>0–3</u>

13. Who usually buys (i.e., selects) your clothes?
    - __x__ I do
    - _____ my mother does (or similar person)
    - _____ sometimes I do; sometimes my mother does

14. With how many social, recreational, or organizational activities were you affiliated during your last year in high school? <u>2 and more</u>

15. Of the activities in No. 14 above, in how many of these (if any) did you hold an office? <u>1 and more</u>

17. Do you drink at all now? <u>yes</u> (yes or no)

18. Do you participate frequently and regularly (once a week or oftener) in some nonorganized athletic activity (e.g., play handball with Joe on Thursdays)? <u>yes</u> (yes or no)

19. How often do you go to church? <u>any response other than "never"</u>

Note—Criterion answers are checked or inserted. No more than 1 point is scored for any one question.

FIGURE 6-1. Sample items from the Biographical Survey III for assessing social competence in college males. From Lanyon (1967a). Copyright 1967 by the American Psychological Association. Reprinted by permission of the publisher and author.

(1979). One additional area that should be noted is the assessment of children, through biographical data reported by teachers and parents. This work is discussed further in Chapter 9.

Multiscale Instruments

Despite the promise of biographical data as a source of assessment information, relatively few structured multiscale instruments have been developed for making comprehensive assessments. One such device is the Minnesota-Briggs History Record, or MBHR (Briggs, 1959; Briggs, Rouzer, Hamburg, and Holman, 1972), which was originally developed to be used with a nonclient informant but was later revised to be a self-report instrument. Items on the MBHR concern the client's life history, including such diverse areas as education, food preferences, and marital status. The client's responses are weighted and scored on seven or eight content scales, such as family disunity, health awareness, and introversion. Recent reviews (Dahlstrom, 1978; Jackson, 1978) indicate that the MBHR has potential as a research and clinical instrument, but that insufficient validity data exist at the present time.

A comprehensive instrument using biographical data for mental health assessment is the Missouri Automated Psychiatric History, or MAPS (Eaton, Sletten, Kitchen, and Smith, 1971). The MAPS consists of approximately 200 questions, each of which is printed on a separate prepunched card. It was designed to be completed by a relative (most commonly a parent or spouse) at the time of patient's admission to psychiatric hospital. Each card is sorted into one of six pockets of an expanding envelope, which is then brought or mailed back to the hospital. Items cover nine general categories, including depression and suicide, work and interpersonal relationships, childhood and adolescence, and genetic factors. Two procedures were employed to check on the accuracy of the information provided: (1) six questions are asked to which the answers are already known, and (2) the number of answers that are clearly "impossible" can be determined. These checks showed satisfactory responding for almost all respondents (Eaton, Altman, Schuff, and Sletten, 1970). In addition, test-retest reliability was reported to be comparable to that found in other studies using relatives as informants.

The MAPS was subsequently refined through factor analytic procedures and shortened to a new instrument of 98 items, entitled the Community Adjustment Profile System, or CAPS (Evenson, Sletten, Hedlund, and Faintich, 1974). Separate norms for men and women were developed for scales assessing 10 separate areas of adjustment, such as depression, work problems, and peculiar behavior. Usable responses on the CAPS were obtainable for about 60 percent of the patient population. A questionnaire form of the instrument was also developed. A number of studies have shown construct validity for the CAPS (Hedlund, Sletten, Evenson, Altman, and Cho, 1977).

Subjective Approaches

In addition to the structured use of objective personal history forms and biographical data blanks, these instruments are also widely used for the assessment of adjustment-related characteristics in an informal or subjective manner. When provided with this diverse array of data, the skilled clinician can develop many hypotheses about the personality characteristics of the respondent, much in the same fashion that many clinicians approach a Rorschach protocol. Besides the content of the blank, potential personality information can be provided by assessing aspects such as how neatly the blank has been completed, how completely information has been provided, and differences in how various questions are answered. The applicant for a job who lists under the category of Health History the fact that he/she had "measles—July, 1937" presumably is rather different in bodily concerns than the applicants who fail to record this rather trivial event.

There are many specific items on the blank whose content can provide relevant material about the personality of the respondent. The youthful applicant who reports owning an expensive sports car, although showing a modest income, has different needs and values from the person reporting several large life insurance policies. At least one commercially available form, the Worthington Personal History Blank (Spencer and Worthington, 1952), is specifically designed to maximize the availability of such data by deliberately minimizing the amount of structure provided for completing the form. For example, there is no information about whether pencil or pen should be used, or how the applicant's name is to be written—whether last name or given name should be written first. It should be noted that there are many other similar sources of written clinical data, including letters, diaries, and other personal documents (Allport, 1961). The obvious problem common to all of them lies in developing adequate methods for evaluating the usefulness and accuracy of the inferences which are drawn by the clinician.

On-Line Computer Technology

A recent development in mental health assessment contexts is the use of on-line computer procedures for collecting biographical data. The client sits in front of a visual display unit and responds to the questions presented there by means of either a typewriter terminal or push buttons. It is also possible for the computer to communicate audibly, through the use of a tape deck and a library of tape-recorded segments arranged for rapid access.

One advantage of on-line procedures is their ability to present branching questionnaires in a form that is easy to work with. For example, one question might ask whether the client is fully satisfied sexually. If the response given is yes, the program moves on to another area of questioning. If the response is no, the program asks a systematic series of questions directed at that topic. Another advantage is that responses can be processed directly by the computer and printed out in some integrated manner. A third advantage is the immediacy with which the report can be available to the clinician. One disadvantage of on-line computer procedures is the initial cost of the equipment and of developing the programs. Therefore, a substantial volume of use would be needed to make the procedure cost-effective. The computer technology aspects of on-line assessment are discussed further in Chapter 10.

An early example of the collection of personal data by computer interaction was described by Stillman, Roth, Colby, and Rosenbaum (1969). These authors developed a computer program which they entitled CASE (for Computer Assisted Special Enquirer). Areas of inquiry include past history, present illness, and mental functioning. Questions can be either multiple choice, to which the client at a typewriter terminal would respond by making an *x,* or open ended, for which the client would type in the information. An illustrative segment of their branching program is shown in Figure 6-2. The authors reported that even severely disturbed patients could answer computer-presented questions without assistance. Another example of the on-line collection of personal data has been described by Johnson and Williams (1975, 1980) as one aspect of a comprehensive computerized assessment system in a mental health context.

Research on Life Events

The relationship between life events and mental health disorders is being increasingly studied as a research area in its own right. Some initial work in this area was done by Langner and Michael (1963), who sought to identify early stressful events in a person's life that were related to later difficulties. Influenced by the writings of Adolf Meyer, interest shifted to a focus on more recent events—within the previous 3, 6, or 12 months—as predictors of current mental health and general stress level. For example, Holmes and Rahe (1967) asked subjects to rate a number of life events according to the amount and duration of change in their accustomed pattern of life that would result from each event. Their Social Readjustment Rating Scale is a list of mean readjustment values for 43 different life events. When the item "death of spouse" was set at a value of 100, "pregnancy" was valued at 40, "change in residence" at 20, and "jail term" at 63. Subsequent researchers have extended the work of Holmes and Rahe into the development of other procedures for assessing stresses associated with life events. For example, Coddington (1972) studied life events as an etiological factor in diseases of children, while Kobasa (1979) attempted to explain why life stresses led to disorders in some people but not others. Kobasa found distinct personality differences between the two groups, which she characterized as differences in *hardiness.*

Overall, it can be said that the use of biographical or life history data for personality assessment has substantial research support. However, there are problems inherent in this method that should not be overlooked. For example, items could be subject to falsification, since many are rather obvious in the sense that the "correct," or socially desirable, answer can readily be ascertained. While this undoubtedly poses a problem in many situations, distortion may not be as widespread as might be thought. For example, Walsh (1967, 1968) showed that data collected by the self-report method were acceptably accurate even when respondents were given financial incentives to distort their responses. Other potential problems involve the coaching of applicants in personnel selection situations and uncertainties as to how much continued cross-validation of scoring procedures is needed. Finally, the clinical or subjective use of the data depends heavily upon the skill and acumen of the individual clinician, and this process requires careful and realistic self-monitoring.

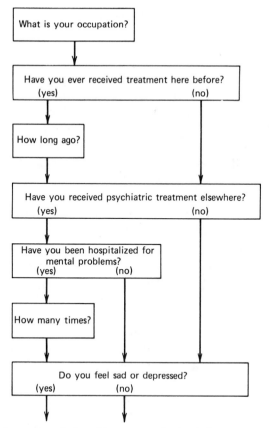

FIGURE 6-2. Sample segment of a branching program for the on-line computer collection of personal data. From Stillman, Roth, Colby, and Rosenbaum (1969). Copyright 1969, the American Psychiatric Association. Reprinted by permission.

INTERVIEWING

The Interview

An *interview* can be regarded as a special kind of conversation between two people: the interviewer (a trained professional, who is attempting to understand and assess the other) and the subject, or interviewee. The interview is distinguished from ordinary conversation by its purposive and probing nature. Much has been written on this complex and involved subject (Bingham and Moore, 1959; Fear, 1978; Haynes and Wilson, 1979; Matarazzo, 1965; S.A. Richardson, Dohrenwend, and Klein, 1965; Sullivan, 1954), and it clearly is beyond our scope to give more than a broad outline of the procedure as used for personality assessment purposes. The role of the interview in personality change or psychotherapy is not discussed.

In general, there are two kinds of information available in the interview: information involved in the *content* of the subject's responses and information involved in the subject's *style,* or manner of relating to the interviewer. In the intake interview in a social service agency or mental hospital, for example, interviewers concentrate upon clarifying patients' presenting complaints, what they have previously done to alleviate these problems, and what they expect from the present situation. The basic question in an intake interview is why each patient is at the agency. In an employment interview, the focus is upon occupational and educational history, job and personal skills, motivation for the present job and for future advancement, and general suitability for work with the employer. The basic question here is whether the applicant is hirable. In a personal or case history interview the concern is with obtaining a more complete set of data about the individual for a specific purpose, such as research or psychotherapy treatment planning. The emphasis here is upon gathering as much data about the person as possible.

The purposes of assessment interviews can be categorized in a variety of different ways, and the preceding samples are offered simply for illustrative purposes. The important point is that, as with a biographical data sheet, the information supplied in an interview is useful for assessment and prediction. Indeed, it can be weighted and scored as in the weighted application blank procedure discussed previously. If this is the case, why should an interview be employed rather than the less time consuming and more readily available application blank or written biographical data questionnaire?

There are at least four reasons why a face-to-face interview might be preferred. First, the interview is less structured and more flexible than the application blank, permitting interviewers to vary their approach and their questions in order to maximize the possibility of openness and truthfulness. (This procedure would obviously not be possible in a highly structured and standardized interview where a predetermined schedule must be followed, such as interviews carried out by public opinion polls.) Second, related to the advantage of flexibility, the opportunity for the interviewer to establish *rapport,* or interpersonal warmth, before proceeding is frequently recognized as another important reason for preferring the interview. Third, there are situations in assessment for mental health purposes in which the client may be sufficiently disturbed or confused as to require careful individual attention in order to successfully communicate the needed information. The fourth advantage of interviewing is that it provides the opportunity to observe the subject directly in an interpersonal situation. The interviewer has an opportunity to observe the subject's reactions, both the obvious ones like blushing and long hesitations, and the more subtle ones like oblique, noninformative answers, all of which suggest that a fuller exploration of the topic under consideration would be appropriate.

One way of conceptualizing the interview is to regard subjects' total behavior as a sample of their interpersonal skills and their manner of approaching and dealing with others. The less structured interviews, which offer subjects few or no clear directions and permit great latitude in the areas to be covered, clearly provide interpersonal behavior samples. Of course, interviewers can deliberately play a role in order to evoke responses to particular kinds of "others." They can be deliberately casual and noncommittal, warm and sympathetic, or cold and rejecting. The OSS Assessment Staff, among others, developed stress interviews where subjects were harassed, criticized, pressured, and otherwise made uncomfortable in order to evaluate their resistance to stress (OSS Assessment Staff, 1948).

It is most important for all professional interviewers to know something about their social stimulus value and to be aware of the modal type of interpersonal situation they establish for their interviewees. There is considerable research evidence (Gottschalk and Gleser, 1969; Kahn and Cannell, 1957) that large differences exist among interviewers and that this may be an important variable in clinical practice and research. The use of the interview as an interpersonal behavior sample obviously requires considerable training and experience on the part of the interviewer in order for this technique to be useful for assessment purposes.

A major difficulty with the interview is the fact that interviewers themselves are fallible instruments. There is much evidence about the subtle cues that interviewers provide, cues of which they may themselves be unaware, that tend to guide and bias the outcome of the interview (Kahn and Cannell, 1957). It is also likely that interviewers tend to avoid probing in certain areas, those in which they themselves are anxious (Bandura, Lipsher, and Miller, 1960). These interviewer biases contribute to the general concern that is expressed about the utility of the interview as an assessment device. In a review of literature on the personnel selection interview, Guion (1976) concluded that the potential for adequate validity existed, but that there were wide differences in validity among different interviewers. Of particular interest are the findings that first impressions carry a disproportionate share of the weight for final decisions, and that negative information appears to carry more weight than positive information. Guion interpreted the research literature as supporting the use of structured rating scales as a means of operationally defining and coding the information obtained from interviewers. The research on objective versus subjective prediction in a clinical context, discussed in Chapter 8, also consistently supports this conclusion.

Interview Rating Instruments

As stated earlier, the most valid use of the interview technique for assessment purposes would seem to be in a structured context. The conclusions of Sawyer's (1966) review are particularly relevant here. Sawyer concluded that clinicians' most useful function was to provide ratings or judgments in as objective a manner as possible, using structured instruments developed for that purpose. In response to this mandate, there has been a rapid development of structured interview procedures, particularly in the mental health area. Many of these instruments are designed for computer scoring and interpretation, using some of the computer technology discussed in Chapter 10. Interview rating instruments are of two types: those that are designed to summarize the interview after it has been conducted, and complete interview guides that are designed to be utilized as a format in conducting the interview.

Interview Summary Instruments.   An early and well known instrument of this nature is the Brief Psychiatric Rating Scale (BPRS) (Overall and Gorham, 1962; Overall and Klett, 1972). Designed to provide a brief and reliable evaluation of symptomatology in hospitalized psychiatric patients, the BPRS consists of 16 ordered-category rating scales, each representing a carefully selected dimension. The basic idea was that each of the scales should represent a "primary dimension" of individual difference in psychiatric symptoms. All dimensions involve seven-point scales ranging from "not present" through "moderate" to "extremely severe." Examples are: somatic concern, anxiety, emotional withdrawal, conceptual disorganization, and guilt feelings. Overall and Klett (1972) have provided a more extensive description of each scale, plus extensive reliability and validity data on the BPRS as a whole.

Another summary instrument of a slightly different nature is the Missouri Automated Mental Status Examination Checklist (MS) (Hedland, Sletten, Evenson, Altman, and Cho, 1977; Sletten, Ernhart, and Ulett, 1970). The MS Checklist consists of a series of rating scales that cover nine areas of functioning: general appearance, motor behavior, speech and thought, mood and affect, other emotional reactions, thought content, sensorium, intellect, and insight and judgment. If any abnormality is observed in an area, it is indicated on the appropriate rating scale with a description of 1, 2, or 3 (mild, moderate, or severe). A total of 119 possible ratings can be made, but the interviewer rates only those items that are relevant. The rating scales are arranged on a single page, and on a second page the patient's standard psychiatric diagnosis is indicated by checking the appropriate box. The interviewer, a psychiatrist, conducts a normal psychiatric interview in which patients are encouraged to tell their own stories in an atmosphere of interest and concern, and the ratings are made at the completion of the interview.

The MS is seen by its developers as a traditional mental status examination in most respects. It was developed through consultation with standard textbooks and rating forms, and it can be completed after a single interview. It is a current status examination and is not a substitute for a longitudinal case history. Some evidence for the construct validity of the MS Checklist is available (Hedland, Sletten, Evenson, Altman, and Cho, 1977).

A somewhat similar instrument is the Mental Status Examination Record (MSER) (Spitzer and Endicott, 1971). The MSER is a four-page computer form designed to provide an objective record of the traditional mental status examination. It contains rather extensive instructions to the rater, including definitions of the terms used. There are 16 traditional mental status categories involving a total of 121 checklist items and 156 rating scales. Not all the items need be rated, but it is suggested that all should be considered. The time required to fill out the form after an interview is said to be five to ten minutes. Computer processing of the MSER yields a score on each of 20 derived scales, such as anger-negativism, hallucinations, somatic concern, and judgment. These scales were derived from factor analysis of the MSER protocols of 2,000 subjects (MSIS, 1973), and they are said to provide rapid identification of the patient's most severely affected domain of behavior. Reliability and validity data are not readily available, however.

Interview Guides. In contrast to the three instruments already described, which were designed to be completed after the interview or observations, the following instruments are intended as structured guides to be utilized by trained interviewers.

Thus, the possibility exists for their use by nonprofessional personnel, and some instruments in this family have been explicitly designed for that purpose, while others are said to be appropriate only for use by mental health professionals. On this topic, a recent study on one such instrument, the Renard Diagnostic Interview (Helzer, Robins, Croughan, and Welner, in press), has shown that lay interviewers with specific training could indeed use that instrument as satisfactorily as psychiatrists.

The Psychiatric Anamnestic Record (PAR) (Spitzer and Endicott, 1971; MSIS, 1973) is basically a highly structured interview schedule that can be administered by personnel with relatively little clinical experience, provided they are specifically trained with the schedule. The format is a four-page booklet containing multiple-choice questions and rating scales designed to cover the information that is usually included in a psychiatric case history. A major section deals with psychopathological signs and symptoms, judged over two time periods: from age 12 up to the last month, and within the last month. The PAR is oriented toward information that is known to be relevant in evaluating degree of disturbance, diagnosis, and probability of improvement. The output is a computer-generated narrative. Validity data on the PAR tend to be limited to subjective evaluations of its clinical utility.

The Current and Past Psychopathology Scales, or CAPPS (Endicott and Spitzer, 1972), represents a combination of the purposes and methodologies of previous instruments. Basically a research instrument, the CAPPS combines an existing instrument for assessing a patient's current status with a "past" section consisting of 130 additional scales and items relating to psychopathology, personality characteristics, and academic, occupational, and interpersonal adjustment. The latter section is an elaborated version of the Psychiatric Anamnestic Record, already described. As with the other instruments in this family, the CAPPS incorporates a highly structured interview schedule, which enables it to be administered by any specifically trained person. The information for completing the CAPPS can be limited to a single source, such as the patient, or it can be additionally based on case records or other informants. The administration booklet contains 477 items and rating scales, plus detailed instructions for administration and rating.

Most of the judgments are recorded on uniform six-point rating scales that take into account both the duration and severity of the characteristic. The output from the CAPPS consists of scores on 26 factor-based symptom summary scales, eight of which are derived from the "current" section and 18 from the "past" section. The output also includes a bar graph of standard scores on the 26 scales. The dimensions reflected in both sets of factors are said to be clinically familiar and are commonly used in describing psychiatric patients. Examples of the scales are: current—disorganization, reality testing-social disturbance, and depression-anxiety; and past—manic, depression-anxiety, and organicity. Endicott and Spitzer (1972) reported a substantial amount of research with the scales, demonstrating high reliabilities and discriminative ability for a variety of subject groups. They also reported the use of data from the CAPPS as the basis for the development of a computer program for providing a psychiatric diagnosis. Such programs are discussed in Chapter 10.

Recent advances have extended the technology of structured interviewing in the mental health industry even further, to address the long-standing problem of the low reliability of psychiatric diagnostic categories. Two major sources of unreliability that lead to disagreement among diagnosticians can be termed *criterion variance* and *information variance* (Spitzer, Endicott, and Robins 1978). To reduce criterion variance, these authors developed a series of carefully defined and reliable rules, termed the Research Diagnostic Criteria. To reduce information variance, structured interview schedules are being developed that are geared to different overall diagnostic categories. For example, the Schedule for Affective Disorders and Schizophrenia, or SADS (Endicott and Spitzer, 1978, 1979), is a structured interview schedule that, when utilized correctly, ensures adequate coverage of critical areas of psychopathology and general functioning so that all the data needed are obtained for making a diagnosis within the domains of schizophrenia and affective disorders. While a great deal of additional work remains to be done in the development of this system, it appears to be a promising and worthwhile project.

QUANTIFICATION OF OBSERVATIONS

In Chapters 5 and 6 thus far we have concentrated on a rather holistic approach to the data obtained in behavioral observations and interview judgments, and we have made passing references to rating procedures and other attempts at quantifying the data. We now examine in greater detail these quantification procedures and some of the inherent problems involved in using them.

A *rating scale* is a form or device by which observers can record their observations or judgments about the behavior of another person in some predetermined, ordered fashion. Rating scales may be filled out either during or after the observation, and the observations can be complete and wide ranging or incomplete and circumscribed. In principle, just about any data can be quantified by rating procedures, although consideration must be given to issues such as interrater agreement and possible rater biases. The form of the rating scale for personality assessment may range from a simple list of adjectives to be checked (e.g., Gough and Heilbrun, 1964) to scales of generalized characteristics such as overall psychological adjustment or extraversion-introversion.

One common procedure for making such ratings is the graphic rating scale. In the simplest form, shown in Figure 6-3, respondents mark a point on the line between the two extremes that best corresponds to the subject's characteristics. It is left to the rater to determine what is meant by different degrees of the dimension, in this case introversion-extraversion. Sometimes, as shown in Figure 6-3, each end of the rating scale is "anchored" with an extended description to characterize each extreme of the dimension. Raters may also be instructed that the different points between the extremes should be taken to represent equal intervals on the dimension. Sometimes the raters are asked to circle one of the numbers, and sometimes the instructions permit the raters to place a mark anywhere at all along the continuum. In the latter case, a number (either a fractional number or the nearest whole number) would be assigned later to each rating.

1	2	3	4	5
Introverted				*Extraverted*
Careful				Enjoys excitement
Thorough				Impulsive
Quiet				Loud
Thoughtful				Socially outgoing
Internalizes				Active
feelings				Verbally facile
Overcontrolled				Externalizes
Contemplative				feelings
Conscientious				Unreliable
Etc.				Etc.

FIGURE 6-3. Graphic rating scale for the trait for introversion-extraversion.

A rating scale can be unipolar or bipolar, depending on the dimension being assessed. The trait of introversion-extraversion is considered bipolar in nature, so that the "neutral" point of the rating scale (Figure 6-3) occurs in the middle, and the numbers representing this dimension could also have appropriately been 2, 1, 0, 1, 2. Other concepts may be unipolar, such as anxiety, leadership, sales ability, and schizophrenia. In these instances, there is no "neutral" point in the middle of the scale, and the low end of the dimension is simply the absence of the characteristic of interest.

A more sophisticated form of rating scale contains anchoring descriptions along all parts of the scale. A good example is seen in the Global Assessment Scale, or GAS (Endicott, Spitzer, Fleiss, and Cohen, 1976), shown in Figure 6-4. This scale was developed "for evaluating the overall functioning of a subject during a specified time period on a continuum from psychological or psychiatric sickness to health" (p. 766). The information needed to make the GAS rating can come from any source, such as case records or a direct interview with the patient. No special skills are said to be necessary to use the scale. Data reported by Endicott et al. show satisfactory reliability for the GAS and also adequate sensitivity to change over time.

Ordinarily, a range of five to seven points on a structured rating scale is regarded as adequate to produce a sufficient dispersion of ratings for discriminating among subjects. If there are only a few judges available, a rating technique allows more opportunity for differentiating among subjects than does a dichotomous task such as an adjective checklist, on which items such as "aggressive" or "flexible" are either endorsed or not endorsed as descriptive of the subject without regard to different degrees of applicability. Satisfactory discrimination on an adjective checklist can be obtained when there are a larger number of judges involved, and the subject's "score" on an item can be the number of times it is checked by the pool of judges.

Rating scales tend to produce fairly good interjudge agreement, and they are widely used in personality research because of the paucity of readily available measures of the behaviors or traits under study. There are, however, certain kinds of

Rate the subject's lowest level of functioning in the last week by selecting the lowest range which describes his functioning on a hypothetical continuum of mental health-illness. For example, a subject whose "behavior is considerably influenced by delusions" (range 21−30) should be given a rating in that range even though he has "major impairment in several areas" (range 31−40. Use intermediary levels when appropriate (eg, 35, 58, 63). Rate actual functioning independent of whether or not subject is receiving and may be helped by medication or some other form of treatment.

100
|
91   No symptoms, superior functioning in a wide range of activities, life's problems never seem to get out of hand, is sought out by others because of his warmth and integrity.

90
|
81   Transient symptoms may occur, but good functioning in all cases, interested and involved in a wide range of activities, socially effective, generally satisfied with life, "everyday" worries that only occasionally get out of hand.

80
|
71   Minimal symptoms may be present but no more than slight impairment in functioning, varying degrees of "everyday" worries and problems that sometimes get out of hand.

70
|
|
61   Some mild symptoms (e.g., depressive mood and mild insomnia) OR some difficulty in several areas of functioning, but generally functioning pretty well, has some meaningful interpersonal relationships and most untrained people would not consider him "sick."

60
|
51   Moderate symptoms OR generally functioning with some difficulty (e.g., few friends and flat affect, depressed mood, and pathological self-doubt, euphoric mood and pressure of speech, moderately severe antisocial behavior).

50
|
|
41   Any serious symptomatology or impairment in functioning that most clinicians would think obviously requires treatment or attention (e.g., suicidal preoccupation or gesture, severe obsessional rituals, frequent anxiety attacks, serious antisocial behavior, compulsive drinking).

40
|
|
31   Major impairment in several areas, such as work, family relations, judgment, thinking, or mood (e.g., depressed woman avoids friends, neglects family, unable to do housework), OR some impairment in reality testing or communication (e.g., speech is at times obscure, illogical, or irrelevant), OR single serious suicide attempt.

30
|
|
21   Unable to function in almost all areas (e.g., stays in bed all day), OR behavior is considerably influenced by either delusions or hallucinations, OR serious impairment in communication (e.g., sometimes incoherent or unresponsive) or judgment (e.g., acts grossly inappropriately).

20
|
|
11   Needs some supervision to prevent hurting self or others, or to maintain minimal personal hygiene (e.g., repeated suicide attempts, frequently violent, manic excitement, smears feces), OR gross impairment in communication (e.g., largely incoherent or mute).

10
|
1   Needs constant supervision for several days to prevent hurting self or others, or makes no attempt to maintain minimal personal hygiene.

FIGURE 6-4. The Global Assessment Scale. From Endicott, Spitzer, Fleiss, and Cohen (1976). Copyright 1976, American medical Association.

rater errors which are particularly bothersome and which should not be ignored. Similar errors are doubtless involved in all personality assessment, but they are seen most clearly in their effects upon ratings. One is the tendency to produce *constant errors* or biases in filling out a rating scale. Thus, one rater may rarely or never use low ratings, while another might rarely use high ratings. A related problem is the *generosity error,* where raters systematically tend to give subjects highly favorable evaluations. Such ratings are of little value since they do not discriminate satisfactorily between individuals. Another related problem exists when raters have only limited opportunities to observe the subject and therefore may not have enough data to make certain ratings. Under these circumstances the so-called *halo effect* may become important, where the rater overgeneralizes from the evidence available, especially if it tends to be positive.

A number of procedures have been developed to reduce rating errors. Constant errors can be reduced by statistically transforming raters' scores into some type of standard score which will compensate for their constant errors and, to a lesser degree, for their leniency errors. Asking for specific behavioral or anecdotal data to support a particular rating is also an effective technique for reducing these errors. The halo effect can be reduced in the same way, especially if there is an opportunity for the rater to use a category like "insufficient data to make this rating." Another technique to reduce rating errors is the *forced-choice* technique (Richardson, 1949; Scott, 1968). Here, the rater is forced to choose which of two traits or phrases, closely matched on favorability, is the more descriptive of the subject.

A further technique that can be used when there are several subjects to evaluate is to have the observer rank-order the individuals on the trait dimension under consideration. When the group to be ranked is rather large, they can be ordered into a specified distribution along the trait dimension such as a seven- or nine-point forced-normal distribution. A "forced" distribution means that the number of individuals to be placed at each of the seven or nine points is specified in advance, and "forced normal" means that these numbers are specified in such a way that the resulting distribution will have approximately the same shape as the normal curve, with relatively few subjects at the most extreme points of the distribution and most of the group in the center. Such ranking procedures, however, are ipsative; that is, they only provide relative data about the group under study and do not indicate how the group would compare with any other group along some absolute dimension of the trait or how an individual from the group would compare with an individual from another group.

An important use of forced-distribution ranking procedures is the *Q-sort* (Block, 1961; Stephenson, 1953). The observer is given a deck of cards, each of which contains a single statement, such as "is basically anxious" or "communicates ideas clearly and effectively." The judge, who may also be the subject (in which case the Q-sort becomes a self-report measure), is then asked to rank-order the statements from most descriptive to least descriptive of the subject, using a forced-normal distribution for the ranking.

The items of the California Q-sort (Block, 1961) have themselves been rated (weighted) by trained clinicians for adjustment, so that this Q-sort for a particular person can be scored individually for adjustment. Another way in which the Q-sort has been used in personality assessment is to ask the subject to sort the cards once as "you actually are" and then again as "you would like to be." The discrepancy between these actual-self and ideal-self Q-sorts has been widely used in psychotherapy research as a criterion measure for personality change (Rogers and Dymond, 1954), with the expectation that successful psychotherapy would reduce this discrepancy. Marks and Seeman (1963), in another interesting use of the Q-sort, developed an "atlas" of Q-sort statements that are empirically correlated with various MMPI profiles.

The Q-sort method is a useful technique for both clinical and research purposes, especially for the description of complex or global personality attributes, but several problems should be noted. One concerns the nature of the items involved in a particular Q-sort deck and involves the problem of whether any manageable group of short statements can satisfactorily describe complex behavior or personality functioning. Another problem is created by the assumption that the descriptive statements can be "forced" into a normal distribution without producing biases. A third involves the fact that unless the Q-sort employed offers a comprehensive and unbiased coverage of the personality domain of interest, comparisons among the Q-sorts of different subjects will not yield satisfactory results.

Peer assessment is the process by which people with the same status, such as classmates or fellow workers, judge each other on particular characteristics. Kane and Lawler (1978) have identified three related methods of peer assessment: rankings, ratings, and nominations. Peer *ranking* has been relatively little researched but has the potential for being the most discriminating method because of its particular psychometric properties.

Peer *rating* is a more commonly used procedure and is generally based upon extended observation in real-life situations. Peer ratings often produce evaluations of the subject which may be rather different from other judgments, a situation which reflects the different values of the peer and superordinate (or subordinate) subcultures. A rebellious college student who leads student protests may be seen as a leader by peers but as a malcontent and troublemaker by professors. Obviously, both kinds of information are relevant, but perhaps for different purposes. Peer ratings appear to be particularly useful for feedback purposes but tend to be less valid and more subject to biases than the other methods (Kane and Lawler, 1978).

In the peer *nomination* technique, each member of the peer group is asked to list or nominate a fixed number of persons who are group members and who are most prominent or visible in particular ways. As part of Peace Corps selection procedures, for example, all the members of a training group would be asked to nominate the five trainees they would: (1) most like to be assigned with overseas; (2) least like to be assigned with overseas, (3) regard as the most successful, and so on. Unpublished research on Peace Corps peer ratings indicates that they were consistently successful in predicting overseas success. Similar findings of the predictive efficiency of peer nominations were reported for military personnel (Downey, Medland, and Yates, 1976) and a variety of other occupational groups. While the peer nomination technique appears to have the highest reliability and validity of the three methods, a serious problem, especially in the context of selection, is the high degree of anxiety about the task and antagonism toward the investigator which may be aroused.

A close variant of the nomination technique is the sociometric rating, developed by Moreno (1934), which is used to study the social structure of small groups. All persons in such a group are asked to choose one or more other group members with whom they would like to work, play, sit near, and so forth; and also to choose those whom they wish to avoid. The patterns of likes and dislikes are then given pictorial representation by plotting them on a sociogram. From the sociogram, the small cliques within the group can be identified, as can the leader, or "star," and the social isolate.

For young children, nominations can be obtained by the "guess who" technique (Hartshorne and May, 1929) where members of the group are asked to "guess who" is the class athlete, the one who plays games best; or who is the class bully, the one who is always annoying or picking on the other children. The number of times each child is nominated under such rubrics constitutes his/her score on that dimension.

Peer ratings are readily obtainable, and they represent quite a useful approach to personality measurement. In the past they have been employed primarily in research and in personnel selection. For other purposes, such as clinical assessment, they have rarely been used in spite of the important vantage which they seem to offer in understanding individual behavior.

The *semantic differential* (Osgood, 1952; Osgood, Suci, and Tannenbaum, 1957) is a rating technique originally developed as a tool for assessing the meaning of concepts. The individual rates the concept or person on a series of seven-point bipolar adjective scales, such as simple-complicated or cruel-kind. Factor analytic studies have shown that the majority of the adjective scales which have been employed in these ratings can be summarized in three factors: (1) evaluation (which incorporates adjective scales such as good-bad and kind-cruel), (2) activity (e.g., fast-slow and active-passive), and (3) potency (e.g., strong-weak and large-small). Wide use has not been made of this tool as a means of clinical personality description; rather, it has been utilized as a research instrument. One good example of research use is Nunnally's (1961) extensive study of public attitudes toward concepts in the field of mental health. Thus, professionals who treat physical disorders received higher ratings on the "evaluative" dimension than professionals who treat mental disorders. Also, the mentally ill were rated by both the public and by general medical practitioners as dangerous, unintelligent, and unpredictable.

Summary

Biographical data and information regarding recent and current events are utilized for assessment in a wide variety of applications. Research in the technology of assessment has demonstrated the great importance of using structured and objective procedures in gathering such data. Considerable use has been made of biographical data for personality assessment purposes, particularly in personnel selection. Personal history data as provided on a formal job application blank can be examined impressionistically as a basis for forming hypotheses about a candidate. The weighted biographical data sheet provides an empirical approach in which a score is determined from weights assigned to various personal and biographical items. Personal history data have also been used empirically to predict the outcome of schizophrenia, and for other specific uses such as the assessment of social competence, shyness, and children's problems. There is increasing interest in the development of structured, multiscale instruments based on biographical data that can be used as an integral aspect of computerized assessment systems for mental health purposes on a large scale. Intuitive or projective interpretations can also be made from an individual's biographical data sheet, although the accuracy of such an approach is not proven. On-line computer procedures for the self-report of biographical data have also been developed. The question of possible falsification of self-reports needs to be considered, although it is generally thought not to be a serious problem.

The interview is a common means of obtaining biographical data and also provides an opportunity for direct observation and for flexibility on the part of the interviewer. Research on the interviewing process suggests that a variety of interviewer biases can operate, and that interviews which are structured or limited in purpose are the most likely to provide valid information. Two kinds of structured instruments are available. Interviewer summary instruments are designed to summarize the interview after completion. A brief instrument of this kind is the Brief Psychiatric Rating Scale, and more extensive forms include the Missouri Automated Mental Status Checklist and the Mental Status Examination Record. Both of the latter instruments are incorporated into comprehensive computerized assessment systems. Interviewer guides are intended as structured guides to be utilized in conducting the interview and require trained interviewers but not necessarily professional personnel. One comprehensive instrument of this type is the Current and Past Psychopathology Scales, which includes 477 items, most of them in a six-point rating scale format, with detailed instructions to the interviewer. The CAPPS yields scores on 26 factor-based symptom summary scales. Recent attention has been paid to the development of instruments that offer increased reliability in assessing patients according to traditional psychiatric diagnostic categories.

How are systematic observations quantified? Perhaps the most common technique is some variant of the rating scale, an approach which can be applied to just about any kind of data. Problems with rating scales include possible rater biases or constant errors, unwillingness to give low or undesirable ratings, and the "halo effect," where a rater overgeneralizes from limited evidence. One method for reducing rater errors is the forced-choice technique, in which the rater is forced to choose which of two descriptions, matched on favorability, is the more applicable. A variant of this technique is the Q-sort, in which the rater arranges a series of cards, each containing a personality statement, in order from least to most descriptive of the individual. Peer assessment, the process by which people with the same status judge each other on particular characteristics, can involve rankings, ratings, or nominations. The semantic differential, another rating procedure originally developed as a tool for assessing the meaning of concepts, also has applicability in personality assessment.

7 PSYCHOMETRIC CONSIDERATIONS

The first six chapters have provided an overview of the nature of personality assessment, its history, and the common methods for performing it. This chapter deals in more detail with two concepts, *reliability* and *validity*, which are basic to an adequate understanding of the scope and limitations of different assessment methods. Also discussed are systematic irrelevancies, or *response distortions*, which affect the utility of personality assessment procedures, including the problem of attempts to present a misleading impression, or *defensiveness* and *faking*.

Reliability, as its name implies, has to do with the reproducibility or dependability of a measure. To take a very simple example, let us say that yesterday we have measured a child's height as 48.3 inches. Today somebody else measures the same child, and gives a report of 48.4 inches. We doubtless would consider that the two measures are in good agreement with each other; that is, we would consider the initial measurement of the child's height to have been verified or reproduced. The .1 inch discrepancy reflects the fact that repeated measurements almost always will be slightly inconsistent or unreliable, while our satisfaction with the result shows that the inconsistency is small enough for the results to be useful to us. Thus, the discrepancy of .1 inch is so small under these circumstances that it can be regarded as inconsequential. In other cases of physical measurement, however, where the tolerance levels are quite small, as in an engine cylinder, such a difference would be practically important, and a higher level of reliability of measurement would be required.

We should note that reliability is not the same as precision. Precision refers to the exactness with which the measurement can be specified; thus, a measuring procedure which permits us to report to the nearest one-thousandth of an inch would be more precise than one permitting a report only to the nearest tenth of an inch. A mechanical gauge which gave a reading of 2.432 inches would have precision to one-thousandth of an inch, but if a second reading gave 2.381 inches, the reliability of the measurement would be nowhere near the precision indicated by the instrument.

The requirement that measurements be made "accurately enough" is also applicable to personality assessment. Compared with the measurement of physical characteristics such as height, personality measurement has always been rather sloppy; that is, somewhat unreliable. Thus, one point of concern affecting any decision to utilize a personality assessment device should be its reliability, and such instruments ordinarily have some index of reliability available for the potential user. We shall return to the matter of reliability in a moment.

In personality measurement there is an additional difficulty, which is not present with the common physical measurements. In common physical measurement there are generally agreed-upon standards against which measurements are made. There is no question that a yardstick (or a meterstick) is appropriate for measuring linear distances, like body height. In personality assessment, however, questions are frequently raised about the legitimacy of the measuring device for assessing or evaluating the dimension under scrutiny. For example, can one really measure depression by counting the number of achromatic color responses given on the Rorschach? In this case, there is not only the question of a reliable count of the number of these responses but there is the further and more serious problem of demonstrating that counting achromatic color responses results in a legitimate measure of depression, in the sense that the markings on a yardstick result in a valid measure of height. (It is interesting to note that the legitimacy or validity of the measuring instruments employed also becomes a problem in physical measurement in cases where very high degrees of precision are required.) Since it is necessary to be able to measure something with adequate reliability before we can determine whether the measure in fact is related to the concept of concern, we shall discuss reliability first. A practical guide to both reliability and validity in psychological tests has been prepared by the American Psychological Association (1974), and this guide should be studied carefully by all persons who are actively engaged in either the construction or use of personality assessment devices. A analogous guide for specific use in the area of personnel selection has recently been published by the American Psychological Association's Division of Industrial-Organizational Psychology (1980). The latter guide pays particular attention to issues of validity and criterion development, and is a valuable reference source on those topics.

RELIABILITY

Reliability refers to the repeatability or dependability of measurement. In a hypothetical situation where the measuring procedure was completely reliable, it would be assumed that any change in the obtained measure reflected a true change in the attribute under study. Thus, in such a system, an increase of one pound on a scale would indicate that the object has gained exactly one pound of weight; and similarly, an increase in the score on a depression scale indicates that the respondent now is more depressed. *Reliability* is the more generic term, and the terms *consistency* and *stability* are employed to describe instrument-related and time-related reliability, respectively.

Consistency refers to the agreement that is obtained by simultaneously using two or more instruments (e.g., scales, rulers, or tests). Any measuring instrument or set of instruments may be regarded as being drawn from a large population of such instruments (real or hypothetical) that might have been used to measure this particular attribute. Consistency is usually evaluated by simultaneous testing with another instrument or instruments, hopefully selected randomly from the available population. Although this poses little problem in the measurement of physical dimensions such as height or weight, it raises some difficult problems in personality assessment, problems to which we shall return shortly.

Stability refers to the accuracy of the obtained measurement over time. Obviously, retesting over time may involve consistency as well as stability if another instrument is used to make the second measurement. If the same instrument is used on both occasions, then we have a direct assessment of the stability of the measurement. Failure to obtain complete reliability is thus a consequence of the inconsistencies or errors that are a function of changes occurring in the system over time, or of differences associated with the particular instrument used, or both.

In general, *reliability* refers to many kinds of evidence which attempt to describe the agreement among measurement operations. Each bit of evidence emphasizes or focuses upon a certain source of disagreement or error and may overlook others. Personality measurement involves taking a sample of behavior at a particular time on a particular day in response to a particular set of stimuli, the responses being recorded by a particular examiner according to a particular system. Some sampling errors are associated with each of these "particulars." The particular occasion is a sample from a period of time, and the particular set of stimuli or questions is a sample from the previously mentioned real or hypothetical array of available stimuli. The particular test administrator, observer, or scorer, as well as the scoring system used, are likewise single instances from real or hypothetical populations. It is important to be able to identify how much a particular response or score is likely to change as a function of changes in each of these aspects of measurement. Unfortunately, however, this type of information is rarely available in personality assessment.

Examination of textbooks on psychometric theory (e.g., Ghiselli, 1964; Horst, 1966; Nunnally, 1978) shows that experts differ on the philosophical assumptions to be made about the basis of psychological measurement. These differences in philosophy give rise to some differences in defining exactly what is meant theoretically by reliability and thus lead to differences in the recommended ways of assessing the reliability of a measure. In this chapter we try to steer a middle course through the various approaches, while attempting to avoid inconsistencies as well as issues which are beyond the scope of the book.

We begin with the observation that reliability is closely related to the concept of measurement error. Errors of measurement can be considered to be of two kinds—*systematic* and *random*. If we observed the time from a clock which was always five minutes fast, we would be making a systematic error. If on the other hand, the clock was accurate but was always so distant from us that we were unable to read the minute hand precisely, we would be making a random error. Systematic errors can be thought of as associated with correctable mistakes; random errors, which tend to average about the correct or absolute score, can be regarded as the "fuzziness" left in the observation when all the systematic biases have been identified and removed.

To put it another way, random measurement errors are "built into" the measuring procedure, as when we try to measure to the nearest tenth of an inch with a yardstick marked only in inches, or when we try to assess "depression" with an omnibus paper-and-pencil inventory scale that contains very few items dealing with the reportable clinical aspects of depression that are necessary to cover the concept of depression as it is typically understood. In contrast to these random types of error, which are difficult to avoid, systematic errors are more identifiable and more easily correctable. In a sense, systematic errors are the fault of the test developer or user rather than being inherent in the instrument. We would be risking systematic error if we administered a depression scale to subjects who lived in a different culture (or subculture) from that represented by the available norms, or if we used stressful instructions which were markedly different from those used with the normative population. These potential systematic errors can and should be corrected by developing new norms based on the appropriate cultural group or for the alternate testing conditions.

In their attempts to quantify reliability, psychometric theorists traditionally have concentrated on specifying the contribution of *random errors* to low reliability. Opinions differ on whether and to what extent *systematic errors* also should be considered a source of unreliability of measurement, and hence reflected in a numerical index of reliability. Each of the several commonly used measures of reliability reflects random error; each may also reflect some (but not all) of the sources of systematic error. The most recent revision of the American Psychological Association's (1974) *Standards for Educational and Psychological Tests,* in recognizing that "different methods of estimating reliability take account of different sources of error" (p. 49), recommends that investigators make clear exactly what sources of variability in scores are regarded as contributing to "error" in the particular reliability measure which they report.

Let us now consider the common methods for assessing reliability. The traditional index of reliability is the *reliability coefficient,* which can be regarded either as the correlation between the actual test scores and hypothetical "true" scores, or as the average correlation between the actual test scores and all other possible tests measuring the same characteristic. The following practical approaches to assessing reliability attempt to approximate this definition.

As we have implied, reliability associated solely with random error (errors stemming from the fact that the content of the test is but one sample of the universe of content covering the characteristic of interest) is termed the consistency or internal consistency of a test. This can be assessed in various ways. One method, statistically sophisticated and involving complex assumptions, is by means of the *Kuder-Richardson reliability* formulas (Kuder and Richardson, 1937). The most useful of these formulas involves the percentage of items scored in a particular way, the correlations between the items and the total score, and the standard deviation of the test. These data are entered into a formula which provides a good estimate of consistency, providing the test measures only one statistical factor. The complexities of this approach are beyond our scope here but are considered in detail in most texts on psychometrics. Another procedure is to divide the test into two comparable halves and correlate one half with the other. The obtained correlation is then "corrected" to its expected value for the full length of the test by what is known as the Spearman-Brown prophecy formula. Such an estimate of consistency, often arrived at by contrasting the odd and the even items in a test, is known as the *split-half reliability coefficient*. A similar method for determining consistency is through the use of similar or *alternate* (or *parallel*) *forms* of the test, if they are available. The correlation between the forms is essentially similar to the corrected correlation between the two halves of the same form. When alternate forms are not available, a common compromise has been the use of a retest with the same form, and the correlation between the two sets of scores is termed the *test-retest reliability coefficient*.

Test-retest and alternate-forms correlations express more than the test's consistency. If the subjects remember some of the items when taking a retest, they might give the same answers purely from memory, a systematic effect which would have the result of spuriously increasing the correlation. Or, as previously noted, conditions from one testing session to the next might change, giving rise to unknown sources of systematic error. Yet again, the subjects themselves might change in the characteristic being measured. These last two circumstances would both serve to reduce the size of the reliability coefficient.

What particular method of computing a reliability coefficient should be employed in practice? A simple answer is that the coefficient should reflect the different kinds of errors in which the user is interested. Thus, if we wanted to know the test's reliability in assessing a concept, a consistency measure (Kuder-Richardson or split-half) would be appropriate. If we were interested in the test's stability in repeated administrations and under diverse conditions, then test-retest or alternate-forms reliability would be more appropriate. Hopefully, the test producer should provide both sets of data.

What are acceptable limits for reliability coefficients? To answer this question, we must look at the way in which these coefficients can be used practically. This ordinarily is done by means of the *standard error of measurement*, a quantity derived directly from the reliability coefficient and the standard deviation of the obtained scores. Representing the reliability coefficient by r, and the standard deviation by s, the standard error of measurement is the quantity $s\sqrt{1-r}$. To illustrate the meaning and use of the standard error of measurement, let us utilize the Sc scale of the MMPI. Internal consistency estimates (split-half correlation coefficients) for this scale have been reported to be in the neighborhood of .91 (Dahlstrom, Welsh, and Dahlstrom, 1975, p. 260). The standard deviation of all MMPI scales is 10 for scaled scores. The standard error of measurement can now be calculated from the formula to be $10\sqrt{1-.91}$, or 3. That is to say, if it were possible to carry out the same testing many times over, the Sc scores obtained would average out to be the "true" score, but they would be distributed about this average with a standard deviation of 3.

If a distribution of scores is not markedly asymmetrical, about two out of three scores fall within one standard deviation of the mean. Thus, the chances that the score obtained in any given test administration is within three points of the "true" score are about two out of three. To put it another way, if a respondent obtains a scale score of 55 on *Sc*, the chances are about two out of three that the "true" score is within three points of 55, that is, between 52 and 58. By similar reasoning, since about 95 percent of the scores in a reasonably symmetrical distribution fall within *two* standard deviations of its mean, the chances would be about 95 percent, or 19 in 20, that our respondent's true score would be within six points of 55, that is, between 49 and 61.

Suppose the reliability coefficient (split-half) were only .75 instead of .91, as appears to be somewhat nearer the case with the *D* scale of the MMPI (Dahlstrom, Welsh, and Dahlstrom, 1975, p. 260). With a standard deviation once again of 10, the formula shows the standard error of measurement to be $10\sqrt{1-.75}$, or 5. In practical terms, if a respondent obtained a score of 60 on the *D* scale, and we wanted to establish a range that would be 95 percent certain to include the "true" score, that range would be 50 through 70. Clearly, the lower the reliability coefficient, the less reliance can be placed on a score as an estimate of the "true" degree of the characteristic possessed by the respondent.

In concluding our discussion of reliability, it is worth nothing that Cattell (1964) has proposed three major ways in which "test consistency," the generic term he considers most preferable, might be measured. The first of these is the consistency or agreement of scores over occasions, that is, changes in the same test given to the same people at different times. Cattell calls this consistency "reliability." The second type of consistency is across tests (or parts of a test, or, commonly, single items) and involves the agreement on the same occasion and the same people over the tests (or parts). This consistency would be termed "homogeneity." The last kind of consistency is across people and involves the agreement as to the meaning of scores on the same test applied at the same time to different sets of people. This third type of consistency, labeled "transferability" (or hardiness), would seem to be an especially neglected aspect of reliability in its traditional sense. The transferability or generalizability of a personality assessment device over subcultures or generations is an important factor in determining limitations on its use.

Reliability and Projective Techniques

The quantitative scores derived from projective tests often have low reliabilities when assessed by the methods just described. Since the reliability of a measure sets an upper limit on its potential usefulness or validity, the low reliabilities often have been blamed for the low demonstrated validities in research investigations of these tests. On the other hand, it has also been argued that the usual methods for assessing reliability are not applicable to projective instruments. For example, the split-half method is said to be inappropriate for the Rorschach because it is impossible to divide the 10 cards in such a way as to obtain comparable halves. Test-retest reliability has been held inapplicable because a retest is regarded as a different psychological experience from the original test, and because projective techniques are said to be particularly sensitive to slight changes in the subject. Indeed, some proponents of projective tests seem to assume that such instruments are completely reliable and that the observed changes in test responses over time reflect real changes in the individual. Since many of the characteristics tapped by these tests, such as mood or energy level, do fluctuate over time, there is a certain cogency to this assumption. However, any real appreciation of the problems of reliability of measurement must lead to the conclusion that many, if not most, of these fluctuations are a function of the marginal reliability of the instruments.

There are certain measurement problems which contribute to unreliability in any test, but which tend to be particularly troublesome with projective devices. One problem has to do with test construction. In general, the stimulus materials used in projective tests have not been chosen with any thought toward ensuring that the various scoring categories would be adequately represented by the stimuli. For example, the mean number of human movement responses *(M)* for nonpatients on the Rorschach is only three, with a standard deviation of nearly two, while the mean for rare details *(Dd)* is only one (Exner, 1978). The reliability of such measurements is so low as to make the demonstration of validities a virtually impossible task.

It is often true, as with the TAT, that scoring systems were not developed until some years after the stimulus materials were selected. In the TAT, examiners even have a choice as to which stimulus they will employ. This haphazard development of scoring categories has also contributed to low reliabilities. Ratio (and difference) scores, as used in the Rorschach, are particularly vulnerable to low reliabilities. Holtzman, in developing the HIT, took care to select stimulus cards for their specific contribution to certain scoring quantities and, as a consequence, the reliabilities of most of the HIT categories are more satisfactory.

Another problem involves standardization of instructions. Directions for the administration of the Rorschach and a number of other projective instruments are not standardized, and thus the examiner can significantly influence the subject's responses. For example, Gross (1959) administered the Rorschach to 30 patients, and for 20 of them he gave social reinforcement after every human content response by saying "good" or by nodding his head. The reinforced patients gave significantly more human content responses than the remaining 10 patients. The importance of such subtle examiner differences, differences of which the examiner may be unaware, should be clear to the reader.

Even more vexing is the problem that subjects are permitted to give a varying number of responses, of varying lengths. The latter portion of a long response or set of responses is probably different in psychological content from a short response. Short responses on the Rorschach or TAT often tend to contain mainly "popular" or banal material. Also, variability in response length makes statistical comparisons extremely difficult.

There is also the problem of scoring. In some tests, such as the MMPI, scoring is mechanical. That is, little or no subjective judgment of the categorization of a response is involved. The same is true for some of the scoring categories in tests like the Rorschach. Here, for example, determining total number of responses given involves little or no judgment, once the data have been collected. Similarly, measuring the height of a figure drawing, or its total area, is a rather mechanical procedure. But by far the majority of scores derived from projective tests involve some subjective judgment in their determination. For example, does this Rorschach response involve color or human movement? Does this TAT story reflect the need for achievement, or affiliation, or both? In Rorschach tests, unreliability of scoring is aggravated by the fact that the several scoring systems available (Toomey and Rickers-Ovsiankina, 1977), although by no means identical, are similar enough that psychologists often tend to overlook the differences.

The question of scoring reliability is simply one of interjudge or intrajudge agreement, but it must be remembered that unreliability of scoring contributes to overall test unreliability. Murstein (1963, pp. 144–146) has presented a summary table of scorer reliabilities for characteristics scored from the TAT. The median scorer reliability of the 45 studies where reliability was reported as a correlation was .74. With scorer reliabilities as low as this, the problems of achieving acceptable levels of test reliability are indeed large. It is possible, however, to achieve higher scorer reliabilities. Feld and Smith (1958) and Holt (1978) have reported TAT data from several sources that show scorer reliabilities as high as .90. Such high reliabilities require care and effort and are the exception rather than the rule.

Reliability of Global Interpretation

Too close an involvement with these approaches to reliability determination involves a danger of missing what is, for practical purposes, the main issue involved in reliability. Tests are techniques for gathering information about personality and, usually, for making predictions about future behavior based on personality functioning. Thus, our ultimate concern with reliability should be for the reliability of the use to which the test is put. That is, if the Rorschach is employed to provide a comprehensive description of global personality functioning, then the issue is the reliability of the global descriptions, not the reliability of individual scoring categories.

What is involved in assessing global reliabilities? The procedures would be similar to those discussed previously. For example, split-half reliability would be assessed by comparing the interpretations made by examining comparable halves of the test, test-retest reliability would involve the comparison of interpretations made from two different administrations of the test, and interjudge reliability would be determined by comparing the interpretations made of the same test material by different judges. Interexaminer reliability could also be assessed in a similar fashion.

In order to make global personality descriptions which can be statistically compared with one another in this way, some common descriptive framework for personality is required. One typical procedure is to employ a series of rating scales or dimensions which are relevant to the test and to the kind of descriptive information required. Interpretation is then made by having the examiner assign scores or positions on these scales to the subjects following a study of the test protocol. A similar procedure would be to have the examiners answer a number of true-false or multiple-choice questions about the subject. Another common method is the use of the Q-sort technique. A typical Q-sort would consist of 100 cards, each containing a personality statement. The examiner is asked to study the test protocol and then to sort the descriptive statements into nine piles, representing equal intervals from least descriptive of the subject to most descriptive. The number of cards to be placed in each pile is determined in advance, so that every judge provides the same distribution of cards. In all these techniques, rank correlation or percentage agreement methods can be applied to determine a numerical index of reliability. (If one wishes to determine reliabilities involving a single examiner, the number of test protocols being judged should be sufficiently large that the examiner will not be able to remember, or guess, which ones came from the same subject.)

One kind of global approach to assessing reliability, the matching technique, has been especially recommended (Holzberg, 1960), and it is somewhat analogous to the matching procedure for assessing validity, described in Chapter 3. An application of this approach would be to have several examiners prepare a personality description from each of several Rorschach protocols, and then have another group of examiners attempt to match the descriptions to the Rorschachs. A major problem here is that correct matchings often can be made through using obvious cues, such as highly idiosyncratic responses, that are not particularly relevant to personality. This disadvantage is particularly important where the examiners are given a series of test and retest protocols to match, but it is of less concern if they are to match personality descriptions which are prepared in a standardized format.

The kind of reliability established for any assessment procedure should be appropriate for the use to which the procedure is to be put. If predictions about specific events are to be made, it is the reliability of these predictions which should be examined. If global personality descriptions are sought, it is their reliabilities which are at issue. Although there will often be more basic sources of reliability to consider (such as scorer reliability), on which the ultimate reliabilities may depend, it is the reliability of the procedure in use that is the question of ultimate interest.

Generalizability Theory

Mention should be made of one rather different approach to the question of reliability. Cronbach and his associates (e.g., Cronbach, Gleser, Nanda, and Rajaratnam, 1972) have proposed that the most basic issue in reliability is the question of being able to generalize from the observations or measurements involved to some other class of observations. In their view, the study of reliability should therefore be the study of the degree to which the obtained scores are representative of scores generated under other conditions, or from different "universes." Examples would be the study of scores across different scorers, test items, methods, observers, or occasions. As emphasized by Wiggins (1973) in a thorough discussion of this approach, a major advantage is that it forces investigators to be explicit about the particular "universe" to which they are interested in generalizing their observations. It also tends to blur somewhat the traditional distinction between reliability and validity. A good example of a quantitative study of generalizability has been reported by Jones, Reid, and Patterson (1975) on their Behavioral Coding System. In this study, the universes of generalization studied were subjects, observers, and occasions. The complexities of generalizability theory are beyond the scope of this book, and interested readers are referred to the sources named here for further information.

VALIDITY

In Chapter 3 we introduced the general notion of the *usefulness* of a test or assessment procedure, meaning the extent to which it permits us to understand and predict some of a person's nontest behavior. We have also used the word *validity* as more or less synonymous with usefulness. We now explore the concept of validity in greater detail.

The American Psychological Association's (1974) *Standards for Educational and Psychological Tests* considers the topic of validity to involve questions of matters of "what may properly be inferred from a test score; validity refers to the appropriateness of inferences from test scores or other forms of assessment" (p. 25). It has long been recognized that since different tests may have different types of aims, an approach which would be appropriate for demonstrating validity in one test might well be inappropriate for another. Three approaches to the assessment of validity are generally recognized, each being specific to a particular set of aims for a test: *content* validity, *criterion-related (predictive* and *concurrent)* validity, and *construct* validity. This threefold division in the purposes of a test is somewhat artificial, and generally it is necessary to demonstrate that a test possesses validity in more than a single way. Obviously, the establishment of validity requires much more than just the acceptance, by either the target person or the test user, of the personality description or prediction yielded by the test instrument. Forer (1949) clearly indicated the fallacy of such "testimonial" or "personal" validity in a study which demonstrated a uniformly high degree of acceptance by a sample of undergraduates of a single, identical personality description. The students were unaware that they all had received the same feedback. O'Dell (1972) went even further in showing that students believed that such "Barnum" reports were more accurate than real computer-generated test reports on themselves.

Content Validity

Content validity involves showing that the content of the test is representative of the behaviors in which we are interested. Content validity has special relevance for achievement and aptitude tests, where the responses to the test items presumably are samples of the behaviors of concern. Personality assessment by means of behavior samples and situational tests, as discussed in Chapter 5, also involves content validity by the direct elicitation of the relevant responses. For example, suppose we wished to develop a test of leadership, and we arranged for a series of behavioral samples which required the respondent to display behaviors characteristic of his/her responses to situational leadership demands. If these behavioral situations are a representative sample of leadership situations in general (or of some clearly identified subset of situations), and if the amount of artificiality introduced by the testing situation is minimized, we would have a valid test of leadership (or an aspect of it) simply by virtue of the fact that the *content* of the test is a representative sample of the behavior of interest. In a sense, the content validity of a test for a particular purpose is the same as the subjective evaluation of the criterion itself. If, however, the aim of a test is to predict behavior under somewhat modified real-life circumstances, such as leadership in combat, then more than content validity is required.

It sometimes is argued that paper-and-pencil personality inventories are valid simply if they appear to have content (or face) validity; that is, when they are rationally derived. Thus the presence on a depression scale of items referring to the experience of mood disturbance, loss of motivation for daily activities, and psychomotor retardation would be taken as reasonable grounds for the usefulness of the scale. But the clinical behaviors of depression cannot be sampled by the marking of an IBM true-false answer sheet. It is the nontest or real-life correlates of these marking responses that are of interest to us, and these must be demonstrated. Fortunately for test developers, we have already seen that rationality (or content validity) of a scale appears to be a necessary though not a sufficient condition for its usefulness.

Criterion-Related Validities

In personality assessment, because of its practical orientation, we often are most concerned with predictive validity in its various forms. Predictive validity refers to "the accuracy with which we can make guesses about one characteristic of an individual from another characteristic" (Ghiselli, 1964, p. 338). The test or assessment measure is called the "predictor," and the characteristic we are guessing at is known as the "criterion." A straightforward numerical index of predictive validity is given by the correlation between predictor and criterion. Predictive validity is central to the criterion groups approach to test construction. It would be the appropriate type of validity to be demonstrated if, for example, we wished to use patients' average elevations on the MMPI scales at the time of their admission to psychiatric treatment as an index of the length of time they would be hospitalized. The correlation between average elevation and days of subsequent hospitalization would be an index of the validity of average elevation as a predictor of hospitalization.

It is important to ensure that the criterion measure does not become "contaminated" with the predictor, otherwise the correlation may be spuriously high. That is to say, the overall elevation of the patient's MMPI profile in the previous example must be given no part in determining the length of his/her hospitalization. This means that both in the original criterion research and in the subsequent practical use of the predictor extreme care must be exercised in maintaining the confidentiality of the predictor scores. Otherwise such scores become "self-fulfilling prophecies."

There are as many different predictive validities for any given test as there are criteria to predict. The fact that average MMPI elevation might be found to predict length of hospitalization does not ensure its success in predicting likelihood of rehospitalization, even though both criteria might be considered measures of "success of treatment." Moreover, the fact that average elevation is found to predict length of hospitalization in one particular location and with one particular population does not automatically mean that it will be successful in another location. In the latter case, cross-validation with the new population should be carried out. The procedures involved in cross-validation and the dangers of a failure to do so have been discussed in Chapter 4. Cureton (1950) provided an appropriate and amusing illustration of this point. As a general rule, predictive validity should be demonstrated for every use to which an assessment procedure is to be put.

Criterion-related validity does not refer necessarily to prediction in the future, although it may. It is logical, and often useful, to consider prediction to a *concurrent* event, and also *postdiction* to an event that has previously occurred but cannot be measured directly without considerable effort. For example, let us say we wished to determine the nature and degree of the interpersonal needs of a group of college students. One method would be to have trained observers follow them about for a period of time, gathering information from real-life situations. Another would be to arrange a series of situational tests. A third approach could be to administer a paper-and-pencil inventory or have them judge themselves on a variety of rating scales. The inventory or self-ratings would represent attempts to make an economical determination of certain characteristics of the students which exist at that particular time. Validity then would be determined by arranging the more lengthy and costly behavior sample and situational test procedures, for which content validity has presumably been demonstrated, and using them as the criteria with which to compare the paper-and-pencil procedure. If these behavior samples or situational measures were available only at some future time, then we would again have future prediction.

Construct Validity

Construct validity is a term introduced by the American Psychological Association's (1954) original version of the *Standards,* and elaborated by Cronbach and Meehl (1955), to provide a label for a method of demonstrating validity which had been used to some extent prior to that time, but without a complete understanding of the logic and implications of the method. It is relevant where there exists no single definitive or tangible criterion for the quality, trait, or characteristic which is to be assessed.

Cattell (1964) pointed out that validity can be dimensionalized in a number of ways. One way involves the concrete versus the abstract or the particular versus the conceptual dimension. Frequently we are interested in the correlations between scores on a test and such particular or concrete criteria as the number of psychiatric hospitalizations or the number of traffic offenses. Predictive validity studies of this nature have considerable appeal because they are immediately useful and do not require much methodological or theoretical sophistication.

Often, however, we are interested in the validity of relationships involving constructs or abstract terms—such as ego strength, anxiety, or extroversion—for which there are no single commonly accepted measures. While we can demonstrate the predictive validity of a psychiatric hospitalization scale or a criminal recidivism index by means of a single correlation, it is far more difficult to demonstrate the construct validity of an anxiety scale or for a measure of any other generalized, abstract concept in the psychological domain. What is necessary for construct validity is the gradual accumulation of supporting evidence garnered from a variety of research findings, arranged to demonstrate a *network of relationships* among the measure in question and other relevant concepts. The nature and strength of these relationships should be predictable both from the theory or theories in which the concept is embedded and from the generally understood meaning of the concept. Thus, to establish construct validity of a measure of anxiety, as the term is generally understood, one might set out to demonstrate positive relationships between the measure and behavior in temporary stress situations, most forms of psychiatric difficulty, physiological indices such as palmar sweating and heart rate, and certain other behaviors typically regarded as related to anxiety. In addition, it should be demonstrated that *no* relationship exists between the measure and certain charac-teristics that are presumed to be independent of anxiety, such as height or intelligence. Establishment of construct validity for an instrument might best be thought of as a continuing program in which the meaning of the construct is gradually sharpened and reified by the nature of the relationships into which it is found to enter, and by which the meaning of the construct may become clarified as unexpected relationships are discovered. In the last analysis, since there is no single coefficient or specifiable group of coefficients that, a priori, are acceptable as clearly "demonstrating" the construct validity of a measure, judgments about the degree of construct validity possessed by the device must necessarily be subjective.

The notion of construct validity has been seriously questioned (Bechtoldt, 1959; Sarbin, 1968) on the grounds that it contributes nothing to our theoretical understanding of human behavior or to the accuracy and utility of our practical work. One central issue in the objections to construct validity is the danger that the postulated attribute or construct will be taken for a *real* entity, rather than a convenient explanatory fiction. Sarbin (1968), using the construct of anxiety as the focus of his discussion of this problem, cogently pointed out the pitfalls involved in assuming that such mental states or traits as anxiety exist. The major danger, of course, is an involvement in searching for a verbal answer to questions like "What is anxiety?"—a question which cannot meaningfully be answered. Sarbin argued that our attempts to construct scientific fictions or "myths" are a function of our language system and verbal habits, and that these tendencies need careful attention and control. Nevertheless, much of current research literature involving personality assessment techniques purports to involve construct validation, and so the knowl-edgeable reader should be aware both of what is involved and of the problems inherent in this approach.

Incremental Validity

When tests are used as the basis for prediction in a clinical situation, the determination of the usefulness of the test is not as simple as determining the accuracy of prediction—that is, the predictive validities. As Sechrest (1963) has explained, tests such as the Rorschach are often "interpreted after interviews, reading of case reports, conferences, and the like. It seems clear that validity must be claimed for a test in terms of some *increment* in predictive efficiency over the information otherwise cheaply and easily available" (p. 154). Meehl (1959b) had earlier spoken of the "increment in valid and semantically clear information transmitted" (p. 114), and, as early as 1957, Cronbach and Gleser (1957, 2nd ed. 1965) discussed the same topic at length in regard to personnel selection.

Since the notion of evaluating the usefulness of a test according to its incremental validity in that particular situation seems so obvious and relevant, it may seem surprising that most of the diagnostic tests commonly used in clinical practice show poor incremental validity. This is partly because clinicians are not generally oriented toward constantly evaluating the efficiency of their behavior. The reader is reminded of Hathaway's (1959) estimate that if clinicians were to evaluate their testing activities from an efficiency viewpoint, more than 40 percent of these activities would be abandoned. Research which has evaluated different assessment procedures in terms of their incremental validities is discussed in Chapter 8.

Hits and Misses

The predictive validity of an assessment device has traditionally been expressed in terms of a correlation coefficient between the predictor score and the criterion. If the criterion involves a hit-or-miss situation, such as whether parolees will or will not violate their parole, predictive validity is sometimes more appropriately expressed in terms of the percentage of times the prediction was correct.

Working within the framework of hits and misses (or percentage correct) makes it possible to demonstrate the importance of taking into account the *base rate* of an event; that is, the proportion of times the event occurs in the population of interest. Let us use the example of parole violation. Suppose we know from past experience that 30 percent of our potential parolees are likely to violate their parole. The base rate for parole violation is thus 30 percent, or .30. If we were to predict the future behavior of parolees from this information alone, we would do best if we predict that *no* parolees will violate the conditions of their parole. Since 30 percent will in fact be violators (though we have no way of knowing which 30 percent), we will be wrong 30 percent of the time. That is, we will be 70 percent accurate in our prediction. Suppose now that we have developed a test which has been shown to identify potential parole violators with 65 percent accuracy. Even though the test enables us to do better than the completely chance rate of 50 percent, we would be ahead in terms of predictive accuracy to predict directly from the base rate of 70 percent. Incidentally, once we know that the base rate of nonviolators is 70 percent, the "chance rate" of assignment is really higher than 50 percent. If we randomly assigned *any* 70 out of 100 prisoners to the "nonviolator" category, we would be correct 70 percent of the time, or 49 times. Likewise, randomly assigning the remaining 30 to the "violator" category would result in 9 correct placements. Thus, in making a chance 70/30 assignment, we would be correct 49 plus 9 or 58 percent of the time. Some psychologists would go one step further and consider that "chance" should be identified with the base rate of 70 percent. A detailed analysis of the use of base rate data in evaluating predictive accuracy has been provided by Meehl and Rosen (1955).

In the preceding analyses we have ignored the relative costs of the alternative outcomes. To be more precise, we have taken for granted that both kinds of possible errors—failing to identify violators and mislabeling nonviolators—would be equally costly. In practice, it is likely to be the case that an error in one direction would be more costly than an error in the other. For example, we could imagine that the cost of placing on parole a criminal who later violates parole may be more costly, all values considered, than refusing parole to a person who would not have violated it. Analyses of the problems of taking into consideration values of alternate outcomes have been made by Buchwald (1965), Cronbach and Gleser (1965), Rimm (1963), and Wiggins (1973). These questions involve the efficiency or utility of predictions and are discussed in Chapter 8 under the heading of "Decision Making."

Utilization of base rate data provides insight into the danger of using automatic cutting scores on tests regardless of the population being considered. For example, Hathaway (1956b) reported that on the *K*-corrected *Sc* scale about 60 percent of schizophrenic patients in his psychiatric cross-validation group achieved a *T* score of 70 or greater, whereas only two percent of the normal cross-validation subjects scored in this range. Suppose the scale is used for diagnosis in a clinic where approximately half the patients are schizophrenic and the other half are "normal." Simple calculation shows that calling schizophrenic all patients who score 70 or more will result in 79 percent of all patients being correctly diagnosed. The calculation is portrayed in Table 7-1. Further, of those patients diagnosed schizophrenic by the test, 30/31, or 97 percent are in fact schizophrenic. Most of the errors made will be in the direction of mislabeling schizophrenics as nonschizophrenic, so that a *lower* cutting score (e.g., 65) would raise the overall diagnostic efficiency. The main point is that the use of 70 as a cutting score assures that almost

TABLE 7-1.   Percentage of Patients Diagnosed Schizophrenic or Normal by the *Sc* Scale, Using a Cutting Score of 70, Where 50 Percent Are Actually Schizophrenic and 50 Percent Are Actually Normal

T Score	Actually Schizophrenic	Actually Normal	Total
T score 70 or more (diagnosed schizophrenic)	30 [a,b]	1 [c]	31
T score below 70 (diagnosed normal)	20 [d]	49 [a,e]	69
Total	50	50	100

[a] Correctly diagnosed.
[b] True positives.
[c] False positives.
[d] False negatives.
[e] True negatives.

all patients labeled schizophrenic by the test are, in fact, schizophrenic. The *Sc* scale, in practice, is not quite so successful as portrayed here, because some of the 50 percent who are normal would achieve high *Sc* scores owing to other disorders.

Now suppose we were to give the test to apparently normal college students. Let us assume that about one percent of these students are schizophrenic. If the same cutting score of 70 is used, the test will diagnose 2.6 percent of them as schizophrenic. This situation is represented in Table 7-2. In other words, most of the students scoring 70 or more on the *Sc* scale are *not schizophrenic*. Conceptualizing the prediction in terms of hit-and-miss and base rates makes it clear that although the predictive accuracy is much higher for college students (97.6 percent) than for patients (79 percent), the test entirely fails in its function when used with the population for which it was not intended. This, however, is not to deny that the high *Sc* scoring college students would tend to be different in some way or other from the lower scoring students, and these differences can be ascertained from specific validity studies conducted on college students.

This example on the danger of using automatic cutting scores also points up another problem of predictive accuracy, that of predicting events which occur infrequently. Thus, Table 7-2 suggests that it would probably be wasted effort to try to employ the *Sc* scale for the efficient identification of the few schizophrenics among a college population. The problem of predicting infrequent events has been dealt with in detail by Rosen (1954), using suicide as the infrequent event of interest. Estimating the suicide rate among psychiatric patients as .0033, and assuming a "correct" prediction rate of 75 percent, Rosen presented hypothetical data to show that even if the cutting score on a suicide detection index were raised so high that only 2.5 percent of the actual suicide cases were correctly identified, more than 98 percent of those patients called "suicide" would have been incorrectly labeled. Needless to say, the same problem is present, though often unrecognized, in attempting to identify potential suicide patients by clinical or subjective judgment.

Since the necessity for identifying patients who are potentially suicidal exists regardless of the difficulty of the prediction, ways of dealing with the potential of

TABLE 7-2.   **Percentage of Students Diagnosed Schizophrenic or Normal by the *Sc* Scale Using a Cutting Score of 70, Where 1 Percent Are Actually Schizophrenic and 99 Percent Are Actually Normal**

T Score	Actually Schizophrenic	Actually Normal	Total
T score 70 or more (diagnosed schizophrenic)	0.6 [a]	2.0	2.6
T score below 70 (diagnosed normal)	0.4	97.0 [a]	97.4
Total	1	99	100

[a] Correctly diagnosed.

suicide must be found. Rosen pointed out that since hospital administrators take the attitude that suicide should be prevented at almost any cost, the usual procedure is to err on the side of safety, by identifying an enormous number of "false positives." Thus, almost any patient who shows signs (whether clinical or on a psychometric index) regarded as suicidal will be treated as a potential suicide risk. Also, some improvement in psychometric prediction would result from the careful collection of detailed data over a number of years, in order to permit more precise classification and the identification of certain subgroups of patients for whom suicide might be relatively more frequent. Such data have in fact been obtained by Farberow, Shneidman, and Neuringer (1966), and have been utilized by Diggory (1969) in a cost analysis of suicide prevention, while the edited volume by Neuringer (1974) discusses a variety of psychometric issues in predicting suicide.

Selection Ratios

In discussing criterion-related validities, we have assumed that predictions or decisions are to be made for every client examined. That is, we have had to make a decision for every person involved. Under some circumstances, we have a slightly different problem—that of *selection*. Here, an assignment does not have to be made for everybody. Suppose we are asked to select 10 schizophrenic patients from a ward of 200. Let us say we know from past experience that there are about 100 schizophrenics on the ward, although we do not know exactly who they are. Our chances of performing this selection successfully by administering a test for schizophrenia and selecting the 10 highest scores are quite high, even if the predictive validity of the test is mediocre. The reason for this is that we are not going to make a prediction for the majority of the patients. All we have to do is to make a prediction about the few patients about whom we are most likely to be correct—that is, those with extreme scores.

The *selection ratio* is defined as the number of people to be selected compared to the total number considered. In this example, this ratio is 10 to 200 or .05. The smaller the ratio, the more successful the selection will be, given the same predictive validity for the test. Another factor which influences accuracy of selection is the proportion of suitable patients in the group being considered, that is, the base rate. In this example, the base rate is 100 to 200 or .50. Tables are available (Taylor and Russell, 1939) to indicate the expected accuracy of selection, given a specific predictive validity, base rate, and selection ratio. In our example, suppose the schizophrenia test had a predictive validity correlation coefficient of .4; the Taylor-Russell tables show that we would most likely have successfully identified 8 schizophrenics out of 10. Suppose, however, that there were only 20 patients to select from, still assuming that half are really schizophrenic. The selection ratio would now be 10 to 20 or .50, and the Taylor-Russell tables indicate that our most likely selection would be 6 schizophrenics out of 10, or only slightly above the chance selection of 5 out of 10.

Selection ratios are important where many people are competing for a few openings. Under such circumstances, a test with fairly low predictive validities can be used to provide fairly accurate selection. This situation often arises in the selection of a person to fill a desirable job from among many candidates, and it would also arise where there are limited treatment services available, such as psychotherapy, and many patients desiring treatment.

Moderator Variables

From time to time statisticians have discovered what appear to be tricks for making silk purses out of sows' ears. One of these tricks was seemingly embodied in the Taylor-Russell tables, whose use we have just described for enhancing predictive validity when there is a favorable selection ratio. The use of *moderator variables* is another procedure for achieving enhanced predictive validities under specific circumstances.

The concept of moderator variables was originally identified by Ghiselli (1956, 1963) and by Saunders (1956). A moderator is a piece of information that can be used to predict, for a given respondent or set of respondents, the accuracy of another predictor. For example, if it is known that college grades for compulsive students can be effectively predicted from their aptitude test scores but grades for noncompulsive students cannot, then a measure of compulsivity could be used to moderate the prediction of grades from aptitude test scores—that is, to identify those students for whom the prediction will be relatively accurate and those for whom it will not. If we were to confine our interest to only the highly compulsive students, the predictive validity of college board scores would be higher than if we considered everybody. In other words, we have improved prediction at the expense of working only with those persons for whom we know prediction to be the most valid.

At first glance, the potentialities for improving prediction by the use of moderators in personality assessment seem considerable. The concept is undoubtedly used informally in many situations. For example, if Dr. Jones is known to be expert at teasing out the differential personality dynamics of schizoid individuals who come to the clinic, the intake interviewer may be more likely to send the schizoid clients to Dr. Jones for their personality workup. To extend the principle, there is the possibility for devising a moderator to indicate how much attention should be paid to a patient's Rorschach protocol or MMPI profile in arriving at a psychiatric diagnosis. On a more complex level, it might be possible to determine whether, for a particular patient or group of patients, most attention should be paid to the Rorschach protocol, the Draw-A-Person, the MMPI, biographical information, or any other particular source of data.

Most of the research to date in developing moderator variables has been concerned with the prediction of success in academic or personnel areas. In attempting to enhance the prediction of earnings among cab drivers, Ghiselli (1960a) found that a moderator based on age and education could be used to indicate which of two ability measures (spatial and motor ability tests) was the better predictor. In this study, the spatial test was a better predictor for the older and less educated drivers. Ghiselli (1960b) also showed that it was possible to develop a moderator variable empirically by using a criterion groups approach. The characteristic to be predicted was sociability, as assessed by a questionnaire. The predictor, which showed a low correlation with sociability, was intelligence, defined by a rather arbitrary scale on a self-description inventory. To develop the moderator, two criterion groups were identified. The "predictable" group was composed of those persons whose scores fell at about the same point in the sociability and the intelligence distributions. The remainder constituted the "unpredictable" group. Responses to the self-description inventory were then examined to identify items which discriminated the two groups, and these items formed the moderator scale. Cross-validation on a new sample showed that the scale continued to identify the most predictable individuals.

Although the main area of research with moderator variables has been in enhancing prediction of academic or job success, clinically relevant research has also been done. Fulkerson (1959) has demonstrated that the validity of a personality test for predicting general adjustment was related to the extroversion-introversion, or hysteric-psychasthenic, personality dimension, presumably because the introverted respondents were more careful in their responses. Further, in a study of clinical judgment, Tomlinson (1967) showed, among other things, that the judges with high achievement needs made more accurate client predictions than other judges after interviewing a client directly, but *less* accurate predictions than other judges when observing the client through a one-way mirror. In a study involving psychiatric problems of men in a war combat zone, Clum and Hoiberg (1971) were able to improve their hit rate of successful decisions on whether to return a man to combat duty by using diagnostic categories as a moderator of prediction based on biographical variables.

What is the basis for the utility of moderator variables? In the first two examples, the prediction of grades for college students and success among cab drivers, commonsense or rational explanations can be offered as to why certain subgroups should be more predictable than others. Thus, one would expect that compulsive students might be more likely to work to the limit of their abilities, while the less compulsive students would tend to devote time selectively to the courses which interested them. What is more difficult to explain is the fact that empirical moderator scales, with no obviously relevant content, can be developed in some instances. A discussion of possible psychometric explanations, though beyond our present scope, has been offered by Hobert and Dunnette (1967), and Zedeck (1971) has provided an extensive review and discussion of the whole area.

There are several limitations to the use of moderators in enhancing prediction. First, it may not be possible to develop moderator variables for all predictions. Smith and Lanyon (1968) used biographical data to postdict juvenile offenders who violated their probation, and they then attempted to build an empirical moderator scale, based on MMPI items, to improve the postdiction. Absolutely no improvement resulted, perhaps because the factors determining whether probation would be violated might have been circumstantial and not present or ascertainable until the probation period had begun. Another potential limitation was demonstrated by Bem and Allen (1974), whose work we have discussed in Chapter 2. Bem and Allen were able to show that people differed reliably in the consistency of their behavior in certain areas, and that "consistency" for each trait could be assessed by self-ratings. As anticipated, highly consistent people were much more predictable by their peers than those who were low on self-rated consistency. Thus, it would appear that an overriding moderator might be "consistency," and that some people are simply more consistent or predictable than others, at least in specific areas. If it could be shown that this was a general personality characteristic, then the clinical potential of moderators would be severely limited, because the same person who scored high on a moderator for the MMPI, for example, would score high on moderators for all other sources of personality information.

Although relatively little research has been done with moderator variables in the field of personality assessment, a number of experts in personality assessment and related fields have predicted their increasing importance (e.g., Anastasi, 1967; Goldberg, 1968b). One new area of recent research interest, for example, is the search for moderators of the relationships between stressful life events and psychological disorders in adults (Johnson and Sarason, 1979) and children (Sandler, 1980). It is fair to say that the exploration of moderator variables represents an advance in the technology of personality assessment, since it goes beyond a global search for validity and explores the question of different degrees of validity for different kinds of persons under different circumstances.

RESPONSE DISTORTIONS

Responses to personality assessment procedures are influenced by other variables beside the personality characteristics of the respondents. Although an individual's personality characteristics are generally assumed to be the major determinants of his/her response, we now know on the basis of both research and theory that these responses are complex products of a number of psychological, sociological, linguistic, and other variables, many of which have nothing to do with the purposes for which the assessment procedure was designed. For example, personality test responses may be influenced by a conscious desire to appear well adjusted, or by the obviousness of the "correct" answers to various items. Responses may also be influenced by recent prior experiences, such as viewing a dramatic motion picture film. As a further example, there are subcultural differences in the use of evaluative words such as "often" and "very," which may affect test answers. An understanding of how these systematic irrelevancies—typically termed "response biases," "response sets," or "response styles"—affect the responses to personality assessment devices is necessary both for improving our effectiveness in utilizing our current instruments and for developing new ones. In our discussion we employ the generic term *response distortions*.

Cronbach (1941, 1942, 1946, 1950) was the first to direct attention to response distortions. He was concerned with the distorting effects of generalized tendencies for students to guess when in doubt on true-false classroom achievement examinations. The concern about response distortions was later extended by Cronbach and others to personality measurement instruments, first to those of the self-report variety and then to the Rorschach, TAT, and others. Some critics have even tended toward the extreme position that answers to personality tests reflect little else but response distortions, and that any efforts to use these tests for assessing the underlying response tendencies typically subsumed under the rubric of personality are doomed to failure. Another view, one with which we are in accord, is that response distortions themselves are consistencies in behavior which sometimes permit useful inferences about the personality of the persons who evidence them. The major issue here, and throughout our discussion of personality assessment, is the degree to which inferences made from responses to assessment devices can be shown to have an empirical basis. Responses which are not related to any nontest behaviors of interest constitute, by definition, *error variance,* and strong efforts must be exerted to eliminate or to substantially reduce them. On the other hand, responses which are related to personality-relevant behaviors should be studied and understood, no matter what they are called or what brings them about.

There are two kinds of response distortion. The first, *response style* (Jackson and Messick, 1958), refers to the tendency to distort responses in a particular direction more or less regardless of the content of the stimulus. Examples of response styles are the tendency to answer "true" a disproportionate number of times on true-false inventories, and the tendency to choose a particular numbered alternative, such as alternative "C," in a multiple-choice task. Extreme responding, discussed in Chapter 7 in regard to rating scales, is also a response style. On the Rorschach, the tendency to respond to the whole blot or the color rather than the shape of the blot would also be an example of response style. Since the content of a test stimulus is usually a powerful determiner of the response that will be given, the influence of response styles will become greater as the content becomes more ambiguous. Thus, we have the interesting situation that with instruments whose stimulus content is relatively ambiguous, such as the Rorschach and the TAT, response styles have been deliberately assessed and have been regarded as important indices of personality factors, while with self-report questionnaires, at least until recently, response style parameters have been treated largely as error variance.

The second kind of response distortion, *response set,* refers to the "conscious or unconscious desire on the part of the respondent to answer in such a way as to produce a certain picture of himself. In this traditional usage, an individual may have a set to dissimulate, to malinger, to appear aggressive, to fake good, to get the job, etc." (Rorer, 1965, p. 133). As distinct from response styles, which may be regarded as relatively "contentless," response sets are largely determined by the stimulus content: the clearer or less ambiguous the content, the more susceptible it is to the influence of response sets. Since tests like the Rorschach and the TAT are more ambiguous in stimulus content than the self-report personality questionnaires, it has been assumed that the former are less susceptible to the influence of response sets than the latter, but research evidence discussed later in the chapter indicates that this assumption is not well supported.

It should be recognized that a particular response or pattern of responses could be evoked by either a response style, a response set, or some simultaneous interaction of both a set and a style. Thus "defensiveness" could refer both to the response set of generally revealing very little about oneself and to the response style of choosing the "cannot say" or "uncertain" category on questionnaires which included such a choice. A well-designed program of personality assessment would include provisions for dealing with both aspects of response distortion.

There have been substantial differences of opinion regarding the importance of response styles and sets in the personality assessment enterprise. At one time, a substantial number of psychologists believed that response distortions exerted such a powerful influence on test takers that the results of personality inventories showed little more than the influence of these irrelevant factors (e.g., Edwards, 1957; Jackson and Messick, 1958). Certain aspects of the controversies of that time still remain unresolved. However, to anticipate our conclusions, we shall see that these influences may be significant at times but can be satisfactorily managed through the use of careful test construction procedures. An exception is deliberate dissimulation or faking, which is still a major problem in many uses of personality assessment. We first review the current state of knowledge on response styles, starting our discussion with acquiescence.

Acquiescent Response Style

The response style that has been the most thoroughly researched is that of acquiescence, or the tendency to respond "true" in a true-false questionnaire. In its most extreme form an acquiescent response style would lead to a "true" response to all items, regardless of content, including such items as "I murdered my mother." It would also lead a respondent to answer affirmatively to two contradictory statements; for example "I am happily married" and "I am unhappily married." Fortunately, extreme instances are rarely encountered, and concern about acquiescence has been mainly directed toward its influence on ambiguous items like "I often worry about unfulfilled responsibilities." On this item, a positive response may result from the fact that the respondent does indeed behave in that fashion; but it may also mean that the respondent is uncertain about this behavior and that the response has been determined by an acquiescent response style. Whenever personality questionnaires contain many relatively ambiguous items on which the majority of the keyed responses are in the same direction, the scores are open to the influence of an acquiescent response style.

How significant is acquiescence response style in the practical use of inventories? Despite views such as those of Couch and Keniston (1960), who took the position that acquiescence was itself a useful personality variable, and Rorer (1965), who argued that it is an unavoidable part of our language structure and should be left alone, the best approach would seem to be a recognition that it can exert a small but bothersome influence in responding on personality inventories. It would therefore seem reasonable to make an effort to remove this influence by having a comparable number of "true"-keyed and "false"-keyed items, whenever this can be done without doing violence to the content of the items (e.g., Jackson, 1967/1974; Lanyon, 1973).

Another style or mode of responding to personality test items that has attracted considerable interest is that of making atypical or unusual responses. There are certain modal or usual responses to personality test items that are given by the general population; for example, an affirmative response to the inventory item "My father was a good man," the response of a "a bat" to Card V of the Rorschach, or the drawing of a clothed figure on the Draw-a-Person test. It is presumed that variations or deviations from these usual or modal responses to test items are indicative of some general tendency toward deviance.

This position has been formally articulated by Berg (1955, 1957, 1959) as the Deviation Hypothesis: "Deviant response patterns tend to be general; hence those deviant behavior patterns which are significant for abnormality and thus regarded as symptoms are associated with other deviant response patterns which are in noncritical areas of behavior and which are not regarded as symptoms of personality aberration" (1955, p. 62). Berg (1959) argued that deviant responding is better viewed as a response style rather than a set because the particular stimulus content was unimportant. Further, he believed that ambiguity of content heightened rather than reduced the operation of this factor. However, Hamilton (1968) took the position that item content *was* a significant factor in deviant responding, because each item had to be inspected individually to determine what would be a deviant response for that item.

It is interesting to note that Rorschach viewed deviant responding as an important consideration on his inkblot test. Rorschach initially noted (1942/1951, p. 23) that most responses to his inkblots are determined by the form of the blot, and "in order to avoid subjective evaluation," he developed the "definite range of normal form visualizations"—the so-called good-form, or F+ responses—based upon the actual responses given by 100 normal persons. Rorschach noted that good-form perception was disturbed by various psychopathological states, especially schizophrenia, and he stated that "the more stable the emotions, the better the form visualization" (p. 31). The evaluation of form level accuracy of perception in Rorschach responses by means of the frequency of occurrence of these responses has been more thoroughly studied and reported by Beck et al. (1961), Exner (1974), and others. In contemporary Rorschach interpretation (e.g., Exner, 1974, 1978), the form level as determined by frequency tables and by the examiner's judgment and clinical experience is considered to be an important index of the general level of deviance or psychopathology to be attributed to the subject. Deviant responding is also an important consideration on the MMPI, and here again it is considered to be a useful index of overall degree of psychological disturbance (e.g., Lachar, 1974). The MMPI scale for assessing deviant responding is, coincidentally, also named *F* (for "frequency," in this case).

The Deviation Hypothesis has been severely criticized by a number of students of personality measurement (such as Rorer, 1965; and Sechrest and Jackson, 1962, 1963) on a number of grounds. There appears to be little research evidence to support Berg's view that deviant responding in *any* response situation is predictive of deviant responding in *all* situations. However, it is clear that some aspects of deviant responding, such as Rorschach form level and the MMPI *F* scale, are useful indices of psychopathology. Because these indices are indeed related to the content of the test stimuli, it would not seem appropriate to regard them simply as response styles. Rather, in view of the way in which they are used in the process of personality assessment, it would perhaps be best to view them as an integral aspect of the test procedure.

Extreme Response Style

One further response style is *extreme responding*. This can operate only in tests whose items require subjects to respond on a rating scale or dimension, such as those discussed in Chapter 7. Some persons have a tendency to select the extreme categories (such as "strongly disagree" or "strongly agree") rather than the middle categories, regardless of the content of the item. Although extreme responding sounds rather like deviant responding, Hamilton (1968) differentiated them by pointing out that extreme responding is completely independent of content, while deviant responding involves a specific reaction to the content of the item. Hamilton's review of the research on extreme response style indicated that this phenomenon is a reliable characteristic of respondents and that it is consistently shown more by women than men, by persons with high anxiety, and by persons with poor psychological adjustment. Thus, it would seem appropriate to take note of these small but significant effects when employing rating scales.

Social Desirability Response Set

We concluded earlier that response styles (content-free distortions of responses to personality assessment devices) are relatively minor variables in most of our efforts to evaluate personality. The situation is rather different, however, when we consider response *sets,* the tendency to systematically "slant" responses to personality assessment items. The reader should recall that our definition of response set includes both the deliberate efforts by subjects to bias their answers in a particular direction and also their subtle, unconscious tendencies to make biased responses.

The most ubiquitous of all response sets is that of defensiveness, or the set to "fake good." One recent approach to understanding this problem has been through the study of a special case of defensiveness, the *social desirability* response set, or the tendency to give what the individual regards as socially desirable responses rather than straightforward responses which would more accurately reflect personality. To anticipate our conclusion with regard to social desirability response set, we shall find that persons who respond in a socially desirable fashion "naturally" or unconsciously are probably reflecting their personality characteristics accurately, and that it is the conscious, deliberate attempts to make oneself appear socially desirable that constitute an important source of response distortion. We use the term "social desirability" to refer to the natural production of socially desirable responses, and the term "defensiveness" for the deliberately biased efforts in this direction.

An important impetus for research on social desirability as a response set in personality assessment was a study by Edwards (1953). Edwards obtained college students' ratings of a variety of self-report inventory items on a nine-point scale, according to how desirable they regarded the behavior involved in each item. He then asked another group of students to take these same items as a self-report personality assessment device, and found a very high positive correlation (.87) between the frequency of endorsement of each item by the second group and the mean social desirability ratings of the first. In other words, these college students were, to an overwhelming degree, responding to the items in what they perceived as the socially desirable direction. Edwards (1964) went on to demonstrate that people's scores on the MMPI scales were so highly correlated with their social desirability ratings of the individual items that their actual MMPI profiles could be predicted moderately well from these ratings.

The conclusion that social desirability response set is the most basic, or even a very important, variable which interferes with responses on personality questionnaires has been seriously challenged on methodological, empirical, and theoretical grounds (e.g., Block, 1965; Heilbrun and Goodstein, 1961a; Norman, 1967; Taylor, 1959). The most widely accepted view is that social desirability should be regarded as an important predictor variable in its own right. Normal individuals ordinarily behave in normal, that is, socially desirable ways—indeed, this is what is typically meant by "normal." And as we noted earlier, social undesirability of behavior is perhaps the most important criterion of psychopathology. That psychopathological persons tend to admit being psychologically disturbed by their responses to questionnaire items, such as those on the MMPI, is an easily demonstrable fact; and that their disturbed behavior is socially undesirable is also immediately obvious. As Heilbrun (1964) has noted, the tendency to make socially undesirable responses to personality questionnaires would seem to be sufficiently related to the production of nontest undesirable behavior that a prediction from one to the other is possible. The conclusion that the production of socially desirable behavior is a correlate of adjustment or psychological health seems inescapable, and this conclusion precludes the relegation of social desirability to the category of response distortion. Thus, some of the newer tests such as the Personality Research Form (Jackson, 1967/1974) contain scales to assess social desirability as a personality variable.

In view of the fact that extreme degrees of social desirability are generally agreed to mask or distort other aspects of responding on a test, it is probably wise to take such extremes into consideration whenever possible. For personality inventories assessing characteristics within the normal range, this can readily be done at the stage of item construction, by using items whose correlations with social desirability are relatively small (e.g., Jackson, 1967/1974, 1976). However, the problem is considerably more difficult to handle on inventories assessing psychopathology or other characteristics which are themselves socially undesirable. Here, the control of extreme degrees of social desirability tends to be merged with the control of deliberate faking.

There has been little attempt to study the influence of social desirability in the functioning of projective approaches in personality assessment. Reznikoff (1961) reported insignificant correlations between the social desirability ratings of a series of common TAT themes and their frequency of endorsement, and concluded that social desirability is not an important source of variance in the production of the TAT themes. However, Exner (1978) showed in a Rorschach study that this element "does have a very significant effect on what is actually delivered by the subject" (p. 45). While there is no reason to suppose that the general conclusions which we have drawn in regard to inventories should not also apply to projective techniques, more research is needed before definite conclusions can be drawn.

Defensiveness

A serious problem in the evaluation of personality is the tendency of persons to *deliberately slant* or bias their responses to personality assessment devices. Although the following discussion centers on the problem of defensiveness, or the deliberate efforts of persons to present a favorable or well-adjusted picture of themselves, similar comments could be made about the efforts of individuals to slant their responses on other personality attributes, such as extroversion or persistence. Meehl and Hathaway (1946), in reviewing past efforts to deal with the problem of defensiveness in personality assessment, pointed out that most developers of personality tests (especially tests of the self-report inventory type) were aware of these problems but could offer no effective solution. Indeed, it is the obviousness of the problems connected with personality inventories that accounts in part for the popularity of the projective approaches to personality assessment, because it is widely believed that the projective approach obviates or at least sharply reduces these problems. We shall shortly examine this belief in some detail.

Evidence on the prevalence of defensiveness as a problem in personality assessment comes from a variety of sources. First, normal-appearing personality test profiles are often obtained from psychiatric patients and other deviant individuals who should not produce normal profiles. Second, there is much evidence that a variety of subject groups, such as college students and psychiatric patients, can alter their personality test responses upon request, especially on self-report questionnaires, in order to make a good (or better) impression. It is worth noting that even college students, who ordinarily produce rather normal personality questionnaire profiles, can produce more favorable profiles under "fake good" instructions. This is especially true on inventories with largely obvious items; that is, where the social desirability of responses is quite apparent. For example, Fosberg (1941), using the Bernreuter Personality Inventory, was able to show that the correlation between scores obtained under normal instructions and those secured under "fake good" instructions was quite modest (.11), clearly indicating how a defensiveness set can affect inventory responses of this sort.

On the other hand, there is considerable evidence to suggest that it is not possible for disturbed individuals, especially psychiatric patients, to completely simulate a normal profile, particularly on inventories that involve items that are more subtle; that is, where the social desirability of the responses is not quite so apparent. In one investigation of this aspect of the problem, Grayson and Olinger (1957) demonstrated that only 11 percent of a group of psychiatric patients could fake a normal MMPI profile. While some patients responded to these instructions by producing more deviant profiles, others simply produced a different pattern of abnormality on their profiles. Further, Canter (1963) has demonstrated that the ability to "fake good" is itself related to the relative adjustment of the individual. Using groups of alcoholics and applicants for employment, Canter found that the better-adjusted subjects were the more successful in producing "fake good" profiles on the California Psychological Inventory. Lanyon (1967b) demonstrated a similar effect in the simulation of pathological profiles. In this study, well-adjusted college students were shown to be superior to poorly adjusted students in their ability to simulate an MMPI pattern suggestive of psychopathic personality.

There has been a traditional belief that projective techniques, especially the Rorschach, are not susceptible to this kind of conscious dissimulation. However, even early studies, while not competely consistent, tended to show that the Rorschach was indeed vulnerable to faking in both the good and bad directions (Carp and Shavzin, 1950; Feldman and Graley, 1954; Fosberg, 1938, 1941; Henry and Rotter, 1956). They further suggested that normal subjects were more capable of distorting their responses than psychiatric patients, and that it was somewhat easier to "fake bad" than to "fake good." The results of more recent studies (e.g., Albert, Fox, and Kahn, 1980; Exner, 1978) are mostly consistent with the earlier work. Research on dissimulation with other projective instruments, although quite sparse, tends to support these conclusions. For example, Weisskopf and Dieppa (1951) showed that subjects could successfully dissimulate in both positive and negative directions in producing TAT stories, and generally were more successful at "faking bad," a conclusion also supported by the work of Kaplan and Eron (1965). Holmes (1974) instructed subjects to introduce false projections or to inhibit true projections on the TAT and found that judges were unable to identify either kind of faking. In a study using Rosenzweig's (1945) Picture Frustration Test, Schwartz, Cohen and Pavlik (1964) found that instructional sets to be defensive or to be frank produced predictably different responses from their subjects. Similarly, Meltzoff (1951) was able to show that responses to sentence completion stems could be distorted in both "fake good" and "fake bad" directions.

These studies support the conclusion that the problem of defensiveness and "fake good" dissimulation on projective devices for personality assessment is a serious one. It is particularly interesting to note that, in their clinically oriented guide to Rorschach interpretation, Phillips and Smith (1953) devoted an entire section to the problems involved in interpreting guarded or defensive Rorschach protocols. Not surprisingly, their characteristics of defensive protocols—fewer responses than expected, a reduction in response determinants other than form, and an increase in the number of popular responses—correspond approximately to those characteristics isolated subsequently by Henry and Rotter (1956) in an experimental study of this problem. Unfortunately, with the exception of a group of studies by Exner involving his particular system for the Rorschach, this area has received little research attention, and it is simply ignored in most of the recent textbooks dealing with projective techniques.

Combating Defensiveness

The conscious and deliberate efforts of some test takers to slant their responses (especially in the positive direction) to personality assessment devices of both the inventory and projective varieties constitute a serious problem. Perhaps the simplest and most direct approach in dealing with the problem is to appeal for the cooperation and honesty of test takers in making their responses. But this kind of candor and willingness for self-disclosure involves a fairly complex set of attitudes and may not be as easily obtainable as we would hope. It seems safer to assume that defensiveness will probably be a significant factor in most personality evaluation situations, and to make attempts to evaluate or control it by other strategies.

Detection Procedures.   While students of projective techniques have tended to rely upon subtle clinical signs of dissimulation, workers interested in self-report questionnaires have attempted a variety of other approaches to reducing these problems. One common approach is the use of *detection devices*. Thus, a number of inventories have included special scales in an effort to assess the degree to which test takers are attempting to slant their responses. For example, the Verification scale of the Kuder Preference Record (Kuder, 1951) and the Lie scale of the MMPI give a score indicating the number of times the individual has responded to certain items that are infrequently answered in this fashion. The Verification scale is primarily aimed at identifying subjects who are responding randomly, while the Lie scale attempts to identify persons with naïvely defensive attitudes that would suggest a strong "fake good" set. A typical item from the MMPI Lie scale is "I do not always tell the truth." Those individuals who answer more than a few such items in the naïvely defensive direction are typically regarded as having "faked good," and their protocols are usually considered invalid for either clinical or research use. As discussed earlier in this chapter, the F scale of the MMPI represents an effort to identify those subjects who are responding in a deviant manner, and it contains items which are rarely answered in a particular direction. Because rare responses are usually also socially undesirable or psychopathological, the F scale also serves to identify persons who are attempting to "fake bad." There is a fair amount of research evidence showing that such scales are to some degree effective in identifying dissimulation. The "$F-K$ index," or difference between raw scores on the F and K scales, has also been shown to be successful in this regard (Dahlstrom, Welsh, and Dahlstrom, 1975; Gough, 1950).

Correction Procedures.   Since detection scales offer the psychologist little alternative but to ignore those profiles which clearly indicate dissimulation, some effort has been expended in the development of *correction devices*. Here an attempt is made to assess the degree of defensiveness present in a protocol and then to correct the profile accordingly. The *K* scale of the MMPI, developed empirically to correct for the more subtle aspects of test-taking defensiveness, is a good example of a correction device. Such scales are sometimes termed "suppressor" scales, in accordance with their presumed function of suppressing or correcting for the effects of dissimulation. It has been pointed out in Chapter 4 that the *K* scale was developed by comparing the responses of normal persons with those of psychiatric patients whose scores on the clinical scales were in the normal range, and who could thus be assumed to be "faking good." High scores on this scale are obtained by answering "true" to items such as "I have never felt better in my life than I do now."

The raw *K*-scale score is used directly as a corrective variable and is added, in different fractions, to the respondent's scores on five of the clinical scales *(Hs, Pd, Pt, Sc,* and *Ma)*. The use of the *K* scale in this way has been shown to increase the discriminative power of these scales, particularly in the crucial middle range of score values (Dahlstrom, Welsh, and Dahlstrom, 1972, p. 128). At the same time it should be recognized that suppressor scales are not likely to result in much improvement unless the predictive validity of the original scales is rather high in the first place (Norman, 1963a). Another significant point is that the optimal fractions of the *K* scale to be added can be expected to differ according to the population of interest. Heilbrun (1963) has reported a revised set of *K* correction fractions for improved validity of the MMPI among college students; however, the original set of weights has long become an integral part of the test and is used in virtually all applications. One major exception is seen in the work of Marks, Seeman, and Haller (1974) in developing an actuarial interpretation system for the MMPI profiles of adolescents. These authors found that a greater degree of validity could be obtained if no *K* corrections were used at all. Users of their actuarial interpretation system should first convert raw scores to scale scores using the specially developed adolescent norms, which also differ from the regular norms in other ways beside the absence of *K* corrections.

Forced-Choice Procedures.   Another widely used approach to the control of defensiveness is through the development of *forced-choice items,* with the items matched in pairs (or triplets) for social desirability. Each item in the pair is keyed empirically, or by some other means, as a significant predictor of a behavior of interest. The EPPS, described in Chapter 3, employs this approach. There are a number of problems still unsolved in the forced-choice procedure. First, there is the requirement that the subject choose one of the alternatives, although neither of them may be descriptive of his/her behavior. We thus have no information about the absolute strength of the preference or of the personality characteristic underlying it. Second, the items in a pair, although matched in a general way for desirability, often still differ enough that faking is possible (e.g., Dicken, 1959). Third, as we noted earlier, efforts to eliminate social desirability may reduce the predictive power of the instrument while they are reducing the influence of defensiveness. A review by Scott (1968) of studies comparing the validities of forced-choice and single-stimulus tests reached the more neutral conclusion that the validities achieved with the two approaches did not differ, and that there was no conclusive evidence for the advantage of the forced-choice approach in controlling defensiveness. Thus, it would seem that the forced-choice technique has not proved to be as advantageous a technique for personality questionnaires as had been initially anticipated.

Subtle Items.   Still another technique that has been advocated is the use of *subtle items,* that is, items with empirically demonstrable predictive or concurrent validity but with little or no face validity. We have already seen in Chapter 3, however, that subtle items tend in general to be less valid or useful than the more obvious items. Norman (1963a), who proposed a complex method for controlling dissimulation by carefully eliminating the most obvious items in his scales, came to a similar conclusion, that the use of such scales "constructed for use in one setting with one class of respondents, may not generalize widely" (p. 240). However, the more recent work of Jackson (1971) and Gynther, Burkhart, and Hovanitz (1979), also discussed in Chapter 3, indicates that the use of subtle items as a control for defensiveness may be an approach worth pursuing.

Neutral Items.   Another approach with some potential promise for the control of defensiveness and deliberate faking is the use of items that are relatively neutral in regard to social desirability, as discussed earlier in this chapter. This approach was originally advocated by Buss (1959) and Buss and Durkee (1957) in the assessment of hostility. For example, rather than presenting the item "Sometimes I lose my temper," to which an affirmative response would be socially undesirable, we would rewrite the item as "I'm afraid that I sometimes lose my temper," or "Sometimes I cannot help losing my temper," or "I am concerned about losing my temper," all of which are phrased in a less undesirable manner. Whether this approach is actually successful in reducing defensiveness has not yet been adequately studied, however.

Maximum Performance Tests.   A more radical procedure has been suggested by the work of Wallace (1966, 1967). Instead of regarding personality in terms of traits or typical behaviors, we might think of personality in terms of *abilities* or maximum performance. Thus, a measure of dominance might involve a situational test where subjects would be required to respond as dominantly as possible and would be evaluated on their actual performance in meeting these task expectations. For a test of maximum rather than habitual performance, the problem of faking or defensiveness becomes somewhat irrelevant. Once again, this approach has not yet been seriously studied in the context of an actual assessment procedure.

All of these methods of attempting to handle defensiveness have some merit and all have their strong supporters. At the same time, each of these methods has some clear-cut limitations and none is a completely satisfactory procedure for handling defensiveness in responding to personality questionnaires. Thus, the question of combating defensiveness will be a continuing one in personality assessment. As we will see in Chapter 11, some psychologists (e.g., Lovell, 1967) believe that personality tests should simply not be used at all under certain conditions of heightened defensiveness, such as in personnel selection.

Summary

Reliability has to do with the repeatability of a measure. Reliability across presumably equivalent forms of a measuring instrument is called consistency. Stability refers to reliability over time. Lack of reliability, or measurement error, can be either systematic or random. Systematic errors, or biases, can be corrected for or allowed for. Random error can be regarded as stemming from the fact that the content of a test is simply one small sample of the universe of content covering the characteristic of interest. A number of different practical techniques are available for assessing reliability, and which one is used should depend on what sources of unreliability are to be assessed. The Kuder-Richardson formulas assess only random error and give an estimate of the internal consistency of a test. Split-half reliability also gives an estimate of random error; alternate-forms and test-retest reliabilities estimate varying degrees of random and systematic error. For practical use of reliabilities in determining the accuracy of a test score, the standard error of measurement can be determined from the reliability coefficient and the standard deviation of the obtained scores.

The special problems associated with determining reliabilities of some projective tests have often led to the inappropriate conclusion that reliability considerations should not apply to them. These problems stem from several sources: the fact that the tests were not constructed with the reliability of scoring categories in mind, the lack of standardization of instructions for administering and scoring the tests, and the subjective aspects of scoring. One approach has been to concentrate on the reliabilities of the various uses to which the test results are to be put; that is, the reliability of global interpretations. This approach, in spite of a number of difficulties, is probably the most appropriate for projective techniques.

Validity may be considered as the degree to which an assessment procedure is capable of achieving its aims. Since different tests may have different kinds of aims, an approach that is appropriate for demonstrating validity in one test or situation may be inappropriate for another. Content or face validity is claimed for a test whose content is a representative sample of the behaviors of interest. Criterion-related validities refer to the accuracy with which guesses about a certain characteristic of the individual, the criterion, can be made from another characteristic, the predictor. Construct validity is relevant where there exists no definitive criterion for the characteristic which is to be assessed, so that it is desirable to demonstrate a network of relationships between the measure of interest and a variety of relevant concepts.

In a clinical situation, the simple predictive accuracy of a test is less important than its incremental validity. Incremental validity is the degree to which a test improves the accuracy of the prediction above the level achieved without the test. It is suspected that if closer attention were paid to incremental validities, much present-day routine clinical testing activity would be dispensed with.

As can be demonstrated when accuracy of prediction is evaluated in terms of hits and misses, it is important to know the base rate or frequency of the event of interest in the population. It is also important to know the cost or value associated with making an incorrect decision in one direction or the other. If the problem is one of selection rather than prediction—that is, if a prediction does not have to be made about every subject on whom information is available—then the selection ratio also becomes a factor in determining predictive efficiency.

A moderator is any piece of information that can be used to predict, for a given person, how accurate another prediction is going to be. Thus, increased accuracy in prediction is potentially possible at the cost of making the prediction only for some proportion of the respondents. The majority of the research and interest in moderator variables to date has been in the contexts of academic and personnel predictions, but there is no reason why their use should not be explored for clinical and personality assessment.

Response styles have been defined as tendencies to select disproportionately some response category independently of the content of the test stimulus. Acquiescence, the most widely studied response style, is the tendency to overrespond yes on true-false inventories. In an attempt to determine the degree to which acquiescence style distorts inventory responses, several research strategies have been used, including examination of the correlations between scores on original scales and "reversed" scales, factor analytic studies, and comparison among various measures of acquiescence. The evidence seems to indicate that acquiescence does not exert an important distorting influence on inventory responses, and that previous conclusions to the contrary have not taken into account the contribution of item content. Deviant response style, the tendency to give responses in a deviant direction, has received somewhat less attention than acquiescence, and we have concluded that this style is likewise of little practical importance in personality assessment.

Response sets have been defined as distortions produced by respondents for the purpose of giving a certain picture of themselves. Social desirability, or the natural tendency to respond in a socially desirable direction, may not be such a distorting factor as was once supposed, but may instead reflect actual (socially desirable) characteristics of the respondent. Deliberate efforts to make a good impression by consciously distorting answers, however, pose a serious problem for the validity of assessment devices that has not been adequately resolved. A variety of efforts to combat defensiveness include detection scales such as the Lie scale of the MMPI, correction scales, and built-in controls such as the forced-choice technique and the use of subtle items. However, these solutions also have their problems. Contrary to popular belief, projective techniques are also quite vulnerable to respondents' efforts to slant their responses, although it appears to be somewhat more difficult to deliberately make a good impression than to make a bad one.

8 ASSESSMENT TECHNOLOGY

We have surveyed many of the major procedures and devices involved in contemporary personality assessment and have attempted to explain their underlying rationale and their actual development. In this chapter we discuss some of the principles and processes underlying their use in practical situations, the major challenges and problems involved, and research on ways of improving their accuracy in contemporary practice.

Because psychologists have been engaged in personality assessment for many years, it would be reasonable to suppose that there have evolved fairly standard assessment strategies for use in any particular situation. For example, there ought to be a relatively standard approach to the evaluation of executive potential, or psychopathology, or leadership in particular situations. Unfortunately, this is not the case. There tend to be rather substantial differences among actual practitioners as to which instruments are the most useful in a given instance, and as to what should be done with the responses once they are obtained. In general, the behavior of psychologists in selecting assessment strategies seems to be governed more by tradition and superstition than by relevance or evidence. Commenting upon this state of affairs, Meehl (1956) wrote that assessment devices ought to be chosen "on the basis of their empirically demonstrated efficiency, rather than upon which one is more exciting, more 'dynamic,' more like what psychiatrists do, or more harmonious with the clinical psychologists' self-concept" (pp. 264–265). Hathaway's (1959) similar criticism has already been mentioned.

CLINICIAN VERSUS ACTUARY

The many problems involved with how the scores derived from the chosen assessment instrument or instruments should be used have been of great interest to research-minded assessment psychologists. The reader may wonder why such problems exist, especially for those instruments with demonstrated empirical validity; that is, with known predictive usefulness. In making a specific prediction, one might presume that the size of the validity coefficient (the known correlation of the test score with the behavior to be predicted) should permit us to make a straightforward prediction, by assuming a simple linear relationship between score and behavior. However, most contemporary assessment devices are multiphasic, so that they yield more than one score, and each of these scores has a different predictive relationship with the criterion behavior. The practitioner thus is faced with the decision of how these several scores should be combined into a single predictive statement. Another aspect of this problem is that in any given situation most contemporary psychologists will want to use several different assessment devices, and these devices yield a melange of scores and responses that require integration before any predictions can be made. Still another problem is the fact that many times the accumulated validity data involve a criterion situation that is somewhat different from the one now confronting the psychologist, so that existing validity coefficients are not directly applicable. How psychologists ought to go about using assessment data, how the scores ought to be combined, and how a specific prediction or decision should be made, have been the subjects of rather heated controversy, which crystallized some years ago around comparisons between the *clinical* and *actuarial* modes of operation. We consider this area under the headings of *prediction,* personality *description,* and *decision making.*

Clinical versus Actuarial Prediction

In most practical situations, the professional psychologist has a great variety of data available on a client, such as test scores, interview impressions, and biographical information, and is asked to make one or more predictions from these data. Will this patient improve in intensive individual psychotherapy? Should this manager be promoted? Should this delinquent be paroled or should he be imprisoned? In such situations, the psychologist's task is to integrate the available data and make a single overall prognostic or diagnostic decision. The reader may note that the same problem exists for the physician who is attempting a physical diagnosis or treatment regimen, the stockbroker advising a client whether or not to buy a stock, the potential better at the parimutuel window, and so on.

In the *actuarial approach* to prediction, the predictors (cues, scores, responses, data) are first quantified and then are combined according to a set of rules that have been empirically determined, and that are to be scrupulously followed. On the basis of previously completed research, each of the obtained predictors is given some quantitative weight, and these predictors are then combined into a "best-fitting" actuarial model. The model may be a simple linear regression equation or a more complex configurational one. The important consideration is always that the actual process of decision making in the actuarial mode follows predetermined rules in a strictly mechanical fashion, requiring no human judgment once the procedure is established.

The *clinical approach* to prediction, in contrast to the actuarial approach, permits practitioners to assign their own weights to the predictors and to combine these predictors in a subjective fashion. The clinical approach refers to instances in which psychologists (or physicians, or stockbrokers, or what have you) use their judgment or "intuition" in order to make what they feel are the appropriate adjustments in the given circumstances.

Examples of the two approaches are as follows. A clinical psychologist may note that a particular patient is depressed, rather agitated, somewhat seclusive, and preoccupied with themes of alienation and death. From these observations, the psychologist concludes that the patient is potentially suicidal and recommends that he/she should be watched carefully. This type of procedure, based largely upon the informal accumulated experience of the clinician and his/her private conception of what is involved in suicide, is called the clinical (or case study) method of prediction.

Alternatively, the psychologist might observe the patient's age, marital status, and certain MMPI test scores. The psychologist then consults an actuarial table, which gives the statistical frequency of suicide in persons as a function of such characteristics, and obtains a figure indicating the probability of suicide by that particular patient. This type of procedure, where the prediction derives solely from prior statistical data, is called the actuarial (or statistical) method of prediction.

One of the early attempts to develop an actuarial prediction procedure for personality-related events involved the prediction of the likelihood that prisoners would violate their parole (Burgess, 1928; Glueck and Glueck, 1930; Hart, 1923). In the most comprehensive and influential of these studies, Burgess (1928) utilized the case files of over 3,000 parolees and was able to identify 21 factors in preparole history that were related to parole success. Burgess then "scored" each of the 3,000 case histories by assigning one point for every predictive factor that was present, yielding a "likelihood of nonviolation" score which could range from 0 to 21. Burgess was able to demonstrate that only 1.5 percent of those with scores of 16 through 21 were violators, while in the range of lowest scores (2 through 4), 76 percent were violators. The intermediate scores yielded corresponding intermediate results. These data appear to offer strong support for an actuarial approach to the prediction of parole success, although we shall see later in this chapter that Burgess's failure to deal with the problem of *base rates* flaws his conclusions and raises questions about the practical usefulness of the scores. In particular, these two extreme groups together included less than 10 percent of the total number of parolees. Nevertheless, the actuarial approach has been successfully applied to a wide variety of other problems, including the prediction of academic success in various educational programs and response to different kinds of institutionalization and therapeutic treatments.

Note that the distinction between clinical and actuarial methods does not imply anything about the nature of the data utilized. Case history data, interview impressions, and formal personality assessment scores can be used in both the actuarial and the clinical approach. In the former case, these data are quantified and interpreted according to established rules, while in the latter case the interpretation is subjective and left to the assumed skill of the clinician. As Gough (1962) has written:

> The defining distinction between clinical and actuarial methods is instead to be found in the way in which the data, once specified, are combined for use in making the prediction. If the procedures, however complex mathematically, are in principle such that a clerk, or a machine, or anyone else could carry out the necessary operations and that the result would

be the same in all instances, then the method is actuarial or statistical in the sense here being discussed. If the combining is done intuitively, if hypotheses and constructs are generated during the course of the analyses, and if the process is mediated by an individual's judgment and reflection, then the method is clinical. (p. 530)

Thus, quantified responses to the ambiguous stimuli of projective techniques are a perfectly legitimate source of data for actuarial prediction, so that scores such as the number of "whole" responses *(W)* or percentage of good-form responses $(F+\%)$ could be employed actuarially. More complex indices could also be used. For example, Klopfer, Kirkner, Wisham, and Baker (1951) developed an "ego strength" measure from the Rorschach, involving a weighted score of the number of human movement, animal movement, and inanimate movement responses, plus the use of shading, color, and form determinants. On the basis of these scores, a therapeutic prognostic index was proposed. Similarly, Rose and Bitter (1980) developed the Palo Alto Destructive Content Scale as a means of predicting physical assaultiveness in men from their Rorschach responses, while Kendra (1979) used Rorschach scores to develop actuarial predictors for attempted and actual suicide. In each of these cases, it was the objectification of the data which permitted the application of the actuarial method.

It should be obvious to the reader that the relative efficiency of the clinical and the actuarial approaches can be directly compared. Burgess (1928) compared his actuarial results with clinical predictions made by two prison psychiatrists and concluded that the overall advantage lay with the actuary. Meehl (1954) was the first to draw attention to the fact that, although the two approaches arouse strong partisanship and affect, the question of their relative accuracy is, in the final analysis, a straightforward empirical one. After a rather full discussion of the logic involved in the two approaches, Meehl (1954) summarized all of the studies then available that attempted a direct comparison. These studies, not all of which are relevant to the personality domain, tended to fall into three categories: success in training, parole violation, and recovery from psychosis. Meehl's conclusion was that "in all but one . . . the predictions made actuarially were either approximately equal or superior to those made by a clinician" (p. 119).

Meehl noted several qualifications: (1) too little was known about the skill of the clinicians involved in making the predictions, (2) some of the actuarial predictions were made on the data from which the original prediction rules had been derived (i.e., the prediction rules were not cross-validated), and (3) the predictive efficiencies for individual clinicians were rarely reported, so that it usually was not possible to determine the performance of the most accurate clinicians. Nevertheless, Meehl did conclude that the studies favored the actuary over the clinician. He further noted that, in favor of the clinician, some clinical predictive activity (e.g., during psychotherapy) cannot in principle be duplicated by statistical procedures. On the other hand, the time saved by employing actuarial rather than clinical procedures is an important factor in favor of the actuarial method.

Meehl (1965) more recently summarized the state of the controversy as follows:

Monitoring of the literature yields a current bibliography of some fifty empirical investigations in which the efficiency of a human judge in combining information is compared with that of a formalized ("mechanical," "statistical") procedure. The design and range of these investigations permits much more confident generalization than was true on the eighteen studies available to me in 1954. They range over such diverse substantive domains as success in training or schooling, criminal recidivism and parole violation, psychotherapy (stayability and outcome), recovery from psychosis, response to shock treatment, formal psychiatric nosology, job success or satisfaction, medical (nonpsychiatric) diagnosis, and general trait ascription or personality description. The current "box score" shows a significantly superior predictive efficiency in about two-thirds of the investigations, and substantially equal efficiency in the rest. . . . It would be difficult to mention any other domain of psychological controversy in which such uniformity of research outcome as this would be evident in the literature. (p. 27)

Has clinical prediction *ever* been shown superior to actuarial? The single study (Hovey and Stauffacher, 1953) which Meehl (1954, p. 108) considered to show the superiority of the clinician was later discovered by him to contain a statistical error which nullified this conclusion (Meehl, 1959a). A paper by Lindzey (1965) attempted to demonstrate one clinical situation, the prediction of homosexuality from TAT protocols, in which clinical predictions were superior to an actuarial approach. In the first part of this study using noninstitutionalized homosexuals, both the clinician and the actuary (using 20 objective TAT indices combined in an after-the-fact fashion) obtained a high degree of success in predicting homosexuality. In the second portion of the investigation, when the results were applied to a prison population, the clinical method was reported to be substantially more effective than the actuarial. However, Goldberg (1968a) reanalyzed Lindzey's data and concluded that no reliable evidence of the clinician's superiority had been presented.

A number of psychologists have disputed the correctness of Meehl's conclusions about the proven superiority of the actuarial method. In a detailed critique, Holt (1958) argued that, in defining the problem as clinical *versus* actuarial prediction, Meehl had encouraged competition and controversy rather than attempts to understand the relative contributions of these two approaches. Holt described the process of prediction as involving several steps; a study of the criterion, choice of intervening variables, choice of measures of these variables, data collection, and data combination. Clinical or statistical approaches can be used at any of these steps, so that a prediction process should be characterized as "more clinical than statistical," or "more statistical than clinical." Holt used the term "sophisticated clinical prediction" to describe a procedure employing all these steps but retaining the clinician as a prime instrument, and "naïve clinical prediction" for a procedure in which the clinician does not make a systematic effort to collect the necessary preliminary information before making predictions. Most of the studies of clinical prediction reviewed by Meehl (1954) were, according to Holt, studies of the naïve clinical method, and thus could not be expected to show what experienced clinicians could do if they were really to put their minds to it. Holt emphasized his view that there were prediction problems where it would make best sense to employ a more clinical approach, and also problems where a more actuarial approach would be the method of choice. Thus, for any problem, an attempt should be made to find the optimal combination of the methods.

Another important review of studies comparing clinical and statistical prediction methods was published by Sawyer (1966). Like Holt (1958), Sawyer felt that an important part of the question had been neglected; namely, how the data were collected—whether a clinical or a mechanical *measurement* procedure was employed. This neglect, according to Sawyer, had resulted in an incomplete picture of the issues involved in the clinical-statistical controversy. By Sawyer's criteria, data collection was statistical or mechanical "if rules can be prespecified so that no clinical judgment need be involved in the procedure" (p. 181). Thus, all self-report, biographical, psychometric, and clerically obtained data were regarded as statistical data. Information gained in interview or observation, on the other hand, was regarded as clinical data, since it involved subjective judgment. Allowing additional categories for composite methods, Sawyer classified 45 studies which compared the prediction of behavioral outcomes according to both the mode of data collection and the mode of combination of data. In spite of methodological problems and equivocal results in many of these studies, Sawyer was able to conclude the following: (1) clinical combination of data was inferior to mechanical, no matter how the data were collected; (2) the type of synthesis between clinical and statistical methods which has been suggested by Holt (1958) did not appear promising; and (3) the clinician may serve a useful function in the data *collection* process "by providing, in objective form, judgments to be combined mechanically . . . that is, by assessing characteristics that otherwise would not enter the prediction." Thus, "improvement should result from devising better ways for the clinician to report objectively the broad range of possibly relevant behavior he perceives" (p. 193).

Holt's (1970) rebuttal to Sawyer's conclusion was simply to continue his earlier arguments that the actuaries had oversimplified the whole area of inquiry, that they had not used adequate scientific standards in their work, and that clinical methods were still very much worthwhile. Relatively little research has been published in this area in the recent past; rather, researchers have turned their attention to the further study and development of actuarial methods. This work is discussed in later sections of the present chapter, and its extension into the field of automated interpretation is described in Chapter 10.

The reader might question why the clinician may be able to identify important predictors but not be able to utilize them in making predictions as consistently as the actuary. The clinician is simply not as reliable as the formula or the computer. Humans have their "bad days," they are influenced by boredom and fatigue, and they can be distracted by interpersonal and environmental circumstances. All of these human foibles interfere with the consistency with which the clinician can apply his/her expertise. These effects tend to be reasonably "random" and they add error to the clinician's judgments, attenuating their accuracy. On the other hand, formulas, computers, and statistical tables ordinarily are not subject to such errors, a fact which almost certainly helps account for their greater accuracy.

The Clinician as Hypothesis Builder

A safe conclusion to be drawn from the foregoing discussion is that once *empirical* relationships have been established between cues and citeria, the clinician can profitably be supplanted by an actuarial model of the phenomenon to be predicted. This suggests that an important role for the assessment clinician, perhaps the most important role, is the identification or discovery of new predictors or cues that will enhance predictive accuracy.

An example of the role of the clinician as a hypothesis generator can be found in the work of Meehl and Dahlstrom (1960), who developed a set of rules for discriminating between the MMPI profiles of patients who, independently of the MMPI, had been unequivocally diagnosed as either neurotic or psychotic. Meehl and Dahlstrom initially used their clinical judgment to sort the profiles, and then wrote a series of sequential, mechanical rules which attempted to duplicate their clinical judgment. Kleinmuntz (1963), using an essentially similar approach, was able to develop a computer program for distinguishing between the MMPI profiles of normal and maladjusted college students.

But even the hypothesis-generating role of the clinician can in principle be supplanted by the computer. Goldberg (1965), using the same MMPI profiles as Meehl and Dahlstrom (1960), compared their rules with 29 clinical judges and with a wide variety of other potentially discriminative rules and indices, some based directly on clinical experience and some which were more or less arbitrary and had no known clinical significance. One of the more interesting findings was that it was one of the latter rules—the linear combination of scores $(L + Pd + Pa - Hy - Pt)$—which proved to be the best discriminator between neurotics and psychotics. Goldberg (1970) also showed that simplified mathematical representations of the clinicians' judgments were more accurate than the original judgments themselves. However, the empirically developed rule given previously outperformed even these representations. In principle the Goldberg procedure—that is, the empirical development of hypotheses—could be extended to any predictive situation. The efficiency of an assortment of different hypotheses or indices—indeed all possible indices which could be generated—thus could be examined by a computer, bypassing the need for the clinician even to generate hypotheses or offer judgments. This nontheoretical approach precisely corresponds to the empirical approach to test construction discussed earlier in Chapter 4, and embodies both the same advantages and the same disadvantages.

Clinical versus Actuarial Description

The failure to demonstrate the superiority of clinical over actuarial prediction led some clinicians to turn to personality *description* as an area in which the clinician's special abilities should be more clearly apparent. For example, Halbower (1955) compared the accuracy of personality descriptions generated by clinicians from patients' MMPI profiles with descriptions which were generated from MMPI profiles by actuarial procedures. First he identified, and defined by specific rules, four MMPI "types" which were relatively common in his patient sample. For example, the "code 13" type was defined by the following rules: *Hs* and *Hy* ≥ 70; *D* $< Hs$ and *Hy* by at least 10 scale points; either *K* or *L* $>$ both *?* and *F*; *F* ≤ 65; and scales *Pd, Mf, Pa, Pt, Sc, Ma,* and *Si* all ≤ 70. To construct "cookbook" or actuarial descriptions of each profile type, he selected at random nine patients whose MMPI profiles fitted the type. Each patient's therapist then completed a 154-item Q-sort which involved the ranking of personality descriptive statements from "most like the patient" to "least like the patient." The mean of the five most similar Q-sorts was designated as the acturial description of that type. To compare the accuracy of these cookbook descriptions with those made clinically, two additional patients fitting each MMPI profile type were selected, and the therapists' Q-sorts were again used as the criterion. Not one of the individual clinicians' readings of an MMPI profile correlated as strongly with the criterion as did the cookbook reading. Halbower repeated the comparison using patients drawn from a different population and achieved identical results.

The possibility that more accurate patient personality descriptions could be obtained from an MMPI cookbook than from a clinician led Marks and Seeman (1963) to develop a relatively comprehensive cookbook for describing the majority of psychiatric patients. Using MMPI profiles from the psychiatric patients of a midwestern medical center, they were able to develop 16 different profile types which accounted for 78 percent of the patients in their sample. The authors reported much normative information about their profile types (including other psychometric information, case history details, presenting symptoms, diagnosis, and course in treatment), expressing the data in terms of percent of occurrence and giving a comparison with patients in general. This cookbook was reissued in revised form a decade later with much simplified rules for classifying patients into the same 16 profile types (Marks, Seeman, and Haller, 1974). While the change increased the percentage of patients whose profiles fitted the rules, thus countering a major criticism of the original cookbook (see following discussion), no new data were presented as to the validity of the simplified rules.

A similar handbook of MMPI profile interpretations was developed by Gilberstadt and Duker (1965). They developed 19 profile types, using a similar approach to that employed by Halbower and by Marks and Seeman. Based upon a careful reading of the case histories of the male psychiatric patients that fitted each of these profile types, Gilberstadt and Duker reported the most likely diagnosis and an extended clinical personality description of each type. They also reported a list of complaints, traits, and symptoms that statistically differentiated each type from patients in general.

A third MMPI interpretive cookbook was developed by Drake and Oetting (1959) for describing college students. Basing their analyses on the three highest and two lowest MMPI scales of the profiles of more than 4,000 college students who had sought counseling, they identified statistically nearly 700 different patterns. They then examined the counseling case materials and independently compiled a list of problems, descriptive phrases, and other items descriptive of these individuals. The cookbook lists the various code patterns, their frequencies, and the personality descriptions that were significantly associated with each pattern.

An interpretative MMPI cookbook for adolescents was developed by Marks, Seeman, and Haller (1974). These authors first developed eight new sets of MMPI norms (without *K* corrections), covering males and females separately in the following four age groups: 14 and below, 15, 16, and 17–18. The MMPI responses of approximately 1,800 "normal" adolescents from six different states were involved in establishing these norms. They then identified 834 white, nonretarded adolescent patients aged 12–18 from 74 different psychological treatment settings over 30 states, involving a total of 172 different therapists. All of these patients had been in treatment for at least 10 sessions.

To develop the cookbook, the profiles of the 834 treatment cases were determined using the new adolescent norms and were then categorized according to the two highest scales, regardless of the absolute values of these two scales. If a code type had less than 10 cases, the first and third highest scales were used. By this procedure, the authors were able to classify more than 98 percent of the 834 treatment cases. The cookbook presents descriptions of 29 different code types, based on a number of data sources such as adjective checklists filled out by both patients and therapists, a descriptive Q-sort and other data supplied by the therapist, and an objective case history form.

Another recent addition to the MMPI literature on objective interpretation systems is the work of Megargee (1977, 1979) and his colleagues on a prison population. Megargee's primary aim was to develop a "reliable, valid, economical typology for classifying criminal offenders" (1979, p. 305). The first step in this project was to use Veldman's (1967) "hierarchical profile analysis" procedure for the purpose of finding groups of profiles that were similar to one another. After identifying nine such groups, the researchers used a lengthy trial-and-error procedure to develop objective rules for defining each type. A wide variety of case information was available about each inmate, including presentence investigation reports, family data, educational and vocational achievement, adjustment reports while in prison, and postprison behavior. These data were used to develop modal descriptions of each of the nine code types. Megargee (1979) reported that more than 85 percent of offenders in a wide range of settings could be assigned a specific type within his system.

A number of other objective interpretation systems exist, both for the MMPI and other tests, within the context of automated or computerized interpretation systems that are offered on a commercial basis. Because these systems are not available for use except through their commercial outlets, and because little or no information about their development or validity is available, they are discussed in Chapter 10 in the context of automated interpretation and its associated problems. One exception is the recently published cookbook for the Personality Inventory for Children (PIC) (Wirt, Lachar, Klinedinst, and Seat, 1977), which is available for individual use and which also forms the basis for a commercially available interpretation program (Lachar and Gdowski, 1979). The PIC and its cookbook are described in Chapter 9.

There has been little research to cross-validate these cookbooks by evaluating their adequacy in other populations. Rather, most of the initial research activity was directed at showing that only relatively small percentages of patients could be covered by the 1963 Marks and Seeman rules and the Gilberstadt and Duker rules (e.g., Huff, 1965; Klett and Vestre, 1967; Payne and Wiggins, 1968; Sines, 1966). As we shall see in Chapter 10, more recent research efforts in the development of objective interpretation systems have tended to involve two areas: the practical development of commercially available computer interpretation systems for a number of different tests, and the objective use of interview and biographical data. There is also a body of research literature studying the relative merits of different actuarial strategies, to which we now turn.

Research on Actuarial Strategies

Once it had been established that actuarial predictions and descriptions were equal to, or better than, clinical judgments, research attention turned to a closer study of actuarial procedures themselves. Is there one particular actuarial approach or model that consistently tends to result in more accurate outcomes? This research question was initially addressed in the simplest of contexts—namely, dichotomous prediction situations. For example, Goldberg's (1965) study on the prediction of neurosis versus psychosis from MMPI profiles examined a wide variety of actuarial or objective predictors. Some of these predictors were *linear,* involving individual MMPI scales or simple additive combinations of scales, and some were *configural,* such as the sums of the squares of certain scale scores, the number of "signs" of a particular kind, and the Marks and Seeman profile types. Goldberg's conclusion from this aspect of his study was that "simple linear combinations of scale scores were more accurate than configural models" (p. 1). This conclusion directly contradicted Meehl's (1954) early hypothesis, in which he stated that because the judgment process of clinicians is believed to be highly configural in nature, the most accurate actuarial predictors should be configural. (Research which helps to clarify the underlying nature of the clinical judgment process is described later in this chapter.)

Not content with his original findings, Goldberg (1969) tried out a variety of additional configurational procedures. Once again, he was led to the same conclusion: "neither . . . moderated regression analyses, profile typologies, the Perceptron algorithm, density estimation procedures, Bayesian techniques, nor sequential analyses . . . have been able to improve on a simple linear function" (p. 523). More recent studies by Giannetti, Johnson, Klingler, and Williams (1978) and by Pritchard (1977), involving methodological improvements over earlier studies, reached the same conclusion regarding the superior accuracy of linear over configural predictors.

More recently, Dawes (1979; Dawes and Corrigan, 1974) has demonstrated that the superiority of linear models in the prediction of complex events is widespread, not only in psychological predictions but on a much more general level, involving such disparate areas as sex, business, violence, and politics. A current controversy in this research concerns the importance of the individual weights given to each of the terms in the linear predictive function (e.g., Pruzek and Frederick, 1978; Wainer, 1978), and whether it makes any practical difference if these weights are not selected with any particular care.

There is a great deal still to be learned about the technology of constructing actuarial prediction systems in personality assessment. Almost all of the research described here has been limited to consideration of simple dichotomous predictions, such as whether an MMPI profile reflects neurosis or psychosis. In real life, however, the problems facing psychologists developing actuarial systems are much more complex. For example, are the basic profile categories or "types" best formed on the basis of high-point profile codes (e.g., Marks, Seeman, and Haller, 1974), or natural clusters of profiles which are then defined more precisely by complex rules (e.g., Marks and Seeman, 1963; Megargee, 1977), or by some other method? Lachar, DeHorn, and Gdowski (1979) have recently addressed this question for the Personality Inventory for Children, and they concluded that both systems may be useful. Whether or not the same conclusion would apply to a different test, such as the MMPI, would require further research. Another topic of considerable importance in constructing actuarial systems, the development of ways to include information about the population base rates of variables to be predicted, is discussed in Chapter 10.

Some General Considerations

There are a number of general points to be made about actuarial and clinical approaches as applied both to personality prediction and description. First, it should not be forgotten that any instrument of demonstrated predictive usefulness (validity) can be used in either a clinical or an actuarial manner.

Second, little is yet known about the degree to which actuarial or cookbook descriptions can be generalized from the original sample upon which they were constructed. Certainly, the research to date on two MMPI cookbooks that describe psychiatric patients suggests that some caution may be necessary, as does Goldberg's (1968) critique of Lindzey's (1965) findings with the TAT. At the same time, the ultimate contribution of actuarial techniques to clinical psychology will depend upon their generality, since the time and effort required to develop such cookbooks can only be justified when the results can be broadly applied.

Third, there is a general issue pertaining to the clinician of exceptional predictive skill. In studies which have reported the success rates of individual clinicians, it is common to find that some clinicians are consistently more accurate in their predictions than others. It has therefore been advocated that more effort should be directed toward identifying such clinicians and having them train others. Goldberg (1970), on the other hand, argued that it would be more useful to employ the most accurate clinicians in the development of actuarial formulas that would then supplant the clinicians altogether. His research evidence showed strong support for this position.

A related point was made by Pritchard (1980), who argued that there were certain situations in which clinical input into a prediction might be desirable and justifiable. For example, there are many instances in which the costs or utilities associated with different sources of error should be taken into account (see later discussion). Pritchard also believed that clinical or subjective review of an actuarial prediction would be in order whenever a clinician had an ethical responsibility to an individual client. Dawes's (1980) response to these suggestions for using clinical input was that actuarial procedures would be superior to the subjective approaches in these situations also, and that clinical input was therefore still unjustified.

Our final comment concerns the relative economy of the clinical and actuarial procedures. Although one advantage claimed from actuarial over clinical methods is the ultimate savings in time, there will be situations in which the clinical method will be more economical, especially if the two methods yield roughly comparable accuracy. Such a situation was described by Johnston and MacNeal (1967), who compared methods of predicting length of stay in a psychiatric hospital. Here, actuarial prediction from case history and behavioral variables was about as accurate as clinical prediction made by the professional staff while handling their routine professional assignments. Since the clinical approach involved considerably less time and effort than the actuarial, it would appear that the clinical approach was clearly the method of choice.

BASE RATES

The term *base rate,* or the relative frequency of an event (disorder, symptom, behavior) in the population of interest, was introduced in Chapter 7, and examples were presented showing the importance of knowing the base rate of a disorder before making a prediction about its presence or absence for a particular individual. Although the intelligent understanding and use of base rate information would greatly increase the effectiveness of personality assessment in practical situations, psychologists have been relatively slow to accept the importance of base rates and to incorporate this information into their clinical work.

The matter was first brought to prominence by Meehl and Rosen (1955) in their discussion of the hit-and-miss validity of predictive devices. Meehl and Rosen pointed out that the more the base rate diverges from .5 (i.e., a 50/50 division in the population), the greater will be the difficulty in prediction. In some cases, the overall hit-and-miss success rate will be *lower* if the test is used than if all persons were simply regarded as belonging to the more frequent category. For example, in Table 7-2 the hit rate (correct diagnosis) was only 97.6 percent, as compared with 99 percent if everybody were to be called "normal."

Cureton (1957) showed that for a valid predictor, it should always be possible to find a cutting score that will result in a greater overall proportion of correct predictions than would result from "using the base rate"; that is, by regarding everybody as belonging to the more frequent category. Thus, if the cutting score in Table 7-2 were to be raised to, let us say, 100, the result might well be as depicted in Table 8-1. Here, the success rate is 99.1 percent, a very modest improvement over the base rate of 99 percent but an improvement nonetheless. However, it is doubtful whether a cutting score of 100 would be useful in practice, because the great majority of the actual schizophrenics would not have been identified as such by the test. (We recognize that it *would* in fact be possible to devise a situation where the base rate could never be exceeded no matter what cutting score was employed—for example, if the variability of scores in the less frequent condition

TABLE 8-1.   Hypothetical Percentage of Patients Diagnosed Schizophrenic or Normal by the *Sc* Scale, Using a Cutting Score of 100, Where 1 Percent Are Actually Schizophrenic and 99 Percent Are Actually Normal

T score	Actually Schizophrenic	Actually Normal	Total
T score 100 or more (diagnosed schizophrenic)	0.2[a]	0.1	0.3
T score below 100 (diagnosed normal)	0.8	98.9[a]	99.7
Total	1.0	99.0	100.0

[a]Correctly diagnosed.

was substantially smaller than the variability of scores in the more frequent condition. The point is, however, that hit-and-miss success rates can be manipulated simply by altering the cutting score.)

In making a particular prediction, it is probable that no single test will be uniformly optimal for all population base rates and relative outcome values. Satz, Fennel, and Reilly (1970) have provided an excellent illustration of this point, reporting hit-and-miss percentages for the prediction of brain disease from five neurological tests and one neuropsychological test. Three different hypothetical base rates for brain disease were then considered (.8, .5, and .2). The data clearly showed that two of the tests that gave a relatively poor showing on overall percentage hit-and-miss figures were in fact the most effective when the base rate for brain disease was as low as .2. These tests, which made almost no "false positive" errors (calling normal persons brain diseased) but correctly identified only a moderate percentage of the actual brain-diseased patients ("true positives"), proved most likely to be correct when the great majority of the subjects were *not* brain diseased.

Decision Making

In a practical assessment situation, the interest is usually not so much in the hit-and-miss success rate as is the overall *usefulness* or *efficiency* of a test. Referring again to Table 7-2, for every 1,000 subjects tested, a cutting score of 70 on the *Sc* scale would identify a group of 26, but only six of them would actually be schizophrenic (i.e., "true positives"). However, we might well be willing to accept this state of affairs if we plan to employ much more extensive and costly procedures for a further evaluation of the 26 thus identified. The benefit would be that we are saved the expense of evaluating the entire 1,000 in this manner. The price we pay consists of (1) failing to identify four pathological persons—the "false negatives," and (2) the cost of the screening procedure.

These questions involving costs and benefits fall in the area of *decision making,* a topic which is becoming increasingly important in personality assessment. The development of a decision-making orientation in the field of personality assessment came about in two ways. The first was an outcome of the Meehl and Rosen (1955) paper, which had implied, perhaps without intent, that percentage accuracy was the all-important criterion in diagnosis or classification. This paper elicited a number of rejoinders (e.g., Buchwald, 1965; Karson and Sells, 1956; Rimm, 1963) which insisted that it was the *utility* of a classification, not its accuracy, that should be used as the ultimate criterion for judging it. Taking account of utility involves a quantitative determination of the different consequences of the various possible classifications in terms of their costs to all concerned. For example, what would the overall costs be to the individual, to the family, to those professionals concerned with the treatment, and to society generally, of institutionalizing a patient at a given time; and, conversely, what would these costs be if the patient were to be maintained in the home?

The second important influence leading toward a decision-making orientation in personality assessment was the appearance of the first edition of the book *Psychological Tests and Personnel Decisions,* by Cronbach and Gleser (1957/ 1965), who offered a clear decision-making framework for the use of psychological tests, as an alternative to more traditional orientations. Among the issues raised was that of the expected utility or "payoff" of a particular kind of information in terms of the cost of obtaining this information relative to its yield in predictive accuracy. In other words, the cost of the testing program must be weighed against the increased efficiency of the selection process. Further discussion of this and other practical applications of the decision-making approach have been provided by Arthur (1966, 1969), Cole and Magnussen (1966), and Cronbach and Gleser (1965). Breger (1968), Lanyon (1971, 1972), and Runyon (1977) have also emphasized a decision-making orientation in their discussions of psychological assessment, while an extensive technical discussion of this topic has been provided by Wiggins (1973).

Specifically, the decision-making approach focuses upon the consequences of various courses of action. Instead of describing a person according to such traditional personality dimensions as dominant, tolerant, and anxious, or classifying him/her according to traditional psychiatric categories, such as depressed, schizophrenic, and brain damaged, the decision-making approach deals with the various courses of action open to those persons who are performing the assessment. For example, if a psychiatrist requests a "personality evaluation" of a patient so that a decision can be made whether to discharge the patient, keep him/her under intensive care, or send him/her to the back ward, these three options become the possible alternatives to be studied. There is no criterion for the accuracy of assessment, in the sense that a description of being high in dominance can be verified against peer ratings or the holding of leadership positions, or a diagnosis of schizophrenia can be checked for accuracy against a panel of expert judges, or a diagnosis of brain damage can be checked against physiological exploration. Rather, the criterion is one of cost and utility—the value of the decision. The aim is to make the decision-assessment that results in the most useful outcome, all things considered. The technical aspects of decision-making strategies in psychological assessment situations (e.g., Cronbach and Gleser, 1965; Rorer, Hoffman, and Hsieh, 1966; Wiggins, 1973) are quite complex and beyond the scope of this book. However, it is worth looking at a general approach to complex decision making, *operations research,* which has developed in quite a different context.

Operations Research

During World War II, the British government was faced with the problem of allocating its limited war resources to a wide variety of possible activities. The criterion for allocation was simple in principle—to maximize the effectiveness of these resources. Mathematical techniques were developed to assist in the kind of decisions that were necessary under these circumstances. After the war, it was realized that the decisions that had been faced were essentially the same as those facing business and industry in countless ways. For example, how many salesmen should a company hire, and where should they be sent, to sell the maximum amount of the company's products at the least cost? Or, how many check-out counters should a supermarket have in order to preserve an optimal balance between saving on clerks' time and losing customers because of their waiting too long? Again, how many plants should a company have, and where should they be located, in order to strike an optimal balance between the cost of transporting raw materials, on the one hand; and the cost of transporting finished goods to their markets, on the other? The field of expertise in the complex engineering, mathematical, and business skills needed to approach such problems has come to be known as *operations research.* For a classic account of some of the techniques of this field, the reader is referred to Ackoff and Rivett (1963) for a brief introduction, and to Hillier and Lieberman (1967) for a more detailed treatment.

Ways in which the technology of operations research can be applied to personality assessment and to the broader context of decision making within mental health contexts have been described by Halpert, Horvath, and Young (1970) and by Lyons (1980). Although definite progress has been made in this area, the major difficulty continues to be the development of adequate criteria of *utility,* a task which involves the quantification of the different values associated with the various possible decisions. In business and industry, the criterion of utility traditionally employed is simple: monetary profit. Relationships can be quantified in terms of the money involved, and a system can then be devised which presumably will result in the greatest profit. A similar approach is possible in the context of psychological assessment; the assessment situation, however, is not quite so straightforward. A major problem is the determination of the values to be placed on the alternate available decisions. The values will at times be monetary, but a more important component is the social or cultural values involved. For example, how much is it worth, socially, to a person to avoid confinement in a psychiatric hospital? Or, how much is it worth to a community to have a particular person confined in a psychiatric hospital where his/her bizarre actions will not threaten others? Despite an interesting collection of papers by Shelly and Bryan (1964) on the quantification of values, ways of determining such mental health related values and incorporating them into decision-making processes need still to be developed in order to make full use of the potential of operations research technology.

It can be argued that social and cultural values are too complex to be quantified, and that it is foolish to hope for any success along these lines. However, these values are implicitly estimated whenever an actual decision is made about a psychiatric patient, whether or not the decision maker is explicit about them. In other words, we cannot and do not avoid making judgments about these values in our actual behavior. The situation might be seen as analogous to skilled clinicians who integrate personality assessment information in their heads and make a diagnoses or predictions about the respondent. They have combined certain specific pieces of information according to certain specific rules, whether or not they were aware of doing so. A task for the future is to understand and make explicit these implicit processes and values.

Mention should also be made of another term often used to describe this orientation: *systems analysis*. This is a much more general term than operations research and is loosely used to refer to the employment of complex quantitative procedures and computers to problems involving a very large number of variables. It is used more specifically to refer to the analyses of complex situations where an attempt is made to identify *all* the variables which interact and influence the outcomes of interest. The situation, defined by those variables which need to be taken into account, is then called a "system," and any part of any operation involved in quantifying processes within the system may become labeled as "systems analysis." Thus, in the context of assessment, Nathan (1967) has developed extensive sets of diagnostic rules for classifying psychiatric patients into traditional psychiatric categories, and he has referred to his work as a "systems-analytic" approach to the diagnosis of psychopathology. Nathan's work should not be confused with decision making as previously discussed, since the decisions to which he is referring concern placement into traditional diagnostic categories, and not alternate treatments or other courses of action.

In conclusion, let us refer back to the actuarial work of Burgess (1928) on parole violation. In his sample, 28.5 percent of all the parolees violated their parole; or, to put it a different way, the base rate for parole violation was 28.5 percent. Thus, we would have been correct 71.5 percent of the time if we had predicted that all parolees would be nonviolators. Gough (1962) reanalyzed Burgess's data and demonstrated that, if optimal cutting scores had been used (those that would give the greatest number of placements in the correct groups of violators and nonviolators), the overall predictive accuracy would have been 76 percent, only four percent greater than the accuracy of predicting that all the parolees would be nonviolators. Whether or not the use of the actuarial data would have been justified in this setting (as opposed to following the base rate and predicting that there would be no violation at all) would depend on the efficiency or optimality of the decisions that would follow, or more specifically, on the relative costs associated with each kind of predictive error.

COMPARISON OF DATA SOURCES

It may only be a slight exaggeration to say that many psychologists, when assigned a task in personality or clinical assessment, administer to the respondent a standard battery of psychological assessment instruments, and that they usually follow the same procedure *no matter what* information is being sought or what question is to be answered. Part of the reason for their behavior undoubtedly lies in the type of request sometimes made of them. It has been traditional for hospital psychologists to receive a referral "for psychologicals," in much the same way that the patient would be referred "for urinalysis" or "for chest X-rays." Thus, using a preestablished battery of assessment instruments becomes a habit. A moment's thought will indicate at least two deficiencies in this approach. First, every patient is different, so that the task of finding things out about one patient is never quite the same as finding them out about another. Second, it would seem reasonable to expect that, for any given assessment task (whether or not we include the particular patient as part of the definition of the task), there would be one particular combination of instruments and procedures that is optimal for the task.

In Chapters 3 and 4 we discussed the various approaches to the construction of personality assessment devices. A significant part of that discussion was devoted to an examination of the ways in which individual items are selected to form a scale. The underlying principle in this work was that each item should contribute something unique to the total product and should complement every other item, so that the concept or domain to be assessed would be fully represented.

The same principle should apply when a group of tests are assembled for the purpose of evaluating a particular patient. In order to do so, however, we would need to know exactly what is contributed by each test to the assessment task as a whole. For example, what patient characteristics are best assessed by the Rorschach? What does an interview contribute that cannot easily be learned by other methods? What are the strongest contributions of the MMPI? Unfortunately, there is no systematic body of research that addresses these questions directly, and such research would be an expensive and large-scale task. However, a number of individual studies are relevant to this area, and indeed, permit us to draw some fairly firm conclusions. To anticipate, the findings are consistent with the general theme that the more *independent* methods or sources of data that are employed, the more valid will be the resulting assessment. Let us now review the evidence in this area.

Contributions of Assessment Instruments

Several studies have been carried out to evaluate the different contributions of various assessment instruments to making a traditional clinical psychodiagnostic evaluation of psychiatric patients. One such study was done by Kostlan (1954). Kostlan collected four kinds of information from each of five male psychiatric outpatients: social case history, the Rorschach, the MMPI, and the Stein (1947) sentence completion test. In order to compare the relative utility of each kind of information in providing an accurate personality description, 20 clinicians, all of whom had at least two years of psychodiagnostic experience, were presented with different combinations of three out of the four kinds of data. Their analyses were then compared with those of criterion judges, using a lengthy checklist of personality descriptive items. The surprising finding was that clinicians who did not have access to a social case history gave personality descriptions which were no more accurate than those made on the basis of "minimal data" alone (age, occupation, education, marital status, and reason for referral to the clinic)! It was also found that the "minimal data" permitted descriptions which were better than chance, and that the most accurate descriptions were those based on combinations which included both the social case history and the MMPI.

Another study was carried out by Sines (1959), who utilized clinical psychology graduate student trainees as judges. Sines first obtained biographical data on a structured self-report questionnaire from each of 30 patients. Each patient was then interviewed and tested with the Rorschach and the MMPI by one of five trainees, with counterbalancing of the order in which these three kinds of information (interview, Rorschach, and MMPI) were obtained. The trainees performed Q-sort personality descriptions of each patient, first using the biographical data alone, and again after each new kind of information was added. Comparisons were then made with a criterion Q-sort description, so that it was possible to compare, for example, the accuracy of a personality description made from the biographical data sheet alone with the description made from that source plus any one or more of the three additional sources of information. According to Sine's report, the clinicians formed specific descriptions fairly quickly, and the descriptions changed little with the addition of data over and above the biographical data sheet. The interview was the only device which consistently resulted in an increased accuracy of description. In fact, there was some evidence that beyond a certain point, accuracy tended to decrease as more data were available.

The most extensive study of the ability of clinical psychologists to make traditional psychiatric diagnoses from assessment instruments was carried out by Little and Shneidman (1959). The instruments involved were the MMPI, the TAT, the Rorschach, and Shneidman's (1951) Make-a-Picture-Story Test, each instrument being considered singly. Forty-eight psychologists—12 who were considered expert with each of the four tests—made a diagnosis about four subjects. The subjects were selected (unknown to the judges) to include one subject each with a psychotic, a neurotic, and a psychophysiological disorder, and one normal or nonpsychiatric subject. Additional personality descriptions were also sought from each of the judges. For criterion purposes, psychiatrists made diagnoses from extended case history data for each of the subjects. Although the results of this study are complex, findings of note were the disappointingly low agreement of the test judges both among themselves and with the criterion diagnoses, and the generally low validities (if such a term is appropriate in the present context) of the test judges' interpretations.

Another study comparing personality descriptions from several sources of assessment data was that of Golden (1964), who attempted to determine whether descriptions based on clinical tests increased in accuracy as a function of the number of tests employed. Thirty experienced clinical psychologists were asked to judge five of the patients utilized in the Little and Shneidman study. After reading the minimal data sheet and again after reading each of the Rorschach, MMPI, and TAT protocols, the judges were asked to complete the Little and Shneidman personality questionnaire for the patient. The judges' responses were then compared for accuracy with those of highly experienced professionals who had access to extensive case history data. Golden reported that a better-than-chance personality description could be provided from the information contained in the minimal data sheet plus any one of the tests, but that the accuracy of description did not increase significantly as more tests became available.

A more recent and somewhat simpler study by Wildman and Wildman (1975) reached similar conclusions. Six clinical psychologists were asked to review test data obtained from 10 nurses and 10 psychiatric patients, and to determine which tests came from each group. Tests employed were the Bender-Gestalt, House-Tree-Person, MMPI, TAT, and Rorschach. In general, judgments made on the basis of combined data from two different tests were less accurate than those made from the most accurate individual test, which was the MMPI.

A related study in the area of normal personality characteristics was conducted by Scott and Johnson (1972). The aim was to compare the validity of assessments made from *direct* tests, such as self-report questionnaires, with those made from *indirect* tests, such as predicted consequences of hypothetical events and imaginative stories written about TAT pictures. Criteria for the predictions were provided by friends' ratings. The findings tended to support the superiority of the direct measures and did not provide any evidence for the superiority of indirect measures. These conclusions were criticized by McClelland (1972) on the grounds that the criteria involved opinions rather than behaviors, and by Mischel (1972) for the same reason and a number of others. However, Mischel reviewed a variety of other evidence on the same topic and concluded that in general, "findings support the utility of direct as compared to indirect approaches to personality measurement" (p. 319).

What conclusions can be drawn from these studies? For one thing, the studies rather consistently demonstrate that, as sources of data for psychological prediction or description, personality tests do not fare as well as case history data. There is also the suggestion that a single test adds about as much to the case history data as do a number of them, and that it does not much matter which test is utilized. To the extent that this is true, the economics of professional time and effort would favor self-report inventories such as the MMPI. Some criticism can be leveled at Sines's (1955) study, and to a lesser degree also to Kostlan's (1954), for using relatively inexperienced diagnosticians, although it is shown later that the relationship between clinical experience and diagnostic acumen is largely an open question. Also, whatever weaknesses are implied in this criticism, it must be noted that the studies did tend to mirror actual clinical practice in the tests used and in the level of *some* clinical workers.

In defense of the clinician's rather poor showing in the previously reported studies, several points can be raised. (1) These kinds of comprehensive personality descriptions are no longer requested on the near-universal basis that was once the case. The reasons for this state of affairs probably have to do with efficiency and with the limited use made of such descriptions, as illustrated by Meehl's (1960) report that psychotherapists do not find them particularly useful when they begin therapy with a patient. (2) The studies were concerned with general personality descriptions, and not with the assessment and prediction of specific traits and behaviors. We might expect the clinicians to show a higher level of predictive accuracy when dealing with specific behaviors. Little research has been reported, however, comparing the differential usefulness of various instruments and techniques in helping the clinician to make specific predictions. (3) Systematic attention should be given to determining the unique advantages of each of the major assessment instruments and techniques, with the aim of eventually using them only for these unique purposes. (4) All of these studies were conducted prior to the development of a substantial research base for MMPI interpretation, as embodied in the various actuarial systems described earlier in this chapter. Thus, one would expect that the MMPI (and any other test with actuarial interpretation data) would make a better showing than was demonstrated in the studies discussed here. The more specific the actuarial rules, of course, the less relevant is the question of the clinician's degree of experience with the test.

Multimethod Assessment

The studies described in the preceding section have thrown some light on the question of the nature and optimal amount of data that should be collected in order to make a prediction or assessment in personality or psychodiagnosis. Let us now approach the question from a different angle, that of the literature on construct validity. In their classic paper on this topic, Campbell and Fiske (1959) pointed out that in the assessment of any trait or characteristic, one can draw upon a variety of different data sources, or *methods*. The greater the number of independent methods which yield data that are related to each other, the more substantial is the construct validity of the trait. Thus, the greater the variety of methods that are represented in the predictors, the more robust the prediction will be.

The data sources must be relatively independent, however. It is of little use to have a great deal of predictive data based on a single method or on highly similar methods, since the correlations among different trait scores based on a single method may at times be higher than correlations among different methods assessing the same trait. That is to say, each method is subject to its own characteristic biases, which could significantly influence all scores based on that method. For example, a person's scores on a normal personality inventory which assessed socially desirable traits could all be significantly correlated simply because of the influence of social desirability. Similarly, data gathered through interviews could be subject to a common bias due to the interviewer's positive (or negative) feelings about the client.

What is the meaning of the work of Campbell and Fiske for practical assessment situations? It means that much more emphasis should be placed on gathering data by different methods, rather than on the use of data gathered by a single method or by closely related methods. We are now in a position to understand better the results of the Kostlan (1954), Golden (1964), Little and Shneidman (1959), and Sines (1959) studies reviewed earlier. Traditional tests might be viewed as representing a single method or a closely related group of methods. The unique contributions of biographical data and interview data to the accuracy of assessment can be understood by viewing these data sources as representing somewhat different methods. However, since all three methods are related in being self-report procedures, we might expect that sum total of their contributions would be fairly modest, as indeed was found.

Since it would appear that the use of a traditional assessment battery results in a redundancy of data within this rather narrow group of methods, one way to improve the efficiency of assessment, if not its accuracy, would be to use abbreviated forms of each of the traditional data collection methods; for example, a brief, structured interview, a brief biographical data sheet, and a brief self-report inventory. Such an approach was suggested by Lanyon (1972). Also consistent with the multimethod philosophy is the *assessment center* method, which we have described briefly in Chapter 1. Here, the assessors construct the entire assessment procedure around the goal of maximizing the number of different data collection methods that can be employed. A recent utility theory analysis of the assessment center method has demonstrated its efficiency even when validities are relatively low (Cascio and Silbey, 1978). Indicative of the growing recognition of the need for multiple methods in assessment is the recent text by Nay (1979) entitled *Multimethod Clinical Assessment*. This book describes a wide range of methods and also considers approaches to the integration of the data. Ironically, no mention is made of the use of traditional psychological tests, indicating that despite the title of the book, Nay failed to recognize fully the significance of the concept "multimethod."

FACTORS AFFECTING CLINICAL ACCURACY

The very core of the personality assessment enterprise is the validity or accuracy of the descriptions and predictions that are offered. There is a growing interest in studying factors which may be related to accuracy independent of the particular assessment modality that is employed. Let us review the research evidence regarding these factors.

Accuracy and Expertise

First we consider the accuracy of judgments based upon or utilizing interpersonal cues. We are referring to the cues available to all of us in our dealings with other people: content and style of speech, manner of dress, and all those other subtleties that are regarded as contributing to our intuitive impressions about other people. Much of the early research on clinical judgment based upon interpersonal cues has been summarized by Taft (1955) and by Vernon (1964). It would appear from their summaries that the ability to judge others is neither entirely general nor entirely specific. That is to say, there is no such person as a uniformly accurate judge of others, although there is some degree of generality to this ability. It is not related to age (in adults) nor strongly to sex, although there is a slight difference in favor of women. The ability to successfully judge others is positively related to intelligence, artistic and dramatic interests, good emotional adjustment, and social detachment, and is negatively related to authoritarian attitudes. Also, judgments are more accurate when the judges are motivated to make accurate judgments and when they come from cultural backgrounds which are similar to those of the persons being judged.

What about the effect of professional training in psychology or psychiatry? Taft's (1955) early review was not encouraging in this regard, suggesting that experienced clinical psychologists might be no more accurate in making judgments based upon interpersonal cues than are clinical psychology graduate students, and that neither group might be as accurate as certain groups of nonpsychologists, such as physical scientists and perhaps personnel workers. More recently, Ziskin (1975, 1977) reviewed a variety of studies investigating the clinical judgment skills of experienced and inexperienced judges in psychiatric and psychological settings, and concluded that there was little or no evidence of a relationship between experience and accuracy.

If the experienced clinician is no better able than the inexperienced clinician to make so-called intuitive judgments about persons, what about ability to make subjective judgments from formal assessment instruments? Goldberg (1968b) summarized a variety of relevant research studies and concluded that here too, the amount of general professional training and clinical experience of different psychologists was not systematically related to their ability to make accurate judgments from clinical psychological assessment instruments. The tests utilized and predictive tasks involved included the Bender Visual-Motor Gestalt Test to identify brain pathology (Goldberg, 1959), human figure drawings to discriminate between psychiatric and normal adolescents (Hiler and Nesvig, 1965), and the MMPI to discriminate between psychiatric and medical patients (Oskamp, 1962).

It should be clearly understood that these findings refer to the use of diagnostic tests when interpreted subjectively or clinically. As we have repeatedly seen, the use of objective interpretation rules, when available, is generally superior to the subjective approach. In regard to the use of human figure drawings, we have seen in Chapter 3 that the unreliability of this procedure places such a low ceiling on attainable validities as to remove this test from serious consideration as a predictor in its current form. Finally, we will see in Chapter 9 that psychological procedures for the assessment of brain dysfunction have recently undergone quite a revolution, so that major reliance is no longer placed on tests like the Bender-Gestalt. Thus, the reader should understand that Goldberg's (1968b) conclusion and its later affirmation by Ziskin (1975) apply to the subjective interpretation of traditional diagnostic tests, and not to some of the more contemporary approaches.

Because the traditional subjective approach is, nevertheless, our only choice in many instances, their findings must be taken seriously. Let us therefore try to explain them and explore their implications. As noted previously, one important issue in clinical judgments and predictions is the low consistency of clinical judgment among clinicians (i.e., low interjudge reliability) who are using different sources of data, and even when using the same data. For example, in their study of the reliability of clinicians using four data sources (MMPI, Rorschach, Wechsler-Bellevue Intelligence Scale, and a simple vocational history), Goldberg and Werts (1966) concluded that the "judgments of one clinician working from one data source bear no systematic relationship to those of another clinician working from another data source, even though both judges are ranking the same patient on the same trait" (p. 199). Little and Shneidman (1959) found that their clinicians did not agree among themselves on the judgments made either from different data sources or from the same source. In this context, it is noteworthy that Oskamp (1962) did find a positive relationship between accuracy of judgment and the amount of specific experience his judges had with the MMPI. This finding might result from the fact that the MMPI signs for making the discriminations required by Oskamp were reasonably clear-cut in the research literature; hence experienced MMPI workers would probably know of them, and thus have a specific advantage over the inexperienced judges.

Training in Judgmental Accuracy

The finding that there is a great deal of unreliability even among experienced clinicians in their judgments suggests that predictive accuracy could be increased if clinicians were aware of the most predictive cues and used them in their predictions. Oskamp (1962) provided data to support this contention by showing that otherwise naïve undergraduates who were given relevant training in the MMPI soon increased their judgmental accuracy to that of the most experienced judges. On the other hand, Goldberg (1968b) reported that judges only demonstrated a stable increase in their ability to discriminate psychotic from neurotic MMPI profiles if they were given the values for a valid actuarial index for making this decision. Simply informing them of the existence and nature of the index only resulted in a temporary increase in accuracy.

Goldberg (1968b) reported another kind of training for increasing clinical predictive accuracy, involving immediate feedback about accuracy of prediction, which was even less successful. Naïve (undergraduate), middle (graduate), and expert (experienced doctoral level) judges were trained over a 17-week period in discriminating between psychotic and neurotic MMPI profiles. In this period, more than 4,000 training profiles were shown to the judges, who made a decision for each and were provided with immediate feedback about their accuracy. The judges also saw another 6,000 test profiles. The only group to show more than a negligible increase in accuracy as a result of this training were the naïve judges, although the level of accuracy they reached was still substantially below that of the middle-level and expert judges, and even they were still below the ceiling of accuracy provided by actuarial prediction.

Sechrest, Gallimore, and Hersch (1967) also studied several methods of improving clinical accuracy in naïve (undergraduate) judges, who were asked to predict the traits of anxiety and pleasantness in subjects from their sentence completion responses. These authors showed that providing immediate feedback after each judgment did result in superior performance, but there was also some evidence to indicate that this superiority may have been due to enhanced motivation rather than to any specific information imparted.

Schroeder (1972) believed that the effect of feedback would be enhanced if judges first developed explicit hypotheses about the nature of the person and the judgment task, and then applied the feedback to these hypothesized relationships. The results of this study showed that predictive accuracy was indeed greater when judges applied the feedback to the *basis* for prediction rather than simply to the predictor-outcome relationship. In a study involving the same principle, Strasburger and Jackson (1977) showed that accuracy of prediction increased when their judges were provided with information about valid constructs that mediated the relationship between the predictor and the target to be predicted.

These findings suggest several tentative generalizations that might be made regarding the relationship between accuracy of prediction and clinical training. (1) It would seem that a major source of inaccuracy is simply lack of information about the valid cues or predictors for the behavior to be judged. It would appear that general clinical experience by itself is not sufficient, nor even experience with a particular assessment device as a measure for general personality description. What appears to be minimally necessary is some awareness of the specific cues or "signs" that are predictive of the behavior under scrutiny. (2) Inexperienced judges who are provided the correct signs will improve their accuracy *if* they use the signs, but some motivation may be necessary in order to have the judges continue to use the signs. (3) In the absence of previously developed empirical signs, it is possible for judges to develop and "learn" signs by repeatedly making judgments and receiving feedback about the accuracy of these judgments, but once again they must be motivated to do so. However, there is the considerable danger that this "learning" will be illusory and erroneous in nature, as demonstrated by Chapman and Chapman (1971) and discussed in Chapter 11. (4) Knowledge or explicit hypotheses by the judges about the theoretical relationship between predictor and target results in improved accuracy. (5) If specific empirically developed signs or cues are available, then they are probably better used in an actuarial rather than a clinical manner.

Accuracy and Amount of Information

A very much related issue concerns the relationship between the amount of information available to the judge and accuracy of prediction. Again, the commonplace notion is that the more information or data the clinician has available, the more accurate will be the prediction. Indeed, this rationale typically underlies the use of a "battery" of tests with a patient in order to make a comprehensive personality description. However, we have already seen that it is the variability in the *methods* by which the data are gathered that increases accuracy, not merely the fact of having a lot of data. This point is well made in a study by Turner (1966), who used only a single personality assessment device, the Rorschach. In this study, personality predictions were made about patients by clinicians who had varying amounts of the Rorschach protocol available to them, as follows: (1) free associations to the blots only, (2) free associations plus a marked location chart showing which areas of the blots were involved in the responses, (3) both of these plus inquiry information to help pinpoint the formal variables which determined the response, and (4) all of the foregoing plus a summary scoring sheet (psychogram) of all of the scoring results. The results showed that there were no increases in accuracy as a function of increased data for either experienced or inexperienced clinical judges. Presumably, the four data sources were so similar that the latter three did not add any information beyond what was contained in the first.

The major point which emerges from this and similar these studies is that it is important to identify the relevant sources of information for the particular descriptive or predictive task at hand, and that in routine practical situations, attention should be directed toward collecting only the data that are relevant. While there is always the hope that extended data may contain further potentially useful predictors, uncovering such predictors is a different task from routine practical assessment. On the basis of these conclusions, we should not be surprised to learn that certain aspects of personality assessment may be considerably simpler than we had earlier believed. In this connection, Peterson (1965) demonstrated that the two major personality dimensions of maladjustment and introversion-extraversion could be assessed as reliably by simple ratings as by more complicated measures such as personality inventories. Similarly, it has been shown that a combination of a few biographical facts, such as whether or not the patient has ever been married, is of substantial predictive usefulness in the prognosis of schizophrenia. In summarizing his work in clinical inference, Hathaway (1956a) concluded that "the power of a few items as sources of generalization is greater than is usually expected. It is also suggested that inaccuracy enters when the percipient (or clinician) attempts to use additional data that are often less reliable" (p. 249).

A word should be said about the reliability of the criterion to be predicted upon the overall accuracy of prediction. In many prediction studies in mental health, the criteria themselves are somewhat vague and unreliable, as are the traits and characteristics which they represent; for example, neurosis, psychosis, anxiety, and depression. Naturally, the unreliability of a criterion measure sets a ceiling on the validities, or correlations with predictors, that can be achieved. It can be shown mathematically that the lower the ceiling on validity in any given prediction, the less useful will it be to have multiple predictors. In other words, if the best prediction that can be achieved is rather inaccurate to begin with, this ceiling on accuracy will usually be reached with the contributions of just one or two predictors. Thus, we should not be too surprised to find that multiple sources of predictive information did not add much to accuracy in the studies reviewed here. On the other hand, the additional predictors would presumably be useful if the criteria could be made more reliable.

Accuracy and Confidence

Another issue that has concerned personality assessment investigators is the relationship between the accuracy of clinicians' judgments and their degree of confidence in the judgments. This question came to light as a result of an extensive study conducted by Kelly and Fiske (1951) in an attempt to predict success in the Veterans' Administration training program in clinical psychology. In trying to find reasons for their generally disappointing results, Kelly and Fiske discovered that the confidence of judges in a prediction was *inversely related* to the accuracy of that prediction. Somewhat more comforting was Oskamp's (1962) report that, in discriminating between MMPI profiles of psychiatric and medical patients, confidence in any judgment was negatively related to the general clinical experience of the judge. Similarly, Goldberg (1959) reported that inexperienced judges were more confident than experienced judges in their predictions of organic brain pathology from the Bender-Gestalt test. In another study by Oskamp (1965), the judges' confidence levels increased as more information about the patient was made available, but, as noted elsewhere, the accuracy of judgments did not increase.

These studies suggest that degree of confidence in the accuracy of one's judgments could be related either to lack of experience, lack of knowledge, lack of accuracy, or to some combination of these interrelated factors. In a series of papers on the general topic of confidence in one's judgments, Fischoff and his colleagues have shown that overconfidence is typical of the judgment process in a wide variety of settings (Fischoff, 1975; Fischoff and Beyth, 1975; Fischoff, Slovic, and Lichtenstein, 1977; Lichtenstein and Fischoff, 1977). Their findings may be summarized as follows. (1) People are consistently overconfident in their judgments. (2) Once knowledge of outcomes is available, people consistently overestimate what they think they knew before having outcome knowledge. (3) At least in some situations, with increasing knowledge comes decreasing overconfidence, until the point may be reached where very knowledgeable persons display a moderate degree of underconfidence.

It appears from these findings that clinicians should be trained right from the beginning to be aware of the pervasive relationship between inexperience and overconfidence, and to assess their level of confidence more realistically. Oskamp (1962) demonstrated that such training was indeed feasible. On a broader level, there is a clear warning implicit in the findings that we should not be beguiled into confidence simply on the basis of having available a considerable amount of information. A clear understanding of how to use the available information for descriptive and predictive purposes is required.

THE PROCESS OF CLINICAL JUDGMENT

Thus far we have been concerned with the *outcome* or consequences of the clinical judgment process; that is, with the effectiveness or accuracy of judgment. Interest has recently developed in the actual *process* of clinical judgment; that is, the question of exactly how the clinician operates.

In the dispute over clinical versus actuarial modes of prediction, Meehl (1959a) suggested that one potential advantage of clinicians was their ability to combine the available data in a complex, configural way that could not easily be reproduced mathematically. We shall now examine the available evidence to see whether this is indeed how the process of clinical judgment operates. Since we have already seen that the most accurate actuarial predictors tend to be linear ones, we might suspect that Meehl's assertion will be found wrong.

In order to determine whether clinicians utilize simple additive combinations of data in making predictions, or whether they employ complex configural combinations, it is necessary to make elaborate statistical analyses of the data available to the clinician. Basically, these analyses involve some measure of the amount of "nonlinearity" utilized by the judge in decision making, and several methods for doing this have been developed (Hoffman, Slovic, and Rorer, 1968; Hursch, Hammond, and Hursch, 1964). One fairly consistent finding (Hammond and Summers, 1965) has been that it makes just as much sense to call the clinical judgment process "linear" as to call it "nonlinear." Using a different statistical procedure, Rorer, Hoffman, Dickman, and Slovic (1967) and Hoffman, Slovic, and Rorer (1968) were able to show that some judges *do* utilize configural combinations of signs in their judgments, but that in general, the contribution of these "nonlinear" elements is negligible when the contribution of the "linear" elements to the judgment is determined. Among the judgment tasks examined in these studies were decisions, based on behavioral data, whether to give weekend passes to psychiatric patients, and the differential diagnosis of malignancy of a gastric ulcer from X-ray data. These data tend to argue against Meehl's (1959a) position that clinical judgment typically involves the configural combination of data.

In another study, Wiggins and Hoffman (1968) used multiple correlation techniques to determine which of three "mathematical models" best described the judgment process used by each of the 29 clinical judges in discriminating psychotic and neurotic profiles. They reported that although a configural or nonlinear model distinguished 16 of the 29 judges, the superiority over a linear model was small. In other words, what most judges use when making complex predictions can be as well described by a single additive combination of weighted signs as by a more complex configural combination. Goldberg (1971) extended this study by examining five additional nonlinear models, including two that had been proposed by Einhorn and Bass (1971), of which one had been reported to outperform linear models. Once again, he showed that a "linear model provided a better representation of the judgments made by all clinicians than did either of Einhorn and Bass's models, and only the logarithmic provided the linear model with any real competition" (p. 458).

Earlier in this chapter we saw that linear models based on empirical data provide more accurate predictions than do nonlinear models. We have now seen that the clinical judgment process also appears to be better represented by linear rather than nonlinear models. Although we are not necessarily arguing that a simple linear model *explains* the behavior of the clinician in making a prediction, it seems clear that the linear model duplicates (or improves upon) the *results* of the clinicians' behavior. One reason for this (Goldberg, 1970) could be simply that equations are perfectly reliable, whereas human clinicians are not.

A different type of approach to the study of the judgment process was taken by Tversky and Kahnemann (1974), whose work, while not directly involving applied areas, helps shed light on why actuarial predictions consistently outperform human judges. These authors identified three important factors which typically operate in the human judgment process and which serve to reduce its accuracy. The first is *representativeness:* In making judgments, people typically rely excessively on familiar associations between the predictor materials and the criterion targets. Thus, a student who is shy, meek, and orderly may be judged to be enrolled in library science rather than in psychology because those characteristics are stereotypic of librarians. However, a far more compelling factor in the judgment process should have been the fact that psychology majors outnumber library science majors 20 to 1, leading to the actuarial judgment that the student will almost certainly be a psychology major. The operation of the representativeness factor is another way of describing the failure of many judges to take into account the base rates of the criterion categories in the population.

The second factor identified by Tversky and Kahnemann was termed *availability* and refers to the process of basing a judgment on the ease with which instances can be brought to mind. For example, the decision of a clinician to call a new patient "schizophrenic" might be unduly influenced by the fact that he/she had just interviewed several other schizophrenic patients. The third factor, *anchoring,* refers to the fact that judges typically select a preliminary judgment and then adjust it according to subsequent evidence. According to Tversky and Kahnemann, these adjustments are typically insufficient.

Obviously, research on the process of clinical judgment has just begun. Yet such research is essential if we are to understand this critically important process and train others in it. It would seem important for researchers in this area to become familiar with the overall psychological literature on the judgment process as a basis for developing hypotheses that can be tested within the context of personality assessment.

Summary

Psychologists have recently begun to show an interest in studying and comparing various aspects of personality assessment procedures in order to find out which are the most useful. Most of this research has been done on comparisons of actuarial (mechanical, statistical, clerical) and clinical (subjective, intuitive, experiential) procedures for prediction. Meehl, who brought this research area before the public eye in 1954, concluded that, whenever it was possible to formulate them, mechanical predictive rules were generally equal or superior in accuracy to the subjective predictions of clinicians using the same data. Subsequent research has not changed this conclusion, although it has suggested that a useful function of clinicians is in quantifying their behavioral observations; that is, in the domain of measurement rather than prediction. Actuarial techniques have also been applied to the description of personality, and "cookbooks" are available to yield personality descriptions of patients who possess certain types of profiles on the MMPI and other tests.

Research on actuarial strategies has shown consistently than linear models yield more accurate predictions than configural ones, and this finding has considerable generality beyond the field of personality assessment. Ultimately, the importance of actuarial procedures in personality assessment will depend upon their generality; that is, the extent to which descriptive or predictive rules derived on one population are valid for another. The reader is again reminded that in assessing the usefulness of an actuarial sign for prediction or description, it is essential to take into consideration the base rate of the sign, or its frequency of occurrence in the population being consieered.

The topic of decision making is becoming increasingly important in personality assessment. In psychological assessment, contrary to medical assessment, a diagnosis or description cannot usually be checked against any real or verifiable criterion. Therefore, interest has developed in making choices among the options or outcomes available; that is, concentrating on the decision to be made. The adoption of a decision-making orientation makes available to psychologists the developments in decision-making technology from other fields and, in particular, the procedures utilized in business and industry known as "operations research." A major problem with their application to personality assessment is that, associated with each possible outcome, there must be a quantifiable criterion of utility. In business and industry, these criteria may be specified in terms of monetary value; however, when decisions are to be made about people *qua* people, social and personal values become involved, and these are difficult to quantify.

Other aspects of the accuracy of personality assessment have also been studied. Whenever various data sources have been compared for their contribution to a valid comprehensive personality description, biographical information has been shown to be at least as powerful as the commonly used clinical tests. Further, it appears that there is a definite ceiling to the amount of data which it is worthwhile to collect, and that the validity of the resulting assessment is not increased by adding more data; in fact, the validity may even be lowered. Also, the more independent methods or sources of data that are employed, the more valid will be the resulting assessment.

Another fairly consistent finding is that general training and experience in clinical psychology does not seem to make a judge more accurate, either in making interpersonal judgments or in judgments from test materials. A possible explanatory factor is the lack of reliability among clinical judges; this underscores the importance of identifying the particular cues that are relevant in making the judgments. Clinicians' confidence in their judgments may sometimes increase even though their accuracy does not; however, it appears that specific training could rectify this difficulty. Another important factor in the learning and making of more accurate judgments is the need for high motivation on the part of the judges. Research on the process of clinical judgment shows that this process is better represented by linear rather than nonlinear models.

9 SPECIAL APPLICATIONS

There are a number of areas in mental health and related disciplines where personality assessment procedures have traditionally been used in certain accepted ways. While some of these uses are valid and appropriate, for others there are questions as to whether the uses may have evolved out of necessity or opportunity without regard to validity. In this chapter we briefly review four of these areas of application: assessment involving special *demographic factors,* the assessment of *children, law-related applications,* and *neuropsychological assessment.* To anticipate our conclusions, we will see that some of the current uses of personality assessment procedures in these areas are not appropriate, but that there may be other defensible ways, either potential or currently available, to handle the questions of concern.

SPECIAL DEMOGRAPHIC FACTORS

The utility of a personality assessment procedure can be affected by demographic variables in two ways: Different demographic groups might vary (1) in their *normative responses* and (2) in the external *validity,* or empirical correlates, of their scores. Both sources of variation must be considered, whether the assessment procedure is an objective one, such as MMPI code book interpretation, or subjective, such as the clinical interpretation of TAT stories. We briefly review the literature regarding the effect on each of these two factors of sex, age, and ethnic background. The examples given tend to involve inventories because it is only there that relevant empirical information is available.

Sex

Psychologists involved in developing objective tests have known for many years that males and females differ normatively on many aspects of responding that are not directly sex related. These differences are reflected, for example, in the procedure for converting raw scores to scale scores on the MMPI. Thus, a raw score of 30 on the Depression scale is equivalent to a T score (standard score) of 82 for males but only 71 for females. Possible explanations for this and similar differences are that women and men differ in their willingness to admit or report certain kinds of behaviors, thoughts, and feelings; that there are valid normative differences between the sexes; or that the meaning of certain items is different for men and women. In any event, test users should be aware of these normative differences and should be sure to use the appropriate set of norms.

The second possibility for a difference is in validity. Do the valid correlates of scales or projective test interpretations differ for men and women? Empirical studies involving psychodiagnostic instruments such as the MMPI suggest that they may. For example, Dahlstrom, Welsh, and Dahlstrom (1972) reported an extensive unpublished adjective checklist study by Hathaway and Meehl which showed many differences in the way in which males and females who scored high on specific MMPI scales were described by their acquaintances. More recently, the code book developed by Lachar and Gdowski (1979) for the actuarial interpretation of the Personality Inventory for Children contains separate lists of empirical correlates of each scale for boys, girls, and the combined sample. On the other hand, many researchers have chosen to emphasize those correlates of their scales which apply equally to men and women. In developing their actuarial code book for MMPI interpretation, Marks and Seeman (1963) found that their empirically developed interpretations tended to apply about equally well to men and women, and showed an overall validity correlation with external criteria of about .5.

In general, then, it would seem appropriate to expect that different norms will apply to males and females on many assessment devices, and empirical interpretive materials should be utilized cautiously unless they are known to apply specifically to the patient's sex.

Age

It is known that age, like sex, affects responses to personality assessment devices both normatively and in validity. For example, in regard to norms, the Psychological Screening Inventory (Lanyon, 1973, 1978) shows a small but steady decline in scores on the Social Nonconformity scale with increasing age from 16 to 60 for both males and females, and a smaller decline in scores on the Expression scale. It should be borne in mind that because these data are cross-sectional rather than longitudinal in nature, they cannot be said to represent potential changes that might take place with aging, but only currently existing differences between age groups. As with the sex variable, some test differences of this nature are presumably due to real-life differences as a function of age, and some are due to other factors. In regard to differences in validity with age, there is no particular reason to expect significant variation within the middle adult age ranges, although little or no research exists in this area. The younger age groups (adolescents and children) require special consideration, as discussed in a separate section of this chapter.

The elderly also require special consideration. One source of material on this topic is the edited volume by Storandt, Siegler, and Elias (1978), which documents specific changes in responses to certain tests with increasing age, but gives no systematic normative or validity data. A more specific review, emphasizing the MMPI, has been published by Gynther (1979a). A somewhat different approach to aging was taken by Cresswell and Lanyon (1981), who attempted to specify the particular problems that were most likely to require assessment in a chronic psychogeriatric setting and evaluated the validity of various screening instruments to assess them in that particular setting. Four problem areas were identified: deterioration due to brain damage, depression, overall psychopathology, and prognosis. It was found that the Mental Status Questionnaire (Kahn, Goldfarb, Pollack, and Peck, 1960), a simple 10-item instrument, was the most effective in the preliminary screening of both deterioration due to brain damage and overall severity of disorder. A number of other instruments that have been developed specifically to assess different aspects of the personality and social functioning of the elderly were reviewed by Cresswell (1978).

Ethnic Background

As with the demographic variables of age and sex, by far the greatest amount of research on the effect of ethnic background on personality assessment devices has involved the MMPI. A significant amount of this work has been done by Gynther (1972, 1979b) in the investigation of test differences between Black and White respondents. On both the MMPI and other personality inventories, stable differences have been reported both for normal adults and for psychiatric patient groups. The meaning and effects of these differences can be interpreted in several different ways, however. One possibility is that the MMPI gives invalid results for Blacks, leading to the potential for racial discrimination. Another is that these differences reflect valid personality differences between Blacks and Whites. A third and perhaps the most likely possibility is that these differences "are determined by a complex interaction of various factors" (Gynther, 1979b, p. 134) such as educational level and social status. One way of handling the problem would be to develop specific tests or scales for Blacks, and Gynther, Lachar, and Dahlstrom (1978) have taken a step in that direction with the development of an MMPI *F* scale for Blacks.

Pritchard and Rosenblatt (1980) criticized the research methods that have been most commonly employed to investigate racial/ethnic differences in the MMPI. They concluded that the soundest research strategy, which would involve an examination of the accuracy of predictions made within racial subgroups on the basis of the MMPI, has produced no evidence that the MMPI makes more errors for Blacks than for Whites. Clearly, more research is needed in this area.

The relatively small amount of research involving Mexican Americans, American Indians, and Asian Americans was also summarized by Gynther (1979b), who concluded that each of these groups appear to have some degree of uniqueness in their responses on personality inventories. Thus, it is not yet clear how much caution should be observed in using the MMPI with such groups. The *translation* of inventories into other languages is an entirely different matter, and this requires considerable sophistication in the translation process as well as substantial study of the translated form, which should be regarded as a new and unvalidated instrument until proven otherwise. Technical information regarding the translation of inventories has been provided by Brislin, Lonner, and Thorndike (1973) and by Butcher and Pancheri (1976).

PERSONALITY ASSESSMENT WITH CHILDREN

The theory and the technology of assessment that are described throughout this book apply equally to adults and to children, and some of the specific assessment procedures already described have been specifically applicable to children. However, we have chosen to discuss the topic separately because it requires two particular considerations that are less relevant with adults. First, the development of norms (whether explicit or implicit) and the demonstration of validity are complicated by the necessary assumption that there may be major differences among children at different age levels. Second, self-report devices would appear to be more limited in applicability, particularly with young children. The assessment of children has been approached in four different ways: with *projective* techniques, with *inventories,* from a *behavioral* viewpoint, and with *checklists* and *rating scales.*

Projective Techniques

The use of projective techniques, interpreted subjectively, has traditionally been the method of choice in the assessment of children. It has usually been supplemented by material gained through various play techniques and whatever other interactions in which the child could be persuaded to engage, and the data have typically been integrated within a framework employing psychoanalytic concepts. Palmer's (1970) book *The Psychological Assessment of Children* illustrates this approach. According to a survey by Brown and McGuire (1976), the vast majority of personality or diagnostic assessments with children have relied heavily on projective instruments.

The problems of reliability and validity with projective tests, discussed in Chapters 3 and 7, are magnified in the assessment of children, since each age grouping might be viewed as involving a different application of the test; somewhat analagous, perhaps, to different ethnic groups. Thus, not only must it be expected that the norms will differ across age groupings, but there is no reason to suppose that a predictive or descriptive correlate that is valid for five-year-olds, for example, will also be valid for ten-year-olds.

One way of approaching the validity problem has been to adopt the theoretical viewpoint that children's personality development is systematic and progressive in a holistic sense, in the same way that the original construction of the Stanford-Binet Intelligence Scale was based on the assumption that intellectual development is systematic and progressive. Thus, administration of the Stanford-Binet results in a "mental age," which might be higher or lower than the child's chronological age. Developmental deficits can then be pinpointed, together with areas in which the child is mentally advanced for his/her age. The work of Ames, Learned, Metraux, and Walker (1952) represents an attempt to apply this approach to the Rorschach.

Ames and her colleagues tabulated and discussed the Rorschach responses of 650 boys and girls between the ages of two and ten, reporting the mean number of responses in each formal scoring category at different ages. Some categories (such as *FM,* or animal movement) show a systematic trend in frequency during a particular age range, while some do not. Even where age trends are apparent, however, they are for the most part too small to be significant. Further, the mean number of responses per child in most categories is so small that the reported differences between age groupings are highly unreliable.

A more global problem with the developmental approach to the interpretation of child Rorschach responses of Ames and her colleagues is that there is no firm evidence that particular responses have valid meaning at any age level for children, let alone across different age levels. At most, the Ames et al. norms can be regarded as portraying the typical responses of children at different ages as summarized by the traditional Rorschach scoring categories, information which is frequently used subjectively in offering clinical hypotheses about individual respondents. Koppitz (1963) presented a somewhat analogous approach to the use of the Bender-Gestalt test for personality assessment with children, and this work embodies the same difficulties and constraints as that of Ames et al.

To conclude, the use of most projective techniques with children continues to be a highly subjective enterprise that does not meet generally accepted scientific standards. There are several exceptions to this conclusion, two of which involve structured procedures discussed earlier in this book: the Blacky Pictures Test and such structured sentence completion procedures as the Rotter Incomplete Sentences Blank (Rotter and Rafferty, 1950) and the Incomplete Sentences Task (Lanyon, 1972). The nature and validity of these instruments has been discussed in Chapter 3.

Personality Inventories

In this section we discuss the use of inventories that are completed by the children themselves rather than by an informant. As with projective techniques, evidence of their validity for use with preadolescent children is sparse. For adolescents, adequate validity data exist for some instruments.

One well-known test is the California Test of Personality (Thorpe, Clark, and Tiegs, 1953), which was published in various forms over the years 1939–1953 for use with children from kindergarten through age 14. In view of its lack of published validity information and consistently poor reviews in the *Mental Measurements Yearbook,* it is not recommended for use. Another set of children's personality inventories is based on Cattell's Sixteen Personality Factors Questionnaire: the Early School Personality Questionnaire (ESPQ), for ages 6–8; the Children's Personality Questionnaire, for ages 8–12; and the Junior–Senior High School Personality Questionnaire, for ages 12–18. All are similar in nature to the 16 PF and share its theoretical orientations and methodological perspective. The ESPQ for 6 to 8-year-olds is read aloud to the children. All of these inventories suffer from the same problems as described in Chapter 4 for the 16 PF test, such as lack of specificity as to the procedures involved in selecting the items for each scale and a relative absence of empirical validity data.

The MMPI, although originally constructed for use with adults, has been commonly used with adolescents and is considered by some authorities to be suitable for use as young as age 12 (e.g., Marks, Seeman, and Haller, 1974). The development of an actuarial interpretation system for adolescents by these authors has been described in Chapter 8. Examination of the empirical correlates of their adolescent MMPI code types shows that they differ considerably from empirical correlates of adult code types, demonstrating that validities for personality tests cannot be assumed to generalize from adults to adolescents. Because the correlates for adolescents were based on a fairly large and varied sample, and are strictly empirical in nature, they can be recommended for use on a general basis except when one's client population has particular characteristics that could reduce the validity.

We have by no means discussed all personality inventories applicable to children and adolescents. However, a more complete review would lead to similar conclusions. Certain adult inventories (such as the MMPI and the California Psychological Inventory) are appropriate for adolescents in those uses for which validity data are specifically available. Other inventories such as the Personality Research Form and the Jackson Personality Inventory were developed and validated primarily with college students and are therefore directly applicable to that population. Relatively few inventories have been designed especially for children, and none are described by recent reviewers as having much potential.

Behavioral Appraoches

Behavioral assessment is an area which has recently grown considerably in importance and is the subject matter of Chapter 6 in this text. The major contemporary impetus to its development has been the growth of behavior modification and behavior therapy, in both research applications and practical settings involving individual clinical cases and single case experimental studies. Although there are no differences in principle between the application of behavioral assessment to adults and children, it has become popular more rapidly with children than with adults, perhaps for two reasons. First, there are fewer viable alternative approaches to the assessment of children. Second, systematic observers—a basic necessity in behavioral assessment—are more readily available with children, in the form of parents and teachers. As emphasized in Chapter 6, although behavioral assessment is a promising approach for many topics and problems involving children, increased attention to psychometric considerations such as standardization, norms, validity, and reliability is needed if its potential is to be fulfilled.

Structured Checklists and Rating Scales

In this section we discuss procedures that require observers to make ratings or other judgments about a child. There is fine line between what is typically called "behavioral assessment" and what is viewed as the use of structured checklists and rating scales. A convenient distinction is that checklists and rating scales are used to make global reports of the habitual occurrence of behaviors, while the behavioral assessor observes and records *each instance* of behavior as it actually occurs.

One recent instrument is the Personality Inventory for Children (PIC) (Wirt, Lachar, Klinedinst, and Seat, 1977). Although termed an "inventory," the PIC is classified here as a checklist because it is completed by a person other than the child, typically the mother. The development of the PIC was in many ways similar to that of the MMPI. Initially, 600 items were written to represent 11 content areas: those regarded as primary areas of personality functioning in children, plus areas which were thought to be useful to the practicing clinician. This item pool served over a number of years as the basis for the construction of a total of 33 scales. Some were constructed empirically, in the manner of MMPI scales, and some were developed on a rational basis. Of the 33, a total of 16—four validity scales and 12 clinical scales—were ultimately selected for inclusion in the published form of the test, while the remaining 17 are regarded as supplemental scales to be used if desired. There are four separate PIC profile sheets: separately by sex and separately by ages 3–5 and 6–16. The development of norms involved nearly 2,400 children in the age range 6–16 and about 200 children aged 3–5. Three of the four validity scales—Lie, *F* (deviant responding), and Defensiveness—are similar to those of the MMPI, while the fourth (Adjustment) is an overall screening scale for poor psychological adjustment. The following descriptions of the clinical scales are paraphrased from the *Manual* by Wirt et al. (1977).

Achievement (ACH): an empirical scale to identify children whose academic achievement is below expectation

Intellectual Screening (IS): an empirical scale to identify children whose difficulties could be due to impaired intellectual functioning

Development (DVL): a content-based scale to assess poor intellectual and physical development

Somatic Concern (SOM): a content-based scale to assess various health-related variables

Depression (D): a content-based scale composed of items judged to reflect childhood depression

Family Relations (FAM): a content-based scale designed to assess family effectiveness and cohesion

Delinquency (DQL): an empirical scale to assess delinquent tendencies

Withdrawal (WDL): a content-based scale to measure withdrawal from social contact

Anxiety (ANX): a content-based scale to assess various manifestations of anxiety

Psychosis (PSY): an empirical scale to discriminate children with psychotic symptoms from normals and from disturbed but nonpsychotic children.

Hyperactivity (HPR): an empirical scale to identify children displaying symptoms typically associated with the "hyperkinetic syndrome"

Social skills (SSK): a content-based scale to measure characteristics which reflect effective social relations in childhood

A considerable amount of information about the test is given in the *Manual* (Wirt et al., 1977), including empirical validity data for most but not all of the scales. More recently, Lachar and Gdowski (1979) have conducted a major validity study involving the development of an actuarial interpretation system for the PIC. Subjects were 200 children (mostly aged 6−12) and 231 adolescents (aged 13−17) evaluated at an urban university-affiliated clinic over a 16-month period. Several hundred items of criterion information were available on these children, including a preappointment questionnaire usually filled out by the child's mother, teacher ratings and school information, and diagnostic interview information. Lachar and Gdowski reported those criterion items that correlated significantly with high or low scores on each of the scales, separately by sex and age grouping and also in combination. Also reported was the range of scores on each of the scales where the relationship with a criterion variable was the strongest, and the results of the study were used as the basis for the development of an automated interpretation program. Because of its careful development and its reliance for the most part on empirical data, the PIC would seem to be potentially a useful instrument, although much more validity information is needed. In particular, justification is needed for the decision to employ only two age categories: 3−5 and 6−16 for the original test norms, and below 12 and 13−17 for the actuarial interpretation study of Lachar and Gdowski.

Another checklist with considerable potential is the Child Behavior Check List (CBCL) and its accompanying Child Behavior Profile (CBP) (Achenbach, 1978; Achenbach and Edelbrock, 1979). Designed to obtain parents' reports of their children's competencies, the CBCL consists of 118 behavior problem items to be rated 0, 1, or 2, plus seven multidimensional items related to social competencies. The initial item pool for the CBCL was developed on the basis of existing literature on the assessment of children's problems plus the case histories of 1,000 psychiatric cases. Some items are quite specific in content (e.g., "runs away from home", "sleeps less than most children"), while others are inferential (e.g., "suspicious").

The behavior problem items served as the basis for constructing six separate sets of scales—by sex and by three different age groupings: 4−5, 6−11, and 12−16. Scales involve clusters of items identified through factor analyses of CBCL responses on several hundred children in each of the six age/sex groupings from mental health settings. Each of the resulting six forms of the CBP has either eight or nine scales, and in many cases the scale names or concepts are the same across forms, although the particular items constituting an identically named scale may differ from form to form. For example, scales entitled Somatic Complaints, Aggressive, and Hyperactive occur on at least four of the six forms. The three social competence scales—Activities, Social, and School—are the same for all six forms and consist of behavioral items which reflect each of the three categories. Reliability data are available for some of the scales, although the small number of items on some scales poses a potential problem for adequate reliability. There is little evidence for external validity as yet; however, the care that was involved in developing the scales suggests the potential for satisfactory validity.

Beside the two instruments already described, there are a number of others which would also appear to have potential for adequate validity but which are, like the PIC and the CBP, too new to evaluate adequately. For example, the Louisville Behavior Checklist (LBC) (Miller, 1977a) and the School Behavior Checklist (SBC) (Miller, 1977b) were designed to help parents and teachers communicate their impressions and concerns about children at home and in the classroom. Each has a form for children aged 4−6 and another for children aged 7−13. True or false responses are requested to items such as "finds it hard to talk to others" and "not dependable; irresponsible." The 20 scales of the LBC and nine scales of the SBC are, for the most part, based on factor analytic procedures. As stated previously, demonstrations of empirical validity are needed for both tests.

The final instrument to be described in this category is the Adaptive Behavior Inventory for Children, or ABIC (Mercer, 1979). The concept of adaptive behavior refers to "the child's ability to perform the social roles appropriate for persons of his or her age and sex in a manner that meets the expectations of the social systems in which he or she participates" (Mercer, 1979, p. 102). Although the concept is as much related to intelligence as it is to personality, the ABIC does have some similarity to other instruments that are designed to assess overall adjustment. It is similar in some ways to the Vineland Social Competence Scale (Doll, 1953, 1965), in that the interviewer asks an informant, typically the mother, a series of age-graded questions about the degree to which the child currently engages in a wide variety of behaviors that are believed to be adaptive in one of five social systems. The six scales represent each of these social systems: family, community, peer relations, nonacademic school roles, and earner/consumer, plus a sixth nonspecific area of adaptation, termed "self-maintenance." The 242 items were refined from a much larger pool developed from previous scales and from interviews with mothers of normal and retarded children. Norms are available for each of the six scales for age groupings at three-month intervals in the age range 5−11. Separate tables for Black, Hispanic, and White children are also presented.

The ABIC is one part of a much larger assessment battery, the System of Multicultural Pluralistic Assessment, or SOMPA, developed by Mercer (1979) to provide for the comprehensive or multidimensional evaluation of children in educational settings, taking sociocultural differences into account. However, the ABIC can be employed separately, and it appears to have the potential for satisfactory validity in the context of a social skills approach to general adjustment and mental health.

ASSESSMENT IN LAW-RELATED SETTINGS

The use of psychologists and other mental health professionals in the legal and correctional systems has increased substantially in recent years. These developments are reflected in the recent appearance of several new textbooks and journals, and in the formation of the American Board of Forensic Psychology for the purpose of examining and designating psychologists with specific expertise in the area. In addition, a new division of the American Psychological Association, on Psychology and Law, was recently formed to associate the American Psychology – Law Society with nationally organized psychology. Together with this increased activity have come significant criticisms of its utility (e.g., Group for the Advancement of Psychiatry, 1974; Morse, 1978; Ziskin, 1981), expressing the concern that mental health professionals may be overstepping the limits of their expertise, and questioning the ultimate utility of psychologists in certain law-related settings, in view of the common good. We review a number of specific uses of personality assessment in forensic psychology and attempt to put them in proper perspective.

Insanity Evaluation

Perhaps the best known use of psychiatrists and psychologists in court settings is as expert witnesses on the question of whether a defendant was insane at the time of committing the offense (and therefore worthy of special consideration). Although very few defendants indeed are ultimately found not guilty by reason of insanity, this issue has generated a great deal of scholarly activity over the years. Legal experts themselves disagree on the exact nature of the concept of insanity, and they also disagree on why special consideration should be given to defendants who are found to have suffered from it (e.g., Fingarette and Hasse, 1979; Stone, 1975). Because the language and concepts of the law are different from those of behavioral science, it is doubtful that even a precise definition of insanity would have a clear counterpart in psychology or psychiatry. Thus, it should not be surprising that a great deal of subjectivity is usually involved in the assessment of insanity.

Different legal jurisdictions have different definitions of insanity. The most conservative is the M'Naghten Rule, which originated in 1843. Under this rule, the defendant must be shown to have been "labouring under such a defect of reason, from disease of the mind, as not to know the nature and quality of the act he was doing; or, if he did know it, that he did not know he was doing what was wrong." The insanity laws in the majority of states now include a broader definition of insanity (Stone, 1975). For example, some include the irresistible impulse test, in which defendants are also legally insane if they knew the difference between right and wrong but found themselves overwhelmed by an irresistible impulse.

The necessity for showing that the defendant was insane *at the time of the offense* and not simply at the time of examination presents additional difficulties. The most straightforward cases are those in which defendants have a history of psychosis, such as schizophrenia, accompanied by evidence (other than the offense itself) that they were obviously psychotic at the time of the offense. In most other cases there is substantial ambiguity, and little can be said about the process of making the assessment except that those who do so rely heavily on the accumulation of their subjective or clinical experience.

Competency to Stand Trial

According to McGarry, Curran, Lipsitt, Lelos, Schwitzgebel, and Rosenberg (1973, p. 20), the common-law criteria for competency to stand trial are: (1) an ability to cooperate with one's attorney in one's own defense, (2) an awareness and understanding of the nature and object of the proceedings, and (3) an understanding of the consequences of the proceedings. The reader should distinguish clearly between the evaluation of competency, involving the defendant's general mental condition at the time of trial, and insanity, involving special aspects of the defendant's condition at the time of the alleged offense. The assessment of competency has been traditionally approached from a psychiatric viewpoint, as with the evaluation of insanity. However, Sales (1980) and others have pointed out that the terms "competent" and "incompetent" are unfortunate ones, since they imply a permanent illness or incapacity, while the situation requires only the assessment of the person's *current ability* to stand trial, which may be temporarily but not permanently affected by various factors.

There have been two noteworthy attempts to develop structured, quantifiable procedures for assessing competency to stand trial. The first is described as a screening instrument for the purpose of distinguishing, "at the earliest possible stage, the competency issue from other legal and mental health issues" (Lipsitt, Lelos, and McGarry, 1971, p. 105). These authors developed the Competency Screening Test, a 22-item sentence completion instrument with stems relevant to the legal criteria of competency. Responses are scored on a three-point scale (2, 1, or 0) with the aid of a structured scoring manual, reflecting different levels of competency. For example, with the sentence stem "When I go to court, the lawyer will . . .," the response "defend me" would be scored 2, while the response "put me away" would be scored 0. Lipsitt et al. showed significant differences on the test between groups of men who had been judged incompetent and those who had not, and concluded that the instrument could facilitate competency screening procedures.

A much more elaborate instrument, the Competency Assessment Instrument (CAI), was developed by McGarry et al. (1973) in the context of a major project to clarify and improve theory and practice of the assessment of competency on a broad basis. The CAI consists of a 13-item interview schedule representing "functions related to the accused's ability to cope with the trial process in an adequately self-protective manner" (McGarry et al., 1973, p. 24), and it is intended to cover all possible grounds for the finding of incompetency. The interview schedule is shown in Figure 9-1. A detailed manual which accompanies the CAI defines the intentions of each item and gives sample interview questions and scoring examples. A subsequent study by the same authors showed that the manual could be successfully used to train personnel in administering and scoring the CAI with adequate reliability. McGarry et al. emphasized that the ultimate decision regarding the weight to be put on any or all of the items should be the responsibility of the court, taking into consideration all factors relevant to the particular defendant. Although a great deal of work remains to be done in the further development of competency assessment procedures, the approach taken by the CAI appears to be a promising one.

Jury Selection

Another of the law-related areas in which psychologists have recently become involved is jury selection. More accurately, the process should be called "juror

	Total	Severe	Degree of Incapacity Moderate	Mild	None	Unratable
1. Appraisal of available legal defenses	1	2	3	4	5	6
2. Unmanageable behavior	1	2	3	4	5	6
3. Quality of relating to attorney	1	2	3	4	5	6
4. Planning of legal strategy, including guilty plea to lesser charges where pertinent	1	2	3	4	5	6
5. Appraisal of role of:	1	2	3	4	5	6
a. Defense counsel						
b. Prosecuting attorney	1	2	3	4	5	6
b. Judge	1	2	3	4	5	6
d. Jury	1	2	3	4	5	6
e. Defendant	1	2	3	4	5	6
f. Witnesses	1	2	3	4	5	6
6. Understanding of court procedure	1	2	3	4	5	6
7. Appreciation of charges	1	2	3	4	5	6
8. Appreciation of range and nature of possible penalties	1	2	·3	4	5	6
9. Appraisal of likely outcome	1	2	3	4	5	6
10. Capacity to disclose to attorney available pertinent facts surrounding the offense including the defendant's movements, timing, mental state, actions at the time of the offense	1	2	3	4	5	6
11. Capacity to realistically challenge prosecution witnesses	1	2	3	4	5	6
12. Capacity to testify relevantly	1	2	3	4	5	6
13. Self-defeating v. self-serving motivation (legal sense)	1	2	3	4	5	6

Examinee _____ Examiner _____

Date _____

FIGURE 9.1. Interview schedule and rating sheet for the Competency Assessment Instrument. From McGarry et al. (1973).

rejection,'' since both prosecution and defense attorneys are allowed the opportunity (in a procedure termed the *voir dire*) to question potential jurors from a preliminary pool and to reject a certain number of them with or without stated reasons for doing so. It is the possibility of rejecting potential jurors with personality characteristics or attitudes antagonistic to an attorney's interests that has attracted the participation of psychologists.

Three approaches to this task have been explored (Hersleb, Sales, and Berman, 1979). The first is to enlist the aid of a network of family members, friends, and supporters of the defendants in the hope that one or more of them will know most of the prospective jurors and will be able to describe their relevant personality characteristics and attitudes. A second approach is to study the nonverbal behavior of each prospective juror during the *voir dire* and to use this information to rate each of them on relevant traits and attitudes. A third procedure is to try to determine, through a general population survey in the jurors' town, the relationship between demographic variables (such as age, sex, education, and religion) and relevant traits and attitudes. Such demographic information can then be elicited during the *voir dire*.

The validity of each of these three procedures rests in part on the assumption that juror traits and attitudes are related to jury decisions. There is a growing body of evidence to give some support to this assumption, for such variables as authoritarianism, liberalism, social approval, and punitiveness (Hepburn, 1980). However, validity also requires a demonstration that the data sources can accurately predict traits and attitudes, and it is here that the evidence is less favorable. For example, despite the popular belief that nonverbal attributes and behaviors form a useful basis for personality assessment, there are no convincing data to show that this is the case in the context of jury selection (Suggs and Sales, 1978). Nor is there any empirical evidence that data on jurors collected by the network procedure can be useful for this purpose. With regard to the population survey procedure, although no general relationships have been demonstrated between demographic variables and juror attitudes and traits, some consistent findings have emerged for particular geographic locations (Hepburn, 1980). Thus, the survey procedure is, at the present time, the only one with some demonstrated potential for validity.

Numerous unanswered legal and ethical questions have been raised about the participation of social scientists in the jury selection process (Hersleb, Sales, and Berman, 1979; Tapp, 1976). For example, is the constitutional right to an impartial jury violated if only one side uses these procedures? Are psychologists violating their own ethics by diminishing the civil or legal rights of others? Although these questions will not become critical until the utility of social scientist participation is convincingly demonstrated, they nevertheless must be considered by any psychologist who becomes involved in this work.

Dangerousness and Violence

One of the most common questions asked of mental health professionals in legal and correctional settings has to do with whether a particular defendant or inmate is dangerous or potentially violent. ''Dangerousness'' is another concept that is defined in legal terms but does not have a direct counterpart in the language of psychology. Traditionally, the origin of dangerous conduct has been assumed to lie within the individual. However, more recent views focus on the interaction between the person and the particular environment or social situation (Schwitzgebel, 1978; Shah, 1978). Thus, people are likely to engage in dangerous behavior only in particular contexts, such as a threat to self-esteem in the presence of a member of the opposite sex. In fact, from a strict behavioral view, "dangerousness" for any given person could be taken to refer to a class of behaviors, each cued and maintained by different events.

Other definitional problems have been raised by Stone (1975), who pointed out that many dangerous acts of great social impact (such as lawmakers who fail to impose strict sanctions on drunken drivers) are simply not viewed as dangerous, while criminal law has tended to overreact to other "dangerous" acts, such as exhibitionism. Thus, the use of the label "dangerous" is to some extent a matter of personal preference. A useful definition has nevertheless been offered by Shah (1978), who wrote that "dangerousness" refers to an increased likelihood of engaging in dangerous behavior or violence, defined as "acts that are characterized by the application of or the overt threat of force and that are likely to result in injury to other persons" (p. 224).

Little has as yet been published on the assessment of dangerousness in terms of person-environment interaction. A number of attempts have been made to develop questionnaire scales that discriminate dangerous and nondangerous groups defined in various ways, such as according to nature of the legal offense. For example, a number of special MMPI scales have been offered for the prediction of hostile or assaultive behavior (Gearing, 1979). The greatest amount of research effort has involved the Overcontrolled Hostility (O-H) Scale of Megargee and Mendelsohn (1962), which has shown some degree of success. Another MMPI indicator with some promise is the high 4-3 pattern. Neither of these two indicators is anywhere near accurate enough for satisfactory prediction on an individual basis, which has traditionally been approached in a subjective manner based on all available information. There appear to be no published studies comparing the relative accuracy of actuarial and clinical prediction in this area.

One further difficulty with the assessment of dangerousness is that the behavior has relatively low base rates. Thus, the predictive problems associated with infrequent events, as discussed in Chapters 7 and 8, apply here. In particular, the use of any cutting point that would correctly identify the majority of "dangerous" persons would also yield an extremely high false positive rate, so that nearly everybody identified as dangerous would in fact be dangerous. Therefore, it would seem that the necessary conditions for the prediction of dangerous behavior would involve populations (1) where the proportion of dangerous people is substantial and (2) for whom a large false positive rate is acceptable. A slightly more positive note has recently been sounded by Monahan (1981) in his book on this topic. It should be emphasized that the use of clinical or subjective methods of prediction would fare no better than objective procedures, since the same predictive principles are applicable even though they may not be made explicit.

Assessment in Child Custody Cases

Until the 19th century, children were generally regarded as the personal property of the father and automatically stayed with him if the marriage collapsed (Halleck, 1980). With the development of more appropriate rights for women, this custom gradually gave way in favor of a preference toward awarding custody to the mother, particularly for young children. More recently, courts have emphasized their responsibility to do whatever is in the best interests of the child, and judges often have considerable discretion in interpreting this policy. It is here that behavioral science professionals have recently been invited to contribute. Since the adversarial nature of the decision-making process often impedes the task of determining the child's best interests, it is often recommended that behavioral scientists should represent the court, or the child, or both parties, rather than one side alone (Halleck, 1980).

The assessment question, that of determining the child's best interests, is a legal and sociological as well as a psychological one. Schwitzgebel and Schwitzgebel (1980) presented a list of 10 "standards" that were adopted by the Michigan Legislature in an attempt to specify what these best interests are. Severeral of them involve psychological matters: the love and affection between parent and child; capacity and willingness of each parent to continue providing love, affection, and child-rearing guidance; the mental health of each parent; and the potential permanence of the custodial home. In an extensive survey of the opinions of mental health professionals regarding the best interests of the child, Woody (1977) found that the most prominent psychological factors identified were similar to those given here, and they were seen as applying equally to both mother and father.

The aspects of assessment in child custody that are relevant for psychologists thus have to do with the general mental health of the competing parents, the nature and quality of the emotional relationship that each of them has with the child, and the likely long-term effects on the child of each of the potential custodial environments. Such assessments are most appropriately performed by psychologists with specific training and experience in the assessment of parent-child relationships, and would be enhanced if the professional has a good working knowledge of the empirical literature in child development. One final point to be emphasized is that the psychologist's contribution is only part of the total question of "suitability," and that the court retains responsibility for making the overall determination, based on both psychological and nonpsychological factors.

Classification in Correctional Settings

Administrators of prisons have traditionally utilized some systematic means of assigning inmates to various facilities, living quarters, and work and rehabilitation programs. There are two major ways in which classification is useful: to facilitate *management,* and to facilitate *rehabilitation.* In regard to management, the factors to be considered typically include whether the inmate can be placed in a large dormitory or whether an individual or shared room is more appropriate; whether there is a suicidal risk; whether there is an increased risk of harassment from other inmates, as with child molesters, for example; whether the inmate is known to be militant and therefore requires careful management; and whether the inmate is known to be in danger from other inmates. Factors that are relevant in classification for rehabilitation include, in addition to those already listed, educational level, skills and abilities, interests, and job-related personality patterns.

It can be seen that much of the classification task does not involve psychological variables at all, but rather demographic and educational factors or aspects of behavior that are listed directly in court and correctional documents. Thus, the classification task is primarily a clerical one in many instances. However, some of the relevant factors—such as suicide potential, sexual deviance, and personal interest patterns—fall within the realm of personality assessment, broadly defined. Because the goals of classification differ from institution to institution, the first step in developing a classification system should be to determine exactly what the goals of the system are for that particular setting. Once that is done, sources of data to assess the variables of interest are assembled, together with information about the base rates of these variables among the population at hand. The extent to which specific cutting points should be used depends on real-life constraints. For example, if there are only 50 single cells, they would be necessarily assigned to the 50 persons judged to need them most in view of the system's goals. However, if there were an unlimited number, then an "optimal" cutting point would be used, either explicitly or implicitly, in deciding which inmates to house singly and which in group settings.

Recently, classification systems have been developed that are based on a single personality inventory, such as the MMPI or the 16 PF Questionnaire. For example, as discussed in Chapter 8, Megargee (1977) and his colleagues reported the painstaking development of a system involving 10 MMPI "types," analogous to the MMPI code book types developed by Marks and Seeman (1963) and by Gilberstadt and Duker (1965). Although there are definite demographic and personality-related differences among these types (Edinger, 1979; Megargee and Bohn, 1979), it would seem that the use of test responses alone as predictors in building a classification system is an indirect and inefficient method of approaching classification except for factors that are strongly related to measurable personality variables.

NEUROPSYCHOLOGICAL ASSESSMENT

The assessment of psychological deficits resulting from brain damage has traditionally been called the assessment of "organicity." Davison (1974) suggested a more precise way of viewing this endeavor, in terms of *impairment in adaptive functioning,* which is described as a "broad concept including decrements in intellectual, sensory-motor, and personality functioning" (p. 2).

The belief that "organicity" is a unitary phenomenon is an early and traditional one, and it was embodied in the views and recommendations of such authorities as Piotrowski (1937) and Schafer (1948). In the unitary approach, the results of traditional psychodiagnostic tests such as the Rorschach and the Bender-Gestalt were examined for "signs of organicity," and there was continuing interest in the search for the "best" single test of "organicity." With the development of the field of clinical neuropsychology as a separate discipline there came a more scientific and differentiated approach to the assessment of impairments in adaptive functioning due to brain damage. Lezak (1976) differentiated three different areas of functioning that are relevant for neuropsychological assessment: intellectual, personality/emotionality, and control functioning. By far the greatest amount of attention has been paid to the assessment of intellectual functions, which Lezak further divided into four areas: perceptive, memory and learning, cognition, and expressive.

It is for the assessment of these intellectual areas (or, more accurately, the assessment of deficits in these areas) that extensive neuropsychological test batteries such as the Halstead-Reitan and the Luria Tests have been developed (Golden, 1979; Lezak, 1976). There is increasing evidence that test batteries and other individual test procedures are useful in assessing difficulties in intellectual and other functions, and that they may be of assistance in determining the location of the brain damage (e.g., Lewis, Golden, Moses, Osmon, Purisch, and Hammeke, 1979) and in discriminating organic disorders from functional disorders such as schizophrenia (Heaton, Baade, and Johnson, 1978). However, the procedures for the assessment of personality and control functions in patients suspected of brain damage are no different from those that would be used in assessing these characteristics in other patients.

The current state of the field may thus be viewed as follows. Psychological assessment of persons suspected of brain damage is a complex task involving a wide variety of neuropsychological tests and is directed mainly toward the evaluation of intellectual, speech, and other performance functions. A working knowledge of brain function is required for the satisfactory use of these procedures. Assessment of personality or psychodiagnostic matters is still approached through the use of the same procedures that would be used with other patients, except that neuropsychological tests can be helpful in differentiating between brain damage and functional difficulties as the cause of a disorder. The use of tests such as the Rorschach to assess "organicity" was popularized before the development of current knowledge in neuropsychology and has little demonstrated validity in this regard. Other traditional tests for "organicity" such as the Bender-Gestalt and Block Design may have specific roles for assessment of particular functions in certain test batteries, but except for certain gross screening purposes it is misleading to consider that they can have a useful role when employed in isolation.

Summary

The utility of personality assessment procedures can be affected by demographic variables in two ways: demographically different groups can vary in their normative responses and in the validity of their scores. For example, males and females differ normatively on many tests and also in their empirical correlates, although in many cases the overlap is great enough that a single set of interpretive material is sufficient. Age also affects responses, although variations within the middle-adult years is probably small. Assessment of the elderly requires special consideration, both because of differences in norms and validity, and because some of the problems requiring assessment in the elderly are somewhat specific to that age group. Another demographic variable affecting responses is ethnic background, and stable differences have been found on such tests as the MMPI between Whites, Blacks, and other ethnic groups. The practical significance of these differences is the subject of some controversy, however.

Personality assessment with children is more complex than with adults, and there is no reason to expect that either the norms or the validity of a test developed for adults will be applicable to children and adolescents, or even that one childhood age group will be comparable to another in norms or validity. The most common procedure for the assessment of children has been through the use of projective tests, and this practice continues to be popular despite the fact that empirical validity data are lacking for all but a few instruments. A number of personality inventories are available for use with children and adolescents, but relatively few have adequate validity for these uses. Behavioral approaches to the assessment of children employ the same principles and procedures as described in Chapter 6 on behavioral assessment in general, and have recently increased in popularity. Considerations of reliability and validity need attention here also. The most rapidly growing personality assessment procedure for children is the use of structured checklists and rating scales which are completed by informants such as parents and teachers. Two recent and potentially important instruments of this type are the Personality Inventory for Children and the Child Behavior Check List. Both are too new to permit an adequate assessment of their potential validity.

The use of psychological assessment in law-related settings has increased substantially in recent years. Perhaps the best-known use is in insanity evaluations. Because insanity is a legal concept and not a psychological one, and because there is even disagreement as to its legal meaning, its assessment is usually a highly subjective enterprise. Psychologists are also called upon to assess competency to stand trial, which is perhaps best viewed as the defendant's current ability to cooperate with an attorney and to be aware of the nature and consequences of the court proceedings. A potentially useful device for guiding such evaluations is the Competency Assessment Instrument. Psychologists have approached the question of jury selection in three different ways: (1) through the development of a network of friends in the hope that each prospective juror will be known to at least one network member, (2) the study of prospective jurors' nonverbal behavior, and (3) the study of their demographic characteristics. All methods rest on the assumptions that juror traits and attitudes can be predicted from these information sources and that traits and attitudes are related to juror decisions. There is relatively little evidence to support these assumptions.

The assessment of dangerousness and potential for violence is another law-related question. Psychologists have had limited success in this area for several reasons: the concept of dangerousness has no consistent psychological definition; dangerous conduct is viewed by many psychologists as being a product of person-environment interactions; and the base rates of dangerous behavior are quite low, leading to high false positive rates. Child custody decisions represent another area in which the input of psychological assessment is often sought. The relevant question is to determine the best interests of the child, several aspects of which are psychological in nature: the degree of love and affection between parent and child; the capacity of each parent to provide love, affection, and child-rearing guidance; and the mental health of each parent. The development of classification systems for correctional settings is also viewed by many persons as involving personality assessment. However, more detailed study shows that classification is in large part a clerical task based on demographic data. Input from the area of personality assessment may be useful for certain classification questions such as sexual deviance, psychosis, and job-related interest patterns. Actuarial systems based on a single personality test are relatively inefficient.

It has been traditional to try to assess problems in the neuropsychological area through the use of personality and intelligence tests. In this approach, the underlying question has been a simplistic one: the presence or extent of "organicity," with emphasis on finding the single best test for this purpose. Now that clinical neuropsychology has developed as a separate area of inquiry, it is recognized that brain damage can result in a great variety of deficits. Contemporary assessment procedures involve lengthy batteries to assess the many different areas of possible deficit, and they require a good working knowledge of brain functions on the part of the assessor.

10 AUTOMATED PERSONALITY ASSESSMENT

Automated devices for the assessment of personality have been part of the entertainment industry for many years. In the penny arcades, for example, there have traditionally been machines which would list a number of trait-descriptive adjectives. When the user inserted a penny and held the handles, some random combination of the traits would light up, calling the user "prudent, bashful, and aggressive" or something equally unlikely.

In this chapter we consider the systematic use of automated procedures in personality assessment. This field has, of course, been made possible by the development of computers, although there were various early attempts to construct automated procedures through mechanical means. Automation in personality assessment is gaining in popularity, after its early development in the 1960s and a period of relatively slow growth in the 1970s. Automation has been applied in three major ways: (1) to the *administration* of an assessment procedure, (2) to *scoring*, and (3) to *interpretation*. Following a discussion of the development of the field, each of these topics is reviewed in turn. There are two necessary bases for the successful application of automated procedures to personality assessment, both of which have been discussed in earlier chapters. The first is the availability of assessment devices that can yield objective scores, such as the MMPI. The second is the availability of research knowledge concerning the relative advantages of using objective (vs. subjective) interpretation systems and a technology for developing such systems. This material has been reviewed in Chapter 8.

It is important to understand that the notion of actuarial description and prediction is independent of automation. The use of computers in personality assessment would not have been possible without the prior development of actuarial systems, but actuarial systems can be used without computers. The specific positive contribution of the computer has to do with the saving of time and effort, and the resultant economic advantages. There is also a qualitative difference between the manually applied objective rules of the actuarial code books and the rules developed for computer application. Because the rules for computer use can be many times more complex, and because the computer can search through a much larger library of statements than would be economical for a secretary, a different type of product is possible—a whole interpretive system rather than a limited number of interpretive statements.

Psychologists and other mental health professionals began to become interested on a large scale in the possibilities for automation in the 1960s, as this technology began to filter into human service fields in general. In psychology and mental health, applications of automation have been attempted in a rather wide variety of areas, including ability testing, case history taking, interviewing, preparation of reports, record-keeping, behavioral observations, ward nursing notes, aspects of psychotherapy and behavior therapy, vocational guidance, and others. There is no single review of all this work, although accounts of some of it have been prepared by Hedland and Hickman (1977), Lanyon, (1974), and Sidowski, Johnson, and Williams (1980).

The serious work on automated personality assessment began in the early 1960s. The necessary groundwork had been laid previously in regard to the validity of actuarial description and prediction (e.g., Meehl, 1954, 1956), and several actuarial description systems had already been developed (e.g., Drake and Oetting, 1959; Marks and Seeman, 1963). Around that time, psychologists at the Mayo Clinic were faced with the stereotyped and repetitive task of writing MMPI interpretations for patients referred for psychiatric screening (Rome et al., 1962; Swenson and Pearson, 1964, 1966). The volume of referrals was so high, with more than 170,000 patients registered annually at the clinic, that they felt it would be appropriate and convenient to program their interpretive statements and to have the computer score the MMPI responses and print out the appropriate interpretations.

There were several factors about the Mayo Clinic situation which made it particularly suited to an automated procedure, and possibly laid the groundwork for the overly ready acceptance of automated interpretation and the resulting difficulties for which it has been criticized (Adair, 1978c; Butcher, 1978c). First, the population was quite homogeneous, so that most of the interpretive needs could be covered with relatively few statements. Second, the procedure was designed for screening only, which further simplified the interpretive task because it meant that responsibility for decision making was not vested in the interpretations. The printout was designed to avoid technical and emotional words, underscoring the intention that the process was simply intended as a screening. Third, the psychology staff could easily police the use of the system, since they had control over the use of the printouts and could readily communicate with the referral sources. Fourth and perhaps most important, the setting was a medical one, in which physicians were accustomed to "ordering tests."

It is worth noting that the vast preponderance of activity in automated personality assessment has been in medical settings. There are two possible reasons for this fact. First, the kinds of questions involving invasion of privacy and confidentiality that have tended to limit assessment procedures in other large-scale settings such as schools and businesses have not arisen to any extent in medical settings. Second, as already indicated, there is the reality that routine testing is an integral aspect of a medical setting. In fact, it is possible that automated assessment would not have developed at all had it not been for physicians' willingness to order the MMPI just like any other test (such as X-rays or urine analysis). Unfortunately, this willingness has not always been based on an accurate understanding of its nature, as indicated by Rome (1962):

> This instrument, originally designed as a pencil-and-paper test, taps these psychological currents, and somewhat like the more familiar electrocardiograph, the electroencephalograph and the determining apparatus for basal metabolic rate, reports them in either a digital or an analogical form. (p. 62)

Several years after the Mayo developments, Fowler (1967, 1969) constructed a more complex program for the automated interpretation of the MMPI. His procedure was essentially a subjective one, involving approximately 2,000 cases over a four-year period. Contrary to the nature of the Mayo Clinic program, which was intended for its own population only, Fowler wished his program to have general applicability, and for that reason he included cases from a variety of other human service settings. The Fowler program was test marketed through the pharmaceutical company Roche Laboratories before moving into full-scale commercial operation on a national basis (Fowler, 1966). Shortly afterward, the Mayo Clinic program began commercial operation through the Psychological Corporation (Pearson and Swenson, 1968). Several other commercial services soon appeared, and the *Eighth Mental Measurements Yearbook* (Buros, 1978) lists seven such services for the MMPI.

In another early development, the Institute of Living, a private psychiatric hospital in Hartford, Connecticut, began an extensive investment in automation in the early 1960s, including an MMPI program and other personality assessment procedures (Glueck and Reznikoff, 1965). Some initial steps toward the development of an automated interpretation program for Cattell's 16 PF questionnaire were reported by Eber (1964). Perhaps the most ambitious project of all was the one undertaken by Piotrowski toward an automated interpretation system for the Rorschach, also reported initially in 1964.

For a time following these initial developments, the field of automated personality assessment tended to be viewed as more or less synonymous with the automated interpretation of the MMPI. More recently, a broader range of developments have taken place. This increased activity could be due in part to at least three influences: a natural and legitimate progression toward greater technological sophistication in the mental health and human services industries, the recognition that the potential for commercial profit exists in this area, and the current general movement in psychology toward applied and professional enterprises. Many psychologists have strong reservations about the appropriateness of these developments, and they believe that a great deal more technical and professional knowledge is first needed. These reservations are discussed later in thd chapter.

AUTOMATED ADMINISTRATION

Since automation is relevant only in instances where there is a potential saving of time and effort, and since the administration of personality inventories involves

little or no professional time, the automated administration of assessment procedures has been more fully developed in areas other than personality. There is a small
body of literature on the automated administration of ability tests, for example.
These include the Wechsler Adult Intelligence Scale (Elwood and Griffin, 1972),
the Raven Progressive Matrices, and others (Gedye and Miller, 1969). Procedures
generally involve the on-line use of computer technology, either with a commercial
computer or a unit that is custom-built for the particular purpose. The use of on-line
computer technology has also been developed for gathering biographical and case
history data, as mentioned in Chapter 7.

One attempt to extend automated on-line administration into the field of
personality inventories has involved the MMPI. Kleinmuntz and McLean (1968)
programmed their computer to make determinations, after the respondent had
completed different subsets of items, as to whether scores on each scale could be
estimated within specific probability limits. Although this procedure is of some
academic interest, it would appear not to generate sufficient savings of professional
time and effort to justify its practical use.

A particular area in which we could expect that automated administration might
be justifiable on an economic basis is the use of projective techniques. To date, the
only such use appears to be the procedure designed by Veldman (1967) for his
One-Word Sentence Completion Test, in conjunction with an automated scoring
procedure. Each sentence stem is presented in typewritten form by the computer,
and the subject responds by typing a single word on the computer keyboard. The
computer then conducts an inquiry by typing out one of a number of specific
questions about the subject's response. For example, if the subject is given the stem
"What I want most is . . ." and responds "Happiness," the computer asks: "Are
you unhappy now?" If the subject responds "Yes," the computer asks "Why?"
Another area of potential utility for automated administration of tests is the
assessment of brain damage. Such tests ordinarily tend to be long and tedious
(Lezak, 1976), but since many of the procedures are objective or clerical they could
well be appropriate for automation. No attempts of this nature appear to have been
made, however.

The problems and concerns which accompany the use of automated test
administration procedures are the same as those which arise when any change is
made in the standardized procedure for administering a test. Because the nature of
the task is changed, norms must be reestablished, the validity of the scores must be
reevaluated, and the reliability of the automated procedure must also be established.
These issues have not yet arisen significantly in regard to personality assessment but
will become salient as automation is extended beyong inventories.

AUTOMATED SCORING

Procedures for automated scoring of personality assessment devices have been
available for many years, in the form of machine scoring for personality inventories.
Other than the need to ensure the accuracy of scoring, which involves adequate
preparation of the answer sheets and maintenance of the equipment, this would
seem to be a noncontroversial area.

There has been some interesting work in the automated scoring of projective techniques. One impetus for these developments is that they are preliminary to attempts to construct automated interpretation procedures. Related is the potential advantage of being able to collect large amounts of validity data in a standardized form. Such data pools would then permit the kinds of large-scale validity studies which have been possible with personality inventories, but whose absence with projective techniques has hampered the establishment of the level of empirical validities that most psychologists seek. One significant problem has been that since responses to projective stimuli are open-ended, any automated scoring system has the potential for violating the integrity of the procedure. Whether the result is indeed detrimental would be, of course, a matter for empirical study.

Two major projects in this area have been those of Gorham, Holtzman, and their associates with the Holtzman Inkblot Technique (Gorham, 1967; Gorham, Moseley, and Holtzman, 1968) and the work of Veldman with his One-Word Sentence Competion Test (Veldman, 1967; Veldman, Menaker, and Peck,1969). In each of these projects, the researchers began by setting a limit on the length of the response. For the HIT, each response was limited to six words; with Veldman's test, responses were limited to a single word. The next step in each case was to develop a library of possible response words and to store them in the computer. For the HIT, the six words of a response were each listed separately without regard to order. For Veldman's test, words were reduced to generic form or word stems, so that, for example, the words LOVE, LOVING, LOVES, and LOVED were all represented by the stem LOV. Gorham listed 6,100 words, accounting for 95 percent of his response material, while Veldman's 4,336-item response dictionary included 98 percent of his material.

The next step was to use the computerized data as a basis for generating scores on relevant and potentially useful variables. For the HIT, Gorham employed a combination of empirical analyses and expert judgment to assign each of his 6,100 words a weight on 17 of the scoring categories of the test. Veldman followed a similar procedure in assigning weights on a rational basis to his items on 25 different variables. Both groups of researchers showed that the computer-based scores had about the same reliability as hand scoring. That is to say, the correlations between hand scorers were about the same as those between computer scoring and hand scoring (Gorham, 1967; Veldman, Menaker, and Peck, 1969).

Another significant application of automation to the scoring of projective responses has been in the use of computer programs for content analysis. For example, Goldberg (1966) reported the use of the General Inquirer program (Stone, Bales, Namenwirth, and Olgivie, 1962) to score or at least to structure the content of responses on a regular sentence completion test. Smith (1968) reviewed the use of the General Inquirer program in structuring the content of TAT stories. Further afield than formal personality assessment, Kleinmuntz (1972) reviewed the use of the same program to structure other kinds of narrative materials in order to extract personality-relevant information, while Rae, Pautler, Kanderscheid, and Silbereld (1977) reported its use in scoring the Free Association Test developed by Gottschalk and Gleser (1969).

The utility of scores and indices generated from projective test responses by automated scoring procedures is a matter to be approached empirically, since it cannot be assumed that validity data which apply to scores generated through hand scoring are necessarily applicable to scores based on computer scoring, even though reliabilities may be comparable. Except for some unpublished data (Holtzman and Gorham, 1972), no validity information is yet available for any of the systems mentioned here. Further, the next logical step of automated interpretation has not been initiated for these tests.

AUTOMATED INTERPRETATION

The bulk of the literature in automated personality assessment is in the area of interpretation. This is an area of considerable professional activity at the present time, and as already noted, there is concern that scientific and professional considerations have been overshadowed by commercial motivations. The literature on automated interpretation should be viewed as including the literature on actuarial interpretation, such as the technology of developing actuarial programs and the assessment of their validity, as discussed in Chapter 8 and later in the present chapter. Questions that are unique to automated interpretation have to do with the effects of large-scale application, and at the present time these are mainly professional and ethical questions.

The development of an automated interpretation system requires the following: a personality test whose responses are in summary form that can be directly utilized as input to a computer, a library of interpretive statements and a program which selects those that are validly associated with particular responses, and a way of integrating the output and delivering it to the user. Let us examine the developments in each of these areas.

Input

For objective inventories, the input question has posed no problem; input simply consists of scores on the scales of the inventory. In addition, as many special scales can be scored as desired, and special indices can be computed such as Wiggins' MMPI content scales (Wiggins, Goldberg, and Appelbaum, 1971) and Goldberg's various MMPI indices for discriminating among broad diagnostic groups (Goldberg, 1972a). Most programs also include indices and scores which are unique to that program.

The situation regarding automation of projective test interpretation is much more complex, and while there have been some attempts in this area, it appears that the complexities will continue to be such as to outweigh the advantages for all but a few highly selected uses. As stated earlier, the attempts at developing automated scoring procedures for projective techniques have not led to automated interpretation systems. However, Piotrowski (1964, 1980) has reported an ambitious attempt to automate the interpretation of Rorschach responses, based on manual scoring. Piotrowski's initial purpose in developing his program was to provide a means of adequately validating his Rorschach interpretation system, perceptanalysis. The program, termed CPR (computerized perceptanalytic Rorschach), has been under continuous evolution for approximately 20 years. Although the literature on the program is somewhat inconsistent in its terminology, a recent form contains about 330 parameters, or primary variables, plus many more rules, or statements based on parameters and combinations of parameters.

One of the persistent problems in the use of Piotrowski's program has been the length of time required to code each record in preparation for computer processing, said to be up to eight hours in the 1969 version of the program (Piotrowski, 1969). More recently, the coding has been done by trained professional coders, but no information is available regarding the efficiency or success of this procedure. Further, the task of establishing the validity of the procedure has not yet been undertaken.

Development of Interpretive Statements

The development of an interpretive statement library and a program for selecting specific statements according to the particular set of test scores is the core of actuarial personality assessment and its extension into automated personality assessment. There are two approaches to generating an interpretive program: empirical, or actuarial; and subjective, or clinical. *Empirical* development involves the empirical determination of the relationships between test indices and patient characteristics, for a particular population. A number of sets of purely empirical data exist for the MMPI, some of them packaged for use in actuarial interpretation "by hand" (e.g., Drake and Oetting, 1959; Gilberstadt and Duker, 1965; Marks and Seeman, 1963; Marks, Seeman, and Haller, 1974; Megargee, 1977). However, none have been programmed for automated use in purely empirical form. Rather, the automated programs which make use of them do so in combination with a variety of subjectively developed material, so that the programs lack the desirable characteristics of a purely empirical program.

The *subjective* approach to automated interpretation refers to the procedure of compiling an accumulation of interpretive statements about a test from all possible sources, and tying each statement to specific scores or cutting points on the basis of clinical judgment. This was the procedure employed by Piotrowski in developing his computerized perceptanalytic Rorschach, and also by Swenson and Pearson (1964, 1966) in developing their interpretive rules for the Mayo Clinic MMPI program. Another way to employ the subjective approach was demonstrated for individual indices by Meehl and Dahlstrom (1960) and by Kleinmuntz (1963), who coded their clinical expertise into objective rules which simulated the performance of individual expert clinicians in sorting MMPI profiles into two or more categories. Incidentally, Goldberg (1970) showed that objective predictions made from tidied-up versions of such rules could surpass the predictions made by the experts on cross-validation.

It should be understood that the term "subjective" development does not mean that none of the interpretive statements have known empirical correlates. It means that the program is based on a general pool of knowledge about the test and not on specific study of a given population. Thus, while it does not mean in any sense that subjectively developed programs are invalid, it means that there is no built-in assurance that validity will probably exist for any particular population. Thus, validity cannot be taken for granted but must be demonstrated on a use-by-use basis. Just how rigorously this rule needs to be applied is discussed in a later section.

Output

The task of preparing and delivering output from an automated personality assessment program is for the most part a clerical one. The typical output consists of several pages of printed copy in a format that is more or less standardized. There are orienting statements with appropriate cautions and disclaimers; general descriptive materials, either in narrative form or as a series of short paragraphs or statements; standard scores; a plotted profile; and a variety of supplemental information involving such areas as critical items, supplemental scales, and diagnostic categories. The process of extending actuarial "by-hand" interpretations to computer-produced output is essentially clerical, although the added step of constructing narratives out of individual statements complicates the task of establishing validity and adds further nuances of meaning, some of which may be unintended.

Because almost all the work in automated personality assessment that has been carried through to the point of delivering routine output has involved inventories, the foregoing material applies specifically to them. However, the same considerations would seem to apply to projective assessment if an automated program were to be developed to that point.

Available Programs

The personality test most heavily involved in automated interpretation has been the MMPI. The *Eighth Mental Measurements Yearbook* (Buros, 1978) listed and reviewed seven commercially available MMPI programs, all of them developed subjectively. Other tests for which automated interpretation programs are commercially available include the Temperament and Values Inventory (Johansson, 1977), the Millon Clinical Multiaxial Inventory (Millon, 1977), several of Cattell's tests (the 16 PF Questionnaire, the High School Personnality Questionnaire, the Children's Personality Questionnaire, and the Clinical Analysis Questionnaire), the California Psychological Inventory (see Adair, 1978b; Butcher, 1978b), and the Personality Inventory for Children (Lachar and Gdowski, 1979; Wirt, Lachar, Klinedinst, and Seat, 1977). This list does not include a number of programs which are available in the assessment of vocational and career interests.

Most of these programs have been subjectively developed and have no independently demonstrated validity basis for the uses that are offered. In most cases, there is not even a published description as to how the computer program was developed. Possible exceptions include Lachar's (1974) MMPI Automated Psychological Assessment program (see Adair, 1978a; Butcher, 1978a) and the Lachar and

Gdowski (1979) program for the Personality Inventory for Children. Use of the Millon Clinical Multiaxial Inventory is currently available *only* through computer scoring and interpretation, and although the manual contains a considerable amount of statistical information about the development of the automated interpretation program, validity data are limited to the subjective judgments of clinicians who received the reports.

TECHNICAL CONSIDERATIONS

Let us now examine the major technical questions, mainly psychometric in nature, that underly the development and use of automated personality assessment procedures. These questions have to do with the methodology of constructing programs and the methodology of validating them. Except for the topic of clinical versus actuarial prediction, the amount of research in this area is modest, and many important questions remain unanswered. Once again, it should be noted that although this technology also forms the basis for actuarial "by-hand" interpretive programs, the addition of computers to the interpretive process magnifies its importance.

Technology of Program Construction

As reviewed in Chapter 8, the earliest question historically in the technnology of program construction was the one asked (and answered affirmatively) in the 1950s by Meehl (1954, 1956)—namely, whether actuarial interpretation was a legitimate enterprise. The next set of questions were those raised in the 1960s by Goldberg (1965, 1968) and others, and had to do with the best kinds of actuarial strategies to follow in personality assessment and clinical diagnosis. Findings have continued to show that linear predictive indices outperform nonlinear ones, and that predictions based on automating the clinical skill of the expert can outperform the expert, although empirically selected predictors do best of all. Similar findings have since been reported for a wide variety of other tasks in human prediction and decision making (Dawes and Corrigan, 1974).

Questions regarding the relative merits of different kinds of indices which might be used as a basis for interpretive statements have received essentially no research attention. MMPI researchers, after their initial disappointment that scores on individual scales did not provide the levels of predictive validity that had been originally hoped for, discovered that patterns of scales worked somewhat better (e.g., Marks and Seeman, 1963). The most recent trend has been to base interpretations on the simplest possible patterns, such as the two or three highest scales ("two-point" and "three-point" codes). Nearly all of this work has involved the MMPI, and it is quite possible that it may not be as useful with other inventories (e.g., Lachar, DeHorn, and Gdowski, 1979).

Other relevant topics which have received little attention include the use of population *base rates* of relevant characteristics and *relative values* associated with different predictions or decisions. The massive differences that the use or omission of such data can make to interpretive utility were illustrated years ago by Meehl and Rosen (1955), Rimm (1963), and others. Until recently, however, few published prediction systems in personality assessment employed base rate data to improve accuracy. One of the few to do so was that of McEachern, Taylor, Newman, and Ashford (1968), involving demographic and other case history data for making practical decisions about juvenile offenders. Recent uses of base rate technology have been made by Lachar and Gdowski (1979) and by Millon (1977). Ways of approaching the inclusion of data on relative values of alternative predictions or outcomes have generated a small literature, and several authors have indicated some of the necessary considerations (e.g., Buchwald, 1965; Cronbach and Gleser, 1965; Wiggins, 1973). Some possible applications of both types of data are suggested in the following section.

Validity

The reviewers of automated personality assessment in the *Eighth Mental Measurements Yearbook* (Buros, 1978) raised serious questions about the inadequate attention paid to validity by the developers of automated programs. To quote Butcher (1978c): "The validation efforts to date have not been very convincing mostly because the methods employed will not produce uncontaminated and unambiguous results" (p. 944). These words tend to understate the problem, since for most programs there have been no serious attempts to demonstrate validity.

Requirements for Demonstrating Validity. What would constitute an adequate demonstration of validity? The question is analogous to the validity question involved in constructing an individual scale consisting of separate items. In constructing a scale, if the item selection procedures have involved both empirical and rational considerations, and if the sample sizes have been relatively large, then we can anticipate that the scale will continue to be valid when used with the same population, although there will be some shrinkage in validity from the initial correlations. A usual additional requirement in establishing adequate validity for a scale is to show that the scale has some generality; that is, to show that it also discriminates or predicts for several different populations. As indicated in Chapter 3, Jackson (1971) has successfully argued that in place of empirical selection of items, one can sometimes substitute careful internal consistency procedures, involving a theoretical definition of the concept and correlations between each item and a preliminary measure of the concept.

The requirements for demonstrating the validity of an interpretive program that has been developed empirically are analogous to those for demonstrating the validity of an individual scale that has been developed by the empirical method. They were fully applied by Halbower (Meehl, 1956) in his initial demonstration of the feasibility of constructing actuarial interpretation programs. In Halbower's procedure, patients were selected whose MMPI profiles fitted one of several specific patterns. Judges who knew the patients then performed criterion Q-sorts describing them, and an average Q-sort pattern was established for each of the three MMPI patterns. Validity for the program was demonstrated by the significance of the correlations between MMPI-based Q-sorts and criterion-based Q-sorts for an independent sample of patients from the same institution. Halbower also did a second validity study, using patients from a different institution in the same city, and demonstrated validity for his program there also.

What would be the requirements for demonstrating the validity of an interpretive program that was developed by a subjective rather than an empirical procedure? Again, let us first examine how validity would be established for a subjectively developed individual scale. The procedure utilized to develop such a scale would probably have consisted of assembling a group of items that appear to be good candidates for validity on the basis of general accumulated folklore or clinical hunches, with little or no statistical refinement of these items. There would be no compelling basis for concluding that such an assemblage of items would be sufficiently valid for prediction with any *particular* population, and it would therefore be necessary to demonstrate empirical validity for every use to which the scale is to be put. Once we had consistently shown such validity in a variety of relevant settings, we could begin to have some confidence about validity in other relevant settings without continued empirical demonstrations. But until substantial validity had been established in a number of different settings, a demonstration of validity would be required for each new application.

The same validity requirements should apply to automated interpretation programs that have been assembled on a subjective basis. Use with each different population should require a specific empirical demonstration of validity for that population, and only after a variety of successful demonstrations had been accomplished could we be confident about likely validity in other related settings.

There are some approaches to the development of automated interpretation programs that are best characterized as intermediate between the empirical approach and the subjective approach. Here, interpretive statements are selected nonstatistically, but on the basis of established empirical validity in related settings. We might call this the "sophisticated subjective approach." The primary basis for establishing validity for such a program would still involve an empirical demonstration of validity for each population with which the program is to be used. However, the stringency of these requirements would diminish toward those of the empirical approach to the extent that both of the following conditions are met. (1) The population for which the interpretive statements have shown prior validity is highly similar to the one with which the program is going to be used. Two aspects of similarity need to be considered: demographic characteristics and base rates of relevant difficulties. (2) The interpretive statements which comprise the program simply embody the prior empirical findings and are not embellished in any way.

Under what circumstances might these conditions be met? The most likely would be when an automated program is developed in a large hospital, agency, or clinic for in-house use, and where the program personnel are able to exercise active control over the way it is used. The original use of the Mayo Clinic MMPI program within the institution itself is such an example. Another can be seen in the MMPI programs of the type that have been developed specifically for particular populations in Veterans Administration services and are coordinated and monitored through a single source (e.g., Gilberstadt, 1970). Each homogeneous type of VA population would require its own program, of course, and the question of what constitutes a homogeneous population would need to be addressed empirically.

Methods of Validation.   What techniques are appropriate for demonstrating the validity of automated interpretation programs? The most satisfactory procedure would be to compare programmed interpretations with independently developed patient descriptions, either statement by statement or on a global level. We have already seen that Halbower and Meehl used this approach on a global level. Unfortunately, a review of existing validity studies shows that the most common procedure has simply been to ask clinicians to rate the accuracy of statements or reports about individual patients. Simple ratings cannot provide useful validity data because there is no control for the personal biases of the raters, which could be a major determinant of their responses. One way of adding controls would be to submit to each rater two kinds of statements: those that the program has identified as applicable to a patient and some that have been identified as irrelevant. The raters' task would be to judge the accuracy of both kinds of statements without knowing which is which, and the ratings of the irrelevant statements would serve as a base line over which the relevant statements would be expected to show a significant increment in their correlations with the criteria.

Let us address the troublesome question of how much generalized validity can be assumed for an interpretive program when applied in an unrestricted manner to new populations. It would seem clear that, in the absence of empirical evidence, there is no reason to assume that *any* interpretive program would be valid for a broad range of human services populations across the country. Rather, in order to have an adequate chance of possessing acceptable validities, programs should be tailored to specific populations and decision situations. The technology for this tailoring would involve the use of base rate data and information on relative utilities.

As an illustration, for automated interpretation programs that are designed for use with a particular population, a simple method for improving accuracy would be to tie cutting points directly to actual population base rates. For example, if 30 percent of the population of interest are known to lack adequate social skills, then the cutting point on the scale or index used for making statements about inadequate social skills would be chosen to separate out 30 percent of respondents. The use of population base rate data could be further extended by expanding a computer interpretation program to include the capacity for responding differently to different population base rates. These data would be entered into the computer as input together with the test scores. Because most commercially available programs are intended for use with a variety of populations, their potential validity could be substantially increased if they could respond to the unique base rate pattern of any given population in this manner. Such a procedure would represent a beginning toward the goal of ''individualizing'' automated interpretation programs.

The use of data on the relative utilities of different decisions or diagnoses, as discussed in Chapter 8, has to do with the relative importance of different kinds of errors. It is relevant, for example, in dealing with the obvious fact that on a suicide prediction device, a false negative error (a person whom the test failed to identify and who later suicided) is much more serious than a false positive error (a person who was mistakenly tagged as a potential suicide). Rorer, Hoffmann, and Hsieh (1966) showed that the ratio of the relative "values" of the different types of errors, if quantified, can be directly viewed as a multiplier of the base rate, and can be entered directly into the calculation for determining the optimal cutting point. Thus, depending on the relative costs and benefits associated with different types of errors, an automated interpretation program might at times be deliberately designed to "overlabel" or to "underlabel." Such variations could either be written directly into the program or entered on a job-by-job basis.

PROBLEMS IN APPLYING AUTOMATION

A variety of professional, ethical, and practical problems can be identified in connection with automated personality assessment. In response to certain of these problems, the American Psychological Association's Council of Representatives in 1966 adopted a set of interim standards for automated test interpretation practices (APA, 1967). Eichman's (1972) subsequent review of computerized scoring and interpretation services in the *Seventh Mental Measurements Yearbook* indicated that these standards were "for the most part sensible and practical guidelines which are easy to follow" (p. 251). By 1978 it had become clear that ethical and professional issues were by no means as simple as they had originally appeared. In reviewing automated interpretation in general, the two separate reviewers in the *Eighth Mental Measurements Yearbook* (Adair, 1978c; Butcher, 1978c) spent more than half of their review space on problems, concerns, dangers, and cautions.

The most important problem has already been identified—namely, the commercial offering of programs for which adequate validity has not been established. Another important problem is one which is common to the development of any technology. The sheer initial cost of developing and validating an adequate system for automated personality assessment is extremely high, putting it out of range of almost everybody except commercial operations. There is thus the danger that commercial considerations will take precedence over scientific and professional ones, and the reviewers in the *Eighth Mental Measurements Yearbook* believe that this has often been the case.

The remaining problems can be broadly grouped under the heading of *ethical considerations* but are closely related to the issues of validity and cost as already described. To quote from Adair's (1978c) review: "The writer was impressed with a curious dichotomy that appears to exist between the professional psychologist who is obliged to uphold the ethics of the profession and the entrepreneurial psychologist who is obliged to make a profit in order to maintain a position in the market" (p. 940). To quote from Butcher's (1978c) review: "The computer approach to personality assessment has been oversold and users place more stock in scientific truths than is actually deserved'' (p. 943). Both reviewers believed that the 1966 APA interim standards for automated test scoring and interpretation practices were *not* adequate to deal with these concerns. Both reviewers also pointed specifically to misleading literature which has been mailed out by some of the services, and to the fact that many users of the services simply do not know enough about personality assessment to decide what part of the information returned to them is usable and what is not. The problem is compounded by the air of finality and correctness which tends to exist about anything that comes out of a computer, creating an inappropriate willingness on the part of users to trust the printout.

These criticisms do not necessarily apply to all automated personality interpretation services. For example, Adair (1978a) and Butcher (1978a) wrote positively about the Automated Psychological Assessment system developed by Lachar. They pointed out that in the development of this system, care was taken to avoid many of the difficulties pointed out here. Thus, there would appear to be no reason in principle why satisfactory systems cannot be developed. Because of the nature and extent of the criticisms, it would appear to be a matter of some urgency for the profession of psychology to take responsibility for upgrading and policing its standards for automated personality assessment. The unattractive alternative is the distinct possibility that another body, such as an arm of the federal government, might step in and insist upon constraints that could seriously hamper future developments that would be in society's best interests.

OTHER APPLICATIONS OF AUTOMATION

This chapter has thus far described automation in traditional personality test procedures. There have been a number of parallel developments involving the automation of other procedures and tasks that are related to personality assessment, and these are next reviewed briefly. All of them involve the mental health industry.

Automated Diagnosis

Because one of the end products of a comprehensive assessment of a patient is often a psychiatric diagnosis, a number of attempts have been made to develop actuarial programs that classify patients into diagnostic categories. One example was mentioned in Chapter 6: the diagnostic program (termed DIAGNO II) developed by Endicott and Spitzer (1972). This computer program employs a logical decision-tree model, and the output is one of 46 diagnoses based on the first edition of the American Psychiatric Association's *Diagnostic and Statistical Manual of Mental Disorders* (DSM I). The schematic flowchart for DIAGNO II is shown in Figure 10-1. A later revision of the program, termed DIAGNO III, was developed to yield one or more of the 79 psychiatric diagnoses listed in the second edition of the *Manual*, DSM II (Spitzer and Endicott, 1974). Another computer diagnosis application involves the use of the decision-tree rules of the Research Diagnostic Criteria, discussed in Chapter 7, as the basis for decisions (Greist, Klein, and

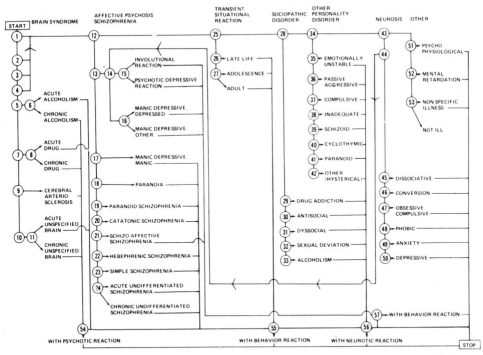

FIGURE 10-1. Schematic flowchart for the DIAGNO II computer program. From Spitzer and Endicott (1969). Copyright 1969, the American Psychiatric Association. Reprinted by permission.

Erdman, 1976). A further example is seen in the Missouri Actuarial Report System, or MARS (Altman, Evenson, Hedland, and Cho, 1978), which yields a comprehensive automated report including statements about the probabilities of different diagnostic categories.

In a recent review of computer diagnostic programs, Hedland, Evenson, Sletten, and Cho (1980) identified two basic models that have been employed: the logical decision-tree model and the statistical model. Both have been shown to agree with clinicians' diagnoses about as well as clinicians agree among themselves. It was concluded that the logical decision-tree model was probably the more valid for routine uses, but that supplemental statistical models could provide additional information in borderline or questionable cases.

Automated Progress Reports

Another use of computers in mental health assessment has been the development of methods for generating routine reports on patient progress. The input to the computer typically involves responses on a structured checklist or multiple-choice questionnaire, and the output can be in either graphic or narrative form. An example is the Automated Nursing Note system developed at the Institute of Living (Glueck, Gullotta, and Ericson, 1980; Rosenberg, Glueck, and Bennett, 1967). In this system, the nursing staff completes a daily checklist on each patient on a computer-readable form from which standardized scores on 13 factor scales are generated. Scales involve common concepts such as thought disorganization, depressive behavior, anxiety, and negativism. Output consists of a narrative report plus a printed or graphic display of the standard scores on the behavior factors. In addition, a display of 10 weeks of scores for any factor can be viewed on a cathode-ray tube terminal, giving a visual display of patient changes over that time period. Two graphic displays of such information are shown in Figure 10-2.

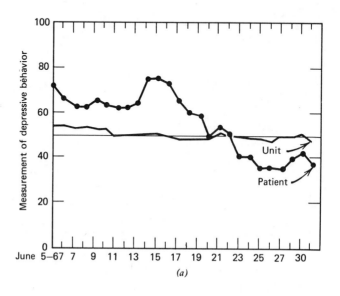

(a)

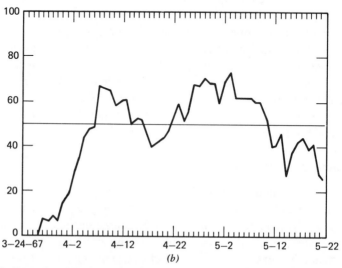

(b)

FIGURE 10-2. Examples of graphical data derived from automated progress reports: *(a)* A recovering depressed female patient. *(b)* Anxiety in a sociopath, using running seven-day mean scores. From Rosenberg and Glueck (1967). Reproduced by permission.

Comprehensive Psychiatric Assessment Systems

Some of the structured interview and biographical data instruments discussed in Chapter 7 form part of comprehensive and interlocking systems of instruments developed for use on a statewide or multistate basis. There are two major systems of this type: the Multi-State Information System (MSIS), centered at the Rockland State Hospital in New York, and the Standard System of Psychiatry (SSOP) of the State of Missouri. The impetus for the development of these systems was cost-efficiency, recognizing that with the extremely large volume of patients available on a statewide basis, considerable savings could result once the initial expenditures for development and start-up were made. Planning for both of these systems began in the 1960s. Each incorporates instruments for the objective recording and processing of case history data, mental status examination results, and inpatient behavior, with a variety of additional instruments for such purposes as alcohol history, social functioning, and periodic review. Outputs vary according to the need being served by the procedure and include narrative reports, summary reports, graphic representations, diagnostic suggestions, and cumulative summaries on individual patients or groups of patients. Detailed accounts of these systems are beyond the scope of this chapter but are available elsewhere (e.g., Hedlund, Sletten, Evensen, Altman, and Cho, 1977; MSIS, 1976).

The most important advantage claimed for comprehensive automated assessment systems is their economy. Other benefits include the maintenance of a comprehensive and standardized master file of all patient data in the system in readily accessible form, the availability of rapid longitudinal monitoring procedures for individual patients, and the provision of a standardized data base for clinical research and for program evaluation. Objections include substantial opposition from some professional staff members who believe that the patient-doctor relationship must necessarily be an individual matter; objections to specific instruments as "too long," "too abstract," etc.; and possible sabotage or improper use by staff members who have negative reactions to the system. Perhaps the most important objection concerns the threat to confidentiality that is generated by the availability of a statewide comprehensive, easily accessible data library of highly personal material. Such problems of confidentiality are discussed further in Chapter 11.

Despite these concerns, the use of automated processing procedures for assessment information in mental health systems is becoming more and more widespread. Thus, a recent review by Hedlund, Evenson, Sletten, and Cho (1980) showed that the vast majority of state departments of mental health utilized computers in some capacity, and that about half of these used them in some clinical function. The edited volume by Sidowski, Johnson, and Williams (1980) provides a detailed introduction to this area.

Summary

Automated procedures in personality assessment procedures tend to be synonymous with the use of computers. This field received its impetus in the early 1960s as a response to routine high-volume assessment needs in particular institutional settings, but it has since become a commercial enterprise on a national basis. Automation is not a significant aspect of the administration of personality tests, mainly because its most ready application is with inventories, which already require minimal professional time and effort to administer. Some on-line computer procedures for administration have been proposed, however. Automated scoring has been available for inventories for many years. Some interesting beginnings have been made in the automated scoring of projective tests, involving the development of libraries of possible response words together with a limitation on the length of each response.

The bulk of the literature in automated personality assessment is in the area of interpretation. The development of an automated interpretation system requires three steps: personality test responses in summary form, a library of interpretive statements and a valid program for associating them with the test responses, and a way of delivering the output. For inventories, the input can be a series of scales and indices; for projective techniques, the complexities of developing structured scoring procedures have so far precluded the development of automated interpretation programs. Interpretation programs can be developed either empirically or subjectively. Empirical development involves the determination of interpretive statements that are known to be empirically related to particular test responses, in exactly the same manner as for the empirical selection of individual items to constitute a single scale. Few interpretation programs have been developed in this manner, however. Most have employed the subjective approach, in which interpretive statements about a test are accumulated from all possible sources and are then tied to specific scores or cutting points on the basis of subjective judgment. The task of preparing and delivering automated output is essentially a clerical one and may involve the use of additional computer programs for the construction of narrative prose.

Despite the popularity of automated personality assessment, relatively little research has been conducted on the technical aspects of developing and validating automated programs. It has been well established that linear predictors tend to outperform nonlinear ones, and whenever test profile patterns are used as input to the computer, the simplest patterns, such as high two-point codes, tend to be employed. Relatively little attention has been given to information on population base rates of relevant characteristics or to the relative values associated with different decisions. The lack of validity research on automated interpretation programs has been the subject of serious criticism of the automated assessment enterprise. The same requirements should apply to establishing the validity of such programs as are needed to establish the validity of individual inventory scales or predictive indices. Unfortunately, the most common approach has been simply to rely on clinicians' ratings of the accuracy of statements in the automated report, a procedure which can be subject to obvious biases. Other criticisms have included the inappropriate readiness of commercial enterprises to offer services without the backing of adequate validity and the misleading nature of some of the accompanying advertising materials.

Other applications of automation in personality assessment include diagnostic programs such as the DIAGNO series and the development of methods for generating routine reports on the progress of hospitalized psychiatric patients. Such procedures often form part of a comprehensive and interlocking set of instruments for use on a statewide or multistate basis, which might include the processing of case history data, mental status examination results, and a variety of instruments for more specific purposes. Two such systems are the Multi-State Information System and the Missouri Standard System of Psychiatry.

11 CRITICISMS OF PERSONALITY ASSESSMENT

Psychological tests, including those used for personality assessment, have been criticized for as long as they have existed. Some of these criticisms undoubtedly have arisen from the vague resentments that many of us feel toward being evaluated, especially by examinations of any kind (Amrine, 1965, p. 859). Other criticisms have been based on misunderstandings. For example, Dahlstrom (1969) pointed out that some government employment application forms have required applicants to sign a statement that their answers are true to the best of their knowledge. Applicants could easily become confused if they are also administered one or more personality tests as part of the application procedure. Self-report personality inventories usually instruct respondents that there are no right or wrong answers, and either that the are to give their own opinions of themselves or that they are to give the most appropriate response. Most projective devices are even more ambiguous and require respondents to give their initial, unqualified impression. All such responses are treated simply as behaviors and not necessarily as "true" or factual information. With such conflicting instructions and attitudinal sets, one can easily understand why respondents could become confused as to whether or not there are supposed to be "right" answers, and also how cautious they should be about their responses. Incidentally, such contradictions point up the importance of having the personality tests administered by, or at least supervised by, qualified professionals, who can make certain that the respondents understand the nature of the task.

Most of the traditional criticisms are more serious than those just described. In 1965, in response to a gradual build-up in public sentiment against psychological testing, two sets of congressional hearings were held. The House Special Subcommittee on Invasion of Privacy of the Committee on Government Operations conducted an inquiry "because of a large body of evidence that certain activities and operations of federal agencies were being carried out concerning which serious questions could be raised. . . . There is the matter of psychological or personality testing of government employees and job applicants by federal agencies. Many federal workers are subjected to extensive tests on their sex life, family situations, religion, personal habits, childhood, and many other matters'' (Gallagher, 1965, p. 955). The other inquiry was conducted by the Senate Subcommittee on Constitutional Rights of the Committee on the Judiciary, which made its investigation for similar reasons (Ervin, 1965). The testimony involved in these inquiries covered a much wider variety of issues than the avowed purposes of the hearings, showing that there was a broad range of dissatisfactions and criticisms voiced by a variety of different people, including a number of psychologists. There might also be some truth in Dahlstrom's (1969) suggestion that psychological tests were to some extent used as a scapegoat for the public's concern and anxiety over the development of ''an increasingly precise psychotechnology.''

Whatever the reasons for the congressional hearings, they served the purpose of forcing psychologists to face many criticisms of psychological tests and testing practices which had previously been minimized, avoided, or denied. The hearings also had the effect of spurring psychologists to initiate a number of reforms which have now become part of the established expectations for psychologists involved in psychological assessment (e.g., American Psychological Association, 1974, 1977). Another positive outcome of the lengthy debates and soul-searching generated by the hearings was the clarification of some complex ethical and moral issues in regard to psychological testing in general. In this chapter, we deal with some of them that are particularly relevant to personality assessment.

Criticisms of personality assessment might be grouped roughly into two kinds. In the terminology of the popular critic Martin Gross (1965), personality tests have been criticized as *inaccurate* and also *immoral*. Messick (1965), a prominent researcher in personality assessment procedures, formulated the criticisms by saying that ''some tests are poor in quality and that tests are often misused'' (p. 138).

Out of the flurry of defenses offered on behalf of personality tests, a reasonable viewpoint on their use can be delineated (e.g., Anastasi, 1967; Messick, 1965). The *use* of personality tests in the past has certainly been inaccurate and immoral in some instances. Other uses have been both accurate and moral. It remains to sort out the accurate uses from the inaccurate, and the moral from the immoral. We discuss these two areas under the headings of *use* and *moral issues*.

USAGE OF PERSONALITY ASSESSMENT DEVICES

Problems in the use of personality tests are of two kinds. First, there are the problems involved in the misuse of a valid test; for example, a test which has been shown to be valid for one purpose is used for another. Second, there are the problems involved in using a test that has no clearly demonstrated validity for any purpose. We deal first with the problems involved in using tests which do have established valid uses. In these cases, the criticism would seem to be more appropriately directed at the test users than at the test itself.

Improper Usage

The improper application of otherwise valid tests has probably been, and undoubtedly will continue to be, among the worst of all the abuses of personality assessment technology. In a sense, all such abuses should be considered to be a result of inadequate understanding by the test users of the nature of the test and the critical issues involved. Thus, two of the four policy implications regarding testing that were delineated by the American Psychological Association (1970) involve improper use; namely, protection of the individual against "unwarranted *inferences* by persons not equipped with the requisite knowledge" and against "unfavorable evaluation based on obsolete information" (p. 265).

Use in Personnel Selection.   One obvious and serious misuse of personality tests has been their employment by untrained users and in inappropriate circumstances for personnel work in industry. This indictment applies particularly to the use of tests intended for use in psychiatric settings, such as the Rorschach and the MMPI. Some possible reasons for this practice are as follows. There is the need of personnel managers to identify persons with potential emotional disturbances. There is also the fact that the personnel manager's formal academic training in personality measurement is quite likely to have stressed these instruments and their validity in identifying psychopathology, whereas in practice he/she is more often concerned with assessing aspects of normal personality functioning, especially those related to job success and management potential. Further, some personnel officers may be indirectly motivated by a desire to gain some of the status of professional psychologists, or to engage in the psychological voyeurism that is legitimized in that profession. It is noteworthy that a basic cause of the 1965 congressional hearings was the use of the MMPI by the State Department in a limited, though routine, manner. It is this kind of misuse of personality measures in personnel selection which led Gross (1962, 1965) and Alex (1965) to claim that all personality tests are invalid, and to imply strongly that this was true in virtually all situations. Thus, Gross (1965) stated: "The results of many careful experiments that have attempted to validate personality testing have all proven the tests to be worthless" (p. 959).

In response to this criticism, it must be agreed that abuses of personality tests certainly do occur. One direction for professional psychologists to take in counteracting them is to restrict the use of such tests to persons qualified to use them properly.

Such a policy was formally adopted by the American Psychological Association (1970) in its statement that "decisions about what assessment procedures are to be used and how they are to be handled should be based on persons competent to make them" (p. 266). In the same vein, the latest edition of the American Psychological Association's (1974) *Standards for Educational and Psychological Tests* includes a completely new section on standards for the use of tests. The 25 standards in this section cover four broad areas: qualifications and concerns of users, choice or development of test or method, administration and scoring, and interpretation of scores. Responsible and ethical use of tests by psychologists requires a familiarity with these standards, as well as with the more general *Ethical Standards of Psychologists* (American Psychological Association, 1977) and the *Casebook on Ethical Standards of Psychologists* (American Psychological Association, 1967). In an early paper, Forehand (1964) discussed some of the difficulties which would result from the elimination of the use of personality tests in making practical decisions. His discussion clearly indicates that many of the problems raised by Gross might in fact be intensified if tests were to be eliminated.

Mention should be made of the various volumes of the *Mental Measurements Yearbook* (e.g., Buros, 1978) and the unwitting role they have played in aiding the test critics. Examination of these volumes will show that there are an enormous number of personality assessment devices available for use, most of them unvalidated in any more than a rudimentary way. The vast majority of these tests, fortunately, are little used in practical situations. For the relatively few tests that are more widely used, the status of their validity, although far from what we might hope, tends to be somewhat better. These yearbooks, however, unwittingly provide abundant ammunition for those who wish to attack personality tests, since they imply (correctly, but misleadingly) that almost all existing published tests have little or no demonstrable validity. A more accurate characterization would be that the validity of some of the more widely used tests (such as the Rorschach, TAT, and MMPI), when employed by adequately trained persons under appropriate conditions, can be satisfactory.

The problem of faking on personality tests is another focus for criticism, one that becomes especially important when tests are used in personnel work. The practical question is whether any valid information can be elicited from respondents if they do not wish to reveal themselves. Our earlier discussion of the faking problem in Chapter 7 led us to a tentative answer that the validity of information gained under these circumstances is doubtful at best, although the evidence is by no means all in. Lovell (1967) has reached a similar conclusion and has reasoned on this basis that personality tests should therefore not be used at all in personnel selection situations. On the other hand, Dahlstrom (1969), while agreeing with the conclusion, suggested that personality tests ethically *could* be used in personnel situations, since respondents are protected by having the opportunity to protect their privacy (through faking) if they so desire. Interestingly, the latest edition of the *Principles for the Validation and Use of Personnel Selection Procedures,* published by the Division of Industrial/Organizational Psychology of the American Psychological Association (1980), makes no mention of faking as a problem, but subsumes it within an extensive and detailed discussion of validity in general. Thus, the view is implicitly taken that if the topic of validity, "the degree to which inferences from scores on tests or assessments are justified or supported by evidence" (p. 2), is properly addressed, the question of faking need not be considered separately.

Failure to Consider Base Rates.   A serious area of concern that seems to have been overlooked by the lay critics of personality tests is the problem posed by base rates, an issue discussed earlier in Chapters 7 and 8. The failure to recognize and understand this complex, technical issue by unsophisticated critics should not be surprising, since many professional psychologists are also unaware of its importance.

At the risk of boring the reader, let us again consider how the failure to take base rates into account may result in the misuse of an otherwise valid test. A clear example of this problem is offered by Seeman (1969) in his reanalysis of the results of Hall and LaDriere (1969), who reported that the number of "conceptually inadequate" responses given on the Similarities subtest of the Wechsler Intelligence Scale for Children had diagnostic usefulness in the detection of cerebral pathology. Seeman noted that, if it was assumed that approximately 25 percent of children seen in child guidance clinics were actually cerebrally damaged (almost certainly an overestimate) and the actual cutting score recommended by Hall and LaDriere was employed, accurate diagnoses would be made only 37 percent of the time and inaccurate ones would be made 63 percent of the time, even though there is no question about the "validity" of the "conceptually inadequate" sign. Thus, the failure to take into account the frequency of occurrence of the event to be predicted could result in an unwarranted application of an otherwise valid predictive sign. Once again, the ultimate choice of whether or not to use the sign should depend on the relative costs and values involved.

Discrimination against Minority Groups.   There are a number of other criticisms of personality testing that, although not so obviously connected with insufficient technical understanding of testing problems, can be indirectly linked to it. One is the issue of racial and other forms of discrimination through the use of tests. Most of the complaints that tests result in unfair discrimination against certain minority groups have until now been made in regard to the use of ability tests, but there is no reason to suppose that personality tests are free of discriminatory biases. This topic has been discussed in more detail in Chapter 9. In regard to ability tests, Brim (1965) suggested that minority groups should be favorably rather than unfavorably inclined toward the use of properly constructed tests, because tests provide an objective standard for assessment. In fact, this is one clear way to identify unfair discriminatory practices. The application of this point to the assessment of personality is unclear, however. It should be noted that the social values underlying the personnel use of personality tests relate to their ability to identify and eliminate unconventional and difficult persons, and the validity of personality tests for accomplishing such a purpose is also a measure of their "bias." The resolution of this dilemma would appear to involve a reconsideration of the underlying social values rather than an attack upon personality tests. In general, the issues with regard to personality and other tests and discrimination are difficult and complex, and the best current insurance against unfair practices is a thorough understanding of the underlying social, psychometric, and ethical principles by test users.

The Experience Controversy.   One aspect of the argument concerning use of personality tests by technically unsophisticated persons is more controversial than those discussed previously. We are referring, in the context of clinical diagnosis, to claims that expertise with such instruments as the Rorschach requires more than just training with that instrument, but rather intensive experience plus a comprehensive theoretical understanding of both general personality theory and the rationale of the particular test. It follows from this position that many studies which have failed to demonstrate validity for these clinical instruments are inadmissable as evidence because inexperienced clinicians were employed in the study. The issue is not one of marginal versus moderate training (as was the case when the personnel uses of tests were discussed) but moderate versus elaborate training.

There is little research evidence on this question of the necessity for prolonged and intensive training, and the evidence that does exist is inconsistent. On the positive side, Goldberg (1959) demonstrated that an expert in the Bender-Gestalt test did much better in diagnosing presence or absence of brain damage than did a number of other judges. However, in the extensive study of psychiatric diagnosis conducted by Little and Shneidman (1959), in which care was taken to select the country's leading practitioners of the tests studied, results were unimpressive. It may be significant that Goldberg's Bender-Gestalt expert spent some 20 hours on the 30 protocols in order to achieve his result, and this would be consistent with our conclusion offered in Chapter 8 that the motivation of the judges plays an important part in their clinical accuracy. But even if it can be consistently demonstrated that highly trained clinicians are superior to those with minimal training, the question remains as to whether their superiority would be sufficient to justify the effort and expense of the additional training.

Unwarranted Applications   Personality tests are widely used, albeit ethically and in good faith, for purposes for which they simply were not intended and for which they are inappropriate. For example, it is not uncommon for psychologists to make an estimate of intelligence from TAT stories or a Rorschach protocol. In a similar vein, the far-reaching attempts which have been made to extend the use of the MMPI can be seen from a scrutiny of Lanyon's (1968) collection of the mean MMPI profiles of a large variety of subject groups. It can also be clearly seen from this collection that the more psychopathological the subjects, the better the discriminations that could be made among their profiles. For example, the MMPI was almost completely ineffective in differentiating good and poor automobile drivers. On the other hand, there are wide and obvious differences between psychopaths and neurotics. As noted earlier, this should surprise nobody, since the MMPI was built for the specific purpose of making the latter type of discriminations, and not the former kind. A similar comment can be made about the TAT, which was devised to describe personality needs and traits, not psychopathology. Despite continuing claims for the utility of the TAT for this purpose (e.g., Bellak, 1975), there are still no substantial data to contradict Eron's (1948) findings of relatively few differences between the TAT responses of college students and those of schizophrenic patients.

Another kind of unwarranted application of personality tests that should be mentioned is the routine development of careful psychodynamic formulations on patients in clinical settings. Although such formulations might be of use in lengthy psychodynamically oriented treatment—though even this has been questioned (Meehl, 1960)—the value of such a procedure in most settings, which depend on other kinds of treatment approaches, is obscure. This point has led to a number of articles reviewing the "decline of psychological testing" (e.g., Cleveland, 1976; Lewandowski and Saccuzzo, 1976). Probably a more accurate view, however, is that the nature of the assessment enterprise has changed, away from lengthy assessment batteries involving a number of projective tests and toward shorter, more objective instruments (cf. Buros, 1978, p. xxxvii).

Unwarranted Criticisms.   Some of the criticisms of personality testing that have been set forth by popular writers (e.g., Gross, 1962; Whyte, 1956) can be attributed to the naïvete of the critics, who appear not to have understood the psychometric principles involved. Many of the complaints made by Gross (1962, Ch. 5) about the MMPI fall into this category. For example, it was inexplicable to him that a correction score such as the *K* scale could improve validity, or that a high score on the *Sc* scale should not invariably indicate schizophrenia. Another such criticism concerns the admissibility of subtle items. Thus, Gross found it somehow inequitable that a person who denies belief in the second coming of Christ should be, to use his term, "penalized" on the depression scale, and he was unable to comprehend the argument that the depressive patients in the original criterion group did in fact differ from the normal groups in their responses to this item. Hathaway (1964) went to considerable pains to explain and illustrate some of these psychometric points which may not be obvious to the layman.

Generalized Test Invalidity

We now turn to those criticisms which are more appropriately directed at the tests (or their authors) rather than at the users. We shall concentrate upon those problems of validity that result from test development procedures that do not pay adequate attention to the usefulness of the test in some or other specific respects. As indicated previously, an excellent discussion of this topic may be found in the *Principles for the Validation and Use of Personnel Selection Procedures,* second edition (Division of Industrial/Organizational Psychology, American Psychological Association, 1980).

The Criterion Problem.   We first discuss the problems that occur if a personality assessment device is developed without regard to any clear-cut criterion. It will be remembered from our earlier discussion that when the empirical approach to test construction is used, test developers have a clear idea of what dimensions of personality they want to assess, and they try to make these dimensions operational by specifying definite criterion groups or by some other clearly described procedure. If correctly applied, the rational and theoretical approaches to test construction also include a clear idea of what dimensions or attributes of personality are to be assessed (expressed in either rational or theoretical terms) and reliable methods of defining these dimensions. In all of these cases there are relatively clear-cut definitions which lead to criteria against which the test can be evaluated. Problems begin for personality assessment when there is no clear-cut specification of the criterion—what we are trying to assess.

The problem of criteria has been particularly acute with some of the projective devices and rationally based inventories, but it is by no means absent even for instruments with originally specified criteria. One example is the MMPI scales. The scales were constructed in order to predict patients' assignment to psychiatric diagnostic categories, and the criteria originally employed were the diagnostic categories to which the patients had already been assigned. Hathaway (1959) and Meehl (1959b) have both pointed out that since psychiatric diagnosis is relatively unreliable, and to some extent arbitrary, one might seriously question why so much attention should be given to these nebulous categories. That is, why attempt to develop an instrument which is concerned, from the first, with predicting an event that is arbitrary and unreliable? The ceiling for the predictive accuracy of such scales is set by the reliability of the criterion diagnosis, so that no further improvement in the instrument is possible beyond this level of accuracy.

These are at least two ways to resolve the dilemma of improving a test when no adequately clear-cut referent or criterion exists for what is being assessed. One, proposed by Hathaway (1959), would be to give the assessment result equal status with the criterion. Looking at the issue of psychiatric diagnosis in this light, a patient could then be called "schizophrenic" from a Rorschach or MMPI record just as validly as from a psychiatric examination. Incongruities among various sources of data would be resolved by clinical judgments. Another way to resolve the problem would be to employ factor analytic procedures and then to adopt factor scales as "basic" psychological variables, recognizing that the initial construction had been based on fallible data. The merits of this procedure were examined in Chapter 4.

In general, persons engaged in developing techniques of personality assessment have paid far too little attention to the specific aims of their assessment procedures, and to the development of adequate criteria for what is to be assessed. With respect to the assessment of specific behaviors, Holt (1958) wrote:

> First, if we are to predict some kind of behavior, it is presupposed that we acquaint ourselves with what we are trying to predict. This may be called job analysis or a study of the criterion. Perhaps these terms sound a little fancy when their referent is something that seems so obvious to common sense. Nevertheless, it is surprising how often people expend a great deal of time and effort trying to predict a kind of behavior about which they know very little without even thinking that it might help if they could find out more. (p. 2)

This shortcoming was initially pointed many years ago by Toops (1944), who suggested that comparable amounts of time should be given to developing the criterion and to perfecting the assessment instruments. Similar warnings and criticisms were offered by Taft (1959) and by Stern, Stein, and Bloom (1956). These writings discussed two large-scale personality assessment studies, the OSS study (OSS Assessment Staff, 1948) and the VA assessment study of training in clinical psychology (Kelly and Fiske, 1951; Kelly and Goldberg, 1959), respectively. Neither of the studies was particularly successful in its aims because of inability to specify clearly in advance the nature of the criterion behavior. A more sophisticated approach to a complex assessment problem was used by Laurent

(1962), who wished to employ personality and other data to select management trainees with the greatest potential for success. In order to cope with the criterion problem, Laurent first developed a composite criterion for "success" by factor-analyzing a variety of available measures of success, such as position level and salary history. The resulting primary factor was adopted as a criterion of overall success and could be used as the target for the predictions.

The foregoing studies deal with complex or multiple assessment projects, but similar criterion problems are encountered in developing instruments to assess individual personality characteristics. Many researchers fail to demonstrate predictive validity for projective devices because the tests were constructed without reference to reliable and easily definable criteria. Rather, each investigator is free to choose whichever dimensions of personality are of interest in the investigation. The resulting melange of investigations has produced largely negative findings, but there can never be the "definitive" study if there is no definitive criterion.

This discussion perhaps can best be summarized by referring to Ebel's (1964b) viewpoint, in which tests that are clearly proposed to be a shortcut method for avoiding more elaborate methods of behavioral assessment are distinguished from those that are not. For the "shortcut" tests, the criterion for test construction must be the "more elaborate method of assessment," and validity is assessed by the correspondence between the two measures. In such cases, the criterion scores would be produced by a measurement procedure that is superior in important ways (e.g., more comprehensive, more reliable) to the test, so that the test is a poorer but more convenient measure of the comprehensive method. In personality assessment, the major problem is usually that a "more elaborate method" for evaluating personality functioning does not exist at this time. It is also true, however, that appropriate criteria could sometimes be developed in the manner utilized by Laurent (1962). An example can be seen in the work of B. Lanyon (1972), who constructed careful criteria as a basis for the empirical development of a three-scale sentence completion test, as described in Chapter 3.

Illusory Correlation.   Another serious problem which involves the validity of certain assessment procedures specifically applies where tests are interpreted by common sense or by an accumulated fund of clinical information, as is the case with much interpretation of projective drawings and, to some extent, with the Rorschach and similar instruments. The problem was identifed by Chapman (1967) and labeled "illusory correlation" (Chapman and Chapman, 1967). It may be because of illusory correlation that certain tests with doubtful empirical validities continue to be used and are supported enthusiastically by diagnosticians.

The Chapmans had observed that, when college students were shown a series of word pairs carefully arranged so that all possible pairings were presented equally often, they systematically but mistakenly reported that certain words tended to occur together more often than was actually the case. Specifically, the illusion was produced that words with high associative strength for each other (e.g., table and chair, hungry and food) had occurred together more often than words with low associative strength. The Chapmans characterized this effect as "analogous to the well-known Muller-Lyer illusion, in that there is a widely shared systematic error of observation that is not dependent on the observer's having some exceptional prior experience or training'' (Chapman and Chapman, 1967, p. 194).

Reasoning that this illusory correlation might also occur in clinical test interpretation, the Chapmans had college undergraduates observe a series of human figure drawings. On each drawing was arbitrarily written two contrived personality symptom statements which were said to describe the person who produced the drawing. There were six such symptom statements, and each was attached to several different drawings. This observational experience was purportedly designed to teach the subjects the relationship between drawings and symptoms. The subjects, thus having ''learned'' about figure drawings, then were given a written list of the six personality symptom statements and were asked to list under each symptom statement the drawing characteristics which they had observed to be related to it. The correct response in each case was, of course, that there was no systematic relationship between the personality symptom statements and any drawing characteristic whatever. As expected, however, the subjects tended to list as related to each personality symptom those drawing characteristics which had high associative strength for the symptom. For example, the subjects overwhelmingly reported a connection between the personality symptom of suspiciousness and the drawing characteristic of atypical eyes, even though their ''learning'' experience had provided absolutely no basis for such a connection. Further investigation produced the following critical finding: that the ''personality interpretation'' given by the naïve undergraduate subjects corresponded closely to the interpretations given by experienced clinicians! Thus, there are indications that some of the ''clinical lore'' used to interpret projective tests is spurious, and presumably is perpetuated for the same reasons that it originally occurred—because such interpretations ''make sense'' or are ''intuitively correct'' although the empirical evidence for these relationships is not present.

How strong is the illusory correlation effect? Chapman and Chapman (1969) were able to show that it occurred in assessing homosexuality from the Rorschach, and Starr and Katkin (1969) also found the effect on the Incomplete Sentences Blank. A study by Dowling and Graham (1976) reported a similar phenomenon in using the MMPI, although their results are open to other interpretations. Two studies have shown that the illusory correlation effect persisted unchanged even where subjects received specific warnings about its effects plus training in avoiding it (Kurtz and Garfield, 1978; Waller and Keeley, 1978). In a study designed to provide further understanding of this phenomenon, Lueger and Petzel (1979) showed that the greater the amount of information to be processed by the judges, the greater was the illusory correlation effect.

It cannot be concluded that illusory correlation accounts entirely for the discrepancy between the positive claims made by many practicing clinicians for validity of the figure drawing technique and similar tests, and the meager empirical evidence that is available in their support. Nevertheless, the strength and consistency of the research findings is a potent condemnation of relying solely on one's ''experience'' in test interpretation, no matter how confident one might be.

MORAL ISSUES IN USING PERSONALITY ASSESSMENT DEVICES

The criticisms discussed under this heading do not apply only to personality assessment. They are relevant to many other aspects of psychology, including the experimental use of human subjects, as well as to many aspects of other social sciences, such as economics, education, and law. We are referring to situations in which individuals feel personally threatened with regard to either their personal rights and needs, or their social and civil rights. The threats are often so subtle that people may find it difficult to articulate their reasons for feeling concern or threat, and they may even explicitly deny that threat is the real cause for their actions. These concerns are the bedrock of the criticisms which have become identified with the term "invasion of privacy."

Dahlstrom (1969) has distinguished two meanings for the concept of invasion of privacy. The first involves the issue of *confidentiality,* where there may be "certain facts about a person that he would prefer to keep secret [that are] in danger of being revealed to someone who could then use them against him" (p. 268). The second is concerned with *inviolacy* and involves people's unwillingness to have another person impose upon them in a significant way. In Dahlstrom's words, "They consider any intrusion upon their activities as a violation of their private pattern of living" (p. 268). Anastasi (1967, p. 297) has made a similar distinction.

Before considering these two aspects in detail, let us first examine reasons why the invasion of privacy has become such a socially sensitive issue. Willingham (1967) listed six possible contributing or underlying influences. (1) The first is the concern for individual dignity and privacy that has been sensitized by the civil rights movement. Thus, identification of personal characteristics may facilitate socially invidious comparisons. (2) Second, and ironically incompatible with the first, are the demands for social equality, for social scientists to make careful studies and comparisons of social groups, so that the inequalities can be investigated and changes can be initiated. The third and fourth influences, both technological, are (3) the greatly increased availability of research funds and (4) the development of a highly sophisticated computer technology. Complex and extensive research projects are not only tempting for the researcher but are seen as mandatory if behavioral scientists are to maintain an image of competence and respectability in the scientific community. (5) The fifth factor, also ironic, is the social scientists' greater need for involvement in socially meaningful research. These efforts might be seen as a reaction against criticisms leveled at much behavioral research in the past, that this research has been irrelevant to the real problems now confronting society. (6) The public has become highly sensitized to invasion of privacy in a number of areas which are not necessarily psychological in nature, but it has failed to make discriminations among them. Thus, some of the resentments against the use of electronic eavesdropping devices, the large-scale accumulation of personal credit histories, and the collection of personal data in the federal census, have spread to psychology in general and to personality assessment in particular.

Let us now return to our examination of the major complaints about invasion of privacy as they apply to personality assessment. We do so under the two headings suggested by Dahlstrom, although the two categories will be seen to overlap to some extent.

Confidentiality

Problems relating to confidentiality are present not only with personality assessment data but with any personal information revealed to a clinical psychologist or counselor, and for that matter to a physician, lawyer, or minister. According to Schwitzgebel and Schwitzgebel (1980), only the relationship between laywer and client is always legally privileged. For communications with other professionals, different states grant different degrees of privilege. As of 1980 communication between psychologist and client was legally privileged in 27 states. It should be clearly understood, however, that certain actions by a client result in waiving the privilege. For example, if a client requests a psychological evaluation to be used as support in a legal proceeding such as a child custody case or a criminal defense, the test records are usually subject to subpoena by the court or by the opposing party. On a broader level, ethical issues for psychologists involved with the criminal justice system are extensive and complex. The recent volume edited by Monahan (1980) gives an excellent introduction to these issues and presents the recommendations of the American Psychological Association's Task Force on the Role of Psychology in the Criminal Justice System.

Ethical Considerations.   It seems unnecessary to state that individuals have the right to withhold from you whatever information they wish, unless they have entered into a contract (actual or implied) with you to the contrary. If, in addition, they have reason to believe that you will employ the information against their best interests, they would indeed be foolish to disclose it. The issues, however, are more complex than that. It may seem strange to us now that, at the height of the public controversy over personality assessment, it was often seriously suggested that *all* personality tests should be outlawed! This failure to distinguish their many legitimate and apparently humanitarian uses from their abuses attests to the amount of emotion invested in the issues.

The legal issues involved in confidentiality have recently come to the forefront, perhaps as people realized that legal mechanisms did indeed exist to protect their rights. Together with increased legal activity has come more vigorous debate over what would be ethically appropriate from the professional's viewpoint in many different situations. Although most of the debate has involved psychological and psychiatric treatment rather than assessment, the issues are the same in both cases. In particular, legal imperatives have not always been consistent with ethical views (e.g., Siegel, 1979). It is perhaps fair to say that the issues which gave rise to the congressional hearings in 1965 are now being formulated, debated, and resolved both within the courts and within each of the helping professions, through the continued evolution of laws and ethical principles.

Under what circumstances in personality assessment situations have people been asked to provide personality information which might be used against them?

Perhaps the most blameworthy practice, discussed earlier in the context of validity criticisms, has been the use of psychopathologically oriented assessment devices in the context of personnel selection. The confidentiality problem has arisen here in two ways. First, tests like the MMPI include questions pertaining to sexual and religious practices, information which has little apparent relation to job suitability, but which presumably could afford much opportunity for personal embarrassment and the exercise of prejudices. This is especially true of many of the so-called subtle items. Second, and perhaps more important, the respondents may be revealing information of which they are not aware, and which they would not choose to reveal if given that choice. The person who is asked to respond to the Rorschach inkblots faces just such a possibility.

What are the ethics of the situation? Rather different views have been proposed by Dahlstrom (1969) and Lovell (1967). It should be remembered that the use of personality tests in a mental health or a counseling setting is not at issue. In those instances, clients are seeking professional help for their own problems, and the outcome of the intervention is clearly understood to be for the clients' own benefit. Lovell referred to this type of situation, where there is no conflict of interest between assessor and respondent, as the *client function* of personality testing. Whenever a potential conflict of interest does exist between assessor and respondent, such as in personnel selection, tests are being used in a *personnel function,* and it is this use that has caused concern. Here, Lovell has argued that the use of personality tests is inadmissable on three counts. First, on ethical grounds, it has no place in a free society. Second, on scientific grounds, it is doubtful that adequate validity is possible under these conditions, because of the difficulties of obtaining subject cooperation. Third, on grounds of community service, the public will be best served in the long run if personality tests are not used in this manner.

Dahlstrom (1969) drew attention to a similar dichotomy, initially proposed by Cronbach and Gleser (1965), referring to the use of personality tests in making decisions serving an *individual* and decisions serving an *institution.* Dahlstrom, however, saw no ethical dilemma in either type of decision under normal circumstances. As an example of an institutional use of tests, let us consider the case where a candidate is being screened for an executive position in a particular company. Since the psychologist's loyalties to the company are clear to the candidate, there should be no ethical problem. Further, the applicant can choose to invalidate the procedure if he/she so desires by subtle noncooperation. Conflicts of interest, however, might arise for the psychologist in the event that information of real concern to society in general, such as murder or pyromania, were revealed in the course of the examination. Dahlstrom offered another plausible reason why many persons are conflicted about the use of personality tests in personnel selection. The reason is simply that the outcome of the testing session is often unfavorable to the respondent. In a sense, the information is used in a fashion that is at cross-purposes with the respondent's own interests. As far as actual breaches of confidentiality with undesirable *general consequences* to the respondent are concerned—that is, the use of test results outside of the situation for which they were obtained—the 1965 congressional hearings uncovered little or no evidence of such practices (Brayfield, 1965).

Confidentiality and the question of having to violate it has been a matter of great concern and no little disagreement among psychologists. The appropriate principle in the *Ethical Standards of Psychologists* (American Psychological Association, 1977) states that "information received in confidence is revealed only after most careful deliberation and when there is clear and imminent danger to an individual or to society, and then only to appropriate professional workers or public authorities" (p. 4). Some legal jurisdictions, however, have considered that the psychologist's duty to reveal information is stronger than implied in this ethical statement (Schwitzgebel and Schwitzgebel, 1980). On the other hand, the view has been expressed by some psychologists that psychologists should not break the confidentiality of a client under *any* circumstances (e.g., Siegel, 1979). Clearly, this will be an issue to be debated for some years to come.

The Client's Right to Know.   Another important issue regarding confidentiality is of a different nature—the question of people's rights to know their own test results. Psychologists have traditionally been very reluctant to share this kind of information, reasoning that it might be misleading or harmful to the subject. However, as a result of the debate initiated by the 1965 congressional hearings and the widespread concern over the existence of inaccessible personal records, psychologists have acknowledged both the client's right to know and their own responsibility to present the information in a manner that can be understood and appreciated by the client. Thus, the *Ethical Standards of Psychologists* (American Psychological Association, 1977) includes the principle that "the client has the right to have and the psychologist has the responsibility to provide explanations of the nature and the purposes of the test and the test results in language the client can understand" (p. 6). Exceptions are possible if there is an explicit agreement to that effect in advance. Once again, the current ethical principle is not completely consistent with the laws of different states, some of which permit patient access and some not. This new doctrine is becoming more and more widely accepted, however.

In concluding our discussion of the confidentiality issue, it must not be overlooked that some people *do* have things to hide which may or may not be related to the assessment task at hand, but which would be potentially damaging to them if inadvertently revealed. Thus, in the context of a personality research program involving schoolchildren, Eron and Walder (1961) reported that one of the local citizens who had made efforts to harass the research team was later indicted for a sexual offense, though this was not in any way related to the research. How to permit such people to retain their rights to privacy in situations where the cooperation of a whole group is sought is indeed a difficult dilemma. Even if it is made known that persons who would rather not cooperate need not do so, such persons may become a focus of attention merely by their action in not participating.

The same problem is present whenever questionnaires or inventories are administered with the instructions that respondents may omit any items which they would rather not answer. A glance at the answer sheet for omitted items reveals the areas of greatest personal sensitivity!

Inviolacy

Inviolacy is concerned with situations where there is no threat that the information that people give as part of an assessment procedure will be used against them; rather, we are concerned with the individual's right of personal privacy—the right not to have privacy intruded upon. The question of inviolacy is relevant when people are questioned about aspects of their daily living that traditionally are not openly discussed in Western culture. Thus, items on the MMPI regarding eliminative functions are hardly likely to provide material that might be self-incriminatory; however, in our society, toilet functions are very private matters, and many people are embarrassed to discuss them. In fact, one reason for negative reactions to such self-report items is that merely reading these items arouses anxiety about "taboo" topics. Another type of material which people object to discussing involves their cherished beliefs about human nature. Thus, Bennett (1967) stated that "A great many people seem to take comfort in believing that all children love and respect their parents, accept without question the teachings of their religion and live without sexual curiosity or urge until they attain the married state" (p. 9). In discussing behavioral research, Brim (1967) made the related point that much of the general concern about such research appears to come "not so much from the concern about methods and privacy, but about the inroads that behavioral science is making on ideas" (p. 30). There is the implication that security is found in the familiar, and that to be asked even to consider that there might be alternatives raises anxieties which are turned into aggression toward the test.

Some personality psychologists have placed considerable importance on the "need for inviolacy" as a personality characteristic. Brim (1965) has suggested that such people are also "authoritarian in interpersonal relations, intolerant of diversity in ideology or beliefs, and strongly opposed to most forms of social change" (p. 128). Jourard (1964) has written extensively on the topic of self-disclosure, by which he means one's readiness to be open and share one's self with others. Murray (1938) listed and discussed the need for inviolacy as one of the basic needs in his personality theory. And it has been found that for normal persons, the K (defensiveness) scale of the MMPI appears to be related to personality needs to remain cool, aloof, and wary, and to a general reluctance to reveal onself (Dahlstrom and Welsh, 1960).

To state the issue simply, some people resent being asked certain questions, for a variety of reasons. These reasons do not necessarily concern the use to which the information will be put, but principally involve the negative feelings which result from being forced to confront the anxiety-arousing subject matter. Bennett (1967) has noted, in his excellent analysis of the problem, that every society has established rules or norms under which its members attain more benefits than would result from anarchy. These rules periodically should be, and typically are, scrutinized and changed if found lacking. Those people who wish to initiate these changes have the responsibility for considering the consequences that even thinking about change would have on members of the society. Because such inquiry does cause considerable apprehension and anxiety, a reasonable degree of restraint must be exercised in asking members of a culture to give information about, or even to think about, certain of its important rules. If this restraint is not exercised, the effectiveness and professional image of the would-be changers of a society are bound to suffer. In the case of our contemporary American society, however desirable it may appear in the long run to gather certain information, psychologists and other social scientists will be ineffective and perhaps even seriously damage themselves if they do not recognize and respond to these very basic concerns and facts about social change.

Some positive responses to many of the criticisms previously discussed in this chapter suggest themselves when we consider the public image of psychology, especially of personality assessment. A clear statement of the poor state of this public image was offered by Nettler (1959) in an article entitled "Test Burning in Texas," which described the generalized unfavorable public reaction to a community-wide testing program. Eron and Walder (1961) reported, however, on another personality research program in which comprehensive and thoughtful procedures were instituted to prepare the community for the participation of both parents and children. Although some persons in the community produced publicity that was unfavorable and deliberately misleading, the foresight of the research team and their straightforwardness in dealing with community concerns and anxieties resulted in excellent cooperation from all but a handful of people. We suggest that psychologists might pay more careful attention to their public relations, particularly with regard to disseminating clear and accurate information about assessment procedures, and that this attention could do much to forestall unfavorable public reactions.

Before leaving the general area of invasion of privacy, we should note that there are certain situations in which there should be no question about the legitimacy of gathering personal information about a person for selection purposes; namely, those positions involving the public security. Bennett (1967) has identified three such situations: (1) where an individual may be susceptible to blackmail by unfriendly governments, (2) where a person may be assigned for important public duty overseas, and (3) where the position is that of policeman or guard. Bennett also pointed out that the amount of investigation to which an individual is subjected is proportional to the seriousness of making a poor selection decision. Thus, applicants for loans or credit are often subjected to a detailed investigation in the relevant areas, however private these areas may be. Perhaps the best example of a personality evaluation on an applicant is that given to a candidate for the presidency of the United States. First, his entire background is scrutinized by his rivals for any information which could possibly reflect negatively on him. Then, under guise of determining his position on substantive issues, the candidate is made the target of a blistering stress interview lasting many months, in which a single major error could cost him his goal. The degree of personal stability required to survive such a test is possessed by few, and the candidate who makes the best showing in this lengthy situational test is elected. The same applies, of course, to all political campaigns to some degree. In these circumstances, confidentiality or personal privacy traditionally has no meaning, and American society demands that the lives of important political figures be open to continual public scrutiny.

RESTRICTION OF FREEDOM

One further criticism of personality assessment which merits discussion involves those procedures which are claimed to restrict a person's individual freedom. For example, with regard to ability assessment, the use of intelligence tests in schools has often been criticized on the grounds that children's opportunities tend to be restricted by the categories into which the test scores explicitly or implicitly place them (e.g., for example, Ebel, 1964a). This restriction has been documented in a series of research projects by Rosenthal (1966), who concluded that children tend to perform according to others' expectations of them, and that these expectations tend to get communicated regardless of efforts to control them. Since personality assessment interpretations lead us to develop expectations about others, we may subtly influence these others to fulfill our expectations. For example, if an assessment report suggests that a person is "untrustworthy," our constant suspiciousness may either produce ambiguous behavior, which we then interpret as justifying the label, or we may actually induuce such behavior in the other person by our responses. One trend toward counteracting these effects can be seen in the current efforts to deemphasize the use of psychiatric diagnostic labels for patients in clinics and mental hospitals because they create strong expectations of patient behavior, a point of view which is supported, in rather different ways, by the writings of Szasz (1961) and by the behavioral approach to personality assessment.

Regarding the restriction of freedom, there is a somewhat different criticism which is made of personality assessment in the context of selection—namely, the problem of "prevention of progress by encouraging the mundane and prosaic" (Guion, 1965, p. 372). Suppose a large industrial organization wishes to select the best executive applicants. The organization might follow the time-honored empirical procedure of exhaustively studying the best persons it has recruited for some years and using the results of this study to set the standards for selection. Thus, in the case of a company, a selection battery might be developed to choose applicants similar to the company's best executives over the past 15 years. Once the selection battery is in operation, the company has inadvertently assured itself of hiring executive trainees whose personality is currently adaptive and has been so in the recent past. Unfortunately, however, what is needed is persons who will best fit the company's needs in the future. There may be a serious error in assuming that the kind of executives most suited for running the company yesterday and today will be optimal in the future. At best, the talent pool becomes markedly narrowed by this procedure, and all executives in the company begin to look alike. At worst, if the management happens to be mediocre at the present time, this state of affairs is perpetuated. People with new and different ideas are never given a chance.

Selection programs need not involve this narrowing of talent and perpetuation of the present state of affairs. Once the nature of the present management staff is determined, the selection team in collaboration with management can then decide whether or not to continue this pattern. One reasonable approach might be to determine what trends are occurring in the industry, and to orient the selection criteria toward persons with characteristics most suitable for dealing with these trends. Also, diversity can deliberately be built in. Once the present managers are described, a deliberate plan can be developed to detect persons who differ from them in specified ways. These plans capitalize on the advantages of a selection program—knowing what kinds of people are being selected—without falling into the trap of making the organization's managers increasingly narrow in their outlook.

Summary

Personality assessment practices were subjected to a lengthy and careful scrutiny in 1965, when two sets of congressional hearings were held. Although the avowed purpose of the hearings was to investigate invasion of privacy through the use of personality tests in federal government personnel selection practices, many more issues were explored. Complaints about personality assessment can be grouped under two headings: problems of use and problems involving moral issues.

Use problems are of two kinds: (1) test misuse, involving invalid use of an assessment procedure that has legitimate and validated uses; and (2) generalized test invalidity, involving the use of assessment procedures whose validity has not been established for any purpose. Test misuse is probably the most serious problem of all in the field of personality assessment, and much of the criticism is due to personnel selection practices in industry, particularly the use in this context of psychiatrically oriented instruments. Another potential misuse of personality tests is with cultural minority·groups for whom the tests may not be valid, as has often been the case with the assessment of abilities. There is also a controversy over whether extensive training and experience are necessary for the valid use of projective instruments. A further misuse of personality assessment procedures is the tendency of clinical psychologists to try to derive from certain tests information which the tests were not designed to discover. In response to these concerns, the APA *Standards for Educational and Psychological Tests* now contains an extensive section on standards for the uses of tests.

Concerning generalized test invalidity, one troublesome problem is that some assessment instruments were not designed with reference to any criteria, so that there is no reasonably straightforward use to which one can point as the "purpose" of such an instrument. Another serious problem is that of illusory correlation, which applies to tests that have traditionally been interpreted by reference to an accumulated fund of "clinical lore" or commonsense principles, and refers to the finding that many of these commonsense principles, although reliable, simply have no basis in fact.

There are two kinds of moral issues. One is that of confidentiality, referring to instances where test respondents are afraid that the information which they give might be used in some way against their interests. Once again, the most serious criticism probably arises in the context of personnel selection practices. Another problem arises when a respondent has something to hide that has nothing to do with the assessment at hand, but which may be damaging for other reasons if revealed. The legal issues involved in confidentiality have recently come to the forefront, as people have come to recognize that legal mechanisms do indeed exist to protect their rights. In regard to a different aspect of confidentiality, the APA *Ethical Standards of Psychologists* has recently affirmed people's rights to know their own test results.

The second moral issue is connected with an individual's right to personal inviolacy, or privacy of thoughts and behaviors. Many persons do not wish even to be required to think about certain topics, and being asked for responses to controversial statements is seen as a definite and unwarranted intrusion into their thoughts. However, in personnel selection situations where the public security is involved, a candidate's privacy often must be invaded. This situation might apply in assessing a person's suitability to be a policeman or an armed guard; and for candidates for political office, invasion of privacy has traditionally been the rule.

A final criticism of personality assessment procedures is that they tend to restrict an individual's freedom. This could happen through the "Rosenthal effect," in which a person's expectation of how another will behave sometimes influences the other's actual behavior. Another way in which assessment procedures can cause restriction is in the context of selection, if the criterion on which the selection procedure has been based is narrow and outmoded.

REFERENCES

Achenbach, T. M. The Child Behavior Profile: I. Boys aged 6−11. *Journal of Consulting and Clinical Psychology*, 1978, **46**, 478−488.

Achenbach, T. M., and Edelbrock, C. S. The Child Behavior Profile: II. Boys aged 12−16 and girls aged 6−11 and 12−16. *Journal of Consulting and Clinical Psychology*, 1979, **47**, 223−233.

Ackoff, R. L., and Rivett, P. *A manager's guide to operations research*. New York: Wiley, 1963.

Adair, F. L. Review of MMPI Automated Psychological Assessment. In O. K. Buros (Ed.), *Eighth mental measurements yearbook*. Highland Park, N.J.: Gryphon, 1978. (a)

Adair, F. L. Review of MMPI Behaviordyne Psychodiagnostic Laboratory Service. In O. K. Buros (Ed.), *Eighth mental measurements yearbook*. Highland Park, N.J.: Gryphon, 1978. (b)

Adair, F. L. Review of MMPI computerized scoring and interpreting services. In O. K. Buros (Ed.), *Eighth mental measurements yearbook*. Highland Park, N.J.: Gryphon, 1978. (c)

Albert, S., Fox, H. M., and Kahn, M. W. Faking psychosis on the Rorschach: Can expert judges detect malingering? *Journal of Personality Assessment*, 1980, **44**, 115−119.

Alex, C. *Personality tests: How to beat them and make top scores*. New York: Arco, 1965.

Alker, H. A., and Owen, D. W. Biographical, trait, and behavioral-sampling predictions of performance in a stressful life setting. *Journal of Personality and Social Psychology*, 1977, **35**, 717−723.

Allport, G. W. *Personality*. New York: Holt, 1937.

Allport, G. W. *Pattern and growth in personality*. New York: Holt, Rinehart, and Winston, 1961.

Allport, G. W., and Odbert, H. S. Trait names: A psycho-lexical study. *Psychological Monographs*, 1936, **47** (Whole No. 211).

Allport, G. W., Vernon, P. E., and Lindzey, G. *Study of values*, 3rd ed. Boston: Houghton-Mifflin, 1960.

Altman, H., Evenson, R. C., Hedland, J. L., and Cho, D. W. The Missouri Actuarial Report System (MARS). *Comprehensive Psychiatry*, 1978, **19**, 185−192.

American Psychological Association. Technical recommendations for psychological tests and diagnostic techniques. *Psychological Bulletin*, 1954, 51 (2, pt. 2).

American Psychological Association. *Casebook on ethical standards of psychologists*. Washington, D.C.: Author, 1967.

American Psychological Association. Psychological assessment and public policy. *American Psychologist*, 1970, **25**, 264−266.

American Psychological Association. *Standards for educational and psychological tests.* Washington, D.C.: Author, 1974.

American Psychological Association. *Ethical standards of psychologists, 1977 revision.* Washington, D.C.: Author, 1977.

American Psychological Association, Division of Industrial/Organizational Psychology. *Principles for the validation and use of personnel selection procedures.* Berkeley, Calif.: Author, 1980.

Ames, L. B., Learned, J., Metraux, R. W., and Walker, R. N. *Child Rorschach responses.* New York: Hoeber, 1952.

Amrine, M. The 1965 congressional inquiry into testing: A commentary. *American Psychologist,* 1965, **20,** 859–870.

Anastasi, A. Psychology, psychologists, and psychological testing. *American Psychologist,* 1967, **22,** 297–306.

Angyal, A. *Foundations for a science of personality.* New York and London: Commonwealth Fund and Oxford University Press, 1941.

Ansbacher, H. L. The history of the leaderless group discussion technique. *Psychological Bulletin,* 1951, **48,** 383–391.

Argyle, M. Non-verbal communication in human social interaction. In R. Hinde (Ed.), *Non-verbal communication.* New York: Cambridge University Press, 1972.

Aronson, M. L. A study of the Freudian theory of paranoia by means of the Blacky pictures. *Journal of Projective Techniques,* 1953, **17,** 3–19.

Arthur, A. Z. A decision-making approach to psychological assessment in the clinic. *Journal of Consulting Psychology,* 1966, **30,** 435–438.

Arthur, A. Z. Diagnostic testing and the new alternatives. *Psychological Bulletin,* 1969, **72,** 183–192.

Asch, S. E. Forming impressions of personality. *Journal of Abnormal and Social Psychology,* 1946, **41,** 258–290.

Ashton, S. G., and Goldberg, L. R. In response to Jackson's challenge: The comparative validity of personality scales constructed by the external (empirical) strategy and scales developed intuitively by experts, novices, and laymen. *Jouurnal of Research in Personality,* 1973, **7,** 1–20.

Bales, R. F. *Interaction process analysis.* Cambridge, Mass.: Addison-Wesley, 1950.

Bandura, A. *Principles of behavior modification.* New York: Holt, Rinehart, and Winston, 1969.

Bandura, A., Lipsher, D. H., and Miller, P. E. Psychotherapists' approach-avoidance reactions to patients' expressions of hostility. *Journal of Consulting Psychology,* 1960, **24,** 1–8.

Barker, R., Kounin, J., and Wright, H. F. (Eds.). *Child behavior and development.* New York: McGraw-Hill, 1943.

Barker, R., and Wright, H. F. *One boy's day.* New York: Harper, 1951.

Barker, R., and Wright, H. F. *Midwest and its children: The psychological ecology of an American town.* New York: Harper and Row, 1955.

Barlow, D. H. Assessment of sexual behavior. In A. R. Ciminero, K. S. Calhoun, and H. E. Adams (Eds.), *Handbook of behavioral assessment.* New York: Wiley, 1977.

Barthell, C. N., and Holmes, D. S. High school yearbooks: A nonreactive measure of social isolation in graduates who later became schizophrenics. *Journal of Abnormal Psychology*, 1968, **73**, 313–316.

Bass, B. M. The leaderless group discussion. *Psychological Bulletin*, 1954, **51**, 465–492.

Bass, B. M. *Leadership, psychology and organizational behavior*. New York: Harper and Row, 1960.

Bass, B. M., and Coates, C. H. Forecasting officer potential using the leaderless group discussion. *Journal of Abnormal and Social Psychology*, 1952, **47**, 321–325.

Bechtoldt, H. P. Construct validity: A critique. *American Psychologist*, 1959, **14**, 619–629.

Beck, S. J., Beck, A. G., Levitt, E. E., and Molish, H. B. *Rorschach's test: I. Basic processes*, 3rd ed. New York: Grune and Stratton, 1961.

Bell, H. M. *The adjustment inventory*. Palo Alto, Calif.: Consulting Psychologists Press, 1939.

Bellack, A. S. A critical appraisal of strategies for assessing social skill. *Behavioral Assessment*, 1979, **1**, 157–176.

Bellak, L. *The Thematic Apperception Test and the Children's Apperception Test in clinical use*. New York: Grune and Stratton, 1954.

Bellak, L. *The TAT, CAT, and SAT in clinical use*, 3rd ed. New York: Grune and Stratton, 1975.

Bem, D. J., and Allen, A. On predicting some of the people some of the time: The search for cross-situational consistencies in behavior. *Psychological Review*, 1974, **81**, 506–520.

Bender, L. A visual motor test and its clinical use. *American Journal of Orthopsychiatry*, Research Monograph No. 3, 1938.

Bender, L. *Instructions for the use of the Visual Motor Gestalt Test*. New York: American Orthopsychiatric Association, 1946.

Bennett, G. K. Testing and privacy. In W. W. Willingham (Ed.), Invasion of privacy in research and testing. *Journal of Educational Measurement*, 1967, **4**, 7–10 (Supplement).

Berg, I. A. Response bias and personality: The Deviation Hypothesis. *Journal of Psychology*, 1955, **40**, 60–71.

Berg, I. A. Deviant responses and deviant people: The formulation of the Deviation Hypothesis. *Journal of Counseling Psychology*, 1957, **4**, 154–161.

Berg, I. A. The unimportance of test item content. In B. M. Bass and I. A. Berg (Eds.), *Objective approaches to personality assessment*. Princeton: Van Nostrand, 1959.

Bernal, M. D., Duryee, J. S., Pruett, H. L., and Burns, G. J. Behavior modification and the brat syndrome. *Journal of Consulting and Clinical Psychology*, 1968, **32**, 447–455.

Bernreuter, R. N. *The Personality Inventory*. Palo Alto, Ca.if.: Consulting Psychologists Press, 1939.

Bersoff, D. N. Silk purses into sow's ears: The decline of psychological testing and a suggestion for its redemption. *American Psychologist*, 1973, **28**, 892–899.

Billingslea, F. Y. The Bender-Gestalt: A review and perspective. *Psychological Bulletin*, 1963, **60**, 233–251.

Bingham, W. V. D., and Moore, B. V. *How to interview*, 4th ed. New York: Harper and Row, 1959.

Blanchard, E. B., and Epstein, L. H. *A biofeedback primer*. Reading, Mass.: Addison-Wesley, 1978.

Block, J. *The Q-sort method in personality assessment and psychiatric research*. Springfield, Ill.: Thomas, 1961.

Block, J. *The challenge of response sets*. New York: Appleton-Century-Crofts, 1965.

Block, J. *Lives through time*. Berkeley, Ca.if.: Bancroft Books, 1971.

Bloxom, B. M. Review of the Sixteen Personality Factors Questionnaire. In O. K. Buros (Ed.), *Eighth mental measurements yearbook*. Highland Park, N.J.: Gryphon, 1978.

Blum, G. S. A study of the psychoanalytic theory of psychosexual development. *Genetic Psychology Monographs*, 1949, **39**, 3–99.

Blum, G. S. *The Blacky Pictures*. New York: Psychological Corporation, 1950.

Blum, G. S. *Revised scoring system for the research use of the Blacky Pictures*. Unpublished mimeographed report, 1951.

Blum, G. S. A guide for research use of the Blacky Pictures. *Journal of Projective Techniques*, 1962, **26**, 3–29.

Blum, G. S., and Kaufman, J. B. Two patterns of personality dynamics in male peptic ulcer patients as suggested by responses to the Blacky Pictures. *Journal of Clinical Psychology*, 1952, **8**, 273–278.

Boring, E. G. *A history of experimental psychology.* New York: Appleton-Century-Crofts, 1929.

Bowers, K. S. Situationism in psychology: An analysis and a critique. *Psychological Review*, 1973, **80**, 307–336.

Bray, D. W., and Grant, D. L. The assessment center in the measurement of potential for business management. *Psychological Monographs*, 1966, **80**, 1–17 (Whole No. 625).

Brayfield, A. H. (Ed.). Testing and public policy. *American Psychologist*, 1965, **20**, 867–1005.

Breger, L. Psychological testing: Treatment and research implications. *Journal of Consulting and Clinical Psychology*, 1968, **32**, 176–181.

Brehm, S. S. *The application of social psychology to clinical practice*. Washington, D.C.: Hemisphere, 1976.

Briggs, P. F. Eight item clusters for use with the M-B History Record. *Journal of Clinical Psychology*, 1959, **15**, 22–28.

Briggs, P. F., Rouzer, D. G., Hamburg, R. L., and Holman, T. R. Seven scales for the Minnesota-Briggs History Record with reference group data. *Journal of Clinical Psychology*, 1972, **28**, 431–438.

Brim, O. G. American attitudes toward intelligence tests. *American Psychologist*, 1965, **20**, 123–124.

Brim, O. G. Reaction to the papers. In W. W. Willingham (Ed.), Invasion of privacy in research and testing. *Journal of Educational Measurement*, 1967, **4**, 29–31 (Supplement).

Brislin, R. W., Lonner, W. J., and Thorndike, R. M. *Cross-cultural research methods*. New York: Wiley, 1973.

Brock, T. C., and Guidice, C. D. Stealing and temporal orientation. *Journal of Abnormal and Social Psychology*, 1963, **66**, 91–94.

Brown, S. H. Long term validity of a personal history item scoring procedure. *Journal of Applied Psychology*, 1978, **63**, 673–676.

Brown, W. R., and McGuire, J. M. Current psychological assessment practices. *Professional Psychology,* 1976, **7,** 475−484.

Buchwald, A. M. Values and the uses of tests. *Journal of Consulting Psychology,* 1965, **29,** 49−54.

Buck, J. N. The H-T-P test. *Journal of Clinical Psychology,* 1948, **4,** 151−159. (a)

Buck, J. N. The H-T-P technique: A qualitative and scoring manual, part one. *Journal of Clinical Psychology,* 1948, **4,** 319−396. (b)

Buck, J. N. The H-T-P technique: A qualitative and scoring manual, part two. *Journal of Clinical Psychology,* 1949, **5,** 37−76.

Burgess, E. W. Factors determining success or failure on parole. In A. A. Bruce (Ed.), *The workings of the indeterminate sentence law and the parole system in Illinois.* Springfield, Ill.: Illinois Board of Parole, 1928.

Buros, O. K. *The sixth mental measurements yearbook.* Highland Park, N.J.: Gryphon, 1965.

Buros, O. K. *Seventh mental measurements yearbook.* Highland Park, N.J.: Gryphon, 1972.

Buros, O. K. *Eighth mental measurements yearbook.* Highland Park, N.J.: Gryphon, 1978.

Buss, A. H. The effect of item style on social desirability and frequency of endorsement. *Journal of Consulting Psychology,* 1959, **23,** 510−513.

Buss, A. H. *Psychopathology.* New York: Wiley, 1966.

Buss, A. H., and Durkee, A. An inventory for assessing different kinds of hostility. *Journal of Consulting Psychology,* 1957, **21,** 343−349.

Butcher, J. N. (Ed.) *MMPI: Research developments and clinical applications.* New York: McGraw-Hill, 1969.

Butcher, J. N. Review of MMPI Automated Psychological Assessment. In O. K. Buros (Ed.), *Eighth mental measurements yearbook.* Highland Park, N.J.: Gryphon, 1978. (a)

Butcher, J. N. Review of MMPI Behaviordyne Psychodiagnostic Laboratory Services. In O. K. Buros (Ed.), *Eighth mental measurements yearbook.* Highland Park, N.J.: Gryphon, 1978. (b)

Butcher, J. N. Review of MMPI computerized scoring and interpretation services. In O. K. Buros (Ed.), *Eighth mental measurements yearbook.* Highland Park, N.J.: Gryphon, 1978. (c)

Butcher, J. N., Kendall, P. C., and Hoffman, N. MMPI short forms: Caution. *Journal of Consulting and Clinical Psychology,* 1980, **48,** 275−278.

Butcher, J. N., and Pancheri, F. *A handbook of cross-national MMPI research.* Minneapolis: University of Minnesota Press, 1976.

Campbell, D. T. Factors relevant to the validity of experiments in social settings. *Psychological Bulletin,* 1957, **54,** 297−312.

Campbell, D. T., and Fiske, D. W. Convergent and discriminant validation by the multitrait-multimethod matrix. *Psychological Bulletin,* 1959, **56,** 81−105.

Canter, A. *The Canter background interference procedure for thhe Bender Gestalt test: Manual for administration, scoring, and interpretation.* Iowa City: Iowa Psychiatric Hospital, 1970.

Canter, F. M. Simulation on the California Psychological Inventory and the adjustment of the simulator. *Journal of Consulting Psychology,* 1963, **27,** 252−256.

Carlson, R. Personality. *Annual Review of Psychology,* 1975, **26,** 393−414.

Carp, A. L., and Shavzin, A. R. The susceptibility to falsification of the Rorschach psychodiagnostic technique. *Journal of Consulting Psychology,* 1950, **14,** 230–233.

Cascio, W. F., and Silbey, V. Utility of the assessment center as a selection device. *Journal of Applied Psychology,* 1979, **64,** 107–118.

Cattell, R. B. *Personality: A systematic theoretical and factual study.* New York: McGraw-Hill, 1950.

Cattell, R. B. *Personality and motivation: Structure and measurement.* New York: World Book, 1957.

Cattell, R. B. Validity and reliability: A proposed more basic set of concepts. *Journal of Educational Psychology,* 1964, **55,** 1–22.

Cattell, R. B. *The scientific analysis of personality.* Baltimore: Penguin, 1965.

Cattell, R. B., Eber, H. W., and Tatsuoka, M. M. *Handbook for the Sixteen Personality Factor Questionnaire (16 PF).* Champaign, Ill.: Institute for Personality and Ability Testing, 1970.

Cattell, R. B., Stice, G. F. *Handbook for the Sixteen Personality Factor Questionnaire.* Champaign, Ill.: Institute for Personality and Ability Testing, 1957.

Chapman, L. J. Illusory correlation in observational report. *Journal of Verbal Learning and Verbal Behavior,* 1967, **6,** 151–155.

Chapman, L. J., and Chapman, J. P. Genesis of popular but erroneous psychodiagnostic observations. *Journal of Abnormal Psychology,* 1967, **72,** 193–204.

Chapman, L. J., and Chapman, J. P. Illusory correlation as an obstacle to the use of valid psychodiagnostic signs. *Journal of Abnormal Psychology,* 1969, **74,** 271–280.

Chapman, L. J., and Chapman, J. P. Associatively based illusory correlation as a source of psychodiagnostic folklore. In L. D. Goodstein and R. I. Lanyon (Eds.), *Readings in personality assessment.* New York: Wiley, 1971.

Cleveland, S. E. Reflections of the rise and fall of psychodiagnosis. *Professional Psychology,* 1976, **8,** 309–318.

Clum, G. A., and Hoiberg, A. Diagnoses as moderators of the relationship between biographical variables and psychiatric decisions in a combat zone. *Journal of Consulting and Clinical Psychology,* 1971, **37,** 209–214.

Coddington, R. D. The significance of life events as etiologic factors in the diseases of children: I. A survey of professional workers. *Journal of Psychosomatic Research,* 1972, **16,** 7–18.

Cole, J. D., and Magnussen, M. G. Where the action is. *Journal of Consulting Psychology,* 1966, **30,** 539–543.

Couch, A., and Keniston, K. Yeasayers and naysayers: Agreeing response set as a personality variable. *Journal of Abnormal and Social Psychology,* 1960, **60,** 151–174.

Cresswell, D. L. *Validation of psychogeriatric screening procedures for organicity, prognosis, depression, and psychopathology.* Master's thesis, Arizona State University, 1978.

Cresswell, D. L., and Lanyon, R. I. Validation of a screening battery for psychogeratric assessment. *Journal of Gerontology,* 1981, **36,** 435–440.

Crites, J. O., Bechtoldt, H. P., Goodstein, L. D., and Heilbrun, A. B. A factor analysis of the California Psychological Inventory. *Journal of Applied Psychology,* 1961, **45,** 408–414.

Cronbach, L. J. An experimental comparison of the multiple true-false and multiple multiple-choice tests. *Journal of Educational Psychology,* 1941, **32,** 533–543.

Cronbach, L. J. Studies of acquiescence as a factor in the true-false test. *Journal of Educational Psychology,* 1942, **33,** 401–415.

Cronbach, L. J. Response sets and test validity. *Educational and Psychological Measurement,* 1946, **6,** 475–494.

Cronbach, L. J. Further evidence on response sets and test design. *Educational and Psychological Measurement,* 1950, **10,** 3–31.

Cronbach, L. J. *Essentials of psychological testing,* 3rd ed. New York: Harper and Row, 1970.

Cronbach, L. J., and Gleser, G. C. *Psychological tests and personnel decisions,* 2nd ed. Urbana: University of Illinois Press, 1965.

Cronbach, L. J., Gleser, G. C., Nanda, H., and Rajaratnam, N. *The dependability of behavioral measurement: Theory of generalizability for scores and profiles.* New York: Wiley, 1972.

Cronbach, L. J., and Meehl, P. E. Construct validity in psychological tests. *Psychological Bulletin,* 1955, **52,** 281–302.

Cureton, E. E. Reliability, validity, and baloney. *Educational and Psychological Measurement,* 1950, **10,** 94–96.

Cureton, E. E. Recipe for cookbook. *Psychological Bulletin,* 1957, **54,** 494–497.

Curran, J. P. Pandura's box reopened? The assessment of social skills. *Journal of behavioral assessment,* 1979, **1,** 55–72.

Dahlstrom, W. G. Invasion of privacy: How legitimate is the current concern over this issue? In J. N. Butcher (Ed.), *MMPI: Research developments and clinical applications.* New York: McGraw-Hill, 1969.

Dahlstrom, W. G. Review of the Minnesota-Briggs History Record. In O. K. Buros (Ed.), *Eighth mental measurements yearbook.* Highland Park, N.J.: Gryphon, 1978.

Dahlstrom, W. G., and Welsh, G. S. *An MMPI handbook.* Minneapolis: University of Minnesota Press, 1960.

Dahlstrom, W. G., Welsh, G. S., and Dahlstrom, L. E. *An MMPI handbook. Vol. 1, Clinical interpretation,* Rev. ed. Minneapolis: University of Minnesota Press, 1972.

Dahlstrom, W. G., Welsh, G. S., and Dahlstrom, L. E. *An MMPI handbook. Vol. 2, Research applications,* Rev. ed. Minneapolis: University of Minnesota Press, 1975.

Dana, R. H. Review of the Rorschach. In O. K. Buros (Ed.), *Eighth mental measurements yearbook.* Highland Park, N.J.: Gryphon, 1978.

Davies, J. D. *Phrenology: Fad and science.* New Haven: Yale University Press, 1955.

Davison, L. A. Introduction. In R. M. Reitan and L. A. Davison (Eds.), *Clinical neuropsychology: Current status and applications.* Washington, D.C.: Winston, 1974.

Dawes, R. M. The robust beauty of improper linear models in decision making. *American Psychologist,* 1979, **34,** 571–582.

Dawes, R. M. Apologia for using what works. *American Psychologist,* 1980, **35,** 678.

Dawes, R. M., and Corrigan, B. Linear models in decision making. *Psychological Bulletin,* 1974, **81,** 95–106.

Dean, E. F. A lengthened Mini-Multi: The Midi-Mult. *Journal of Clinical Psychology,* 1972, **28,** 68–71.

Deutsch, M., Fishman, J. A., Kogan, L., North, R., and Whiteman, M. Guidelines for testing minority group children. *Journal of Social Issues*, 1964, **20**, (2, pt. 2), 127–145.

Dicken, C. F. Simulated patterns on the Edwards Personal Preference Schedule. *Journal of Applied Psychology*, 1959, **43**, 372–378.

Diggory, J. C. Calculation of some costs of suicide prevention using certain predictors of suicidal behavior. *Psychological Bulletin*, 1969, **71**, 373–386.

Dion, K. K., Berscheid, E., and Walster, E. What is beautiful is good. *Journal of Personality and Social Psychology*, 1972, **24**, 285–290.

Doll, E. A. *The measurement of social competence*. Minneapolis: Educational Test Bureau, 1953.

Doll, E. A. *Vineland Social Maturity Scale: Condensed manual of directions*. Minneapolis: American Guidance Service, 1965.

Dombrose, L. A., and Slobin, M. A. The IES Test. *Perceptual and Motor Skills*, 1958, **8**, 347–389.

Dowling, J. F., and Graham, J. R. Illusory correlation and the MMPI. *Journal of Personality Assessment*, 1976, **40**, 531–538.

Downey, R. G., Medland, F. F., and Yates, L. G. Evaluation of a peer rating system for predicting subsequent promotion of senior military officers. *Journal of Applied Psychology*, 1976, **61**, 206–209.

Drake, L. E., and Oetting, E. R. *An MMPI codebook for counselors*. Minneapolis: University of Minnesota Press, 1959.

Duff, F. L. Item subtlety in personality inventory scales. *Journal of Consulting Psychology*, 1965, **28**, 565–570.

Eaton, M. E., Altman, H., Scheff, S., and Sletten, I. Missouri Automated Psychiatric History for relatives and other informants. *Diseases of the Nervous System*, 1970, **31**, 198–202.

Eaton, M. E., Sletten, I. W., Kitchen, A. D., and Smith, R. J. II. The Missouri Automated Psychiatric History: Symptom frequencies, sex differences, use of weapons, and other findings. *Comprehensive Psychiatry*, 1971, **12**, 264–276.

Ebel, R. L. The social consequences of educational testing. *School and Society*, 1964, **92**, 331–334. (a)

Ebel, R. L. Must all tests be valid? *American Psychologist*, 1964, **19**, 640–647. (b)

Eber, H. W. Automated personality description with 16 PF data. *American Psychologist*, 1964, **19**, 544. (Abstract)

Edinger, J. D. Cross-validation of the Megargee MMPI typology for prisoners. *Journal of Consulting and Clinical Psychology*, 1979, **47**, 234–242.

Edwards, A. L. The relationship between the judged desirability of a trait and the probability that the trait will be endorsed. *Journal of Applied Psychology*, 1953, **37**, 90–93.

Edwards, A. L. *The social desirability variable in personality assessment and research*. New York: Dryden, 1957.

Edwards, A. L. *Edwards Personnal Preference Schedule*. New York: Psychological Corporation, 1959.

Edwards, A. L. Social desirability and performance on the MMPI. *Psychometrika*, 1964, **29**, 95–308.

Eichman, W. J. MMPI: Computerized scoring and interpreting services. In O. K. Buros (Ed.), *Seventh mental measurements yearbook*. Highland Park, N.J.: Gryphon, 1972.

Einhorn, H. J., and Bass, A. R. Methodological considerations relevant to discrimination in employment testing. *Psychological Bulletin*, 1971, **75**, 261−269.

Ekehammar, B. Interactionism in personality from a historical perspective. *Psychological Bulletin*, 1974, **81**, 1026−1048.

Elwood, D. L., and Griffin, H. R. Individual intelligence testing without the examiner: Reliability of an automated method. *Journal of Consulting and Clinical Psychology*, 1972, **38**, 9−14.

Endicott, J., and Spitzer, R. L. Current and Past Psychopathology Scales (CAPPS). *Archives of General Psychiatry*, 1972, **27**, 678−687.

Endicott, J., and Spitzer, R. L. A diagnostic interview: The Schedule for Affective Disorders and Schizophrenia. *Archives of General Psychiatry*, 1978, **35**, 837−844.

Endicott, J., and Spitzer, R. L. Use of the Research Diagnostic Criteria and the Schedule of Affective Disorders and Schizophrenia to study affective disorders. *American Journal of Psychiatry*, 1979, **136**, 52−56.

Endicott, J., Spitzer, R. L., Fleiss, J. L., and Cohen, J. The Global Assessment Scale: A procedure for measuring overall severity of psychiatric disturbances. *Archives of General Psychiatry*, 1976, **33**, 766−771.

Endler, N. S., and Magnusson, D. Toward an interactional psychology of personality. *Psychological Bulletin*, 1976, **83**, 956−974.

England, G. W. *Development and use of weighted application blanks.* Dubuque, Iowa: Brown, 1961.

Eron, L. D. Frequencies of themes and identifications in the stories of schizophrenic patients and non-hospitalized college students. *Journaal of consulting Psychology*, 1948, **12**, 387−395.

Eron, L. D., and Walder, L. Test burning: II. *American Psychologist*, 1961, **16**, 237−244.

Ervin, S. J. Why Senate hearings on psychological tests in government? *American Psychologist*, 1965, **20**, 879−880.

Evenson, R. C., Sletten, I. W., Hedlund, J. L., and Faintich, D. M. CAPS: An automated evaluation system. *American Journal of Psychiatry*, 1974, **131**, 531−534.

Exner, J. E., Jr. *The Rorschach: A comprehensive system.* New York: Wiley, 1974.

Exner, J. E., Jr. *The Rorschach: A comprehensive system*, Vol. 2. New York: Wiley, 1978.

Eysenck, H. J. The logical basis of factor analysis. *American Psychologist*, 1953, **8**, 105−114.

Eysenck, H. J. *The structure of human personality*, 2nd ed. London: Methuen, 1960.

Farberow, N. L., Shneidman, E. S., and Neuringer, C. Case history and hospitalization factors in suicides of neuropsychiatric hospital patients. *Journal of Nervous and Mental Disease*, 1966, **142**, 32−44.

Faschingbauer, T. R. A 166-item written short form of the group MMPI: The FAM. *Journal of Consulting and Clinical Psychology*, 1974, **42**, 645−655.

Faschingbauer, T. R., and Newmark, C. S. *Short forms of the MMPI.* Lexington, Mass.: D. C. Heath, 1978.

Fear, R. A. *The evaluation interview*, Rev. 2nd. ed. New York: McGraw-Hill, 1978.

Feld, S., and Smith, C. P. An evaluation of the method of content analysis. In J. W. Atkinson (Ed.) *Motives in fantasy, action, and society.* Princeton, NJ: Van Nostrand, 1958.

Feldman, M. J., and Graley, J. The effects of an experimented set to simulate abnormality on group Rorschach performance. *Journal of Projective Techniques,* 1954, **18,** 326–334.

Festinger, L., Riecken, H. W., and Schachter, S. *When prophecy fails.* Minneapolis: University of Minnesota Press, 1956.

Fingarette, H., and Hasse, A. F. *Mental disabilities and criminal responsibility.* Berkeley: University of California Press, 1979.

Fischoff, B. Hindsight ≠ foresight: The effect of outcome knowledge on judgment under uncertainty. *Journal of Experimental Psychology: Human Perception and Performance,* 1975, **1,** 288–299.

Fischoff, B., and Beyth, R. "I knew it would happen": Remembered probabilities of once-future things. *Organizational Behavior and Human Performance,* 1975, **13,** 1–16.

Fischoff, B., Slovic, P., and Lichtenstein, S. Knowing with certainty: The appropriateness of extreme confidence. *Journal of Experimental Psychology: Human Perception and Performance,* 1977, **3,** 552–564.

Flanagan, J. C. The critical incident technique. *Psychological Bulletin,* 1954, **51,** 327–358.

Forehand, G. A. Comments on comments on testing. *Educational and Psychological Measurement,* 1964, **24,** 853–859.

Forehand, R., and Scarboro, M. E. An analysis of children's oppositional behavior. *Journal of Abnormal Child Psychology,* 1975, **3,** 27–31.

Forer, B. R. The fallacy of personal validation: A classroom demonstration of gullibility. *Journal of Abnormal and Social Psychology,* 1949, **44,** 118–123.

Forer, B. R. A structured sentence completion test. *Journal of Projective Techniques,* 1950, **14,** 15–29.

Fosberg, I. A. Rorschach reactions under varied instructions. *Rorschach Research Exchange,* 1938, **3,** 12–20.

Fosberg, I. A. An experimental study of the reliability of the Rorschach psychodiagnostic technique. *Rorschach Research Exchange,* 1941, **5,** 72–84.

Fowler, R. D. *Three approaches to the automatic interpretation of the MMPI: Purposes and usefulness of the Alabama program.* Presented at the annual meeting of the American Psychological Association, Chicago, September 1965.

Fowler, R. D. *The MMPI notebook: A guide to the clinical use of the automated MMPI.* Nutley, N.J.: Roche Psychiatric Service Institute, 1966.

Fowler, R. D. Computer interpretation of personality tests: The automated psychologist. *Comprehensive Psychiatry,* 1967, **8,** 455–467.

Fowler, R. D. The current status of computer interpretation of psychological tests. *Supplement to the American Journal of Psychiatry,* 1969, **125,** 21–27.

Frank, L. K. Projective methods for the study of personality. *Journal of Psychology,* 1939, **8,** 389–413.

Freeburg, N. E. The biographical information blank as a predictor of student achievement: A review. *Psychological Reports,* 1967, **20,** 911–925.

Freedman, B. J., Rosenthal, L., Donahoe, C. P. Jr., Schlundt, D. G., and McFall, R. M. A social behavioral analysis of skill deficits in delinquent and nondelinquent adolescent boys. *Journal of Consulting and Clinical Psychology,* 1978, **46,** 1448–1462.

Fulkerson, S. C. Individual differences in response validity. *Journal of Clinical Psychology,* 1959, **15,** 169–173.

Gallagher, C. E. Opening remarks. In Testimony before House Special Subcommittee on Invasion of Privacy the Committee on Government Operations. *American Psychologist*, 1965, **20**, 955–988.

Galton, F. Measurement of character. *Fortnightly Review*, 1884, **42**, 179–185.

Gamble, K. R. The Holtzman Inkblot Technique: A review. *Psychological Bulletin*, 1972, **77**, 172–194.

Garfield, S. L., and Sundland, D. M. Prognostic scales in schizophrenia. *Journal of Consulting Psychology*, 1966, **30**, 18–24.

Gauquelin, M. *Cosmic influences on human behaviors*. New York: Stein and Day, 1973.

Gearing, M. L. II. The MMPI as a primary differentiator and predictor of behavior in prison: A methodological critique and review of the recent literature. *Psychological Bulletin*, 1979, **86**, 929–963.

Gedye, J. L., and Miller, E. The automation of psychological assessment. *International Journal of Man-Machine Studies*, 1969, **1**, 237–262.

Geer, J. H. The development of a scale to measure fear. *Behavior Research and Therapy*, 1965, **3**, 45–53.

Geer, J. H. Sexual functioning: Some data and speculations on psychophysiological assessment. In J. D. Cone and R. P. Hawkins (Eds.), *Behavioral assessment*. New York: Brunner/Mazel, 1977.

Ghiselli, E. E. Differentiation of individuals in terms of their predictability. *Journal of Applied Psychology*, 1956, **40**, 374–377.

Ghiselli, E. E. Differentiation of tests in terms of the accuracy with which they predict for a given individual. *Educational and Psychological Measurement*, 1960, **20**, 675–84. (a)

Ghiselli, E. E. The prediction of predictability. *Educational and Psychological Measurement*, 1960, **20**, 3–8. (b)

Ghiselli, E. E. Moderating effects and differential reliability and validity. *Journal of Applied Psychology*, 1963, **47**, 81–86.

Ghiselli, E. E. *Theory of psychological measurement*. New York: McGraw-Hill, 1964.

Gianetti, R. A., Johnson, J. H., Klingler, D. E., and Williams, T. A. Comparison of linear and configural MMPI diagnostic methods with an uncontaminated criterion. *Journal of Consulting and Clinical Psychology*, 1978, **46**, 1046–1052.

Gilberstadt, H. *Comprehensive MMPI code book for males*. Minneapolis: Veterans Administration Hospital, 1970.

Gilberstadt, H., and Duker, J. *A handbook for clinical and actuarial MMPI interpretation*. Philadelphia: Saunders, 1965.

Gilbert, J. *Interpreting psychological test data*, Vol. 1. New York: Van Nostrand Reinhold, 1978.

Gleser, G. C., and Ihilevich, D. An objective instrument for measuring defense mechanisms. *Journal of Consulting and Clinical Psychology*, 1969, **33**, 51–60.

Glueck, B. C., Gullotta, G. P., and Ericson, R. P. Automation of behavior assessments: the computer-produced musing note. In J. B. Sidowski, J. H. Johnson, and T. A. Williams (eds.), *Technology in mental health care delivery systems*. Norwood, N.J.: Ablex, 1980.

Glueck, B. C., and Reznikoff, M. Comparison of computer-derived personality profile and projective psychological test findings. *American Journal of Psychiatry*, 1965, **121**, 1156–1161.

Glueck, S., and Glueck, E. T. *500 criminal careers*. New York: Knopf, 1930.

Goffman, E. *The presentation of self in everyday life.* Garden City, N.Y.: Doubleday, 1959.

Goheen, H. W., and Mosel, J. N. Validity of the Employment Recommendation Questionnaire: II. Comparison with field investigations. *Personnel Psychology,* 1959, **12,** 297–302.

Goldberg, J. B. Computer analysis of sentence completions. *Journal of Projective Techniques and Personality Assessment,* 1966, **30,** 37–45.

Goldberg, L. R. The effectiveness of clinicians' judgments: The diagnosis of organic brain damage from the Bender-Gestalt test. *Journal of Consulting Psychology,* 1959, **23,** 24–33.

Goldberg, L. R. Diagnosticians vs. diagnostic signs: The diagnosis of psychosis vs. neurosis from the MMPI. *Psychological Monographs,* 1965, **79** (9, Whole No. 602).

Goldberg, L. R. Seer over sign: The first good example? *Journal of Experimental Research in Personality,* 1968, **3,** 168–171. (a)

Goldberg, L. R. Simple models or simple processes? Some research on clinical judgments. *American Psychologist,* 1968, **23,** 483–496. (b)

Goldberg, L. R. The search for configural relationships in personality assessment: The diagnosis of psychosis vs. neurosis from the MMPI. *Multivariate Behavioral Research,* 1969, **4,** 523–536.

Goldberg, L. R. Man vs. model of man: A rationale, plus some evidence, for a method of improving on clinical inferences. *Psychological Bulletin,* 1970, **73,** 422–432.

Goldberg, L. R. A historical survey of personality scales and inventories. In P. McReynolds. (Ed.), *Advances in psychological assessment,* Vol. 2. Palo Alto, Calif.: Science and Behavior Books, 1971. (a)

Goldberg, L. R. Five models of clinical judgment: An empirical comparison between linear and nonlinear representations of the human inference process. *Organizational Behavior and Human Performance,* 1971, **6,** 458–479. (b)

Goldberg, L. R. Man vs. mean: The exploitation of group profiles for the construction of diagnostic classification systems. *Journal of Abnormal Psychology,* 1972, **79,** 121–131. (a)

Goldberg, L. R. Parameters of personality inventory construction and utilization: A comparison of prediction strategies and tactics. *Multivariate Behavioral Research Monograph,* 1972, No. 72-2. (b)

Goldberg, L. R. Some recent trends in personality assessment. *Journal of Personality Assessment,* 1972, **36,** 547–560. (c)

Goldberg, L. R. Differential attribution of trait-descriptive terms to oneself as compared to well-liked, neutral, and disliked others: A psychometric analysis. *Journal of Personality and Social Psychology,* 1978, **36,** 1012–1028. (a)

Goldberg, L. R. Review of the Jackson Personality Inventory. In O. K. Buros (Ed.), *Eighth mental measurements yearbook.* Highland Park, N.J.: Gryphon, 1978. (b)

Goldberg, L. R. *Some ruminations about the structure of individual differences: Developing a common lexicon for the major characteristics of human personality.* Presented to the annual meeting of the Western Psychological Association, Honolulu, April 1980.

Goldberg, L. R., and Slovic, P. Importance of test item content: An analysis of a corollary of the deviation hypothesis. *Journal of Counseling Psychology,* 1967, **14,** 462–472.

Goldberg, L. R., and Werts, C. E. The reliability of clinicians' judgments: A multitrait-multimethod approach. *Journal of Consulting Psychology,* 1966, **30,** 199–206.

Goldberg, P. A. A review of sentence completion methods in personality assessment. *Journal of Projective Techniques and Personality Assessment,* 1965, **29,** 12–45.

Golden, C. J. *Clinical interpretation of objective psychological tests.* New York: Grune and Stratton, 1979.

Golden, M. Some effects of combining psychological tests on clinical inferences. *Journal of Consulting Psychology,* 1964, **28,** 440–446.

Goldfried, M. R. Behavioral assessment: Where do we go from here? *Behavioral Assessment,* 1979, **1,** 19–22.

Goldfried, M. R., and D'Zurilla, T. J. A behavior-analytic model for assessing competence. In C. D. Spielberger (Ed.), *Current topics in clinical and community psychology,* Vol. 1. New York: Academic Press, 1969.

Goldsmith, D. B. The use of the personal history blank as a salesmanship test. *Journal of Applied Psychology,* 1922, **6,** 149–155.

Goodenough, F. L. *Measurement of intelligence by drawings.* Yonkers-on-Hudson, N.Y.: World Book, 1926.

Goodstein, L. D., Crites, J. O., Heilbrun, A. B., Jr., and Rempel, P. P. The use of the California Psychological Inventory in a university counseling service. *Journal of Counseling Psychology,* 1961, **8,** 147–153.

Gordon, L. V. *Gordon Personal Profile manual,* Rev. ed. New York: Harcourt, Brace, and World, 1963.

Gordon, L. V. Clinical, psychometric and work-sample approaches in the prediction of success in Peace Corps training. *Journal of Applied Psychology,* 1967, **51,** 111–119.

Gorham, D. R. Validity and reliability studies of a computer-based scoring system for inkblot responses. *Journal of Consulting Psychology,* 1967, **31,** 65–70.

Gorham, D. R., Moseley, E. C., and Holtzman, W. W. Norms for the computer-scored Holtzman Inkblot Technique. *Perceptual and Motor Skills,* 1968, **26,** 1279–1305.

Gottschalk, L. A., and Gleser, G. C. *The measurement of psychological states through the content analysis of verbal behavior.* Berkeley: University of California Press, 1969.

Gough, H. G. The F minus K dissimulation index for the MMPI. *Journal of Consulting Psychology,* 1950, **14,** 408–413.

Gough, H. G. The construction of a personality scale to predict scholastic achievement. *Journal of Applied Psychology,* 1953, **37,** 361–366.

Gough, H. G. Clinical versus statistical prediction in psychology. In L. Postman (Ed.), *Psychology in the making.* New York: Knopf, 1962.

Gough, H. G. Conceptual analysis of psychological test scores and other diagnostic variables. *Journal of Abnormal Psychology,* 1965, **70,** 294–302.

Gough, H. G. An interpreter's syllabus for the California Psychological Inventory. In P. McReynolds (Ed.), *Advances in psychological assessment,* Vol. 1. Palo Alto, Calif.: Science and Behavior Books, 1968.

Gough, H. G. *California Psychological Inventory: Manual.* Palo Alto, Calif.: Consulting Psychologists Press, 1957 (Rev. ed., 1975).

Gough, H. G., and Heilbrun, A. B., Jr. *Manual for the Adjective Check List.* Palo Alto, Ca.if.: Consulting Psychologists Press, 1964.

Gough, H. G., McClosky, H., and Meehl, P. E. A personality scale for dominance. *Journal of Abnormal and Social Psychology,* 1951, **46,** 360–366.

Gough, H. G., and Peterson, D. R. The identification and measurement of predispositional factors in crime and delinquency. *Journal of Consulting Psychology,* 1952, **16,** 207–212.

Graham, J. R. *The MMPI: A practical guide.* New York: Oxford, 1977.

Grayson, H. M., and Olinger, L. B. Simulation of "normalcy" by psychiatric patients on the MMPI. *Journal of Consulting Psychology,* 1957, **21,** 73–77.

Greist, J. H., Klein, M. H., and Erdman, H. P. Routine on-line psychiatric diagnosis by computer. *American Journal of Psychiatry,* 1976, **133,** 1405.

Gross, M. L. *The brain watchers.* New York: Random House, 1962.

Gross, M. L. Testimony before House Special Subcommittee on Invasion of Privacy of the Committee on Government Operations. *American Psychologist,* 1965, **20,** 958–960.

Group for the Advancement of Psychiatry. *Misuse of psychiatry in the criminal courts: Competency to stand trial.* New York: Author, 1974.

Guilford, J. P. *An inventory of factors STDCR.* Beverly Hills, Calif.: Sheridan Supply Company, 1940.

Guilford, J. P. (Ed.) *Printed classification tests.* Washington, D.C.: Government Printing Office, 1947.

Guilford, J. P. *Personality.* New York: McGraw-Hill, 1959.

Guilford, J. P., and Martin, H. G. *Personnel Inventory: Manual of directions and norms.* Beverly Hills, Calif.: Sheridan Supply Company, 1943. (a)

Guilford, J. P., and Martin, H. G. *The Guilford-Martin inventory of factors GAMIN: Manual of directions and norms.* Beverly Hills, Ca.if.: Sheridan Supply Company, 1943. (b)

Guilford, J. P., and Zimmerman, W. S. *The Guilford-Zimmerman Temperament Survey: Manual of instructions and interpretations.* Beverly Hills, Ca.if.: Sheridan Supply Company, 1949.

Guion, R. M. *Personnel testing.* New York: McGraw-Hill, 1965.

Guion, R. M. Recruiting, selection, and job replacement. In M. D. Dunnette (Ed.), *Handbook of industrial and organizational psychology.* Chicago: Rand McNally, 1976.

Gynther, M. D. White norms and Black MMPIs: A prescription for discrimination? *Psychological Bulletin,* 1972, **78,** 386–402.

Gynther, M. D. Review of the California Psychological Inventory. In O. K. Buros (Ed.), *Eighth mental measurements yearbook.* Highland Park, N.J.: Gryphon, 1978.

Gynther, M. D. Aging and personality. In J. N. Butcher (Ed.), *New developments in the use of the MMPI.* Minneapolis: University of Minnesota Press, 1979. (a)

Gynther, M. D. Ethnicity and personality: An update. In J. N. Butcher (Ed.), *New developments in the use of the MMPI.* Minneapolis: University of Minnesota Press, 1979. (b)

Gynther, M. D., Burkhart, B. R., and Hovanitz, C. Do face-valid items have more predictive validity than subtle items? The case of the MMPI *Pd* scale. *Journal of Consulting and Clinical Psychology,* 1979, **47,** 295–300.

Gynther, M. D., and Greer, S. B. Accuracy may make a difference, but does a difference make for accuracy? A response to Pritchard and Rosenblatt. *Journal of Consulting and Clinical Psychology,* 1980, **48,** 268–72.

Gynther, M. D., Lachar, D., and Dahlstrom, W. G. Are special norms for minorities needed? Development of an MMPI *F* scale for Blacks. *Journal of Consulting and Clinical Psychology,* 1978, **46,** 1403–1408.

Halbower, C. C. *A comparison of actuarial versus clinical prediction to classes discriminated by MMPI.* Doctoral dissertation, University of Minnesota, 1955.

Hall, C. S., and Lindzey, G. *Theories of personality,* 3rd ed. New York: Wiley, 1978.

Hall, L. P., and LaDriere, L. Patterns of performance on WISC similarities in emotionally disturbed and brain damaged children. *Journal of Consulting and Clinical Psychology,* 1969, **33,** 357–364.

Halleck, S. L. *Law in the practice of psychiatry: A handbook for professionals.* New York: Plenum, 1980.

Halpert, H. P., Horvath, W. J., and Young, J. P. *An administrator's handbook on the application of operations research to the management of mental health systems.* Washington, D.C.: National Clearinghouse for Mental Health Information, NIMH, 1970.

Hamilton, D. L. Personality attributes associated with extreme response style. *Psychological Bulletin,* 1968, **69,** 192–203.

Hammer, E. F. (Ed.) *The clinical application of projective drawings.* Springfield, Ill.: Thomas, 1958.

Hammer, E. F. Projective drawings. In A. I. Rabin (Ed.), *Projective techniques in personality assessment.* New York: Springer, 1968.

Hammond, K. R., and Summers, D. A. Cognitive dependence on linear and nonlinear cues. *Psychological Review,* 1965, **72,** 215–224.

Hart, H. Predicting parole success. *Journal of Criminal Law and Criminology,* 1923, **14,** 405–413.

Hartmann, D. P., Roper, B. L., and Bradford, D. C. Some relationships between behavioral and traditional assessment. *Journal of Behavioral Assessment,* 1979, **1,** 3–21.

Hartshorne, H., and May, M. A. *Studies in deceit.* New York: Macmillan, 1928.

Hartshorne, H., and May, M. A. *Studies in the nature of character: II. Studies in service and self-control.* New York: Macmillan, 1929.

Hartshorne, H., May, M. A., and Shuttleworth, F. K. *Studies in the nature of character: III. Studies in the organization of character.* New York: Macmillan, 1930.

Hartwell, S. W., Hutt, M. L., Andrew, G., and Walton, R. E. The Michigan Picture Test: Diagnostic and therapeutic possibilities of a new projective test for children. *American Journal of Orthopsychiatry,* 1951, **21,** 124–137.

Hase, H. D., and Goldberg, L. R. Comparative validities of different strategies of constructing personality inventory scales. *Psychological Bulletin,* 1967, **67,** 231–248.

Hathaway, S. R. Clinical intuition and inferential accuracy. *Journal of Personality,* 1956, **24,** 223–250. (a)

Hathaway, S. R. Scales 5 (masculinity-femininity), 6 (paranoia), and 8 (schizophrenia). In G. S. Welsh and W. G. Dahlstrom (Ed.), *Basic readings on the MMPI in psychology and medicine.* Minneapolis: University of Minnesota Press, 1956. (b)

Hathaway, S. R. Increasing clinical efficiency. In B. M. Bass and I. A. Berg (Eds.), *Objective approaches to personality assessment.* Princeton: Van Nostrand, 1959.

Hathaway, S. R. MMPI: Professional use by professional people. *American Psychologist,* 1964, **19,** 204–210.

Hathaway, S. R., and McKinley, J. C. A multiphasic personality schedule (Minnesota): I. Construction of the schedule. *Journal of Psychology,* 1940, **10,** 249–254.

Hathaway, S. R., and McKinley, J. C. *Minnesota Multiphasic Personality Inventory: Manual.* New York: Psychological Corporation, 1951.

Haynes, S. N. *Principles of behavioral assessment.* New York: Gardner, 1978.

Haynes, S. N., and Wilson, C. C. *Behavioral assessment.* San Francisco: Jossey-Bass, 1979.

Heaton, R. K., Baade, L. E., and Johnson, K. L. Neuropsychological test results associated with psychiatric disorders in adults. *Psychological Bulletin,* 1978, **85,** 141–162.

Hedlund, J. L., Evenson, R. C., Sletten, I. W., and Cho, D. W. The computer and clinical prediction. In J. B. Sidowski, J. H. Johnson, and T. A. Williams (Eds.), *Technology in Mental Health Care Delivery Systems.* Norwood, N.J.: Ablex, 1980.

Hedlund, J. L., and Hickman, C. V. Computers in mental health: A national survey. *Journal of Mental Health Administration,* 1977, **6,** 30–52.

Hedlund, J. L., Sletten, I. W., Evenson, R. C., Altman, H., and Cho, D. W. Automated psychiatric information systems: A critical review of Missouri's Standard System of Psychiatry (SSOP). *Journal of Operational Psychiatry,* 1977, **8,** 5–26.

Heider, F. *The psychology of interpersonal relations.* New York: Wiley, 1958.

Heilbrun, A. B. Revision of the MMPI *K* correction procedure for improved detection of maladjustment in a normal college population. *Journal of Consulting Psychology,* 1963, **25,** 161–165.

Heilbrun, A. B. Social-learning theory, social desirability, and the MMPI. *Psychological Bulletin,* 1964, **61,** 377–387.

Heilbrun, A. B., Jr. Review of the Edwards Personal Preference Schedule. In O. K. Buros (Ed.), *Seventh mental measurements yearbook.* Highland Park, N.J.: Gryphon, 1972.

Heilbrun, A. B., and Goodstein, L. D. Social desirability response set: Error or predictor variable? *Journal of Psychology,* 1961, **51,** 321–329. (a)

Heilbrun, A. B., and Goodstein, L. D. The relationships between individually defined and group defined social desirability and performance on the Edwards Personal Preference Schedule. *Journal of Consulting Psychology,* 1961, **25,** 200–204.

Helmrich, R., Bakeman, R., and Radloff, R. The Life History Questionnaire as a predictor of performance in Navy divers training. *Journal of Applied Psychology,* 1973, **57,** 148–153.

Henry, E. M., and Rotter, J. B. Situational influences on Rorschach responses. *Journal of Consulting Psychology,* 1956, **20,** 457–462.

Henry, W. E. *The analysis of fantasy.* New York: Wiley, 1956.

Hepburn, J. R. The objective reality of evidence and the utility of systematic jury selection. *Law and Human Behavior,* 1980, **4,** 89–101.

Hersleb, J. D., Sales, B. D., and Berman, J. J. When psychologists aid in the *voir dire:* Legal and ethical considerations. In L. E. Abt and I. R. Stuart (Eds.), *Social psychology and discretionary law.* New York: Van Nostrand Reinhold, 1979.

Hertz, M. R. *Frequency tables for scoring responses to the Rorschach inkblot test, 3rd ed.* Cleveland: Western Reserve University Press, 1951.

Heymans, G., and Wiersma, E. Beitrage zur Speziellen Psychologie auf Grund einer Massenunterschung. *Zeitschrift für Psychologie,* 1906, **43,** 81–127 and 258–301.

Hiler, E. W., and Nesvig, D. An evaluation of criteria used by clinicians to infer pathology from figure drawings. *Journal of Consulting Psychology,* 1965, **29,** 520–529.

Hill, E. F. *The Holtzman Inkblot Technique.* San Francisco: Jossey-Bass, 1972.

Hillier, F. S., and Lieberman, G. J. *Introduction to operations research.* San Francisco: Holden-Day, 1967.

Hobert, R., and Dunnette, M. D. Development of moderator variables to enhance the prediction of managerial effectiveness. *Journal of Applied Psychology,* 1967, **51,** 50–64.

Hoch, A., and Amsden, G. S. A guide to the descriptive study of personality. *Review of Neurology and Psychiatry,* 1913, **11,** 577–587.

Hoffman, N., and Butcher, J. N. Clinical limitations of three Minnesota Multiphasic Personality Inventory short forms. *Journal of Consulting and Clinical Psychology,* 1975, **43,** 32–39.

Hoffman, P. J., Slovic, P., and Rorer, L. G. An analysis-of-variance model for the assessment of configural cue utilization in clinical judgment. *Psychological Bulletin,* 1968, **69,** 338–349.

Hogan, R. Review of the study of values. In O. K. Buros (Ed.), *Seventh mental measurements yearbook.* Highland Park, N.J.: Gryphon, 1972.

Hogan, R. Review of the Personality Research Form. In O. K. Buros (Ed.), *Eighth mental measurements yearbook.* Highland Park, N.J.: Gryphon, 1978.

Hogan, R., DeSoto, C. B., and Solano, C. Traits, tests, and personality research. *American Psychologist,* 1977, **32,** 255–264.

Holmen, M. G., Katter, R. V., Jones, A. M., and Richardson, I. F. *An assessment program for OCS candidates* (HumRRO Technical Reports, 1956-26). Alexandria, Va.: Human Resources Research Organization, 1956.

Holmes, D. S. The conscious control of thematic projection. *Journal of Consulting and Clinical Psychology,* 1974, **42,** 323–329.

Holmes, T. H., and Rahe, R. H. The Social Readjustment Rating Scale. *Journal of Psychosomatic Research,* 1967, **11,** 213–218.

Holt, R. R. Clinical and statistical prediction: A reformulation and some new data. *Journal of Abnormal and Social Psychology,* 1958, **56,** 1–12.

Holt, R. R. Yet another look at clinical and statistical prediction: Or, is clinical psychology worthwhile? *American Psychologist,* 1970, **25,** 337–349.

Holt, R. R. *Methods in clinical psychology.* Vol. 1, *Projective assessment.* New York: Plenum, 1978.

Holt, R. R., and Luborsky, L. *Personality patterns of psychiatrists.* New York: Basic Books, 1958.

Holtzman, W. H., and Gorham, D. R. *Automated scoring and interpretation of the group-administered Holtzman Inkblot Test by computer in group psychological assessment.* Symposium presented at the annual convention of the American Psychological Association, Honolulu, 1972.

Holtzman, W. H., Thorpe, J. S., Swartz, J. D. and Herron, E. W. *Inkblot perception and personality: Holtzman inkblot technique.* Austin: University of Texas Press, 1961.

Holzberg, J. D. Reliability re-examined. In M. A. Rickers-Ovsiankina (Ed.), *Rorschach psychology.* New York: Wiley, 1960.

Horst, P. *Psychological measurement and prediction.* Belmont, Calif.: Wadsworth, 1966.

Hovey, H. B., and Stauffacher, J. C. Intuitive versus objective prediction from a test. *Journal of Clinical Psychology,* 1953, **9,** 349−351.

Huff, F. W. Use of actuarial description of abnormal personality in a mental hospital. *Psychological Reports,* 1965, **17,** 224.

Hughes, J. F., Dunn, J. F., and Baxter, B. The validity of selection instruments under operating conditions (The Prudential Insurance Company of America). *Personnel Psychology,* 1956, **9,** 321−324.

Humm, D. G., and Wadsworth, G. W. The Humm-Wadsworth Temperament Scale. *American Journal of Psychiatry,* 1935, **92,** 163−200.

Hundleby, J. D. Review of the Study of Values. In O. K. Buros (Ed.), *Sixth mental measurements yearbook.* Highland Park, N.J.: Gryphon, 1965.

Hursch, C. J., Hammond, K. R., and Hursch, J. L. Some methodological considerations in multiple-cue probability studies. *Psychological Review,* 1964, **71,** 42−60.

Hutt, M. L. *The Hutt adaptation of the Bender-Gestalt test,* 3rd ed. New York: Grune and Stratton, 1977.

Jackson, D. N. The dynamics of structured personality tests, 1971. *Psychological Review,* 1971, **78,** 229−248.

Jackson, D. N. *Personality Research Form: Manual.* Goshen, N.Y.: Research Psychologist Press, 1967 (Rev. ed., 1974).

Jackson, D. N. *Jackson Personality Inventory: Manual.* Port Huron, Mich.: Research Psychologists Press, 1976.

Jackson, D. N. Review of the Minnesota-Briggs History Record. In O. K. Buros (Ed.), *Eighth mental measurements yearbook.* Highland Park, N.J.: Gryphon, 1978.

Jackson, D. N., and Messick, S. Content and style in personality assessment. *Psychological Bulletin,* 1958, **55,** 243−252.

Jackson, D. N., and Messick, S. Response styles on the MMPI: Comparison of clinical and normal samples. *Journal of Abnormal and Social Psychology,* 1962, **65,** 285−299.

Jacobs, A., and Schlaff, A. *Falsification scales for the Guilford-Zimmerman Temperament Survey.* Beverly Hills, Calif.: Sheridan Supply Company, 1955.

James, L. R., Ellison, R. L., Fox, D. G., and Taylor, C. W. Prediction of artistic performance from biographical data. *Journal of Applied Psychology,* 1974, **59,** 84−86.

Jarnecke, R. W., and Chambers, E. D. MMPI content scales: Dimensional structure, construct validity, and interpretive norms in a psychiatric populalion. *Journal of Consulting and Clinical Psychology,* 1977, **45,** 1126−1131.

Johannson, C. B. Manual for the *Temperament and Values Inventory.* Minneapolis: NCS/Interpretive Scoring System, 1977.

Johnson, F. A., and Greenberg, R. P. Quality of drawing as a factor in the interpretation of figure drawings. *Journal of Personality Assessment,* 1978, **42,** 485−495.

Johnson, J. H., and Sarason, I. G. Moderator variables in stress research. In I. G. Sarason and C. D. Spielberger (Eds.), *Stress and anxiety,* Vol. 6. New York: Halstead, 1979.

Johnson, J. H., and Williams, T. A. The use of on-line computer technology in a mental health admitting system. *American Psychologist,* 1975, **3,** 388−390.

Johnson, J. H., and Williams, T. A. Using on-line computer technology to improve service response and decision-making effectiveness in a mental health admitting system. In J. B. Sidowski, J. H. Johnson, and T. A. Williams (Eds.), *Technology in mental health care delivery systems*. Norwood, N.J.: Ablex, 1980.

Johnston, R., and McNeal, B. F. Statistical versus clinical prediction: Length of neuropsychiatric hospital stay. *Journal of Abnormal Psychology*, 1967, **72**, 335–340.

Jones, E. E., and Nisbett, R. E. *The actor and the observer: Divergent perceptions of the causes of behavior*. New York: General Learning Press, 1971.

Jones, S. L., and Lanyon, R. I. Relationship between adaptive skills and outcome of alcoholism treatment. *Journal of Studies on Alcohol*, 1981, **42**, 521–525.

Jones, R. R., Reid, J. B., and Patterson, G. R. Naturalistic observation in clinical assessment. In P. McReynolds (Ed.), *Advances in psychological assessment*, Vol. 3. San Francisco: Jossey-Bass, 1975.

Jourard, S. *The transparent self*. Princeton, N.J.: Van Nostrand, 1964.

Jung, C. G. The association method. *American Journal of Psychology*, 1910, **21**, 219–269.

Kahn, R. L., and Cannell, C. F. *The dynamics of interviewing*. New York: Wiley, 1957.

Kahn, R. L., Goldfarb, A. I., Pollack, M., and Peck, A. Brief objective measures for the determination of mental status in the aged. *American Journal of Psychiatry*, 1960, **117**, 326–328.

Kane, J. S., and Lawler, E. E. III. Methods of peer assessment. *Psychological Bulletin*, 1978, **85**, 555–586.

Kanfer, F. H., and Phillips, J. S. *Learning foundations of behavior therapy*. New York: Wiley, 1970.

Kanfer, F. H., and Saslow, G. Behavioral analysis: An alternative to diagnostic classification. *Archives of General Psychiatry*, 1965, **12**, 529–538.

Kantor, R. E., Wallner, J. M., and Winder, C. L. Process and reactive schizophrenia. *Journal of Consulting Psychology*, 1953, **17**, 157–162.

Kaplan, M. F., and Eron, L. D. Test sophistication and faking in the TAT situation. *Journal of Projective Techniques*, 1965, **29**, 498–503.

Karson, S., and O'Dell, J. W. *A guide to the clinical use of the 16 PF*. Champaign, Ill.: Institute for Personality and Ability Testing, 1976.

Karson, S., and Sells, S. B. Comments on Meehl and Rosen's paper. *Psychological Bulletin*, 1956, **53**, 335–337.

Kazdin, A. E. Self-monitoring and behavior change. In M. J. Mahoney and C. E. Thoreson (Eds.), *Self-control: Power to the person*. Belmont, Calif.: Wadsworth, 1974.

Kazdin, A. E. *History of behavior modification*. Baltimore: University Park Press, 1979.

Kelly, E. L., and Fiske, D. W. *The prediction of performance in clinical psychology*. Ann Arbor: University of Michigan Press, 1951.

Kelly, E. L., and Goldberg, L. R. Correlates of later performance and specialization in psychology. *Psychological Monographs*, 1959, **73** (12, Whole No. 482).

Kelly, G. A. *The psychology of personal constructs*. New York: Norton, 1955.

Kendra, J. M. Predicting suicide using the Rorschach Inkblot Test. *Journal of Personality Assessment*, 1979, **43**, 452–456.

Kent, G. H., and Rosanoff, A. J. A study of association in insanity. *American Journal of Insanity*, 1910, 67, 37–96 and 317–390.

Kent, R. N., O'Leary, K. D., Diament, C., and Dietz, A. Expectation biases in observational evaluation of therapeutic change. *Journal of Consulting and Clinical Psychology,* 1974, **42,** 774–780.

Kincannon, J. C. Prediction of the standard MMPI scale scores from 71 items: The Mini-Mult. *Journal of Consulting and Clinical Psychology,* 1968, **32,** 319–325.

Kitay, P. M. Review of the Bender-Gestalt Test. In O. K. Buros (Ed.), *Seventh mental measurements yearbook.* Highland Park, N.J.: Gryphon, 1972.

Kleinmuntz, B. MMPI decision rules for the identification of college maladjustment: A digital computer approach. *Psychological Monographs,* 1963, **77** (14, Whole No. 577).

Kleinmuntz, B. Review of the Roche MMPI Computerized Interpretation Service. In O. K. Buros (Ed.), *Seventh mental measurement yearbook.* Highland Park, N.J.: Gryphon, 1972.

Kleinmuntz, B., and McLean, R. S. Computers in behavioral science: Diagnostic interviewing by digital computer. *Behavioral Science,* 1968, **13,** 75–80.

Klett, W. G., and Vestre, N. D. Demographic and prognostic characteristics of psychiatric patients classified by gross MMPI measures. *American Psychologist,* 1967, **22,** 562. (Abstract)

Klopfer, B., Ainsworth, M. D., Klopfer, W. G., and Holt, R. R. *Developments in the Rorschach technique: I. Technique and theory.* New York: Harcourt, Brace and World, 1954.

Klopfer, B., and Davidson, H. H. *The Rorschach technique: An introductory manual.* New York: Harcourt, Brace, and World, 1962.

Klopfer, B., Kirkner, F., Wisham, W., and Baker, G. Rorschach prognostic rating scale. *Journal of Projective Techniques,* 1951, **15,** 425–428.

Klopfer, W. G., and Taulbee, E. S. Projective tests. *Annual Review of Psychology,* 1976, **27,** 543–567.

Knutson, J. F. Review of the Rorschach. In O. K. Buros (Ed.), *Seventh mental measurements yearbook.* Highland Park, N.J.: Gryphon, 1972.

Kobasa, S. Stressful life events, personality and health: An inquiry into hardiness. *Journal of Personality and Social Psychology,* 1979, **37,** 1–10.

Komaki, J., Collins, R. L. ,and Thoene, T. J. F. Behavioral measurement in business, industry, and government. *Behavioral Assessment,* 1980, **2,** 103–124.

Koppitz, E. M. *The Bender Gestalt test for young children.* New York: Grune and Stratton, 1963.

Korchin, S. J. *Modern clinical psychology.* New York: Basic Books, 1976.

Kostlan, A. A method of the empirical study of psychodiagnosis. *Journal of Consulting Psychology,* 1954, **18,** 82–88.

Kuder, G. F. *Examiner manual for the Kuder Preference Record.* Chicago: Science Research Associates, 1951.

Kuder, G. F., and Richardson, M. W. The theory of the estimation of test reliability. *Psychometrika,* 1937, **2,** 151–160.

Kurtz, R. M., and Garfield, S. L. Illusory correlation: A further exploration of Chapman's paradigm. *Journal of Consulting and Clinical Psychology,* 1978, **46,** 1009–1015.

Lachar, D. *The MMPI: Clinical assessment and automated interpretation.* Los Angeles: Western Psychological Services, 1974.

Lachar, D., and Alexander, R. S. Veridicality of self-report: Replicated correlates of the Wiggins MMPI content scales. *Journal of Consulting and Clinical Psychology,* 1978, **48,** 1349–1356.

Lachar, D., DeHorn, A. B., and Gdowski, C. L. Profile classification strategies for the Personality Inventory for Children. *Journal of Consulting and Clinical Psychology,* 1979, **47,** 874–881.

Lachar, D., and Gdowski, C. L. *Actuarial assessment of child and adolescent personality: An interpretive guide to the Personality Inventory for Children.* Los Angeles: Western Psychological Services, 1979.

Lang, P. J. Fear reduction and fear behaviors: Problems in treating a construct. In J. M. Schlien (Ed.), *Research in psychotherapy,* Vol. 3. Washington, D.C.: American Psychological Association, 1968.

Lang, R. P., and Lazovik, A. D. Experimental desensitization of a phobia. *Journal of Abnormal and Social Psychology,* 1963, **66,** 519–525.

Langner, T. S., and Michael, S. T. *Life stress and mental health.* New York: Free Press of Glencoe, 1963.

Lanyon, B. P. Empirical construction and validation of a sentence completion test for hostility, anxiety, and dependency. *Journal of Consulting and Clinical Psychology,* 1972, **39,** 420–428.

Lanyon, B. P., and Lanyon, R. I. *Incomplete Sentences Task: Manual.* Chicago: Stoelting, 1980.

Lanyon, R. I. Measurement of social competence in college males. *Journal of Consulting Psychology,* 1967, **31,** 495–498. (a)

Lanyon, R. I. Simulation of normal and psychopathic MMPI personality patterns. *Journal of Consulting Psychology,* 1967, **31,** 94–97. (b)

Lanyon, R. I. *A handbook of MMPI group profiles.* Minneapolis: University of Minnesota Press, 1968.

Lanyon, R. I. Development and validation of a psychological screening inventory. *Journal of Consulting and Clinical Psychology,* 1970, **35** (1, pt. 2), 1–24.

Lanyon, R. I. Mental health technology. *American Psychologist,* 1971, **26,** 1071–1076.

Lanyon, R. I. A technological approach to the improvement of decision making in mental health services. *Journal of Consulting and Clinical Psychology,* 1972, **39,** 43–48.

Lanyon, R. I. *Psychological Screening Inventory: Manual.* Goshen, New York: Research Psychologists Press, 1973.

Lanyon, R. I. *Psychological Screening Inventory: Manual,* 2nd ed. Port Huron, Mich.: Research Psychologists Press, 1978.

Lanyon, R. I. *The new technology of mental health care.* Final Report, National Institute of Mental Health, Grant No. MH20233, 1974.

Lanyon, R. I., and Lanyon, B. P. Behavioral assessment and decision-making: The design of strategies for therapeutic behavior change. In M. P. Feldman and A. Broadhurst (Eds.), *Theoretical and experimental bases of the behavior therapies.* London and New York: Wiley, 1976.

Lanyon, R. I., and Lanyon, B. P. *Behavior therapy: A clinical introduction.* Reading, Mass.: Addison-Wesley, 1978.

Lanyon, R. I., and Manosevitz, M. Validity of self-reported fear. *Behavioral Research and Therapy,* 1966, **4,** 259–263.

Laurent, H. *The early identification of management potential.* Paper presented to the American Psychological Association, St. Louis, September 1962.

Lee, R., and Booth, J. M. A utility analysis of a weighted application blank designed to predict turnover for clerical employees. *Journal of Applied Psychology,* 1974, **59,** 516–518.

Levy, L. H. *Psychological interpretation.* New York: Holt, Rinehart, and Winston, 1963.

Lewandowski, D. G., and Saccuzzo, D. P. The decline of psychological testing. *Professional Psychology,* 1976, **7,** 177–184.

Lewis, G. P., Golden, C. J., Moses, J. A., Jr., Osmon, D. C., Purisch, A. D., and Hammeke, T. A. Localization of cerebral dysfunction with a standardized version of Luria's neuropsychological battery. *Journal of Consulting and Clinical Psychology,* 1979, **47,** 1003–1019.

Lewis, J. L., and Lanyon, R. I. *Validity of the MMPI, the FAM, and the Psychological Screening Inventory with state hospital patients.* Paper presented at the annual meeting of the Western Psychological Association, San Diego, Calif., April 1979.

Lezak, M. *Neuropsychological assessment.* New York: Oxford University Press, 1976.

Lichtenstein, S., and Fischoff, B. Do those who know more also know more about how much they know? *Organizational Behavior and Human Performance,* 1977, **20,** 159–183.

Lindsley, O. R. Operant conditioning methods applied to chronic schizophrenia. *Diseases of the Nervous System,* 1960, **21,** 66–78. (Monograph Supplement).

Lindsley, O. R. A reliable wrist counter for recording behavior rates. *Journal of Applied Behavior Analysis,* 1968, **1,** 77–78.

Lindzey, G. *Projective techniques and cross-cultural research.* New York: Appleton-Century-Crofts, 1961.

Lindzey, G. Seer versus sign. *Journal of Experimental Research in Personality,* 1965, **1,** 17–26.

Lindzey, G., and Kalnins, D. Thematic Apperception Test: Some evidence bearing on the "hero assumption." *Journal of Abnormal and Social Psychology,* 1958, **57,** 76–83.

Linehan, M. M. Content validity: Its relevance to behavioral assessment. *Behavioral Assessment,* 1980, **2,** 147–159.

Lipinski, D., and Nelson, R. O. Problems in the use of naturalistic observation as a means of behavioral assessment. *Behavior Therapy,* 1974, **5,** 341–351.

Lippmann, W. *Public opinion.* New York: Harcourt, Brace, 1922.

Lipsitt, P. D., Lelos, D., and McGarry, A. L. Competency for trial: A screening instrument. *American Journal of Psychiatry,* 1971, **128,** 105–109.

Little, K. B., and Shneidman, E. S. Congruencies among interpretations of psychological test and anamnestic data. *Psychological Monographs,* 1959, **73,** (6, Whole No. 476).

Loevinger, J. Objective tests as instruments of psychological theory. *Psychological Reports,* 1957, **3,** 635–694.

Lovell, V. R. The human use of personality tests: A dissenting view. *American Psychologist,* 1967, **22,** 383–393.

Lueger, R. L., and Petzel, T. P. Illusory correlation in clinical judgment: Effects of amount of information to be processed. *Journal of Consulting and Clinical Psychology,* 1979, **47,** 1120–1121.

Lykken, D. T. *A tremor in the blood.* New York: McGraw-Hill, 1980.

Lyons, J. P. Operations research in mental health service delivery systems. In J. B. Sidowski, J. H. Johnson, and T. A. Williams (Eds.), *Technology in mental health care delivery systems*. Norwood, N.J.: Ablex, 1980.

MSIS. *Multi-State Information System: A review*. Orangeburg, N.Y.: Rockland State Hospital, 1973.

Machover, K. *Personality projection in the drawing of the human figure*. Springfield, Ill.: Thomas, 1949.

MacKinnon, D. W. IPAR's contribution to the conceptualization and study of creativity. In I. A. Taylor and J. W. Getzells (Eds.), *Perspectives in Creativity*. Chicago: Aldine, 1975.

Mahoney, M. J. Some applied issues in self-monitoring. In J. D. Cone and R. D. Hawkins (Eds.), *Behavioral assessment*. New York: Brunner-Mazel, 1977.

Marks, P. A., and Seeman, W. *The actuarial description of abnormal personality*. Baltimore: Williams and Wilkins, 1963.

Marks, P. A., Seeman, W., and Haller, D. L. *The actuarial use of the MMPI with adolescents and adults*. Baltimore: Williams and Wilkins, 1974.

Marlatt, G. A. Behavioral assessment of social drinking and alcoholism. In G. A. Marlatt and P. E. Nathan (Eds.), *Behavioral approaches to alcoholism*. New Brunswick, N.J.: Rutgers Center of Alcohol Studies, 1978.

Marx, M. H., and Hillix, W. A. *Systems and theories in psychology*, 2nd ed. New York: McGraw-Hill, 1973.

Mash, E. J., and Terdal, L. G. *Behavior therapy assessment: Diagnosis, design, and evaluation*. New York: Springer, 1976.

Matarazzo, J. D. The interview. In B. B. Wolman (Ed.), *Handbook of clinical psychology*. New York: McGraw-Hill, 1965.

McClelland, D. C. Opinions predict opinions: So what else is new? *Journal of Consulting and Clinical Psychology,* 1972, **38,** 325–328.

McClelland, D. C., Atkinson, J. W., Clark, R. A., and Lowell, E. L. *The achievement motive*. New York: Appleton-Century-Crofts, 1953.

McEachern, A. W., Taylor, E. M., Newman, J. R., and Ashford, A. E. The juvenile probation system: Simulation for research and decision-making. *American Behavioral Scientist,* 1968, **11,** 1–46.

McFall, R. M., and Lillesand, D. V. Behavior rehearsal with modeling and coaching in assertive training. *Journal of Abnormal Psychology,* 1971, **77,** 313–323.

McFall, R. M., and Marston, A. An experimental investigation of behavioral rehearsal in assertive training. *Journal of Abnormal Psychology,* 1970, **76,** 295–303.

McGarry, A. L., Curran, W. J., Lipsitt, P. D., Lelos, D., Schwitzgebel, R. K., and Rosenberg, A. H. *Competency to stand trial and mental illness*. Rockville, Md.: National Institute of Mental Health, 1973.

McKee, M. G. Review of the Edwards Personal Preference Schedule. In O. K. Buros (Ed.), *Seventh mental measurements yearbook*. Highland Park, N.J.: Gryphon, 1972.

Meehl, P. E. Configural scoring. *Journal of Consulting Psychology,* 1950, **14,** 165–171.

Meehl, P. E. *Clinical vs. statistical prediction*. Minneapolis: University of Minnesota Press, 1954.

Meehl, P. E. Wanted—A good cookbook. *American Psychologist,* 1956, **11,** 263–272.

Meehl, P. E. A comparison of clinicians with five statistical methods of identifying psychotic MMPI profiles. *Journal of Counseling Psychology,* 1959, **6,** 102–109. (a)

Meehl, P. E. Some ruminations on the validation of clinical procedures. *Canadian Journal of Psychology,* 1959, **13,** 102–128. (b)

Meehl, P. E. The cognitive activity of the clinician. *American Psychologist,* 1960, **15,** 19–27.

Meehl, P. E. Seer over sign: The first good example. *Journal of Experimental Research in Personality,* 1965, **1,** 27–32.

Meehl, P. E. *Making a new MMPI.* Memorandum to Robert R. Golden, February 23, 1979.

Meehl, P. E., and Dahlstrom, W. G. Objective configural rules for discriminating psychotic from neurotic MMPI profiles. *Journal of Consulting Psychology,* 1960, **24,** 375–387.

Meehl, P. E., and Hathaway, S. R. The K factor as a suppressor variable in the MMPI. *Journal of Applied Psychology,* 1946, **30,** 525–564.

Meehl, P. E., and Rosen, A. Antecedent probability and the efficiency of psychometric signs, patterns, or cutting scores. *Psychological Bulletin,* 1955, **52,** 194–216.

Megargee, E. I. *The California Psychological Inventory handbook.* San Francisco: Jossey-Bass, 1972.

Megargee, E. I. (Ed.) A new classification system for criminal offenders. *Criminal Justice and Behavior,* 1977, **4,** 107–216.

Megargee, E. I. Development and validation of an MMPI-based system for classifying criminal offenders. In J. N. Butcher (Ed.), *New developments in the use of the MMPI.* Minneapolis: University of Minnesota Press, 1979.

Megargee, E. I., and Bohn, M. J., Jr. *Classifying criminal offenders: A new system based on the MMPI.* Beverly Hills, Calif.: Sage, 1979.

Megargee, E. I., and Mendelsohn, G. A. A cross-validation of twelve MMPI indices of hostility and control. *Journal of Abnormal Psychology,* 1962, **65,** 431–438.

Meltzoff, J. The effect of mental set and item structure upon responses to a projective test. *Journal of Abnormal and Social Psychology,* 1951, **46,** 177–189.

Messick, S. Personality assessment and the ethics of assessment. *American Psychologist,* 1965, **20,** 136–142.

Mercer, J. R. *System of Multicultural Pluralistic Assessment: Technical manual.* New York: Psychological Corporation, 1979.

Milgram, S. *Obedience to authority.* New York: Harper and Row, 1974.

Miller, L. C. *Louisville Behavior Checklist: Manual.* Los Angeles: Western Psychological Services, 1977. (a)

Miller, L. C. *School Behavior Checklist: Manual.* Los Angeles: Western Psychological Services, 1977. (b)

Millon, T. *The Millon Clinical Multiaxial Inventory: Manual.* Minneapolis: NCS/Interpretive Scoring Systems, 1977.

Mills, R. B., McDevitt, R. J., and Tonkin, S. Situational tests in metropolitan police recruit selection. *Journal of Criminal Law, Criminology, and Police Science,* 1966, **57,** 99–106.

Mischel, W. *Personality and assessment.* New York: Wiley, 1968.

Mischel, W. Direct versus indirect personality assessment: Evidence and implications. *Journal of Consulting and Clinical Psychology,* 1972, **38,** 319–324.

Mischel, W. Toward a cognitive social learning reconceptualization of personality. *Psychological Review,* 1973, **80,** 252–283.

Mischel, W. *Introduction to personality,* 2nd ed. New York: Holt, Rinehart, and Winston, 1976.

Mischel, W. On the future of personality measurement. *American Psychologist,* 1977, **32,** 246–254.

Mischel, W. On the interface of cognition and personality: Beyond the person-situation debate. *American Psychologist,* 1979, **34,** 740–754.

Mitchell, J. V., and Pierce-Jones, J. A factor analysis of Gough's California Psychological Inventory. *Journal of Consulting Psychology,* 1960, **24,** 454–456.

Mogar, R. E. Three versions of the F scale and performance on the semantic differential. *Journal of Abnormal and Social Psychology,* 1960, **60,** 262–265.

Monahan, J. (Ed.) *Who is the client? The ethics of psychological intervention in the criminal justice system.* Washington, D.C.: American Psychological Association, 1980.

Monahan, J. *The clinical prediction of violent behavior.* Rockville, Md.: National Institute of Mental Health, 1981.

Moos, R. H. Behavioral effects of being observed: Reactions to a wireless transmitter. *Journal of Consulting and Clinical Psychology,* 1968, **32,** 383–388.

Moreno, J. L. *Who shall survive?* Washington, D.C.: Nervous and Mental Disease Publishing Company, 1934.

Morgan, C. D., and Murray, H. A. A method for investigating fantasies: The Thematic Apperception Test. *Archives of Neurology and Psychiatry,* 1935, **34,** 289–306.

Morse, S. J. Law and mental health professionals: The limits of expertise. *Professional Psychology,* 1978, **9,** 389–399.

MSIS. *Multi-State Information System: A review.* Orangeburg, N.Y.: Rockland State Hospital, 1973.

MSIS. *Multistate Information System: Brief description.* Orangeburg, N.Y.: Rockland Research Institute, 1976.

Murray, H. A. *Explorations in personality.* New York: Oxford, 1938.

Murray, H. A. *Thematic Apperception Test manual.* Cambridge: Mass.: Harvard University Press, 1943.

Murstein, B. I. *Theory and research in projective techniques (emphasizing the TAT).* New York: Wiley, 1963.

Murstein, B. I. Introduction to Study 49. In B. I. Murstein (Ed.), *Handbook of projective techniques.* New York: Basic Books, 1965.

Murstein, B. I. Effect of stimulus, background, personality, and scoring system on the manifestation of hostility on the TAT. *Journal of Consulting and Clinical Psychology,* 1968, **32,** 355–365.

Nathan, P. E. *Cues, decisions, and diagnosis: A systems-analytic approach to the diagnosis of psychopathology.* New York: Academic Press, 1967.

Nay, W. R. *Multimethod clinical assessment.* New York: Gardner, 1979.

Nelson, R. O. Methodological issues in assessment via self-monitoring. In J. D. Cone and R. P. Hawkins (Eds.), *Behavioral assessment.* New York: Brunner/Mazel, 1977.

Nelson, R. O., and Hayes, S. C. Some current dimensions of behavioral assessment. *Behavioral Assessment,* 1979, 1–16.

Nettler, G. Test burning in Texas. *American Psychologist,* 1959, **14,** 682–683.

Neuringer, C. (Ed.) *Psychological assessment of suicidal risk.* Springfield, Ill.: Thomas, 1974.

Nisbett, R. E., Caputo, C., Legant, P., and Marecek, J. Behavior as seen by the actor and as seen by the observer. *Journal of Personality and Social Psychology,* 1973, **27,** 154−164.

Norman, W. T. Personality assessment, faking and detection: An assessment method for use in personnel selection. *Journal of Applied Psychology,* 1963, **47,** 225−241. (a)

Norman, W. T. Relative importance of test item content. *Journal of Consulting Psychology,* 1963, **27,** 166−174. (b)

Norman, W. T. Toward an adequate taxonomy of personality attributes: Replicated factor structure in peer nomination personality ratings. *Journal of Abnormal and Social Psychology,* 1963, **66,** 547−583. (c)

Norman, W. T. *2,800 personality trait descriptors: Normative operating characteristics for a university population.* Unpublished manuscript, University of Michigan, 1967.

Norman, W. T. Psychometric considerations for a revision of the MMPI. In J. N. Butcher (Ed.), *Objective personality assessment.* New York: Academic Press, 1972.

Norman, W. T., and Goldberg, L. R. Raters, ratees, and randomness in personality structure. *Journal of Personality and Social Psychology,* 1966, **4,** 681−691.

Nunnally, J. C. *Popular conceptions of mental health.* New York: Holt, Rinehart, and Winston, 1961.

Nunnally, J. C. *Psychometric theory,* 2nd ed. New York: McGraw-Hill, 1978.

O'Dell, J. W. P. T. Barnum explores the computer. *Journal of Consulting and Clinical Psychology,* 1972, **38,** 270−273.

Ogdon, D. P. *Psychodiagnostics and personality assessment: A handbook,* 2nd ed. Los Angeles: Western Psychological Services, 1975.

Orne, M. T. On the social psychology of the psychological experiment: With particular reference to demand characteristics and their implications. *American Psychologist,* 1962, **17,** 766−783.

Osgood, C. E. The nature and measurement of meaning. *Psychological Bulletin,* 1952, **49,** 197−237.

Osgood, C. E., Suci, G. J., and Tannenbaum, P. H. *The measurement of meaning.* Urbana: University of Illinois Press, 1957.

Oskamp. S. The relationship of clinical experience and training methods to several criteria of clinical prediction. *Psychological Monographs,* 1962, **76** (28, Whole No. 547).

Oskamp. S. Overconfidence in case-study judgments. *Journal of Consulting Psychology,* 1965, **29,** 261−265.

Oskamp, S., Mindick, B., Berger, D., and Motta, E. A longitudinal study of success versus failure in contraceptive planning. *Journal of Population,* 1978, **1,** 69−83.

OSS Assessment Staff. *Assessment of men.* New York: Rinehart, 1948.

Overall, J. E. and Gorham, D. R. The Brief Psychiatric Rating Scale. *Psychological Reports,* 1962, **10,** 799−812.

Overall, J. E., and Klett, C. J. *Applied multivariate analysis.* New York: McGraw-Hill, 1972.

Overall, J. E., and Gomez-Mont, F. The MMPI-168 for psychiatric screening. *Educational and Psychological Measurement,* 1974, **34,** 315−319.

Owens, W. A., and Henry, E. R. *Biographical data in industrial psychology: A review and evaluation.* Greensboro, N.C.: Richardson Foundation, 1966.

Palmer, J. D. *The psychological assessment of children*. New York: Wiley, 1970.

Pascal, G. R., and Suttell, B. J. *The Bender-Gestalt Test*. New York: Grune and Stratton, 1951.

Passini, F. T., and Norman, W. T. A universal conception of personality structure. *Journal of Personality and Social Psychology*, 1966, **4**, 44–49.

Patterson, G. R., Hops, H., and Weiss, R. L. Interpersonal skills training for couples in the early stages of conflict. *Journal of Miarriage and the Family*, 1975, **37**, 295–303.

Patterson, G. R., Reid, J. B., Jones, R. R., and Conger, R. E. *A social-learning approach to family intervention*. Vol. 1, *Families with aggressive children*. Eugene, Oreg.: Castalia, 1975.

Paul, G. L. *Insight versus desensitization in psychotherapy: An experiment in anxiety reduction*. Stanford, Calif.: Stanford University Press, 1966.

Payne, F. D., and Wiggins, J. S. Effects of rule relaxation and system combination on classification rates in two MMPI "cookbook" systems. *Journal of Consulting and Clinical Psychology*, 1968, **32**, 734–736.

Peak, H. Problems of objective observation. In L. Festinger and D. Katz (Eds.), *Research methods in the behavioral sciences*. New York: Dryden, 1953.

Pearson, J. S., and Swenson, W. M. *A user's guide to the Mayo Clinic automated MMPI program*. New York: Psychological Corporation, 1967.

Peterson, D. R. Scope and generality of verbally defined personality factors. *Psychological Review*, 1965, **72**, 48–59.

Peterson, D. R. *The clinical study of social behavior*. New York: Appleton-Century-Crofts, 1968.

Peterson, R. A. Review of the Holtzman Inkblot Technique. In O. K. Buros (Ed.), *Eighth mental measurements yearbook*. Highland Park, N.J.: Gryphon, 1978. (a)

Peterson, R. A. Review of the Rorschach. In O. K. Buros (Ed.), *Eighth mental measurements yearbook*. Highland Park, N.J.: Gryphon, 1978. (b)

Phillips, L. Case history data and prognosis in schizophrenia. *Journal of Nervous and Mental Disease*, 1953, **117**, 515–525.

Phillips, L., and Smith, J. G. *Rorschach interpretation: Advanced technique*. New York: Grune and Stratton, 1953.

Pintner, R., and Forlano, G. Season of birth and mental differences. *Psychological Bulletin*, 1943, **40**, 25–35.

Piotrowski, C., and Keller, J. W. Psychological test usage in Southeastern outpatient mental health facilities in 1975. *Professional Psychology*, 1978, **9**, 63–67.

Piotrowski, Z. A. The Rorschach inkblot method in organic disturbances of the central nervous system. *Journal of Nervous and Mental Disease*, 1937, **86**, 525–537.

Piotrowski, Z. A. Digital-computer interpretation of inkblot test data. *Psychiatric Quarterly*, 1964, **38**, 1–26.

Piotrowski, Z. A. Personal communication, 1969.

Piotrowski, Z. A. The psychological X-ray in mental disorders. In J. B. Sidowski, J. H. Johnson, and T. W. Williams (Eds.), *Technology in mental health care delivery systems*. Norwood, N.J.: Ablex, 1980.

Pressey, S. L., and Pressey, L. W., "Cross-out" tests, with suggestions as to a group scale of the emotions. *Journal of Applied Psychology,* 1919, **3,** 138–150.

Pritchard, D. A. Linear versus configural statistical prediction. *Journal of Consulting and Clinical Psychology,* 1977, **45,** 559–563.

Pritchard, D. A. Apologia for clinical/configural decision making. *American Psychologist,* 1980, **35,** 676–678.

Pritchard, D. A., and Rosenblatt, A. Racial bias in the MMPI: A methodological review. *Journal of Consulting and Clinical Psychology,* 1980, **48,** 263–267.

Pruzek, R. M., and Frederick, B. C. Weighting predictors in linear models: Alternatives to least squares and limitations of equal weights. *Psychological Bulletin,* 1978, **85,** 254–266.

Rabin, A. I. Projective methods: An historical introduction. In A. I. Rabin (Ed.), *Projective techniques in personality assessment.* New York: Springer, 1968.

Rae, D. S., Pautler, C. P., Kanderscheid, R. W., and Silbereld, J. Free association test (FAT) scoring and analysis program. *Behavior Research Methods and Instrumentation,* 1977, **9,** 31–32.

Rand, S. W. Correspondence between psychological reports based on the Mini-Mult and the MMPI. *Journal of Personality Assessment,* 1979, **43,** 160–163.

Reznikoff, M. Social desirability in TAT themes. *Journal of Projective Techniques,* 1961, **25,** 87–89.

Richardson, M. W. An empirical study of the forced-choice performance report. *American Psychologist,* 1949, **4,** 278–279. (Abstract)

Richardson, S. A., Dohrenwend, B. S., and Klein, D. *Interviewing: Its forms and functions.* New York: Basic Books, 1965.

Rimm, D. C. Cost efficiency and test prediction. *Journal of Consulting Psychology,* 1963, **27,** 89–91.

Roback, H. B. Human figure drawings: Their utility in the clinical psychologist's armentarium for personality assessment. *Psychological Bulletin,* 1968, **70,** 1–19.

Robins, A. J. Prognostic studies in mental disorder. *American Journal of Psychiatry,* 1954, **111,** 434–444.

Rodnick, E. H., and Garmezy, N. An experimental approach to the study of motivation in schizophrenia. In M. R. Jones (Ed.), *Nebraska Symposium on Motivation,* 1957, Lincoln: University of Nebraska Press, 1957.

Rogers, C. R., and Dymond, R. F. *Psychotherapy and personality change.* Chicago: University of Chicago Press, 1954.

Rohde, A. R. *The sentence completion method: Its diagnostic and clinical application to mental disorders.* New York: Ronald, 1957.

Romanczyk, R. G., Kent, R. N., Diament, C., and O'Leary, K. D. Measuring the reliability of observational data: A reactive process. *Journal of Applied Behavior Analysis,* 1973, **6,** 175–184.

Rome, H. P. Rationale. In H. P. Rome et al., Symposium on automation techniques in personality assessment. *Proceedings of the Staff Meetings of the Mayo Clinic,* 1962, **37,** 61–64.

Rome, H. P., et al. Symposium on automation techniques in personality assessment. *Proceedings of the Staff Meetings of the Mayo Clinic,* 1962, **37,** 61−82.

Rorer, L. G. The great response-style myth. *Psychological Bulletin,* 1965, **63,** 129−156.

Rorer, L. G., Hoffman, P. J., Dickman, H. R., and Slovic, P. Configural judgments revealed. *Proceedings of the 75th Annaul Convention of the American Psychological Association,* 1967, **2,** 195−196.

Rorer, L. G., Hoffman, P. J., and Hsieh, K. C. Utilities as base rate multipliers in the determination of optimum cutting scores for the discrimination of groups of unequal size and variance. *Journal of Applied Psychology,* 1966, **50,** 364−368.

Rorschach, H. *Psychodiagnostics.* Bern: Huber, 1942 (New York: Grune and Stratton, 1951).

Rose, D., and Bitter, E. J. The Palo Alto Content Scale as a predictor of physical assaultiveness in men. *Journal of Personality Assessment,* 1980, **44,** 228−233.

Rosen, A. Detection of suicidal patients: An example of some limitations in the prediction of infrequent events. *Journal of Consulting Psychology,* 1954, **18,** 397−403.

Rosenberg, M., and Glueck, B. C., Jr. Further developments in automation of behavioral observations on hospitalized psychiatric patients. *Comprehensive Psychiatry,* 1967, **8,** 468−475.

Rosenberg, M., Glueck, B. C., Jr., and Bennet, W. L. Automation of behavioral observation on hospitalized psychiatric patients. *American Journal of Psychiatry,* 1967, **123,** 926−929.

Rosenberg, S., and Sedlak, A. Structural representations of implicit personality theory. In L. Berkowitz (Ed.), *Advances in experimental social psychology,* Vol. 6. New York: Academic Press, 1972.

Rosenthal, R. *Experimenter effects in behavioral research.* New York: Appleton-Century-Crofts, 1966.

Rosenzweig, S. The picture-association method and its application in a study of reactions to frustration. *Journal of Personality,* 1945, **21,** 3−23.

Rotter, J. B., and Rafferty, J. E. *Manual: The Rotter Incomplete Sentences Blank.* New York: Psychological Corporation, 1950.

Runyan, W. M. How should treatment recommendations be made? Three studies in the logical and empirical bases of decision making. *Journal of Consulting and Clinical Psychology,* 1977, **45,** 552−558.

Sales, B. D. Law and attitudes toward the mentally ill. In J. G. Rabkin, L. Gelb, and J. B. Lazar (Eds.), *Attitudes toward the mentally ill: Research perspectives.* Rockville, Md.: National Institute of Mental Health, 1980.

Sandler, I. N. Social support resources, stress, and maladjustment of poor children. *American Journal of Community Psychology,* 1980, **8,** 41−52.

Sanford, N. Personality: Its place in psychology. In S. Koch (Ed.), *Psychology: A study of a science,* Vol. 5. New York: McGraw-Hill, 1963.

Sanson-Fisher, R. W., Poole, A. D., Small, G. A., and Fleming, I. R. Data acquisition in real time—An improved system for naturalistic observation. *Behavior Therapy,* 1979, **10,** 543−554.

Sappenfield, B. R. Review of the Blacky Pictures. In O. K. Buros (Ed.), *The sixth mental measurement yearbook.* Highland Park, N.J.: Gryphon, 1965.

Sarason, S. B. *The clinical interaction with special reference to the Rorschach.* New York: Harper, 1954.

Sarason, S. B. *The psychological sense of community.* San Francisco: Jossey-Bass, 1974.

Sarbin, T. R. Ontology recapitulates philosophy: The mythic nature of anxiety. *American Psychologist,* 1968, **23,** 411–418.

Sarbin, T. R., Taft, R., and Bailey, D. E. *Clinical inference and cognitive theory.* New York: Holt, Rinehart, and Winston, 1960.

Satz, P., Fennel, E., and Reilly, C. The predictive validity of six neurodiagnostic tests: A decision theory analysis. *Journal of Consulting and Clinical Psychology,* 1970, **34,** 375–381.

Saunders, D. S. Moderator variables in prediction. *Educational and Psychological Measurement,* 1956, **16,** 209–222.

Sawyer, J. Measurement *and* prediction, clinical *and* statistical. *Psychological Bulletin,* 1966, **66,** 178–200.

Schafer, R. *The clinical application of psychological tests.* New York: International Universities Press, 1948.

Schroeder, H. E. Use of feedback in clinical prediction. *Journal of Consulting and Clinical Psychology,* 1972, **38,** 265–269.

Schutz, W. *The FIRO Scales.* Palo Alto, Calif.: Consulting Psychologists Press, 1967.

Schwartz, L. A. Social-situation pictures in the psychiatric interview. *American Journal of Orthopsychiatry,* 1932, **2,** 124–133.

Schwartz, M. M., Cohen, B. D., and Pavlik, W. B. The effects of subject- and experimenter-induced defensive response sets on Picture-Frustration Test reactions. *Journal of Projective Techniques,* 1964, **28,** 341–345.

Schwarz, J. C. Comment on "High school yearbooks: A nonreactive measure of social isolation in graduates who later became schizophrenic." *Journal of Abnormal Psychology,* 1970, **75,** 317–318.

Schwitzgebel, R. K. Legal and social aspects of the concept of dangerousness. In C. J. Frederick (Ed.), *Dangerous behavior: A problem in law and mental health.* Rockville, Md.: National Institute of Mentall Health, 1978.

Schwitzgebel, R. L., and Schwitzgebel, R. K. *Law and psychological practice.* New York: Wiley, 1980.

Scollay, R. W. Personal history data as a predictor of success. *Personnel Psychology,* 1957, **10,** 23–26.

Scott, R. D., and Johnson, R. W. Use of the weighted application blank in selecting unskilled employees. *Journal of Applied Psychology,* 1967, **51,** 393–395.

Scott, W. A. Comparative validites of forced-choice and single-stimulus tests. *Psychological Bulletin,* 1968, **70,** 231–244.

Scott, W. A., and Johnson, R. C. Comparative validites of direct and indirect personality tests. *Journal of Consulting and Clinical Psychology,* 1972, **38,** 301–318.

Sechrest, L. Incremental validity: A recommendation. *Educational and Psychological Measurement,* 1963, **23,** 153–157.

Sechrest, L. Personality. *Annual Review of Psychology,* 1976, **27,** 1–27.

Sechrest, L., Gallimore, R., and Hersch, P. D. Feedback and accuracy of clinical predictions. *Journal of Consulting Psychology*, 1967, **31**, 1−11.

Sechrest, L., and Jackson, D. N. The generality of deviant response tendencies. *Journal of Consulting Psychology*, 1962, **26**, 395−401.

Sechrest, L., and Jackson, D. N. Deviant response tendencies: Their measurement and interpretation. *Educational and Psychological Measurement*, 1963, **23**, 33−53.

Seeman, W. "Subtlety" in structured personality tests. *Journal of Consulting Psychology*, 1952, **16**, 278−283.

Seeman, W. Concept of "subtlety" in structured psychiatric and personality tests: An experimental approach. *Journal of Abnormal and Social Psychology*, 1953, **48**, 239−247.

Seeman, W. *The complete clinician: Constituting some reflections on diagnostic decision-making and on theorizing.* Unpublished manuscript, 1969.

Selltiz, C., Jahoda, M., Deutsch, M., and Cook, S. W. *Research methods in social problems.* New York: Holt, Rinehart, and Winston, 1959.

Schaffer, J. W., Schmidt, C. W., Zlotowitz, H. I., and Fisher, R. S. Biorhythms and highway crashes. *Archives of General Psychiatry*, 1978, **35**, 41−46.

Shah, S. A. Dangerousness: A paradigm for exploring some issues in law and psychology. *American Psychologist*, 1978, **33**, 224−238.

Shaver, K. G. *An introduction to attribution processes.* Cambridge, Mass.: Winthrop, 1975.

Sheldon, W. H., Stevens, S. S., and Tucker, W. B. *The varieties of human physique.* New York: Harper and Row, 1940.

Shelly, M. W., and Bryan, G. L. *Human judgments and optimality.* New York: Wiley, 1964.

Shneidman, E. S. *Thematic test analysis.* New York: Grune and Stratton, 1951.

Sidowski, J. B., Johnson, J. H., and Williams, T. A. (Eds), *Technology in mental health care delivery systems.* Norwood, N.J.: Ablex, 1980.

Siegel, M. Privacy, ethics, and confidentiality. *Professional Psychology*, 1979, **10**, 249−258.

Sines, J. O. Actuarial methods in personality assessment. In B. A. Maher (Ed.), *Progress in experimental personality research.* Vol. 3. New York: Academic Press, 1966.

Sines, L. K. The relative contribution of four kinds of data to accuracy in personality assessment. *Journal of Consulting Psychology*, 1959, **23**, 483−492.

Sletten, I., Ernhart, C., and Ulett, G. The Missouri automated mental status examination: Its development, use, and reliability. *Comprehensive Psychiatry*, 1970, **11**, 315−327.

Smith, J., and Lanyon, R. I. Prediction of juvenile probation violators. *Journal of Consulting and Clinical Psychology*, 1968, **32**, 54−58.

Smith, M. S. The computer and the TAT. *Journal of School Psychology*, 1968, **6**, 206−214.

Soskin, W. F., and John, V. P. The study of spontaneous talk. In R. G. Barker (Ed.), *The stream of behavior.* New York: Appleton-Century-Crofts, 1963.

Spencer, G. J., and Worthington, R. Validity of a projective technique in predicting sales effectiveness. *Personnel Psychology*, 1952, **5**, 125−144.

Spitzer, R. L., and Endicott, J. DIAGNO II: Further developments in a computer program for psychiatric diagnosis. *American Journal of Psychiatry*, 1969, **125**(7), Supplement, 12−21.

Spitzer, R. L., and Endicott, J. An integrated group of forms for automated psychiatric case records: Progress report. *Archives of General Psychiatry,* 1971, **24,** 540–547.

Spitzer, R. L., and Endicott, J. Can the computer assist clinicians in psychiatric diagnosis? *American Journal of Psychiatry,* 1974, **131,** 523–530.

Spitzer, R. L., Endicott, J., and Robins, E. Research Diagnostic Criteria: Reliability and validity. *Archives of General Psychiatry,* 1978, **35,** 773–782.

Spranger, E. *Types of men.* Translated from the 5th German edition of *Lebensformen* by P. J. W. Pigors. Halle: Max Niemeyer Verlag, 1928.

Starr, B. J., and Katkin, E. S. The clinician as aberrant actuary: Illusory correlation and the Incomplete Sentences Blank. *Journal of Abnormal Psychology,* 1969, **74,** 670–675.

Stein, M. I. The use of a sentence completion test for the diagnosis of personality. *Journal of Clinical Psychology,* 1947, **3,** 47–56.

Stein, M. I. *Volunteers for peace: The first group of Peace Corps volunteers in a rural community development in Colombia.* New York: Wiley, 1966.

Stephenson, W. *The study of behavior.* Chicago: University of Chicago Press, 1953.

Stern, G. G., Stein, M. I., and Bloom, B. S. *Methods in personality assessment.* Glencoe, Ill.: Free Press, 1956.

Stillman, R., Roth W. T., Colby, K. M., and Rosenbaum, C. P. An on-line computer system for initial psychiatric inventory. *American Journal of Psychiatry,* 1969, **125,** 8–11 (Supplement).

Stone, A. A. *Mental health and law: A system in transition.* Rockville, Md.: National Institute of Mental Health, 1975.

Stone, P. J., Bales, R. F., Namenwirth, J. Z., and Olgivie, D. M. The general inquirer: A computer system for content analysis and retrieval based on the sentence as a unit of information. *Behavioral Science,* 1962, **7,** 1–15.

Storandt, M., Siegler, I. C., and Elias, M. F. (Eds.) *The clinical psychology of aging.* New York: Plenum, 1978.

Strasburger, E. L., and Jackson, D. N. Improving accuracy in a clinical judgment task. *Journal of Consulting and Clinical Psychology,* 1977, **45,** 303–309.

Stricker, L. J. Review of the EPPS. In O. K. Buros (Ed.), *Sixth mental measurements yearbook.* Highland Park, N.J.: Gryphon, 1965.

Strong, E. K. A vocational interest test. *Educational Record,* 1927, **8,** 107–121.

Strong, E. K. *Vocational interests 18 years after college.* Minneapolis: University of Minnesota Press, 1955.

Stuart, R. B., and Davis, B. *Slim chance in a fat world: Behavioral control of obesity.* Champaign, Ill.: Research Press, 1972.

Suggs, D., and Sales, B. D. The art and science of conducting the *voir dire. Professional Psychology,* 1978, **9,** 367–388.

Sullivan, H. S. *The psychiatric interview.* New York: Norton, 1954.

Swartz, J. Review of the Thematic Apperception Test. In O. K. Buros (Ed.), *Eighth mental measurements yearbook.* Highland Park, N.J.: Gryphon, 1978.

Swenson, C. H. Empirical evaluations of human figure drawings. *Psychological Bulletin,* 1957, **54,** 431–466.

Swenson, C. H. Empirical evaluations of human figure drawings, 1957–1966. *Psychological Bulletin,* 1968, **70,** 20–44.

Swenson, W. M., and Pearson, J. S. Automation techniques in personality assessment: A frontier in behavioral science and medicine. *Methods of Information in Medicine,* 1964, **3,** 34−36.

Swenson, W. M., and Pearson, J. S. Psychiatry—Psychiatric screening. *Journal of Chronic Diseases,* 1966, **19,** 497−507.

Swenson, W. M., Pearson, J. S., and Osborne, D. *An MMPI source book.* Minneapolis: University of Minnesota Press, 1973.

Symonds, P. M. *Diagnosing personality and conduct.* New York: Appleton-Century, 1931.

Szasz, T. *The myth of mental illness.* New York: Hoeber, 1961.

Taft, R. The ability to judge people. *Psychological Bulletin,* 1955, **52,** 1−23.

Taft, R. Multiple methods of personality assessment. *Psychological Bulletin,* 1959, **56,** 333−352.

Tallent, N. On individualizing the psychologist's clinical evaluation. *Journal of Clinical Psychology,* 1958, **14,** 243−244.

Tapp, J. L. Psychology and the law: An overture. *Annual Review of Psychology,* 1976, **27,** 359−404.

Taylor, C. W., and Ellison, R. L. Biographical predictors of specific performance. *Science,* 1967, **155,** 1075−1080.

Taylor, H. C., and Russell, J. T. The relationship of validity coefficients to the practical effectiveness of tests in selection: Discussion and tables. *Journal of Applied Psychology,* 1939, **23,** 565−578.

Taylor, J. B. Social desirability and MMPI performance: The individual case. *Journal of Consulting Psychology,* 1959, **23,** 514−517.

Thommen, G. *Is this your day? How biorhythm helps you determine your life cycle,* Rev. ed. New York: Crown, 1973.

Thoreson, C. E., and Mahoney, M. J. *Behavioral self-control.* New York: Holt, Rinehart, and Winston, 1974.

Thorpe, L. P., Clark, W. W., and Tiegs, E. W. *Manual, California Test of Personality.* Los Angeles: California Test Bureau, 1953.

Thurstone, L. L. *Thurstone Temperament Schedule.* Chicago: Science Research Associates, 1949.

Thurstone, L. L. The dimensions of temperament. *Psychometrika,* 1951, **16,** 11−20.

Tomlinson, J. R. Situational and personality correlates of predictive accuracy. *Journal of Consulting Psychology,* 1967, **31,** 19−22.

Toomey, L. C., and Rickers-Ovsiankina, M. A. *Rorschach psychology,* 2nd ed. Huntington, N.Y.: Krieger, 1977.

Toops, H. A. The criterion. *Educational and Psychological Measurement,* 1944, **4,** 271−297.

Tupes, E. C., and Christal, R. E. *Recurrent personality factors based on trait ratings.* USAF ASD Technical Report, No. 61-97, 1961.

Turner, D. R. Predictive efficiency as a function of amount of information and level of professional experience. *Journal of Projective Techniques and Personality Assessment,* 1966, **30,** 4−11.

Tversky, A., and Kahnemann, D. Judgment under uncertainty: Heuristics and biases. *Science,* 1974, **185,** 1124−1131.

Twentyman, C. T., and McFall, R. M. Behavioral training of social skills in shy males. *Journal of Consulting and Clinical Psychology,* 1975, **43,** 384−395.

Ullmann, L. P., and Krasner, L. *Case studies in behavior modification.* New York: Holt, Rinehart, and Winston, 1965.

Underwood, B. J. *Experimental psychology.* New York: Appleton-Century-Crofts, 1966.

Valins, S., and Nisbett, R. E. *Attribution processes in the development and treatment of emotional disorders.* New York: General Learning Press, 1971.

Van Lennep, D. J. The Four-Picture Test. In H. H. Anderson and G. L. Anderson (Eds.), *An introduction to projective techniques.* Englewood Cliffs, N.J.: Prentice-Hall, 1951.

Veldman, D. J. Computer-based sentence completion interviews. *Journal of Counseling Psychology,* 1967, **14,** 153−157.

Veldman, D. J., Menaker, S. L., and Peck, R. F. Computer scoring of sentence completion data. *Behavioral Science,* 1969, **14,** 501−507.

Vernon, P. E. The validation of civil service selection board procedures. *Occupational Psychology,* 1950, **24,** 75−95.

Vernon, P. E. *Personality assessment: A critical survey.* London: Methuen, 1964.

Vernon, P. E., and Allport, G. W. A test for personal value. *Journal of Abnormal and Social Psychology,* 1931, **26,** 231−248.

Wainer, H. On the sensitivity of regression and regressors. *Psychological Bulletin,* 1978, **85,** 267−273.

Wallace, C. J., and Davis, J. R. Effects of information and reinforcement on the conversational behavior of chronic psychiatric patient dyads. *Journal of Consulting and Clinical Psychology,* 1974, **42,** 656−662.

Wallace, J. An abilities conception of personality: Some implications for personality measurement. *American Psychologist,* 1966, **21,** 132−138.

Wallace, J. What units shall we employ? Allport's question revisited. *Journal of Consulting Psychology,* 1967, **31,** 56−64.

Waller, R. W., and Keeley, S. M. Effects of explanation and information feedback on the illusory correlation phenomenon. *Journal of Consulting and Clinical Psychology,* 1978, **46,** 342−343.

Walsh, J. A. Review of the Sixteen Personality Factors Questionnaire. In O. K. Buros (Ed.), *Eighth mental measurements yearbook.* Highland Park, N.J.: Gryphon, 1978.

Walsh, W. B. Validity of self-report. *Journal of Counseling Psychology,* 1967, **14,** 18−23.

Walsh, W. B. Validity of self-report: Another look. *Journal of Counseling Psychology,* 1968, **15,** 180−186.

Watson, D. L., and Tharp, R. G. *Self-directed behavior: Self-modification for personal adjustment,* 2nd ed. Monterey, Calif.: Brooks/Cole, 1977.

Watson, L. *Supernature.* New York: Anchor/Doubleday, 1973.

Webb, E. Character and intelligence. *British Journal of Psychology Monograph Supplement,* 1915, III.

Webb, E. J., Campbell, D. T., Schwartz, R. D., and Sechrest, L. *Unobtrusive measures: Nonreactive research in the social sciences.* Chicago: Rand McNally, 1966.

Webster, E. C. *Decision making in the employment interview.* Montreal: Industrial Relations Centre, McGill University, 1967.

Weiner, I. B. Approaches to Rorschach validation. In M. A. Rickers-Ovsiankina (Eds.), *Rorschach psychology,* 2nd ed. Huntington, N.Y.: Krieger, 1977.

Weisskopf, E. A., and Dieppa, J. J. Experimentally induced faking of TAT responses. *Journal of Consulting Psychology,* 1951, **15,** 469–474.

Wells, F. L. The systematic observation of the personality—In its relation to the hygiene of the mind. *Psychological Review,* 1914, **21,** 295–333.

Welsh, G. S., and Dahlstrom, W. G. *Basic readings on the MMPI in psychology and medicine.* Minneapolis: University of Minnesota Press, 1956.

Whyte, W. H., Jr. *The organization man.* New York: Simon and Schuster, 1956.

Wiggins, J. S. Substantive dimensions of self-report in the MMPI item pool. *Psychological Monographs,* 1966, **80** (22, Whole No. 630).

Wiggins, J. S. *Personality and prediction: Principles of personality assessment.* Reading, Mass.: Addison-Wesley, 1973.

Wiggins, J. S., Goldberg, L. R., and Appelbaum, M. MMPI content scales: Interpretive norms and correlations with other scales. *Journal of Consulting and Clinical Psychology,* 1971, **37,** 403–410.

Wiggins, N. L., and Hoffman, P. J. Three models of clinical judgment. *Journal of Abnormal Psychology,* 1968, **73,** 70–77.

Wildman, R. W., and Wildman, R. W. II. An investigation into the comparative validity of several diagnostic tests and test batteries. *Journal of Clinical Psychology,* 1975, **31,** 455–458.

Williams, T. R. *Field methods in the study of culture.* New York: Holt, Rinehart, and Winston, 1967.

Willingham, W. W. Foreword. In W. W. Willingham (Ed.), Invasion of privacy in research and testing. *Journal of Educational Measurement,* 1967, **4,** 1–31 (Supplement).

Wirt, R. D., Lachar, D., Klinedinst, J. K., and Seat, P. D. *Multidimensional description of child personality: A manual for the Personality Inventory for Children.* Los Angeles: Western Psychological Services, 1977.

Wittman, P. A scale for measuring prognosis in schizophrenic patients. *Elgin State Hospital Papers,* 1941, **4,** 20–33.

Wolff, W. T., and Merrens, M. R. Behavioral assessment: A review of clinical methods. *Journal of Personality Assessment,* 1974, **38,** 3–16.

Wolpe, J., and Lang, P. J. A fear survey schedule for use in behavior therapy. *Behavior Research and Therapy,* 1964, **2,** 27–30.

Woodworth, R. S. Examination of emotional fitness for warfare. *Psychological Bulletin,* 1919, **16,** 59–60.

Woodworth, R. S. *Dynamic psychology.* New York: Columbia University Press, 1920.

Woody, R. H. Psychologists in child custody. In B. D. Sales (Ed.), *Psychology in the legal process.* New York: Spectrum, 1977.

Yarmey, A. D. *The psychology of eyewitness testimony.* New York: Free Press, 1979.

Zedeck, S. Problems with the use of "moderator" variables. *Psychological Bulletin,* 1971, **76,** 295–310.

Zigler, E., and Phillips, L. Social effectiveness and symptomatic behaviors. *Journal of Abnormal and Social Psychology,* 1960, **61,** 231–238.

Zigler, E., and Phillips, L. Social competence and the process-reactive distinction in schizophrenia. *Journal of Abnormal and Social Psycholog,* 1962, **65,** 215–222.

Ziskin, J. *Coping with psychiatric and psychological testimony,* 2nd ed. Beverly Hills, Calif.: Law and Psychology Press, 1975.

Ziskin, J. *Coping with psychiatric and psychological testimony,* 2nd ed. 1977 Pocket Supplement. Beverly Hills, Calif.: Law and Psychology Press, 1977.

Ziskin, J. *Coping with psychiatric and psychological testimony,* 3rd ed. Vols. 1 and 2. Venice, Calif.: Law and Psychology Press, 1981.

Zubin, J., Eron, L. D., and Schumer, F. *An experimental approach to projective techniques.* New York: Wiley, 1965.

Zuckerman, M. Physiological measures of sexual arousal in the human. *Psychological Bulletin,* 1971, **75,** 297–329.

AUTHOR INDEX

SUBJECT INDEX